Accounts and Audit of Limited Liability Partnerships

Accounts and Audit of Limited Liability Partnerships

Fifth edition

Steve Collings FMAAT FCCA

Bloomsbury Professional

Bloomsbury Professional
An imprint of Bloomsbury Publishing Plc

Bloomsbury Professional Ltd
41–43 Boltro Road
Haywards Heath
RH16 1BJ
UK

Bloomsbury Publishing Plc
50 Bedford Square
London
WC1B 3DP
UK

www.bloomsbury.com

BLOOMSBURY and the Diana logo are trademarks of Bloomsbury Publishing Plc

British Library Cataloguing-in-Publication Data

A catalogue record for this book is available from the British Library.

ISBN: PB: 978-1-78451-752-6
ePDF: 978-1-78451-750-2
ePub: 978-1-78451-751-9

Typeset by Compuscript Ltd, Shannon
Printed and bound by CPI Group (UK) Ltd, Croydon, CR0 4YY

To find out more about our authors and books visit www.bloomsburyprofessional.com. Here you will find extracts, author information, details of forthcoming events and the option to sign up for our newsletters

Preface

The number of Limited Liability Partnerships (LLPs) in the UK which have emerged since the introduction of the Limited Liability Partnerships Act 2000 in 2001 has increased significantly over the years. The popularity of LLPs has increased largely due to the flexibility afforded by such entities by allowing them to maintain a traditional partnership existence in the way that profits are shared among the members, but also offering the members *limited liability* which is usually afforded to companies. The privilege of limited liability does not come without a price tag in the form of the requirement to file, on public record, the LLPs' financial statements at Companies House.

Financial reporting in the UK and Republic of Ireland has changed considerably with the introduction of FRS 102 *The Financial Reporting Standard applicable in the UK and Republic of Ireland*. FRS 102 is based on the provisions found in *IFRS for SMEs* and brings about changes in the way that certain items are accounted for. FRS 102 has been mandatory for many reporting entities for accounting periods starting on or after 1 January 2015; however, it will also become mandatory for small entities for accounting periods starting on or after 1 January 2016. Early-adoption of the standard to accounting periods starting on or after 1 January 2015, but before 1 January 2016, is permissible.

LLPs are also subject to the requirements of the *Statement of Recommended Practice – Accounting by Limited Liability Partnerships* (LLP SORP). The SORP was reissued in July 2014 to reflect the provisions in FRS 102. However, SI 2016/575 *The Limited Liability Partnerships, Partnerships and Groups (Accounts and Audit) Regulations 2016* amended legislation relating to the accounting and audit regulatory frameworks for LLPs. In addition, SI 2016/575 introduced an exemption from certain financial reporting requirements for very small LLPs (referred to as micro-entity LLPs or micro-LLPs) as well as for very small (micro) partnerships, including limited partnerships which are 'qualifying partnerships' under the Partnerships (Accounts) Regulations 2008 (SI 2008/569).

As a consequence of the revisions to the LLP legislation, the LLP SORP was updated and re-issued in January 2017 and the updated LLP SORP is effective for periods commencing on or after 1 January 2016. Early-adoption of the revised SORP is permitted for accounting periods which start on or after 1 January 2015 provided that The Limited Liability Partnerships (Accounts and Audit) Regulations 2016 (SI 2016/575) are applied from the same date.

In this fifth edition, I have incorporated the specific accounting issues relating to micro-entity LLPs that choose to apply FRS 105 *The Financial Reporting Standard applicable to the Micro-entities Regime*. There is an additional chapter (Chapter 14 *Micro-Entities*) which outlines the requirements of FRS 105. I have also updated the remainder of the book to reflect the provisions of the revised legislation as well as to introduce the requirements of FRS 102, Section 1A *Small Entities* which small LLPs, and micro-entity LLPs that chooses not to report under FRS 105, are required to follow. The book has also been comprehensively updated for changes to FRS 102 and legislation since the fourth edition.

My most grateful thanks go to Sarah Laing, CTA, who has updated Chapter 8 on taxation issues. I would also like to thank my editors, Claire Banyard, Claire McDermott and Dave Wright for their support during the production of this edition.

I hope that this book will prove to be a useful reference guide to those dealing with accounting and auditing issues for LLPs and feedback is welcomed, via the publishers, for future editions of this book.

Steve Collings, FMAAT FCCA

January 2017

Contents

Table of Examples

[*All references are to paragraph numbers and appendices*]

Table of Statutes

[*All references are to paragraph numbers and appendices*]

Table of Statutory Instruments

[*All references are to paragraph numbers and appendices*]

Abbreviations and definitions

ASB	=	Accounting Standards Board
CA 06	=	Companies Act 2006
CCAB	=	Consultative Committee of Accountancy Bodies
CGU	=	Cash Generating Unit
EEA	=	European Economic Area
EU	=	European Union
FRC	=	Financial Reporting Council
FRS	=	Financial Reporting Standard (issued by the ASB)
FRSSE	=	Financial Reporting Standard for Smaller Entities
HMRC	=	HM Revenue & Customs
IFRS	=	International Financial Reporting Standard
LLP	=	Limited Liability Partnership
LLPA	=	Limited Liability Partnerships Act 2000
LLPAAR 2008	=	Limited Liability Partnerships (Accounts and Audit) (Application of Companies Act 2006) Regulations 2008
LLP 2001	=	Limited Liability Partnerships Regulations 2001
LMLLPR 2008	=	Large and Medium-sized Limited Liability Partnerships (Accounts) Regulations 2008
SLLPR 2008	=	Small Limited Liability Partnerships (Accounts) Regulations 2008
SORP	=	Statement of Recommended Practice *Accounting by Limited Liability Partnerships*
SSAP	=	Statement of Standard Accounting Practice (issued by the predecessor body to the ASB)
STRGL	=	Statement of total recognised gains and losses
UITF	=	Urgent Issues Task Force (assists the ASB in providing guidance on specific accounting areas; produces UITF Abstracts)

Chapter 1

The law and practice of limited liability partnerships

Signposts

- The Limited Liability Partnerships Act 2000 (LLPA) created the first new major form of legal vehicle available under UK law since the establishment of joint stock companies in 1844 (see **1.1**).
- A limited liability partnership (LLP) is an independent legal entity; it is a body corporate which provides the benefits of a partnership but has a separate legal personality and unlimited capacity to contract (see **1.1**).
- Professional advice should always be sought before transferring an existing entity into an LLP (see **1.1**).
- The LLPA is a short Act of 19 sections but cannot be read in isolation from the regulations which implement the LLPA including the Limited Liability Partnership Regulations 2001, the Limited Liability Partnerships (Application of the Companies Act 2006) Regulations 2009 and the Limited Liability Partnerships, Partnerships and Groups (Accounts and Audit) Regulations 2016 (see **1.2**).
- Before an LLP can be incorporated, two or more persons associated with carrying on a lawful business with a view to profit must have subscribed their names to an incorporation document (see **1.4**).
- LLP status is not applicable for certain activities (for example non-profit making activities) (see **1.4**).
- Unlike limited companies, an LLP has no share capital and there is no requirement to file a memorandum and articles of association on incorporation (see **1.4**).
- Form LL IN01 needs to be completed in order to form an LLP (see **1.5**).
- When a new member is appointed to the LLP, form LL AP01 has to be submitted which gives the new member's details and has to be submitted to the Registrar of Companies within 14 days of their appointment (see **1.5**).
- LLPs must submit annual confirmation statements and maintain a register of People with Significant Control (see **1.6**).
- A members' agreement should be drawn up on formation of an LLP which is a private document and does not have to be filed with the Registrar of Companies (see **1.7**).

- The drawing up of the members' agreement should be considered carefully and the importance of seeking professional advice in this respect cannot be over-emphasised (see **1.7**).
- LLPs must have at least two designated members which will have a number of defined responsibilities and duties including the signing of the accounts and filing of those accounts, appointing the auditors and determining their remuneration, making statutory declaration of solvency on a members' voluntary winding up and filing the various statutory returns (see **1.8**).
- Each member is an agent of the LLP and not of each other and an LLP is not bound by anything done by a member dealing with another person if that member has no authority for that act (see **1.9**).
- If a member is liable to a third party (other than another member) as a result of his own wrongful act or omission in the course of business, the LLP is also liable to that person to the same extent as the member (see **1.9**).
- The Supreme Court has heard a case and held that members of an LLP are to be classed as 'workers' for the purpose of employment legislation and will receive the same levels of protection as employees if they 'blow the whistle' at work (see **1.10**).

1 Introduction

1.1 The Limited Liability Partnerships Act 2000 (LLPA) created the first new major form of legal vehicle available under UK law since the establishment of joint stock companies in 1844. The law came into force on 6 April 2001 and the number of LLPs in existence some 16 years later has seen a significant increase, mainly due to the flexibility the LLP structure offers (the Department for Business Innovation and Skills (which is now superseded by the Department for Business, Energy and Industrial Strategy from July 2016) cited approximately 58,000 LLPs were registered in the UK in May 2016). LLPs were introduced in Northern Ireland in November 2004, with the Limited Liability Partnerships Regulations (Northern Ireland) 2004 implementing the Limited Liability Partnerships Act (Northern Ireland) 2002. The most important feature of the LLP is that it is an independent legal entity – similar to a Limited Liability company which is distinct from its shareholders and is an entity in its own right. An LLP is a body corporate and not a partnership. An LLP, however, provides the benefits of a partnership in that members (who are referred to as 'members' and not 'partners' in the legislation) are free to organise their own internal affairs through a private members' agreement. However, unlike a partnership, an LLP has separate legal personality and unlimited capacity to contract. Members are the agents of the LLP and not of each other. The concept of mutual agency between partners, which results in innocent partners being bound by the acts of fellow partners to the full extent of their personal assets, does not apply to LLPs.

The limitation of members' personal liability will be central to those considering either setting up or transferring their business to an LLP. Its limitations should, however, also be clearly understood and professional advice should always be sought before transferring to an LLP in order to ensure that (a) the requirements are understood, and (b) transferring the partnership to an LLP is appropriate in the business' and partners' interests. Although a member's personal assets should be protected in the event of a catastrophic or 'Armageddon' claim against the LLP to the extent it exceeds the firm's professional indemnity insurance cover and assets, there will still be the need to adopt strict risk management procedures. Professional practices should maintain their indemnity insurance levels and all members will continue (in much the same way as directors in companies) to be personally liable for their own negligent acts and defaults where they have assumed a personal responsibility to a client which has subsequently been relied upon. Where the LLP has client relationships and where it is permitted, terms of engagement should seek to limit personal liability. This is, however, a complex area and legal advice should always be sought.

As a consequence of what was referred to in the House of Lords' debates during the passage of the LLP legislation, as the 'great privilege' of limited liability status, an LLP is required to file accounts with the Registrar of Companies (Companies House) as the price to pay for the affordability of limited liability. Most of the provisions of the Companies Act in respect of the preparation and filing of accounts are therefore applied to LLPs (see Chapter 2). An LLP can, as a body corporate, also grant charges over its undertakings. In addition, most of the provisions of the Insolvency Act 1986 are also applicable to an LLP.

2 The legislation

1.2 The LLPA is a short Act of 19 sections, the longest of which concerns taxation and ensures that the position in respect of LLPs and taxation is the same as for general law partnerships, as well as providing that there is (subject to various conditions being met) tax neutrality on the transfer of a partnership's business to an LLP.

However, the LLPA cannot be read in isolation from the regulations which implement the LLPA, consisting primarily of the Limited Liability Partnership Regulations 2001 (the 2001 Regulations) and the Limited Liability Partnerships (Application of the Companies Act 2006) Regulations 2009 (the 2009 Regulations). The Limited Liability Partnerships, Partnerships and Groups (Accounts and Audit) Regulations 2016 (SI 2016/575) were issued on 10 May 2016 and make amendments to the legislation in respect of the accounting and audit regulatory framework for LLPs. The Regulations themselves are deregulatory in nature and reduce the burden of financial reporting and audit obligations, particularly for small LLPs, so as to achieve alignment with the financial reporting regime for companies, which was changed by virtue of SI 2015/980.

Parts II to IV of the 2001 Regulations make applicable to LLPs the relevant parts of the Companies Act 2006 (CA 2006) and the 2009 Regulations, the Company Directors Disqualification Act 1986, and the Insolvency Act 1986. Part V of the 2001 Regulations applies provisions of the Financial Services and Markets Act 2000 to LLPs. Part VI sets out a set of default rules which will apply to an LLP in the absence of a members' agreement. For the reasons set out later in this chapter, those forming an LLP would generally be ill-advised to allow themselves to be governed by these default rules.

The 2009 Regulations apply certain provisions of the CA 2006 to LLPs, and seek to harmonise some aspects of the operation of LLPs and companies. Consequently, parts of the CA 2006 governing the formalities of doing business, names and trading disclosures, arrangements and reconstructions, registration of charges, as well as registration and disclosure of members' details, have been applied to LLPs. Some of these, including the disclosure requirements, have imposed new obligations on LLPs and their members.

The provisions of the 2001 Regulations have to be read together with the Schedules attached to them, which set out the modifications to the relevant statutes they apply. Publications are available which incorporate these modifications into the actual body of the legislation, which makes it much easier to understand the necessary detail. The 2009 Regulations, however, consist of consolidated text which can be read with limited reference to the CA 2006.

SI 2016/575 (The Limited Liability Partnerships, Partnerships and Groups (Accounts and Audit) Regulations 2016, issued in May 2016, amends the following legislation:

(1) the Limited Liability Partnerships (Accounts and Audit) (Application of Companies Act 2006) Regulations 2008 (SI 2008/1911), which applies to LLPs, with modifications, provisions of the Companies Act 2006 concerning accounts and audit;

(2) the Small Limited Liability Partnerships (Accounts) Regulations 2008 (SI 2008/1912), which applies to LLPs, with modifications, provisions of the Small Companies and Groups (Accounts and Directors' Report) Regulations 2008 (SI 2008/409);

(3) the Large and Medium-sized Limited Liability Partnerships (Accounts) Regulations 2008 (SI 2008/1913), which applies to LLPs, with modifications, provisions of the Large and Medium-sized Companies and Groups (Accounts and Reports) Regulations 2008 (SI 2008/410);

(4) the Small Companies (Micro-Entities' Accounts) Regulations 2013 (SI 2013/3008), which introduced a micro-entities regime for companies that was not applied to qualifying partnerships;

(5) the Partnerships (Accounts) Regulations 2008 (SI 2008/569); and

(6) the Large and Medium-sized Companies and Groups (Accounts and Reports) Regulations 2008 (SI 208/410), which contains provisions regarding the preparation of accounts for large and medium-sized companies.

1.3 In 2015, the Department for Business Innovation and Skills introduced the Companies, Partnerships and Group (Accounts and Reports) Regulations 2015 and the Companies, Partnerships and Groups (Accounts and Reports) (No. 2) Regulations 2015 (SI 2015/1672) in order to implement certain provisions of the EU Accounting Directive (the directive). These made significant changes to the financial reporting framework which companies are subjected to and reduced the administrative burdens associated with the preparation and publications of financial statements for limited companies and qualifying partnerships. In addition, a new micro-entities regime was introduced in SI 2013/3008 but this regime was not applied to qualifying partnerships.

LLPs are not subject to the directive. However, they are subject to a very similar accounting regime to limited companies, including the requirement to file their financial statements with Companies House and similar requirements in respect of audit and accounting issues.

SI 2016/575 introduced similar changes to the financial reporting framework for LLPs, including the creation of a new micro-entities regime (see Chapter 14). The Regulations will allow for a less burdensome financial reporting regime for small LLPs as well as aligning the legislative requirements for LLPs to those of limited companies. This was done to avoid unnecessary complexity for those preparing and using accounts. In addition, groups which include LLPs and companies within their structure will also be able to apply the same reporting requirements across the group.

3 Incorporation

1.4 As a result of its corporate status, the incorporation of an LLP follows much the same procedure as the incorporation of a company. The LLPA states that, before an LLP can be incorporated, 'two or more persons associated for carrying on a lawful business with a view to profit' must have subscribed their names to an incorporation document. This is a wider definition than under the Partnership Act 1890, s 1, which defines the relationship between partners as 'persons carrying on business in common with a view of profit'. 'Persons' includes not only individuals but also corporate entities such as another LLP or company. LLPs are not limited to regulated professions, as had originally been the government's intention, and their uses can be extremely varied and are only likely to be prohibited by illegality. However, LLPs are not applicable for certain activities – for example non-profit making activities.

An LLP has no share capital, and there is no requirement to file a memorandum and articles of association on incorporation. There is no LLP equivalent to the model articles of association that can be adopted by a company.

4 Forming an LLP

1.5 With the increase in use of technology, an LLP can be formed electronically through appropriate software systems. This has become more popular over recent years and many formation agents (or 'incorporation agents') and software providers have produced their own software which, in certain cases, allows their customers to form their own LLP via the formation agent's website. Information relating to software filing and a list of providers can be found on the Companies House website at www.companieshouse.gov.uk.

To incorporate an LLP via paper, Form LL IN01 has to be completed and delivered to Companies House with a registration fee (currently £40 (£20 if you are filing documents in Welsh for an LLP whose registered office is in Wales), or £100 for a 'same day' incorporation – you must write 'Same day incorporation' on the envelope). The forms can be obtained from the Companies House website at www.companieshouse.gov.uk, and various guidance notes are available. Form LL IN01 requires the name of the LLP which is to be registered, the names and addresses of the members, and specification of which members are to be designated members. The duties and obligations of the designated members, which are much like those of a company secretary, are dealt with later in this chapter.

An LLP cannot have the same name as a registered company or another LLP, and vice versa. It is, however, inadvisable to use a shelf LLP to protect a name, in the way in which shelf companies are used, if the LLP business will be transferred to it by a partnership. This is because the stamp duty and stamp duty land tax rules on the transfer of a partnership's business to an LLP (LLPA, s 12) provide an exemption from stamp duty and stamp duty land tax where there is identical membership in the predecessor partnership immediately prior to incorporation of the LLP and in the LLP immediately after transfer to it of the partnership's business. The exemption is, however, only available for a period of 12 months from the date of incorporation of the LLP. In such circumstances, the appropriate route for name protection continues to be the use of a shelf company.

In respect of the members' details which need to be provided to Companies House, a new disclosure regime came into force for LLPs on 1 October 2009. Each member is required to provide a service address to appear on the public record, and a usual residential address which will be kept confidential (although the Registrar of Companies may disclose it to specified bodies in certain circumstances). Both the service address and the residential address may be the same. There is an ongoing duty to notify the Registrar each time the membership of an LLP changes or the personal details of a member change.

Where any new member is appointed to the LLP, Form LL AP01, providing that member's details, has to be submitted to Companies House within 14 days of their appointment. The same applies to the termination of the appointment of a member, the relevant form being LL TM01.

Form LL IN01 also carries a formal statement of compliance, to be completed either by a member or the solicitor engaged in the formation of the LLP, to the effect that the persons named on the form as members are associated for carrying on a lawful business with a view to profit. The nature of the business does not have to be stated.

The Registrar of Companies will issue a certificate of incorporation to the LLP with its own registered number which begins with the prefix OC3. The detailed rules in respect of the display of a registered company's name and details on business stationery and at its premises apply to LLPs and as a consequence it will be important to register the LLP well in advance of the actual transfer of the business to an LLP so that the necessary details are available for the LLP's stationery and signage.

Annual confirmation statements and people with significant control

1.6 From 30 June 2016, the annual confirmation statement will replace the annual return. Every LLP must confirm the information that Companies House holds about it by delivering a confirmation statement. Where information is out of date, the information will need to be updated either before, or at the same time, that the LLP delivers the confirmation statement.

The confirmation statement confirms that information which the LLP is duty-bound to inform Companies House about under section 853A(2) of the Companies Act 2006 (as applied to LLPs) for a relevant confirmation period has been delivered, or is being delivered at the time the statement is made.

> **Focus**
>
> The confirmation statement must be made at least once a year; although an LLP can choose to make a statement more frequently if it so wishes; although a review period cannot be longer than 12 months. Where the LLP makes a confirmation statement early, the next review period will start the day after the date of that confirmation statement.
>
> It is a criminal offence not to file the confirmation statement within 14 days of the end of the review period. If an LLP fails to deliver the confirmation statement within the correct timeframe, Companies House has the power to prosecute the LLP and its designated members.

Confirmation statements can be made via WebFiling or software filing systems. Paper confirmation statements can be completed by using form LL CS01. The statement must contain:

- the LLP's name;
- the LLP's number; and
- the confirmation date.

From 30 June 2016 onwards, LLPs must deliver information to Companies House regarding people with significant control (PSC). A PSC is anyone who meets one, or more, of the following conditions (although an LLP can have more than one PSC):

- holds, directly or indirectly, rights to share in more than 25% of the surplus assets on winding up;
- holds, directly or indirectly, more than 25% of the rights to vote on matters to be decided by a vote of the LLP's members;
- holds, directly or indirectly, the right to appoint or remove the majority of those entitled to be involved in the LLP's management;
- otherwise has the right to exercise, or actually exercises, significant influence or control over the LLP; or
- holds the right to exercise, or actually exercises, significant influence or control over the activities of a trust or firm which is not a legal entity but would itself satisfy any of the first four conditions if it were an individual.

From 6 April 2016, an LLP must also keep a register of PSCs in addition to keeping other information, such as a register of members. An LLP must determine who has a controlling interest in the LLP and then include this information on the register of PSCs. This information must then be filed at Companies House along with the confirmation statement.

Focus

- LLPs must send the information contained in their PSC register to Companies House (unless the LLP chooses to hold the PSC register at Companies House). When LLPs deliver their first confirmation statement, they must include all the information contained in the PSC register. In respect of later confirmations, LLPs which have previously delivered this information will not need to deliver it again if nothing has changed. Where any changes have occurred, then details of the change must be filed, along with the date of the change.

5 The members' agreement

1.7 The default rules set out in the 2001 Regulations are unlikely to be suitable for the majority of LLPs. They draw heavily on the Partnership Act 1890, although the LLPA specifically disapplies partnership law to LLPs. The default rules provide, for example, that each member is entitled to share equally in the capital and profits of the LLP, that every member can take part in the management of the LLP, and that the consent of all existing members is necessary before a new member can be admitted. In addition, differences between members concerning ordinary matters connected with the business may be decided by a majority of the members.

For a business of any size or sophistication, these rules will be inappropriate and incapable of providing a workable management structure. Furthermore, the legislation clearly contemplates LLPs regulating their own internal structure and management, and there are various central issues (for example, the application to LLPs of CA 2006, s 994 regarding the protection of minorities from unfairly prejudicial conduct) which are not addressed in the default rules.

The members' agreement is a private document and does not have to be filed at Companies House. As well as dealing with the usual matters found in a partnership agreement, such as management structure, sharing of profits (and losses), admission of members, contribution of capital, the conduct of members and their departure, there are issues unique to LLPs that must be addressed.

These include the powers and duties of the designated members, the preparation, approval and audit of the statutory accounts, the ability and authority to create fixed and floating charges, and the position of any salaried members. One other major issue is the effect of the company insolvency regime being applicable to LLPs. The members' agreement must deal with the effect of a dissolution, either by acts of the members or by virtue of insolvency. Furthermore, unlike in a partnership, it is possible to have a members' voluntary liquidation of an LLP, and the powers of reconstruction set out in the Insolvency Act 1986 apply to LLPs. The legal opinion set out in Appendix 5 of the LLP SORP in respect of the difference between distribution and allocation of profits (see Chapter 5), means that the profit-sharing mechanism will need to be carefully worded and it is advisable to seek professional advice on this. Whilst the LLP SORP classifies amounts owing to members as either debt or equity, the general principles regarding the distinction between the allocation and division of profits remain unchanged.

Whilst a partnership agreement will often provide the basic structure for a members' agreement, the new, often corporate concepts are technical, and it is fundamentally important to have them correctly drafted and hence the importance of seeking professional input where this is concerned cannot be over-emphasised. The drawing-up of the members' agreement is not a job for the amateur, and the expense of getting it right will stand any LLP in good stead for its commercial future. It will also provide an opportunity for existing partnerships to conduct an extensive review of their current internal arrangements.

6 Designated members

1.8 LLPs have to have at least two designated members, who have a number of defined responsibilities and duties. On incorporation, the LLP will have to state whether all the members are to be designated, or name those who are. This position can be subsequently changed. Companies House must be notified of any changes to the designated members within 14 days of the change, using Form LL CH01. Designated members automatically cease to be designated when they cease to be members. In larger organisations, there will probably be a small group of designated members (ie those who are involved in management and compliance issues) whilst, in the smaller organisation, it may be that each member should assume the role.

The key duties of designated members include the signing (on behalf of members) and filing of the annual accounts, the appointment of the auditors and determining their remuneration, making a statutory declaration of solvency on a members' voluntary winding up, and filing the various statutory returns (for example, the LLP's confirmation statement and the notification to the Registrar of Companies regarding a change in membership in the LLP). There are penalties for breaches of the filing requirements in the form of fines. In most cases, the legislation provides protection for designated members who were not knowingly and wilfully involved in the offence in question, or where they took reasonable steps to avoid an offence occurring.

7 Duties and responsibilities of members

1.9 The relationship between members should be regulated by the members' agreement. As already explained, by virtue of LLPA, s 6(1) each member is the agent of the LLP and not of each other. This is the basis for the protection of members from personal liability in respect of another member's negligence.

Section 6 further provides that an LLP is not bound by anything done by a member dealing with another person if that member has no authority for that act, and that person either knows the member has no authority or does not know or believe the member to be a member of the LLP.

Where a member is liable to a third party (other than another member) as a result of his own wrongful act or omission in the course of the business, then the LLP will be liable to that person to the same extent as the member. The possibility of a member still being liable for his own wrongful acts and omissions is discussed above. Such remaining personal liability may possibly be excluded by clear terms of engagement between the LLP and its clients and, again, this is an area where those considering converting to LLP status would be well advised to take professional advice.

8 Whistleblowing protection

1.10 In a landmark ruling by the UK Supreme Court in 2014, accountants and other professionals who are partners within an LLP and who speak out publicly about wrongdoings within the LLP receive legal protection on the basis that they are classed as 'workers' for the purposes of employment legislation.

Prior to the ruling, partners in LLPs were excluded from legal protection on the grounds that they were not considered to be employees. The ruling follows a three-year legal battle involving a partner at a law firm who was expelled from the partnership after the ex-partner blew the whistle on the managing partner of an associated firm after the managing partner admitted he had paid bribes to secure cases and to secure the outcome of the cases. The firm had tried to prevent a claim by the ex-partner on the grounds that she was not classed as an employee as she had partner status and hence had no protection when she was dismissed for whistleblowing.

The Supreme Court held that members of an LLP are to be classed as 'workers' for the purposes of employment legislation and will receive the same levels of protection as employees if they 'blow the whistle' at work.

The impact of this ruling is likely to be far-reaching and accountants, lawyers and other professionals who are connected with LLPs will have to consider this ruling – particularly where they come across acts of wrongdoing within the LLP.

Chapter summary

- Various legislation is in place governing LLPs and the latest amendments to legislation (at the time of writing) reflect the provisions in SI 2016/575, issued in May 2016, which affects smaller LLPs.
- An LLP is a body corporate and not a partnership.
- The incorporation procedures are similar to those of a company, although an LLP has no share capital and there is no requirement to file a memorandum and articles of association.
- LLPs are formed by completing Form LL IN01 together with the registration fee.
- A members' agreement must be in place, although the default rules set out in the 2001 Regulations are likely to be inappropriate for the majority of LLPs.
- LLPs have to have at least two designated members.
- The duties and responsibilities of the members are regulated by the members' agreement.
- Whistleblowing protection is now in place following a landmark ruling by the UK Supreme Court.

Chapter 2

General accounting requirements and the LLP SORP

Signposts

- Parts 1 to 9 of the Limited Liability Partnerships Accounts and Audit Regulations 2008 deal with the general accounting requirements of LLPs (see **2.1**).
- The size and complexity of the business the LLP undertakes will essentially dictate the level of sophistication of the accounting records maintained by the LLP (see **2.2**).
- Failure to maintain adequate accounting records is an offence and is also a matter which will be referred to in the auditor's report (see **2.2**).
- Regulations say that accounting records should be maintained for three years from the date on which they are prepared, although tax legislation requires that records be retained for a longer period (see **2.2**).
- For the first period after incorporation, the accounting reference date is the last day of the month in which the anniversary of its incorporation falls (see **2.3**).
- The first accounting period cannot be shorter than six months or longer than 18 months and it is possible to change the accounting reference date (see **2.3**).
- LLPs with subsidiaries should ensure that each subsidiary has a uniform year to that of the parent (see **2.3**).
- Extensive changes have been made to the SORP to reflect the new financial reporting frameworks for small LLPs and micro-entity LLPs (see **2.3**).
- The members are responsible for preparing financial statements at the end of each financial year which give a true and fair view of the state of the affairs of the LLP and hence will have to comply with applicable accounting standards (see **2.4**).
- The SORP identifies certain information which must be included within the members' report (see **2.5**).
- An LLP which is the parent of a group may have to prepare consolidated financial statements in addition to its own separate financial statements (see **2.7**).
- There are certain exemptions from preparing consolidated financial statements (see **2.7** and **2.9**).
- Financial statements must be approved by the members of the LLP and signed on their behalf by a designated member (see **2.8**).

- The designated members are responsible for ensuring that the financial statements are delivered to the Registrar of Companies within nine months of the period-end (different deadlines may apply to an LLP's first accounting period) (see **2.8**).
- There are special provisions which apply to small, eligible LLPs (see **2.9**).
- There are choices available for small LLPs as to what financial information is filed with the Registrar of Companies (see **2.9**).
- FRS 102 *The Financial Reporting Standard applicable in the UK and Republic of Ireland* was first issued by the Financial Reporting Council (FRC) in March 2013 and replaces all extant FRSs, SSAPs and UITF Abstracts with effect for accounting periods commencing on or after 1 January 2015. The latest edition of FRS 102 (at the time of writing this fifth edition) is the September 2015 edition which incorporates small entities and the LLP SORP is based on the provisions in FRS 102 (see **2.14**).
- There are notable differences between FRS 102 and previous UK GAAP which are likely to affect the way that amounts are recognised and measured (see **2.15**).

1 Statutory provisions

2.1 The general accounting requirements for LLPs are set out in the Limited Liability Partnerships Accounts and Audit Regulations 2008, Parts 1 to 9. These provisions take the Companies Act 2006 (CA 2006), Part 15 (accounts and reports), which deals with the requirements to prepare accounts, and make such modifications as are necessary to deal with the particular circumstances of LLPs. The requirements in relation to the form and content of an LLP's financial statements are contained in the Small Limited Liability Partnerships (Accounts) Regulations 2008 for small LLPs (see below) which have been amended by virtue of SI 2016/575, issued in May 2016, and the Large and Medium-sized Limited Liability Partnerships (Accounts) Regulations 2008 for all other LLPs. With the exception of the rules with respect to filing of accounts considered in **2.8** below, all of the provisions are applicable to accounting periods that began on or after 1 October 2008.

2 Requirements to keep accounting records

2.2 The level of sophistication of the accounting records maintained by an LLP will vary dependent on its size and the complexity of the business it undertakes. The legal requirements are that the accounting records must be sufficient to record and explain the LLP's transactions and disclose with reasonable accuracy, at any time, the financial position of the LLP. They must also contain sufficient information to enable accounts to be prepared in accordance with the legislation. Additional requirements may be imposed where an LLP is subject to further regulation, such as LLPs that are authorised by the Financial Conduct Authority. Failure to maintain adequate records is an offence and is also a matter which is required to be referred to in the auditor's report (see **3.8**). The accounting records are required to be kept at the registered office unless the members consider it appropriate to keep them elsewhere. The members of the LLP have the right to inspect the records at any time. To the extent that the records are held outside the United Kingdom, accounts and returns with respect to those records must be sent to, and retained in, the United Kingdom.

Whilst the regulations require that accounting records be retained for three years from the date on which they are prepared, tax legislation requires that partnerships are required to keep the records that are needed to make their returns until five years and ten months from the end of the relevant tax year or, if later, the date of completion of enquiries into the returns or the date of expiry of the time limit for making enquiries (TMA 1970, s 12B). For example, records relating to accounts prepared for the year ended 30 April 2011 (which falls in the tax year ending 5 April 2012) would need to be retained until 31 January 2018. There may also be other requirements specific to the nature of the business of the LLP (for example, where it has long-term contracts) which would result in a longer period of retention being necessary.

3 Accounting reference dates and accounting periods

2.3 For the first period after incorporation, the accounting reference date of an LLP (ie the date to which the accounts are prepared) is the last day of the month in which the anniversary of its incorporation falls. In the absence of any application to shorten or lengthen the accounting period (see below), the first accounting period will start on the date of incorporation and end on that accounting reference date. The first accounting period cannot be shorter than six months or longer than 18 months. Subsequent accounting periods will then cover a year from the date of the end of the previous accounting period, unless an application is made to amend the accounting reference date.

To make provision for those LLPs who want to prepare their accounts for a 52- (or 53-) week period, accounts may be prepared to a date which is no more than seven days either side of the accounting reference date.

Where an LLP has subsidiary undertakings, the members should ensure that the financial year of each subsidiary coincides with that of the LLP, unless there is a good reason for it not to. For example, where the regulations of an overseas jurisdiction require a different date.

LLPs are able to change their accounting reference dates, subject to certain restrictions. It is possible to change either:

- the current accounting reference period (and subsequent periods); or
- after the end of the immediately preceding accounting period, for that immediately preceding accounting reference period (and subsequent periods), provided that the period for filing accounts (see **2.8**) has not expired.

An accounting reference period cannot be extended beyond 18 months. In addition, an LLP cannot usually extend its accounting period more than once in any five-year period. The exception is where the LLP becomes a subsidiary or parent of another EEA undertaking, and the change is necessary in order to align accounting reference dates across a group.

4 Form and content of accounts

2.4 The members are responsible for preparing, at the end of each financial year, a profit and loss account (income statement/statement of comprehensive income) and a balance sheet (statement of financial position) which give a true and fair view of the state of the affairs of the LLP at the end of the financial period and of the profit or loss for that financial period. A report to the members (members' report) is also required. The form and content of the balance sheet, profit and loss account and notes to the accounts are set out in the Small Limited Liability Partnerships (Accounts) Regulations 2008 (as amended by SI 2016/575) for small LLPs and the Large and Medium-sized Limited Liability Partnerships (Accounts) Regulations 2008 for all other LLPs.

The fact that the accounts of an LLP, which is not a micro-entity, are required to give a true and fair view means that they also have to comply with all sections of FRS 102 *The Financial Reporting Standard applicable in the UK and Republic of Ireland.* Small LLPs are only required to comply with the disclosure requirements of Section 1A *Small Entities* in FRS 102 (see **2.9**). LLPs which are outside of the small LLPs' regime will, where required, also need to include a cash flow statement (statement of cash flows) and a statement of changes in equity.

Focus

- Unlike previous editions of the LLP SORP, the SORP issued on 26 January 2017 states explicitly at paragraph 59A that a statement of changes in equity does not need to be presented if an LLP has no equity. The SORP requires that where a statement of changes in equity is not included due to the fact that the LLP has no equity and is not replaced as a primary statement by a reconciliation of members' interests, a statement should be made either on the face of one of the other primary statements or in the notes to the accounts that the LLP has no equity and consequently a statement of changes in equity is not given.

The Consultative Committee of Accountancy Bodies (CCAB) regularly reviews the SORP for changes in accounting practice and new developments and therefore the fourth edition, issued on 15 July 2014, was revised in respect of:

- the amendments made to FRS 102 by the Financial Reporting Council (FRC) in July 2014 which relaxed the conditions determining whether a financial instrument was 'basic' (Section 11 *Basic Financial Instruments*) or 'other' (Section 12 *Other Financial Instruments Issues*) and the updated requirements on hedge accounting;
- the amendments made to FRS 102 by the FRC in February 2015 which clarified aspects concerning defined benefit pension accounting;
- the amendments made to UK accounting standards in July 2015 which resulted in:
  - the withdrawal of the Financial Reporting Standard for Smaller Entities (FRSSE);

- amendments made to FRS 102 to add a new section outlining presentation and disclosure requirements for small entities and other changes considered necessary for continued compliance with company law; and
- the publication of FRS 105 *The Financial Reporting Standard applicable to the Micro-entities Regime*; and

- the amendments made to FRS 102 in March 2016 which updated the fair value hierarchy disclosures.

Focus

- Any changes to accounting standards made after 1 August 2016 have not been reflected in the 2016 SORP.

As noted above, the FRSSE is withdrawn in its entirety for accounting periods which start on or after 1 January 2016. As a consequence, small LLPs are moved under the scope of FRS 102, Section 1A *Small Entities* which is examined further in **2.10** below. Section 1A only outlines the presentation and disclosure requirements applicable to small entities; in terms of recognition and measurement, these are based on full FRS 102.

Focus

- Paragraph 27A of the SORP states that small LLPs which qualify for, and choose to, apply the small entities regime are required to comply with the disclosure requirements of Section 1A of FRS 102 rather than the disclosure requirements of the SORP. However, paragraph 27C of the SORP requires LLPs to make the disclosures about how loans and other debts due to members rank in relation to other unsecured creditors. This disclosure is beyond the requirements of Section 1A, but the SORP requires this to be disclosed because LLPs do not have any of the capital maintenance provisions which apply to companies. Therefore, CCAB believe mandating such a disclosure (regardless of the LLP's size) will ensure a true and fair view.

As discussed in more detail in Chapter 5, the SORP also requires disclosure of total members' interests on the face of the balance sheet, as a memorandum item. In respect of small LLPs, the reconciliation of members' interests may be necessary in some instances in order to give a true and fair view. In revising the SORP, the CCAB were of the view that it is not necessary to require all small LLPs to include such a reconciliation, which is consistent with the requirements for small companies which are not required to produce a statement of changes in equity. However, the reconciliation of the movement in members' other interests may be necessary in some instances to ensure a true and fair view. Professional judgement will be required as to whether, or not, this reconciliation is needed.

The LLP SORP was updated in 2014 to comply with the provisions in FRS 102 and the fourth edition of the SORP (which reflected the provisions in FRS 102) became effective for accounting periods commencing on or after 1 January 2015 with early-adoption permissible. The latest edition of the LLP SORP, issued on 26 January 2017, is effective for accounting periods commencing on or after 1 January 2016, with early-adoption permissible. Where early-adoption is taken up, The Limited Liability Partnerships (Accounts and Audit) Regulations 2016 (SI 2016/575) must also be applied from the same date.

Illustrative accounts are set out in Appendices 1 and 2 in this book.

5 The members' report

2.5 Whilst the requirements of the Companies Act 2006 (CA 2006) relating to the form and content of the financial statements are largely reflected in the Regulations, the requirements with respect to preparing a directors' report and the content thereof are not. However, the SORP does require that a members' report is prepared. The reason for including this requirement within the SORP is that it is considered that the financial statements and notes alone cannot provide all the information about the financial performance of the LLP. Some narrative reporting is required in order to provide complete communication with the users of the LLP's annual report.

The SORP requires that the following are included within the members' report:

- the principal activities of the LLP and its subsidiary undertakings, indicating any significant changes during the year;
- an indication of the existence of any branches outside the UK;
- the identity of anyone who was a designated member during the year; and
- the policy of the LLP regarding members' drawings and the subscription and repayment of amounts subscribed or otherwise contributed by members.

LLPs are not, therefore, required to prepare a Strategic Report or detailed business review required of limited companies, nor make the disclosures in respect of corporate governance required of listed companies. There is, however, an increasing trend, particularly amongst larger LLPs, to provide further information about their businesses, resulting in disclosures that are in practice not dissimilar to those of limited companies. The objective of such disclosures is to make the financial statements more understandable and to aid transparency.

Narrative reporting can provide a good opportunity for the members to further explain matters affecting their financial performance, which are either not adequately dealt with within the disclosure requirements of accounting standards or which cannot be included because they are subjective and incapable of verification by the auditors.

In preparing any additional narrative reporting, members of an LLP need to be mindful that they should not prepare anything that could be construed as misleading by users of the accounts or include any additional information which is unnecessary (ie to reduce 'clutter' within the financial statements). Matters to consider include:

- Ensuring that the report is a reasonably balanced reflection of the LLP's financial performance. It is human nature to focus on what has gone well and to not want to discuss what has not gone quite so well. It is unlikely that a balanced view can be given without giving some consideration to both.
- When discussing the future, this needs to be done in a realistic way in order to avoid users placing undue reliance on what may turn out to be over-optimism.
- Anything that is said in the narrative reporting about the financial position and performance of the LLP must be consistent with what is shown in the financial statements. Any inconsistencies will render the financial statements to be misleading.
- Any numbers that are quoted should be capable of reconciliation to the financial statements.

Auditors are not required to give an opinion on information that is presented with the financial statements, such as the members' report, but they are required to draw attention to any matters referred to that are inconsistent with the financial statements. As a consequence, the auditors will request to see all information that will accompany the financial statements before they sign their audit report and will read any accompanying reports to ensure that they are consistent with the financial statements.

6 Statement of recommended practice – accounting by limited liability partnerships

2.6 The current version of the SORP was issued by the CCAB (the five major accountancy institutes in UK and Ireland) on 26 January 2017 and reflects the provisions in SI 2016/575 which amended legislation relating to the accounting and audit regulatory framework for LLPs. SI 2016/575 also introduced an exemption from certain financial reporting requirements for very small (micro) LLPs, and for very small (micro) partnerships, including limited partnerships, which are 'qualifying partnerships' under the Partnerships (Accounts) Regulations 2008 (SI 2008/569).

The SORP was also revised to reflect various changes to UK accounting standards, including the withdrawal of the FRSSE and the transition of small entities to FRS 102 for accounting periods starting on or after 1 January 2016.

Focus

- Micro-entity LLPs preparing their accounts under FRS 105 should not follow the provisions in the SORP, but should, instead, follow the relevant requirements of FRS 105. This is because the LLP SORP is based on the provisions in FRS 102 and there are significant differences between FRS 102 and FRS 105; hence the CCAB concluded that LLPs applying FRS 105 are scoped out of the SORP. Chapter 14 examines the micro-entities' regime in more detail.

Development of the SORP is overseen by a steering committee whose membership is drawn from industries and professions whose members are, or are expected to become, LLPs. An exposure draft of the latest version of the SORP was issued in August 2016, with a final version issued on 26 January 2017.

Whilst there is no legal requirement to comply with the SORP, non-compliance would need to be reported in the accounts, and it is likely that the non-compliance would result in the accounts not giving a true and fair view (this would not, however, apply to micro-entity LLPs applying FRS 105 who are scoped out of the requirements of the SORP). Where the LLP is subject to audit this would result in the auditor's report being qualified as a result of the non-compliance if the non-compliance is material.

The SORP does not provide details of all of the reporting requirements which are applicable to LLPs, but it does provide interpretation of those accounting standards where there are specific issues regarding their application to the circumstances of an LLP. There is a requirement within the SORP (specifically paragraph 132 *Compliance Statement*) that the note to the financial statements which deals with accounting policies should refer to the LLP's compliance with the SORP, together with any non-compliance and the reasons.

Areas of the financial statements dealt with within the SORP, together with the specific paragraphs which deal with those areas, are as follows:

	Paragraphs
The contents of the annual report and financial statements	25–26C
Accounting by small LLPs	27–29
Disclosures	30–31
Members' remuneration and interests	32–74B
Retirement benefits	75–94
Taxation	95–99
Inventories	100–101
Business combinations and group accounts	102–119
Provisions and other implications of section 21 of FRS 102	120–127
Related parties	128–131

7 Groups

2.7 Where, at the end of the financial period, an LLP is a parent undertaking, both individual and group (consolidated) accounts are required. The LLP is not required to present its own profit and loss account (income statement) as part of those group accounts, but must state that it has taken advantage of the exemption contained in Companies Act 2006 (CA 2006), s 408 (as applied to LLPs), and the profit or loss of the LLP must be disclosed in the notes to the accounts. The profit and loss account is, however, still required to be prepared and approved by the members.

Exemption from the preparation of group accounts is available where the LLP is itself a wholly or majority (ie greater than 50%) owned subsidiary, and notice has not been served on the LLP by members holding either, in aggregate, more than half of the remaining interest in the LLP, or 5% in total of the interest in the LLP, that they require group accounts to be prepared (such notice must be served not later than six months after the end of the financial year before that to which it relates). The exemption is also conditional on the following:

- The LLP must be included in consolidated accounts prepared by the parent of a larger group and those accounts are either at the same date as the LLP's own accounts or an earlier date in the same financial year.
- Where the parent is established under the law of an EEA State, the accounts of the parent must be prepared either in accordance with the provisions of the Seventh Directive 83/349/EEC (as modified, where relevant, by the provisions of the Bank Accounts Directive (86/635/EEC) or the Insurance Accounts Directive (91/674/EEC)) or in accordance with EU-adopted International Financial Reporting Standards.
- Where the parent is not established under the law of an EEA State, the accounts of the parent must be prepared either in accordance with the Seventh Directive or an 'equivalent manner'.
- The parent company's accounts must be audited and the auditor's report submitted to the registrar with the financial statements.
- The LLP must disclose that it is exempt from the requirement to prepare group accounts, together with the name of the parent within whose accounts the LLP is included and, if that parent is incorporated outside the United Kingdom, the country in which it is incorporated.
- Copies of the parent's individual and group accounts have to be filed with the Registrar of Companies (ie Companies House). If they are not in English, a certified translation must be attached.

Exemption from the requirement to prepare group accounts is also available to small groups (see **2.9**).

Subsidiaries may be excluded from consolidation in the following circumstances:

- Severe long-term restrictions exist which hinder the LLP from exercising its rights over the assets or management of the subsidiary.
- Control by the LLP is only temporary (ie the interest in the subsidiary is held exclusively with a view to resale) and the subsidiary has not previously been consolidated in the consolidated financial statements.

The Limited Liability Partnerships (Accounts and Audit) (Application of Companies Act 2006) Regulations 2008 also allows a subsidiary to be excluded from consolidation in circumstances where the information necessary for the preparation of group accounts cannot be obtained without disproportionate expense or delay. This exemption is not, however, permitted by accounting standards, and cannot therefore be used by an LLP if the financial statements are to give a true and fair view.

Chapter 11 discusses some of the practical aspects of preparing group accounts.

8 Approval, publication and filing of accounts

2.8 The accounts are required to be approved by the members and signed on their behalf by a designated member. This signature must be on the balance sheet. Obtaining the approval of all members can pose potential practical problems because of the large numbers that could be involved. However, use of electronic communication (email, websites, intranets, etc) should considerably simplify the process.

A copy of the accounts together with the auditor's report (see Chapter 3) is required to be sent to every member no later than the end of the period for filing the accounts with the registrar or, where earlier, the actual date of filing the accounts. The designated members are responsible for delivering the accounts to the Registrar of Companies – in practice, this will most probably be delegated to one person. Delivery to the registrar has to be within nine months of the period end. Where it is the first accounting period and it covers more than 12 months, the period allowed is nine months from the first anniversary of the date of incorporation, or three months from the end of the accounting reference period, whichever expires last.

9 Special provisions applicable to small LLPs

2.9 Qualification as a small LLP is based on the requirements in CA 2006 which have been updated to align the small LLP thresholds to the small company thresholds. The qualifying conditions, of which two or more have to be met, are as follows:

Turnover	Not more than £10.2 million
Balance sheet total	Not more than £5.1 million
Number of employees	Not more than 50

The above thresholds apply to accounting periods starting on or after 1 January 2016. However, an early-adoption clause has been built into the LLP Regulations allowing an LLP to adopt the provisions of SI 2016/575 (and hence the revised thresholds above) for accounting periods beginning on or after 1 January 2015, but before 1 January 2016, if:

- the members of the LLP so decide; and
- a copy of the LLP's accounts for that financial year has not been delivered to Companies House in accordance with section 444, 445 or 446 of the Act as applied by LLPs by the 2008 Regulations prior to the date on which the Regulations come into force.

The government included an early-adoption clause because they estimate that around 400 medium-sized LLPs will qualify to be re-categorised as small under the increased thresholds and hence be able to access a less burdensome small LLP's accounting and audit regime. In addition, the government also estimate that some 40 large LLPs will be re-classified as medium-sized and also be able to access a reduced reporting regime.

Focus

- Where an LLP early-adopts the revised Act, it must also early-adopt FRS 102, Section 1A or FRS 105. It cannot adopt the provisions in the FRSSE (effective January 2015) if, for example, the LLP applies the new legislation for an accounting period ending on 31 December 2015. Similarly, where an LLP early-adopts the revised SORP, it must also early-adopt the revised Regulations.

Balance sheet total is total assets (fixed and current) before taking into account any of the LLP's liabilities.

Where the period covered by the financial statements is shorter than a year, the turnover limit should be pro-rated.

An LLP qualifies as small in the following circumstances:

- If, in respect of the first financial period, it meets the criteria for that period.
- For subsequent financial years, it may qualify if it meets the criteria in both that year and the previous year, and it met the qualifying criteria in the preceding year.

The provisions do not apply if the LLP was, at any time within the financial period, authorised to undertake insurance business, an e-money issuer, a MiFID investment firm or a UCITS management company, carried on insurance business or it was a member of an ineligible group. An ineligible group is one where any of its members is:

- a public company or body corporate whose shares are admitted to trading on a regulated exchange in an EEA state;
- a banking company;
- an authorised insurance business;
- an e-money issuer;
- a MiFID investment firm or a UCITS management company;
- a person who carries on insurance market activity; or
- an authorised person (other than a small company or small LLP) under the Financial Services and Markets Act 2000.

Where an LLP qualifies as small, it is permitted to prepare its accounts using the requirements set out in the Small Limited Liability Partnerships (Accounts) Regulations 2008 (SLLPR 2008) as amended by SI 2016/575, which reduces the amount of disclosure required within the accounts compared to medium-sized and large LLPs. This is referred to as the 'small LLPs regime'. Where financial statements are prepared in accordance with the small LLPs regime, this fact must be disclosed on the balance sheet above the signature.

A small LLP can choose, however, to comply with the requirements of the Large and Medium-sized Limited Liability Partnerships (Accounts) Regulations 2008 (LMLLPR 2008) and make the additional disclosure requirements required under those regulations – although in reality few small LLPs apply the LMLLPR 2008, choosing to take advantage of the reduced disclosures required under the small LLPs regime.

A parent LLP need not prepare group accounts for a financial period if it qualifies as a small group and is not an ineligible group as defined above. The qualification criteria for being a small group are similar to those for individual companies, in that the criteria have to be met:

- in the first financial period, in respect of that period;
- in subsequent periods, in both that period and the preceding period; or
- the group needs to have met the qualifying criteria in the preceding period.

The qualifying conditions are as follows:

Turnover	Not more than £10.2 million net (or £12.2 million gross)
Balance sheet total	Not more than £5.1 million net (or £6.1 million gross)
Number of employees	Not more than 50

Gross figures are the aggregated amounts for the group before eliminating group transactions and balances. Net figures reflect the elimination of intra-group trading and balances.

10 FRS 102, Section 1A *Small Entities*

2.10 Small LLPs which qualify for, and choose to, apply the small entities regime must comply with the disclosure requirements of Section 1A *Small Entities* of FRS 102 rather than the disclosure requirements of the LLP SORP (with an exception relating to the ranking of loans and other debts due to members (see **Focus** box below)). Section 1A of FRS 102 only deals with the **presentation** and **disclosure** requirements of small entities; in terms of **recognition** and **measurement**, these are based on full FRS 102/ the LLP SORP.

Appendix C to Section 1A *Disclosure requirements for small entities* outlines the disclosures required by law and Appendix D *Additional disclosures encouraged for small entities* outlines those disclosures which a small entity should consider making, where it is affected by such disclosures, in order that the financial statements give a true and fair view.

The disclosures in Appendix C deal with:

- accounting policies, including:
  - changes in presentation and accounting policies and corrections of prior period errors; and
  - true and fair override;
- notes supporting the statement of financial position;
- fixed assets, including:
  - fixed assets at revalued amounts; and
  - capitalisation of borrowing costs;
- impairment of assets;
- fair value measurement, including:
  - financial instruments measured at fair value; and
  - indebtedness, guarantees and financial commitments;
- notes supporting the income statement;
- related party disclosures; and
- other disclosures.

Focus

- In total there are some 39 legally required disclosures in the September 2015 edition of FRS 102 which must be made in the small LLP's financial statements where they apply and hence preparers must have a sound understanding of the provisions in Appendix C. In addition, the SORP mandates disclosure in a small LLP's financial statements about how loans and other debts due to members rank in relation to other unsecured creditors in order to give a true and fair view. This is mandated because LLP's are not subject to the capital maintenance provisions which companies are subjected to.

Notwithstanding the reduced disclosure requirements reflected in Section 1A, a small LLP's financial statements must still give a true and fair view (the mere application of the legally required minimum may be insufficient to achieve a true and fair view). The SORP confirms that judgement will be needed when considering whether further disclosures over and above those required by Section 1A should be made in order to ensure that the accounts give a true and fair view. In some situations, facts and circumstances may give rise to some, or all, of the disclosures included in the LLP SORP and the rest of FRS 102 having to be made in order to ensure that the accounts give a true and fair view.

Appendix D to Section 1A outlines five encouraged disclosures which are as follows:

- a statement of compliance with FRS 102, adapted to refer to Section 1A;
- a statement that the LLP is a public benefit entity, if applicable;
- disclosures relating to going concern where there are material uncertainties in relation to the LLP's ability to continue as a going concern;
- dividends declared and paid or payable during the period (although LLP's will not be affected by the payment of dividends as they do not hold share capital); and
- on first-time adoption of FRS 102, an explanation as to how the transition has affected the LLP's financial position and financial performance.

Focus

- The LLP SORP encourages small LLPs to include the reconciliation of movements in members' other interests which are detailed in paragraph 59 of the SORP.

11 Abridged and adapted financial statements

2.11 SI 2016/575 allows a small LLP to draw up abridged financial statements where appropriate to the circumstances of the LLP's business. Abridged financial statements only show those items in the statutory formats which are preceded by letters and Roman numerals; in other words, items preceded with Arabic numerals are omitted. Where the small LLP prepares a Format 1 or a Format 2 balance sheet, note 3 of the notes to the statutory formats must be complied with which says:

> 'Amounts in respect of concessions, parents, licences, trade marks and similar rights and assets must only be included in a company's balance sheet under this item if either—
>
> (a) the assets were acquired for valuable consideration and are not required to be shown under goodwill, or
>
> (b) the assets in question were created by the company itself.'

Where the small LLP prepares a Format 2 balance sheet, note 8 must be complied with which relates to net current assets (liabilities) and says:

> 'In determining the amount to be shown under this item any prepayments and accrued income must be taken into account wherever shown.'

An abridged profit and loss account combines turnover, other income and cost of sales in a Format 1 profit and loss account and turnover, change in stocks of finished goods and work in progress, own work capitalised, other operating income, raw materials and consumables and other external charges in a Format 2 profit and loss account. Therefore, the abridged profit and loss account starts with 'Gross profit or loss'.

In order to draw up abridged financial statements, the **unanimous consent** of **all** the members must be obtained. The agreement by the members is an annual process because members can only consent to abridged financial statements being drawn up in respect of the preceding financial year.

> **Focus**
>
> - Where a small LLP prepares abridged financial statements, the Regulations require a statement to be delivered to Companies House confirming that all members of the LLP have consented to the abridgement. This statement would normally be contained on the balance sheet filed with the registrar.

SI 2016/575 and the LLP SORP also allows LLPs the opportunity of adapting the formats of the balance sheet and profit loss account in a manner which is consistent with EU-adopted IAS 1 *Presentation of Financial Statements*. FRS 102 at paragraphs 4.2A to 4.2D and 5.5B to 5.5C outline the requirements for large and medium-sized LLPs. In respect of small LLPs, FRS 102 outlines the requirements at paragraphs 1AA.3 to 1AA.6 and 1AB.3 to 1AB.4.

Where an LLP chooses to adapt the statutory formats, the information provided must be equivalent to the information required by the formats which are set out in the Regulations. As a consequence, the LLP SORP requires separate disclosure in the balance sheet of:

- loans and other debts due to members (balance sheet item J); and
- members' other interests (balance sheet item K).

In addition, separate disclosure is also required in the profit and loss account in respect of 'Profit or loss for the financial year before members' remuneration and profit shares'.

12 Filing requirements for small LLPs

2.12 A small LLP has a choice as to what financial information is filed with the Registrar of Companies:

- the full financial statements; or
- a copy of the balance sheet which is prepared for the members (whether abridged or not) and the notes thereto (where the designated members of an LLP subject to the small LLPs regime do not deliver a copy of the profit and loss account to the registrar, the copy of the balance sheet delivered must disclose that fact);
- unless the LLP is exempt from audit and the members have taken advantage of that exemption, the notes to the balance sheet must:
  - state whether the auditor's report was qualified or unqualified;

- — where the auditor's report was qualified, disclose the basis of the qualification (reproducing any statement under section 498(2)(a) or (b) or (3), if applicable);
- — where the auditor's report was unqualified, include a reference to any matters to which the auditor drew attention by way of emphasis; and
- — state the name of the auditor and (where the auditor is a firm) the name of the person who signed the auditor's report as senior statutory auditor, or where the conditions in section 506 (circumstances in which names be omitted) are met, that a determination has been made and notified to the Secretary of State in accordance with that section.

Focus

- The concept of 'filleted financial statements' is proving quite popular among small LLPs. The term 'filleted financial statements' is not an 'official' term but refers to the financial statements filed at Companies House where the profit and loss account and any notes to the profit and loss account are removed and the remainder filed at Companies House (in other words the balance sheet, together with the related notes relating to the balance sheet). Accountants' reports for an LLP's financial statements which have not been subject to audit are not (and have never been) a legal requirement; they are a requirement of the relevant professional body and hence it is likely that such reports will continue to be produced. Some professional bodies require member firms to submit a copy of the accountant's report with the financial statements prepared for the registrar in order to distinguish accounts which have been prepared by a qualified firm from those prepared by a non-qualified firm.

13 Provisions applicable to medium-sized LLPs

2.13 At the time of writing, qualification as a medium-sized LLP is based on the requirements in CA 2006. The qualifying conditions, of which two or more have to be met, are as follows:

Turnover	Not more than £36 million
Balance sheet total	Not more than £18 million
Number of employees	Not more than 250

In respect of medium-sized groups, the qualifying criteria are as follows:

Turnover	Not more than £36 million net or £43.2 million gross
Balance sheet total	Not more than £18 million net or £21.6 million gross
Number of employees	Not more than 250

The concept of 'abbreviated' financial statements is repealed for medium-sized entities and therefore the medium-sized LLP must file the annual accounts.

14 International financial reporting standards and interaction with new UK GAAP

2.14 The Large and Medium-sized Limited Liability Partnerships Regulations 2008 permit the use by LLPs of EU-adopted International Financial Reporting Standards (IFRS). The SORP does not deal with the application of EU-adopted IFRS to LLPs and, to date, whilst some large LLPs have chosen to prepare their accounts in accordance with EU-adopted IFRS, the majority remain with UK GAAP. In September 2012, the Department for Business, Innovation and Skills published the Companies and Limited Liability Partnership (Accounts and Audit Exemptions and Change of Accounting Framework) Regulations 2012 ('the Regulations'). The impact of these changes created a number of new exemptions and widened certain existing exemptions in relation to requirements to prepare, file and audit annual accounts under the Companies Act 2006. Specifically, the Regulations were relaxed for LLPs which prepare accounts under EU-adopted IFRS and they now allow LLPs to prepare non-IFRS accounts. If the entity preparing IFRS accounts has not, at any time, during the five years before the first day of the relevant financial year, prepared Companies Act/non-IFRS accounts it will be free to switch. Any change during the preceding five years due to a relevant change of circumstance is to be ignored.

The 2012 Regulations came into force on 1 October 2012.

The Financial Reporting Council (FRC) issued FRS 102 *The Financial Reporting Standard applicable in the UK and Republic of Ireland* in March 2013 which replaced all extant FRSs, SSAPs and UITFs with effect for accounting periods commencing on or after 1 January 2015 and the LLP SORP was revised and re-issued in July 2014 for the consequential effects of FRS 102. FRS 102 was further revised in September 2015 to bring small entities under the scope of the standard mandatorily for accounting periods starting on or after 1 January 2016 (with early-adoption permissible). The SORP was also further revised to reflect these provisions as well as the less burdensome financial reporting regime which small and micro-entity LLPs can take advantage of. The revised SORP is applicable for accounting periods which start on or after 1 January 2016 (with early-adoption permissible. Although where the LLP early-adopts the revised SORP, it must also early-adopt the provisions in SI 2016/575).

FRS 102 is essentially based on the *IFRS for SMEs* which was issued by the International Accounting Standards Board and followed a long consultation by the (now defunct) Accounting Standards Board to overhaul UK GAAP. It had been the intention by the UK and Republic of Ireland standard-setters that the UK would always report under an international-based framework which is what FRS 102 effectively is. FRS 102 overhauls UK GAAP and is regarded as the most significant change in accounting in a generation. Previous UK GAAP had become overly complex in a lot of areas and was considered to be far too voluminous. In contrast to old UK GAAP (at just over 3,500 pages), FRS 102 (September 2015) is 378 pages long and brings with it a modernised way of accounting for many companies and LLPs whilst retaining some of the more established values enshrined in previous UK GAAP (eg use of the revaluation model for fixed assets and the adoption of the 'merger method' of accounting for group reconstructions).

The *Basis for Conclusions* at paragraph BC41 in the SORP acknowledges that the FRC considers there to be space for supplementary guidance, where relevant, in the form of

SORPs. As a consequence, the LLP SORP (as well as many of the other SORPs) had to be updated to bring them in line with FRS 102.

Paragraph BC42 to the LLP SORP acknowledges that whilst many of the changes to the SORP are straightforward and will not affect existing practice, paragraph BC43 does highlight more substantive changes to the SORP following the publication of FRS 102, including:

- Updating the guidance on business combinations and group accounts (paragraphs 102–119) to reflect the fact that FRS 102 only allows merger accounting to be used for group reconstructions and some public benefit entity combinations.
- Updating the guidance on contractual or constructive obligations (paragraph 76) and annuities (paragraph 80) to reflect the fact that FRS 102's requirements relating to financial liabilities differ from previous UK GAAP requirements.
- Updating references throughout to reflect the introduction of the option to produce a single statement of comprehensive income, including an additional exhibit in Appendix 1.

Further changes to the SORP in 2016 considered:

- the amendments made to FRS 102 in July 2014 which relaxed the conditions for determining whether financial statements are 'basic' or 'other' and updated the requirements on hedge accounting;
- the amendments made to FRS 102 in February 2015 which clarified aspects of defined benefit pension scheme accounting;
- the amendments made to UK accounting standards in July 2015 which resulted in:
  - the withdrawal of the FRSSE;
  - amendments made to FRS 102 to add a new section outlining presentation and disclosure requirements for small entities (Section 1A *Small Entities*) and other changes necessary for continued compliance with company law; and
  - the publication of FRS 105 *The Financial Reporting Standard applicable to the Micro-entities Regime* (see Chapter 14); and
- the amendments made to FRS 102 in March 2016 which updated the fair value hierarchy disclosures.

15 The main differences between previous UK GAAP and FRS 102

2.15 Notwithstanding the similarities between the previous UK GAAP and FRS 102, there are some notable differences which are likely to affect the way that amounts are recognised and measured in LLP financial statements and which may need consideration during the transition from UK GAAP to FRS 102 for LLPs.

The notable changes relate to the following issues:

- Accounting policies.

- Defined benefit pension schemes.
- Employee benefits.
- Fixed assets.
- Investment properties.
- Leases.
- Prior period adjustments.
- Revenue recognition.
- Stock valuations.

Accounting policies

2.16 Accounting policies, estimates and errors are covered in Section 10 *Accounting Policies, Estimates and Errors* of FRS 102. Paragraph 10.4 tells financial statement preparers that if FRS 102 does not specifically address a transaction, or other event or condition, an entity's management must develop and apply an accounting policy which is:

- **Relevant** – information is relevant to aid the decision-making process of the users; and
- **Reliable** – will result in the financial statements faithfully representing the financial position, performance and cash flows. In addition, the policy must also reflect the economic substance of the transaction(s)/event(s)/condition(s) rather than reflecting the legal form. To achieve reliability, the policy adopted must also be neutral, prudent and complete in all material respects.

FRS 18 *Accounting policies* was very similar, but in some cases the end result and impact on profit or loss would not necessarily have been the same.

Defined benefit pension schemes

2.17 Section 28 *Employee Benefits* at paragraph 28.18 provides a number of simplifications where the valuation basis (the Projected Unit Credit Method) would require undue cost or effort. Section 28 does not require the use of an independent actuary to provide a valuation as previous FRS 17 *Retirement Benefits* did. However, the entity must be able to measure its obligation and cost under defined benefit pension plans without undue cost or effort. Therefore, in reality, the vast majority of LLPs will have to use the services of an actuary to arrive at the valuations required to include the defined benefit pension plan within the financial statements. Paragraph 28.20 also does not require comprehensive actuarial valuations to be carried out annually.

The SORP acknowledges that the accounting and disclosures will differ depending on whether an LLP's obligation for defined benefit pension obligations falls within the scope of FRS 102 or FRS 103 *Insurance Contracts* and, if the former, depending on whether the obligation falls within the scope of Section 11 *Basic Financial Instruments* or Section 12 *Other Financial Instruments Issues* or Section 21 *Provisions and Contingencies*.

Paragraph 76B includes a flowchart which summarises how to determine which guidance applies to a particular obligation and is reproduced in Chapter 9.

Employee benefits

2.18 The main issue surrounding this area is the fact that under Section 28 *Employee Benefits*, accruals for short-term employee benefits (eg holiday pay) will have to be made. Many entities previously did not account for unpaid holiday pay accrued by the employees at the balance sheet date but not paid under previous UK GAAP in the belief that there was no specific standard which required this. However, FRS 12 *Provisions, contingent liabilities and contingent assets* at paragraph 11(b) did cite accrued holiday pay as a liability. Where the LLP has previously not accounted for unpaid holiday pay entitlement at the year-end, the difficulty is potentially in the calculation of holiday pay that is to be carried over for future use and pulling this information together for the very first time. This is likely to be time-consuming and cumbersome, particularly for large organisations where there is no central record of this information.

Fixed assets

2.19 Previous FRS 15 *Tangible fixed assets* went into a lot of detail about the capitalisation criteria for 'subsequent expenditure'. As a general rule, FRS 15 required subsequent expenditure to be written off to profit or loss unless the expenditure:

- Provided an enhancement of the economic benefits of the asset in excess of the previously assessed standard of performance.
- Related to a component of a tangible asset that had been treated separately for depreciation purposes which was replaced or restored.
- Related to a major inspection or overhaul of the tangible fixed asset that restored the economic benefits of the asset(s) that had been used up by the entity and which had already been reflected in the depreciation charge.

There were several paragraphs dealing with subsequent expenditure in FRS 15. However, FRS 102 does not specifically cover 'subsequent expenditure', but merely states at paragraph 17.15 that day-to-day servicing of property, plant and equipment must be recognised in profit or loss in the periods during which the costs are incurred. Users would therefore be directed to the *Concepts and Pervasive Principles* in Section 2 to FRS 102 to determine whether any subsequent expenditure does, in fact, meet the definition and recognition criteria of an asset outlined at paragraphs 2.15(a) and 2.27(a) and (b).

Paragraph 2.15(a) defines an asset and says that an asset is a resource controlled by the entity as a result of past events and from which future economic benefits are expected to flow to the entity. Paragraphs 2.27(a) and (b) outline the recognition criteria for assets, liabilities, equity, income and expenses. In respect of an asset, an LLP can only recognise an asset on the balance sheet when:

(a) it is probable (ie, more likely than not) that any future economic benefit associated with the item will flow to the entity; and

(b) the item has a cost or value that can be measured reliably.

Paragraph 17.5 deals with 'spare parts and servicing equipment'. Under previous UK GAAP, these were normally carried in the financial statements as stock with recognition taking place as and when such parts/equipment were used in the business. FRS 102 at paragraph 17.5 requires 'major' spare parts and stand-by equipment to be included within the cost of the fixed asset(s) to which it relates when the business is expected to use them for more than one accounting period. The main difference is that FRS 15 did not make reference to 'major spare parts/servicing equipment' and hence the treatment under FRS 102 would essentially mean that the cost of major spare parts/servicing equipment would be recognised within the depreciation charge as opposed to consumption of stock (cost of sales).

Where fixed assets are acquired under deferred payment arrangements (in other words deferred beyond normal credit term), the cost of the asset under FRS 102 must be the present value of all future payments in accordance with paragraph 17.13 of FRS 102. Such issues were not specifically covered in FRS 15 and would mean that under previous GAAP the value of assets would have been under-stated, giving rise to a lower depreciation charge. FRS 102 addresses this issue so that the book value of fixed assets under new UK GAAP will be higher, but this would also have a consequential increase in depreciation charges, thus reducing profitability or increasing losses in an LLP where appropriate.

Investment properties

2.20 SSAP 19 *Accounting for investment properties* required such properties to be measured in the balance sheet at their market value, with any changes in this market value going through the revaluation reserve account (ie reported through the statement of total recognised gains and losses). This was because under previous UK GAAP, investment properties were accounted for under the Alternative Accounting Rules which required changes in market value to go to a revaluation reserve within equity.

Paragraph 16.7 to FRS 102 extinguishes the use of the revaluation reserve account and requires all changes in fair value to be recognised in profit or loss. In contrast to SSAP 19, FRS 102 uses the Fair Value Accounting Rules rather than the Alternative Accounting Rules. The upshot of this treatment is that reported profit or loss would be different than would otherwise have been the case under previous GAAP.

There was a specific scope exemption for groups under SSAP 19 at paragraph 8(b) which confirmed that a property let to, and occupied by, another group member is not an investment property for the purpose of its own accounts or the group accounts. This scope exemption is not carried over into FRS 102 (September 2015) and this may create complications for LLPs which prepare group accounts that have investment property let out to other group members because reclassification may have to take place in both the individual accounts (which will treat the property as investment property) and in the group accounts (which may reclassify the property back to owned property, plant and equipment). The reason that reclassification would take place in the group accounts is because group accounts show the results of the group in line with its economic substance, which is that of a single reporting entity. It follows, therefore, that in the group accounts, the group still owns a property regardless of the fact that it is let out to a group member because the group accounts show the results as if the group structure did not exist, hence it will be reclassified on consolidation as owned property, plant and equipment. It is advisable to carry out an impact assessment on transition to FRS 102 to understand the effect of investment property which is owned by a group.

Leases

2.21 Previous SSAP 21 *Accounting for leases and hire purchase contracts* set out a specific numeric benchmark when determining whether a lease is a finance lease or an operating lease. This benchmark was where the present value of the minimum lease payments equated to 90% or more of the fair value of the asset subjected to the lease and in such cases the lease was treated as a finance lease and capitalised on the balance sheet with a corresponding finance lease creditor.

The classification under Section 20 *Leases* does not refer to a 90% benchmark, but instead offers examples of the various situations that individually, or in combination, would give rise to a lease being classified as a finance lease. The classification criteria are found in paragraphs 20.5 and 20.6 of FRS 102 and are based upon the risks and rewards of ownership of the associated asset and which party retains those risks and rewards as follows:

(a) the lease transfers ownership of the asset to the lessee by the end of the **lease term**;

(b) the lessee has the option to purchase the asset at a price that is expected to be sufficiently lower than the **fair value** at the date the option becomes exercisable for it to be reasonably certain, at the **inception of the lease**, that the option will be exercised;

(c) the lease term is for the major part of the economic life of the asset even if title is not transferred;

(d) at the inception of the lease the **present value** of the **minimum lease payments** amounts to at least substantially all of the fair value of the leased asset; and

(e) the leased assets are of such a specialised nature that only the lessee can use them without major modifications.[1]

There are then three additional situations that individually or in combination could also lead to a lease being classified as a finance lease as follows:

(a) if the lessee can cancel the lease, the lessor's losses associated with the cancellation are borne by the lessee;

(b) **gains** or losses from the fluctuation in the **residual value** of the leased asset accrue to the lessee (eg in the form of a rent rebate equalling most of the sales proceeds at the end of the lease); and

(c) the lessee has the ability to continue the lease for a secondary period at a rent that is substantially lower than market rent.[2]

1 FRS 102, para 20.5(a)–(e).
2 FRS 102, para 20.6(c).

There are a number of factors which can determine whether risks and rewards of ownership have, or have not, been transferred from lessor to lessee and therefore paragraph 20.7 to FRS 102 acknowledges that the examples in paragraphs 20.5 and 20.6 are not conclusive in every respect and consideration must therefore be given to other indicators that risks and rewards may (or may not) have transferred from lessor to lessee and hence there is more judgement required under FRS 102.

Prior period adjustments

2.22 The difference in this area relates to error correction. Error correction is dealt with in Section 10 *Accounting Policies, Estimates and Errors* (paragraphs 10.19–10.23). Paragraph 10.21 requires an entity to correct an error by way of a prior period adjustment if the error is 'material'. In contrast, FRS 3 *Reporting financial performance* required an entity to correct an error by way of a prior year adjustment if the error was 'fundamental'. Fundamental errors were deemed to be those which essentially destroyed the truth and fairness of the financial statements as well as the validity of those financial statements.

The terms 'material' and 'fundamental' could be interpreted differently amongst preparers of financial statements. It is likely, however, that more errors will be corrected by way of a prior period adjustment under FRS 102.

Revenue recognition

2.23 There are some slight variations to the wording relating to the measurement of revenue in Section 23 *Revenue*. For example, in paragraph 23.3, FRS 102 refers to revenue being the fair valuation of the consideration 'received or receivable'. Application Note G to FRS 5 *Reporting the substance of transactions* said that a seller would recognise revenue under an exchange transaction with a customer when, and to the extent that, it obtained the 'right to consideration' in exchange for its performance.

This subtle difference in wording could *potentially* allow for later recognition of profit. It is possible that the Financial Reporting Council could issue further guidance to clarify this point if there is any evidence that entities are abusing the wording in Section 23 and hence disproportionately accelerating or delaying revenue recognition.

Paragraph 23.15 to FRS 102 refers to a 'specific act' and a 'significant act'. The paragraph says that when a specific act is much more significant than any other act, the entity postpones revenue recognition until the significant act is executed. UITF 40 was more prohibitive in that it required revenue to be recognised in line with performance (passing a 'milestone' or the occurrence of a 'critical event') and earning the right to consideration, hence there is more judgement needed in FRS 102.

Paragraph 23.16 of FRS 102 says that if an entity cannot estimate the outcome of a service contract then the entity should only recognise revenue to the extent of the costs incurred. In contrast, paragraph 10 to SSAP 9 *Stocks and long-term contracts* said that where the outcome of a long-term contract could not be assessed with reasonable certainty, no profit should be reflected in profit or loss and suggested showing as turnover a proportion of the total contract value using a zero estimate of profit.

Stock valuations

2.24 SSAP 9 *Stocks and long-term contracts* allowed stock to be valued using the 'last-in first-out' (LIFO) method. Whilst this methodology was permissible in SSAP 9, the standard itself acknowledged that there must have to be justifiable reasons for its use and hence did not favour the use of such a valuation.

Paragraph 13.18 of FRS 102 follows the same stance as *IFRS for SMEs* which outlaws the use of the LIFO method as a basis of inventory valuation.

Chapter summary

- LLPs are subject to requirements in law which dictate the form and content of the financial statements.
- SI 2016/575 made significant amendments to legislation in respect of small and micro-entity LLPs that can now apply a less burdensome financial reporting regime in the preparation of their financial statements.
- The LLP must retain accounting records for minimum timeframes specified in law.
- Accounting reference dates cannot be longer than 18 months and cannot be changed more than one in any five-year period.
- Group members should have uniform accounting reference dates.
- FRS 105 *The Financial Reporting Standard applicable to the Micro-entities Regime* can be used for a micro-entity LLP (see Chapter 14). LLPs using FRS 105 are scoped out of the requirements of the LLP SORP. FRS 105 is used mandatorily for an accounting period starting on or after 1 January 2016 (although early-adoption is permissible).
- Small LLPs are moved under the scope of FRS 102, Section 1A *Small Entities* mandatorily for accounting periods starting on or after 1 January 2016 (although early-adoption is permissible).
- The SORP outlines certain information which must be included in the members' report and LLPs are not legally required to prepare a strategic report.
- The latest version of the LLP SORP was issued in January 2017.
- Small groups need not prepare consolidated financial statements but medium-sized and large groups must prepare such consolidated accounts.
- The members are required to approve the financial statements which are signed on their behalf by a designated member. A copy of the accounts is to be filed at Companies House within nine months of the accounting period end.
- The concept of abbreviated financial statements has been repealed although special provisions apply to small LLPs in respect of what they are required to file at Companies House.

- Section 1A of FRS 102 outlines the presentation and disclosure requirements only. In respect of recognition and measurement of amounts, these are based on full FRS 102.
- Appendix C in Section 1A outlines the legally required disclosures; whereas Appendix D outlines the encouraged disclosures. In all cases, small LLPs must ensure the financial statements give a true and fair view.
- SI 2016/575 allows the preparation of abridged and adapted financial statements. In respect of abridged financial statements, all the members must unanimously agree to the abridgement.
- There are notable differences between previous UK GAAP and FRS 102 which must be understood in order that the financial statements can be correctly prepared.

Chapter 3

The LLP and auditor relationship

Signposts

- Unless covered by exemption, all LLPs are required to appoint auditors and have their accounts audited (see **3.1**).
- Exemption from audit is available for an LLP that qualifies as a small LLP (see **3.2**).
- LLPs which do not have an audit are still required to file their financial statements with the Registrar of Companies (see **3.2**).
- It is the members' responsibility to prepare financial statements which give a true and fair view (see **3.3**).
- There are a range of matters which the auditors are required to communicate with the members of the LLP throughout the entire audit process (see **3.4**).
- An engagement letter should be in place between the LLP and the audit firm which sets out the terms on which the auditor will act and explains the respective responsibilities of the members and the auditor (see **3.5**).
- The 'preconditions' for an audit must be present before the auditor can accept engagement or reappointment as auditor (see **3.5**).
- The auditor may seek representations from the members during the course of the audit, which is usually in written form, and there are certain specific representations which the auditor must obtain to comply with the International Standards on Auditing (UK) (see **3.6**).
- Any deficiencies in internal control should be brought to the attention of the members (see **3.7**).
- At the end of the audit process, the auditor will produce an auditor's report on the financial statements which contains the auditor's opinion as to whether the financial statements give a true and fair view and have been properly prepared in accordance with the financial reporting framework and legislation. There are certain elements that the auditor's report must contain (see **3.8**).
- Auditors also have to report on certain matters by exception (see **3.8**).
- There may be additional reports needed covering an LLP's compliance with certain regulations which is required to be supplied to regulators and the format is usually specified by relevant legislation (see **3.9**).

- If a third party is required to be provided with reports on certain aspects of the LLP's financial information, the auditor may require the third party to be included in the engagement letter before it will report to them (see **3.10**).
- Legislation and certain protocol have to be complied with if an LLP wishes to remove or change its auditors, or if the auditor wishes to vacate office (see **3.11**).
- Regulatory bodies (such as the auditor's professional body) may also have to be notified when the auditor vacates office (see **3.11**).
- A statement of circumstances must be lodged with Companies House within 14 days of the auditor vacating office (see **3.11**).

1 General requirement to appoint auditors

3.1 The requirements with respect to audit are set out in Parts 10 to 14 of The Limited Liability Partnerships (Accounts and Audit) (Application of Companies Act 2006) Regulations 2008.

Unless entitled to the exemptions set out below, all LLPs are required to appoint auditors and have their accounts audited. For the first accounting period, auditors must be appointed no later than 28 days from the time allowed for sending out copies of the LLP's accounts to members (see **2.8**). Thereafter, the regulations require appointment or reappointment for the subsequent year's audit to be made no later than 28 days after the date upon which the financial statements are required to be filed with the Registrar of Companies (Companies House) or, if earlier, the date on which the previous year's financial statements are sent to members under section 423. However, where it is intended that the auditors for the previous financial year should stay in office, no action is required, as the regulations permit the auditors to be deemed as reappointed, unless:

- the members' agreement requires actual reappointment; or
- the deemed reappointment is prevented by the members under section 488; or
- the members have determined the auditor should not be reappointed; or
- the designated members have determined that no auditor should be appointed for the financial year in question.

2 Exemption from audit

3.2 Exemption from audit is available for an LLP that both qualifies as a small LLP in respect of a particular financial year (see **2.9**) and which has turnover of less than £10.2 million and a balance sheet total (total assets before taking account of liabilities) that does not exceed £5.1 million. These thresholds were increased in 2016 by the government (SI 2016/575) and apply for accounting periods starting on or after 1 January 2016, with early-adoption permissible. Audit exemption, however, is not available where the LLP:

- has securities admitted for trading on a regulated market in an EEA state;

- is an authorised insurance company, a banking LLP, an e-money issuer, a MiFID investment firm or UCITS management company;
- is carrying on insurance market business;
- is an employers' association as defined in section 122 of the Trade Union and Labour Relations (Consolidation) Act 1992; or
- is a parent or a subsidiary unless:
  - — throughout the financial period in which it was a subsidiary, it was dormant; or
  - — it is a parent or subsidiary in a small group (see **2.9**) for the definition of a small group). In addition, the group's aggregate turnover should not be more than £10.2 million net (or £12.2 million gross) and the group's aggregate balance sheet total should be no more than £5.1 million net (or £6.1 million gross). It should be noted that the rules with respect to groups require all worldwide interests to be taken into account and not just the UK position. The thresholds for groups were also updated by virtue of SI 2016/575.

An LLP which is exempt from audit is still required to file accounts with the Registrar of Companies and must also circulate a full set of the accounts to each member. The LLP must also file its accounts with the Registrar no later than nine months after the year-end date. Failure to submit the accounts by the filing deadline will result in penalties being levied by Companies House (which are doubled if the accounts were also filed late in the previous year).

Entitlement to the exemption is dependent on inclusion on the balance sheet of the statement set out below, which must be inserted immediately above the signature of the designated member(s):

> 'For the financial year ended [insert year-end date], the LLP was entitled to exemption from audit under section 477 Companies Act 2006 (as applied to LLPs). The members acknowledge their responsibilities for ensuring that the LLP keeps accounting records which comply with section 386 of the Act (as applied to LLPs) and for preparing accounts which give a true and fair view of the state of affairs of the LLP as at the end of the financial year and of its profit or loss for the financial year in accordance with the requirements of section 394 and 395 (as applied to LLPs) and which otherwise comply with the requirements of the Companies Act 2006 (as applied to LLPs) relating to accounts, so far as applicable to the LLP.'

3 Responsibilities of members and auditors

3.3 As noted at **1.6** the members of the LLP have ultimate responsibility for preparing accounts that give a true and fair view. This responsibility remains the same, even in circumstances where the audit firm may have been engaged to assist in the preparation of those accounts.

Micro-entity LLPs (see Chapter 14) preparing their financial statements under the micro-entities' regime and applying FRS 105 *The Financial Reporting Standard applicable to the*

Micro-entities Regime are only required to prepare their financial statements in accordance with the basic legal requirements. Where the micro-entity LLP complies with such legal requirements, the financial statements are presumed to give a true and fair view, even if the partners choose not to make any additional disclosures.

4 Communication between the auditor and the LLP

3.4 In June 2016, the Financial Reporting Council issued revised versions of UK International Standards on Auditing (ISAs). Previously the ISAs were ISAs (UK and Ireland). However, following the transposition of the Audit Regulation and Directive, the ISAs now only relate to the UK. The revised ISAs (UK) are effective for audits of financial statements for periods commencing on or after 17 June 2016 and this book will focus throughout on the revised ISAs (UK).

ISAs (UK) require auditors to communicate with the members of the LLP on a range of matters throughout the audit process, including:

- the terms under which the auditor will act for the LLP, including the respective responsibilities of the auditors and the LLP (see below);
- any relationships between the LLP and the audit firm that may affect, or be perceived to affect, the audit firm's independence;
- the nature and scope of the audit work to be performed;
- the findings from the audit, including:
  - the auditor's views about the qualitative aspects of the LLP's accounting practices;
  - the written representations the auditor will be requesting from management and, where applicable, those charged with governance, in respect of the audit (see **3.6**);
  - the extent of uncorrected misstatements found during the course of the audit;
  - any expected modifications to the auditor's report; and
  - material weaknesses in internal controls identified during the audit.

5 Terms of engagement

3.5 ISA (UK) 210 (Revised June 2016) *Agreeing the Terms of Audit Engagements* sets out the requirements for the auditor and the LLP to agree the terms on which the auditor will act. Ordinarily the terms will be agreed in the form of an engagement letter which will be signed by both parties. The auditor must review the terms of the engagement letter at the commencement of each audit (ie annually) and determine whether the engagement letter should be updated or the LLP reminded of the engagement terms. Appendix 1 to this chapter provides an illustrative letter of engagement in respect of an audit assignment (note – this illustrative engagement letter is not definitive and regard should be had to client-specific matters that may need to be incorporated in the letter of engagement).

The engagement letter issued by the auditor sets out the terms on which the auditor will act and also establishes, in writing, the respective responsibilities of auditors and members. Where the audit firm is to provide other services in addition to the audit (for example, taxation advice), to the extent that these services are also of a recurring nature, they may be included in the same letter or may be the subject of a separate letter dependent on the procedures of the audit firm – in practice many firms issue separate letters to cover such circumstances so that the audit engagement is clearly separate. It is not unusual for the same firm in addition to provide services to individual members (for example the completion of a member's self-assessment income tax return). Such services will be covered by separate letters of engagement between the audit firm and the individual member.

As well as detailing the services being provided, the engagement letter will also set out the limitations in the audit process and it is essential that the members understand the scope of the services being provided to avoid any misunderstanding at a later date. The audit firm will ask that a designated member sign a copy of the letter confirming, on behalf of all members, that they understand and agree with the terms.

Focus

- The importance of an up-to-date and appropriate letter of engagement cannot be over-emphasised. Not only does the engagement letter outline the respective responsibilities of each party, but it is also a means of protection for both parties. It is therefore imperative that both parties (the auditor and the members of the LLP) fully understand the provisions in the engagement letter. In addition, engagement letters should be reviewed at least annually to ensure they are up-to-date because difficulties can, and do, arise where engagement letters are not kept up-to-date.

ISA (UK) 210 (Revised June 2016) requires the auditor to ensure that the 'preconditions' for the audit are present before acceptance of the audit engagement. To ensure that the preconditions are present, the auditor shall:

- establish if the financial reporting framework used in preparation of the LLP's financial statements is acceptable; and
- obtain the members' agreement that they acknowledge and understand their responsibility:
  - to prepare the financial statements in accordance with the applicable financial reporting framework including, where relevant, their fair presentation;
  - for such internal control as the members' deem necessary to enable the LLP's financial statements to be prepared free from material misstatement, whether such misstatement is due to fraud or error; and
  - to provide the auditor with:
    1. access to all the information of which the members are aware which is relevant to the preparation of the financial statements;
    2. any additional information which the auditor may request from management for the purposes of the audit; and

3. unrestricted access to persons within the entity from whom the auditor determines it is necessary to obtain audit evidence.

Example – preconditions not present

An audit firm has been approached by ABC Partnership LLP to audit the LLP's financial statements for the year-ended 30 June 2017. Discussions with the members and the auditor have taken place and during that discussion the designated members refused permission for the auditor to have unrestricted access to anyone within the entity (other than the designated members) to obtain audit evidence as the designated members did not want any other individuals within the LLP discussing financial issues with the auditors.

In this scenario the preconditions for an audit are not fully present because unrestricted access to persons within the entity from whom the auditor determines it is necessary to obtain audit evidence has been refused.

In such cases paragraph 8 to ISA (UK) 210 (Revised June 2016) says that the auditor has to discuss the matter with management (ie obtain reasons why access is restricted). Once discussions have been entered into and the preconditions are still not present, the auditor must not accept the proposed audit engagement. The exception to this would be where the auditor is required by law or regulation to accept the proposed audit engagement.

The recurring nature of the audit appointment means that it may not be necessary to reissue the letter of engagement every year. However, as part of their annual planning process, the auditors will reconsider the content of the letter and decide whether it is necessary to reissue it. This may be required where there is a significant change of management, a significant change in the membership of the LLP, or a change in any relevant legal or professional requirements (such as a change in financial reporting framework). An important point to emphasise is that regulatory bodies which inspect the audit quality of audit firms must be satisfied that the letter of engagement is up-to-date – many audit firms are criticised for failing to have an up-to-date letter of engagement and in some rarer cases firms are criticised for failing to have a letter of engagement on file at all.

6 Written representations

3.6 Some of the evidence obtained by the auditors will come in the form of oral representations from the management of the LLP. In order to clarify understanding of these representations and to enable the auditors to fully document the evidence upon which their opinion is based, the auditors will request written confirmation prior to the auditor's report being signed. The written representation most usually takes the form of a representation letter to the auditors signed on behalf of the LLP by a designated member or members and be prepared on the LLPs letterhead. However, on occasion it may be a letter from the auditors outlining their understanding of the representations received, which is then acknowledged and confirmed in writing by the members.

ISA (UK) 580 *Written Representations* deals with the auditor's responsibilities to obtain written representations from the LLP. This ISA (UK) requires the auditor to ask for a written representation from the appropriate members that they acknowledge their responsibility for the financial statements and that the members have discharged their responsibility for the preparation of the financial statements in accordance with the applicable financial reporting framework including, where relevant, their fair presentation.

In addition, ISA (UK) 580 requires written confirmation from the members of the LLP regarding the following:

- That the members have provided the auditor with all relevant information and access as agreed in the terms of the audit engagement.
- That all transactions have been recorded and are reflected within the LLP's financial statements.
- That the members acknowledge their responsibility for the design and implementation of controls to prevent and detect fraud and that they have disclosed to the auditors their knowledge of fraud or suspected fraud.
- That the members have disclosed to the auditors any events that involve possible non-compliance with the laws or regulations, providing the legal framework within which the LLP conducts its business and which are central to the LLP's ability to conduct its business.
- That information provided regarding the related party and control disclosures in the financial statements is complete. (See **9.37–9.42** for a further discussion of related parties.)
- An explanation of the reasons for not adjusting any misstatements brought to the attention of the members by the auditors.
- The members' assessment of whether the LLP is a going concern (see Chapter 10).
- These confirmations would usually be included in the written representation.

Appendix 1 to ISA (UK) 580 contains a list of paragraphs within other UK ISAs which the auditor should obtain specific representations, including:

- ISA (UK) 240 (Revised June 2016), *The Auditor's Responsibilities Relating to Fraud in an Audit of Financial Statements* – paragraph 39.
- ISA (UK) 250 (Revised June 2016), *Consideration of Laws and Regulations in an Audit of Financial Statements* – paragraph 16.
- ISA (UK and Ireland) 450 (Revised June 2016), *Evaluation of Misstatements Identified during the Audit* – paragraph 14.
- ISA (UK) 501 *Audit Evidence – Specific Considerations for Selected Items* – paragraph 12.
- ISA (UK) 540 (Revised June 2016), *Auditing Accounting Estimates, Including Fair Value Accounting Estimates, and Related Disclosures* – paragraph 22.
- ISA (UK) 550 *Related Parties* – paragraph 26.
- ISA (UK) 560 *Subsequent Events* – paragraph 9.
- ISA (UK) 570 (Revised June 2016), *Going Concern* – paragraph 16(e).

- ISA (UK) 710 *Comparative Information – Corresponding Figures and Comparative Financial Statements* – paragraph 9.
- ISA (UK) 720 (Revised June 2016), *The Auditor's Responsibilities Relating to Other Information* – paragraph 13(c).

An example written representation letter is shown in Appendix 2 to this chapter.

7 Material weaknesses in internal control

3.7 The communication of material weaknesses is usually in the form of a letter of recommendation (often referred to as a management letter or letter of comment) to the LLP. The LLP will usually be requested to include the extent of any action they intend to take as a consequence of the letter of recommendation.

The communication from the auditor will also explain that it is restricted to those matters that come to the attention of the audit firm during the course of their work, and that the audit is not designed to identify all matters that may be of relevance to the members of the LLP.

ISA (UK) 265 *Communicating Deficiencies in Internal Control to Those Charged with Governance and Management* is appropriate where the auditor has discovered deficiencies within internal control and considers it appropriate that such deficiencies warrant the attention of management and those charged with governance of the entity. 'Significant deficiencies' in internal control must be communicated to those charged with governance and paragraph 6(b) to ISA (UK) 265 says that a deficiency is significant when, in the auditor's professional judgement, such a deficiency is of sufficient importance that it warrants the attention of those charged with governance.

A deficiency in internal control exists when the control(s) present will not prevent, detect or correct misstatements arising in the financial statements on a timely basis. This can also be the case when a misstatement(s) arises in the financial statements and necessary controls are missing.

Example – missing internal controls

A firm of accountants operates as an LLP and the financial statements for the year-ended 31 August 2017 are currently being audited. Analytical review procedures have been adopted by the auditor and these have highlighted a disproportionate increase in payroll costs for the accountancy firm which was not expected. The payroll charge has been disaggregated into each respective month and it was noted that for the last six months of the financial year the payroll costs have increased significantly, but staff numbers have remained consistent.

Additional audit procedures have been undertaken which has revealed that two audit teams have claimed overtime payments each month. Examination of the time sheets for each audit team member have been scrutinised and these reveal no additional overtime has been undertaken and the general policy of the firm is that no overtime should be worked on audits unless specifically authorised by the audit engagement partner. A discussion with the payroll supervisor indicates that the audit team merely emails their overtime each month and this is included in the payroll by the payroll supervisor. There are, in fact, no checks undertaken by the partners of the accountancy firm on either the payroll or the overtime worked by the audit teams due to their workloads.

The controls that should be present (ie authorisation of overtime and authorisation of the payroll by a senior official) are not present. Such overtime claims by the audit teams in this example could be indicative of a fraud risk factor and such matters should be brought to the attention of those charged with governance of the LLP.

---

8 The auditor's report

3.8 The auditor's report is generally the only output of an external statutory audit which the members receive. ISA (UK) 700 (Revised June 2016) *Forming an Opinion and Reporting on Financial Statements* establishes the form and content of the auditor's report on the LLP financial statements. The auditor's report itself will contain certain elements as follows:

- **Title:** It will have an appropriate title to distinguish the audit report from other reports in the LLP's financial statements.
- **Addressee:** It will be appropriately addressed to the members of the LLP.
- **Auditor's opinion:** ISA (UK) 700 requires the first section of the auditor's report to include the auditor's opinion and shall have the heading 'Opinion'. The Opinion section must also:
  - identify the entity whose financial statements have been audited;
  - state that the financial statements have been audited;
  - identify the title of each statement comprising the financial statements;
  - refer to the notes, including the summary of significant accounting policies; and
  - specify the date of, or period covered by, each financial statement comprising the financial statements.
- Where the auditor expresses an unqualified opinion, it must use one of the following phrases:
  - In our opinion, the accompanying financial statements present fairly, in all material respects, [...] in accordance with [the applicable financial reporting framework]; or
  - In our opinion, the accompanying financial statements give a true and fair view of [...] in accordance with [the applicable financial reporting framework].
- **Basis for opinion:** The auditor's report must include a section, directly underneath the Opinion section, with the heading 'Basis for Opinion', which:
  - states that the audit was conducted in accordance with International Standards on Auditing (UK) and applicable law;

- refers to the section of the auditor's report which describes the auditor's responsibilities under the ISAs (UK);
- includes a statement that the auditor is independent of the entity in accordance with the relevant ethical requirements relating to the audit, and has fulfilled the auditor's other ethical responsibilities in accordance with these requirements. The statement must identify the jurisdiction of origin of the relevant ethical requirements or refer to the International Ethics Standards Board for Accountants' *Code of Ethics for Professional Accountants* (IESBA Code) (see **Focus** box below); and
- states whether the auditor believes that the audit evidence the auditor has obtained is sufficient and appropriate to provide a basis for the auditor's opinion.

Focus

- In the UK, auditors are subject to the ethical requirements from two sources: the Financial Reporting Council's (FRC) *Ethical Standard* which concerns the integrity, objectivity and independence of the auditor and the ethical pronouncements established by the auditor's professional body. When identifying the relevant ethical requirements in the auditor's report, the auditor must indicate that these include the FRC's *Ethical Standard*, applied as required for the types of entity determined to be appropriate in the circumstances.

- **Going concern**: Where applicable, the auditor must report in accordance with ISA (UK) 570 (Revised June 2016) *Going Concern* (see Chapter 4).
- **Key audit matters**: this only relates to listed entities.
- **Other information**: The auditor shall, where applicable, report in accordance with ISA (UK) 720 (Revised June 2016) *The Auditor's Responsibilities Relating to Other Information.*
- **Responsibilities for the financial statements**: This section of the auditor's report must be headed up 'Responsibilities of Management for the Financial Statements' (or an alternative term which is appropriate in the context of the legal framework in the particular jurisdiction). This section must describe management's responsibility for:
  - preparing the financial statements in accordance with the applicable financial reporting framework, and for such internal control as management determines is necessary to enable the preparation of financial statements which are free from material misstatement, whether due to fraud or error; and
  - assessing the entity's ability to continue as a going concern and whether the use of the going concern presumption is appropriate (including disclosing,

where applicable, any matters relating to going concern). The explanation of management's responsibility for this assessment must also include a description of when the use of the going concern basis of accounting is appropriate.

This section of the report must also identify those responsible for oversight of the financial reporting process, if those responsible for such oversight are different from management. Where those responsible for oversight of the financial reporting process are different from management, this particular section of the report must also refer to 'Those Charged with Governance'.

- **Responsibilities of the auditor**: This section of the auditor's report must be headed up 'Auditor's Responsibilities for the Audit of the Financial Statements' and must:
  - State that the objectives of the auditor are to:
    - (i) obtain reasonable assurance about whether the financial statements as a whole are free from material misstatement, whether due to fraud or error; and
    - (ii) issue an auditor's report that includes the auditor's opinion.
  - State that reasonable assurance is a high level of assurance, but is not a guarantee that an audit conducted in accordance with ISAs (UK) will always detect a material misstatement when it exists.
  - State that misstatements can arise from fraud or error, and either:
    - (i) describe that they are considered material if, individually or in aggregate, they could reasonably be expected to influence the economic decisions of users taken on the basis of the financial statements; or
    - (ii) provide a definition or description of materiality in accordance with the applicable financial reporting framework.

  The auditor's report must also state that in applying ISAs (UK), the auditor exercises professional judgement and maintains professional scepticism throughout the audit. In addition, this section of the report must also describe an audit by stating that the auditor's responsibilities are to:
  - identify and assess the risks of material misstatement of the financial statements, whether due to fraud or error;
  - design and perform audit procedures responsive to those risks;
  - obtain audit evidence that is sufficient and appropriate to provide a basis for the auditor's opinion;
  - obtain an understanding of internal control relevant to the auditor so as to design audit procedures which are appropriate in the circumstances but not for the purposes of expressing an opinion on the effectiveness of the entity's internal control (although if the auditor has a responsibility to express an opinion on the effectiveness of internal control in conjunction with the financial statements audit, the auditor must omit the phrase that the auditor's

consideration of internal control is not for the purpose of expressing an opinion on the effectiveness of the entity's internal control);

— evaluate the appropriateness of the entity's accounting policies and the reasonableness of accounting estimates and related disclosures made by management;

— conclude on the appropriateness of management's use of the going concern basis of accounting and, based on the audit evidence obtained, whether a material uncertainty exists which is related to events or conditions that may cast significant doubt on the entity's ability to continue as a going concern. Where the auditor concludes that a material uncertainty exists, they are required to draw attention in the auditor's report to the related disclosures in the financial statements; or, where such disclosures are inadequate, modify the audit opinion; and

— when the financial statements are prepared in accordance with a fair presentation framework, evaluate the overall presentation, structure and content of the financial statements, including the disclosures, and whether the financial statements represent the underlying transactions and events in a manner which achieves fair presentation.

In a group audit, the auditor's responsibilities section must also state that:

— the auditor's responsibilities are to obtain sufficient appropriate audit evidence regarding the financial information of the entities or business activities within the group to express an opinion on the group financial statements;

— the auditor is responsible for the direction, supervision and performance of the group audit; and

— the auditor remains solely responsible for the auditor's opinion.

The auditor's responsibilities section must also:

— state that the auditor communicates with those charged with governance regarding, among other matters, the planned scope and timing of the audit as well as significant findings from the audit, including any significant deficiencies in internal control;

— for listed entities, state that the auditor provides those charged with governance with a statement that the auditor has complied with relevant ethical requirements regarding independence and communicate with them all relationships and other matters which may reasonably be thought to bear on the auditor's independence and related safeguards; and

— in respect of key audit matters (for listed entities) include a 'Key Audit Matters' section.

> **Focus**
>
> - ISA (UK) 700 (Revised June 2016) permits the Description of the Auditor's Responsibilities for the Audit of Financial Statements section of the report to be included:
>   - within the body of the auditor's report;
>   - in an appendix to the auditor's report; or
>   - by a specific reference within the auditor's report to the location of such a description on a website of an appropriate authority, where law, regulation or national auditing standards expressly permits the auditor to do so.

- **Other reporting responsibilities:** Where the auditor reports on other areas of the financial statements which are in addition to the auditor's responsibilities under the ISAs (UK), these reporting responsibilities must be included in a separate section of the auditor's report headed up 'Report on Other Legal and Regulatory Requirements' unless these topics are the same as those presented under the reporting responsibilities required by ISAs (UK).
- **Reporting by exception**: If the auditor is required to report on certain matters by exception, the auditor must escribe in the auditor's report the auditor's responsibilities for such matters and incorporate a suitable conclusion in respect of such matters.
- **Name of the engagement partner**: The name of the engagement partner must be included in the auditor's report of listed entities (unless such disclosure is reasonably expected to lead to a significant personal security threat).
- **Signature of the auditor**: The auditor's report must be signed.
- **Auditor's address**: The auditor's report must include the location in the jurisdiction where the auditor practises.
- **Date**: The auditor's report must be dated no earlier than the date on which the auditor has obtained sufficient appropriate audit evidence on which to base the opinion on the financial statements. In the UK, the date of the auditor's report is the date on which the auditor signed the report expressing an opinion on the financial statements and must not be signed and dated any earlier than the date on which all of those charged with governance has approved all the information in the annual report.

In addition to reporting on whether the accounts of the LLP give a true and fair view, there are certain other matters which legislation requires auditors to report on by exception. These are as follows:

- Whether adequate accounting records have been maintained.
- Whether the accounts are in agreement with the accounting records and returns.
- Whether the auditors have obtained all of the information and explanations which they consider to be necessary to enable them to perform their audit.

Where the content of any other information accompanying the financial statements including the members' report is inconsistent with the accounts, the auditors may decide that this should be referred to in their auditor's report.

Auditors are also required to report on the circumstances when financial statements do not comply with applicable accounting standards and the SORP, unless the departure is considered necessary in order for the accounts to give a true and fair view and the accounts contain adequate disclosure of the reasons for the departure.

9 Regulatory reports required from auditors

3.9 In some sectors, for example financial services, additional reports covering an LLP's compliance with regulations are required to be given by the auditors to the regulators. The format of these reports is usually specified by the relevant legislation and, to the extent that it is of a recurring nature, will be covered in the letter of engagement.

In certain regulated businesses, legislation places a duty on auditors to report certain rule breaches, sometimes without the prior knowledge of the entity concerned. Such circumstances will usually be referred to in the terms of engagement.

10 Reporting to third parties

3.10 From time to time, third parties may request auditors to provide reports on certain aspects of the financial information of an LLP. The request may come from a trade body (for example the Civil Aviation Authority), a government department (for example, in relation to a grant application), and a whole range of other possible parties. Provision of such reports goes beyond the statutory duties of an auditor and will always require additional terms of engagement to be agreed.

Dependent on the precise nature of the report, the audit firm may require the third party to be included in the engagement letter before it will report to them. Alternatively, the audit firm may carry out the assignment directly for the LLP and only allow the third party access to the report after receiving confirmation that the auditors owe no duty of care to that third party.

11 Changes in audit appointment

3.11 The procedures surrounding the changes in audit appointment mirror those contained in Part 16, Chapter 4 of the Companies Act 2006 (CA 2006) *Removal, Resignation, etc of Auditors* with respect to company audit appointments.

A resigning auditor is required to deposit a written notice of resignation at the registered office of the LLP. The notice of resignation must also be accompanied by a statement setting out any circumstances surrounding the resignation which the auditor considers should be brought to the attention of the members or creditors of the LLP or, where there are no such circumstances, a statement to that effect. A copy must also be lodged with Companies House no later than 14 days following its issuance.

Where the notice of resignation was accompanied by a statement of circumstances, the auditor may lodge, together with his notice of resignation, a requisition calling on the designated members to convene a meeting of the LLP to consider the explanation of the circumstances surrounding the resignation.

The designated members may remove an auditor and appoint a replacement by giving at least seven days' notice to the incumbent auditor. The auditor is entitled to make representations in writing to the LLP and may ask for those representations to be circulated to members. Notice is required to be given to the Registrar of Companies on the prescribed form, which can be obtained from Companies House, within 14 days.

Additional notification requirements are also placed upon both the auditor and the LLP, irrespective of the reason the auditor ceased to hold office. The requirements, which again mirror those in CA 2006, are for the 'appropriate audit authority' to be informed of the change in appointment. Who the appropriate audit authority is, and whether notification is required, will depend upon whether or not the LLP is a 'major audit client'.

Whilst the term 'major audit client' is used in LLPAAR 2008, there is no definition. Determination of the types of entity that will fall within the definition has been left to the Financial Reporting Council (FRC). The parameters are primarily by reference to turnover and external debt, and are subject to regular updating.

Where the LLP is a major audit client, the appropriate audit authority is the FRC and, where it is not a major audit client, the appropriate audit authority is the recognised supervisory body of the audit firm (eg ICAEW, ACCA).

Notification is always required when the LLP is a major audit client and, for other LLPs, it is required in circumstances where the auditor ceases to hold office before the end of his term of office.

The notification is required to include a copy of the auditor's statement to the LLP in relation to the circumstances surrounding their resignation or removal. Where there were no circumstances that are needed to be brought to the attention of members or creditors, the notification to the appropriate audit authority should explain the reason for the change. In the case of major audit clients, notification is required at the same time as the auditor deposits their resignation statement with the LLP. For other LLPs, the period of notification is set by the supervisory body.

The requirements placed upon the LLP are similar to those relating to the auditor, with the necessary notifications being required no later than 14 days after the auditors' statement is deposited with the LLP.

Appendix 1 – example audit letter of engagement

3.12 The following engagement letter is an illustrative letter only and is not to be taken as definitive. Each engagement is different and will inherently require tailored terms.

The members of An LLP

Dear Members,

We are pleased to accept the instruction to act as auditors for your limited liability partnership (LLP) and are writing to confirm the terms of our appointment.

The purpose of this letter together with the attached terms and conditions is to set out our terms for carrying out the work and to clarify our respective responsibilities.

We are bound by the ethical guidelines of [name of professional body], and accept instructions to act for you on the basis that we will act in accordance with those ethical guidelines. A copy of these guidelines can be viewed at our offices on request or can be seen at [insert website URL].

1 Period of Engagement

1.1 This letter is effective from [insert date].

1.2 It replaces our letter dated [insert date]. The previously agreed commencement date for this engagement still applies.

1.3 We will not be responsible for earlier periods. The partnership's previous accountants, [insert name of accountants], will deal with outstanding returns, assessments and other matters relating to earlier periods and will agree the position with the relevant authorities.

2 Scope of services to be provided

2.1 Our audit will be made with the objective of expressing an opinion on the financial statements.

3 Our responsibility to you

3.1 We have set out the agreed scope and objectives of your instructions within this letter of engagement. Any subsequent changes will be discussed with you and, where appropriate, a new letter of engagement will be agreed. We shall proceed on the basis of the instructions we have received from you and will rely on you to tell us as soon as possible if anything occurs which renders any information previously given to us as incorrect or inaccurate. We shall not be responsible for any failure to advise or comment on any matter which falls outside the specific scope of your instructions. We cannot accept any responsibility for any event, loss or situation unless it is one against which it is the expressed purpose of these instructions to provide protection.

4 Your responsibility to us

4.1 The advice that we give can only be as good as the information upon which it is based. Insofar as that information is provided by you, or by third parties with your permission, your responsibility arises as soon as possible if any circumstances or facts alter as any alteration may have a significant impact on the advice given. If the circumstances change therefore or your needs alter, advise us of the alteration as soon as possible in writing.

5 Statutory responsibilities

5.1 As members, you are required by statute to prepare accounts (financial statements) for each financial year which give a true and fair view of the state of affairs of the LLP and of its profit or loss for that period. In preparing those accounts you must:

(a) Select suitable accounting policies and then apply them consistently;

(b) Make judgements and estimates that are reasonable and prudent; and

(c) Prepare the accounts on the going concern basis unless it is not appropriate to presume that the partnership will continue in business.

5.2 It is your responsibility to keep proper accounting records which disclose with reasonable accuracy at any particular time the financial position of the LLP. It is also your responsibility to safeguard the assets of the LLP and for taking reasonable steps for the prevention of and detection of fraud and other irregularities with an appropriate system of internal controls.

5.3 You are also responsible for making available to us, as and when required, all the LLP's accounting records and all other relevant records and related information, including minutes of all members' meetings.

5.4 The intended users of the report are the members. The report will be addressed to the members.

5.5 As independent auditors we will report to you whether in our opinion the accounts of the LLP which we have audited give a true and fair view of the state of the partnership's affairs, and of the profit or loss for the year, and whether they have been prepared in accordance with the Limited Liability Partnerships Act 2000, Limited Liability Partnership Regulations 2008, Statement of Recommended Practice and Companies Act 2006. In arriving at our opinion we are required to consider the following matters, and to report on any in respect of which we are not satisfied:

(a) Whether proper accounting records have been kept by the LLP and proper returns adequate for our audit have been received from branches not visited by us.

(b) Whether the LLP's balance sheet and profit and loss account are in agreement with the accounting records and returns;

(c) Whether we have obtained all the information and explanations which we think necessary for the purpose of our audit; and

(d) Whether the information in the members' report is consistent with that in the audited accounts.

5.6 We have a professional duty to report if the accounts do not comply in any material respect with applicable accounting standards (UK GAAP) and the Statement of Recommended Practice, unless in our opinion the non-compliance is justified in the circumstances. In determining whether or not the departure is justified we consider whether:

(a) The departure is required in order for the accounts to give a true and fair view; and

(b) Whether adequate disclosure has been made concerning the departure.

5.7 Our professional responsibilities also include:

(a) Stating in our report a description of the members' responsibilities for the accounts, where the accounts or accompanying information do not include such description; and

(b) Considering whether other information and documents contained in audited accounts is consistent with those accounts; and

(c) Reporting to you on a timely basis in respect of any issues, such as material weaknesses in your accounting system, which we feel need to be brought to your attention.

5.8 Should you instruct us to carry out any alternative report then it will be necessary for us to issue a separate letter of engagement.

6 Our service to you

6.1 We will conduct our audit in accordance with International Standards on Auditing (UK). Those standards require that we plan and perform the audit to obtain reasonable assurance about whether the financial statements are free from material misstatement whether caused by fraud or error. An audit includes examining, on a test basis, evidence supporting the amounts and disclosures in the financial statements. An audit also includes assessing the accounting principles used and significant estimates made by management, as well as evaluating the overall financial statement presentation.

6.2 When undertaking the assignment we will take due consideration of the contents of the partnership agreement or where one does not exist with the Partnership Act 1890.

6.3 Because of the test nature and other inherent limitations of an audit, together with the inherent limitations of any accounting and internal control system, there is an unavoidable risk that even some material misstatements may remain undiscovered.

6.4 In addition to our report on the financial statements, we expect to provide you with a separate letter concerning any material weaknesses in accounting and internal control systems which come to our notice.

6.5 Our auditing procedures will be carried out in accordance with the International Auditing Standards (UK) issued by the Financial Reporting Council, and will include such tests of transactions and of the existence, ownership and valuation of assets and liabilities as we consider necessary. We shall obtain an understanding of the accounting and internal control systems in order to assess their adequacy as a basis for the preparation of the accounts and to establish whether proper accounting records have been maintained by the LLP. We will need to obtain sufficient relevant and reliable evidence to enable us to draw reasonable conclusions therefrom.

6.6 The nature and extent of our tests will vary according to our assessment of the LLP's accounting and internal control systems, and may cover any aspects of the LLP's operations that we consider appropriate. Our audit is not designed to identify all significant weaknesses in the LLP's systems, but we shall report to the management any significant weaknesses in, or observations on, the LLP's systems which come to our notice and which we think should be brought to management's attention. Any such report may not be provided to third parties without our prior written consent.

Such consent would be granted only on the basis that such reports are not prepared for the interests of anyone other than the LLP in mind and that we accept no duty or responsibility to any other party as concerns the reports.

6.7 The responsibility for safeguarding the assets of the LLP and for the prevention and detection of fraud, error and non-compliance with law or regulations rests with the management. We will plan our audit so that we have a reasonable expectation of detecting material misstatements in the accounts resulting from irregularities, fraud or non-compliance with law or regulations, but our examination should not be relied upon to disclose all such material misstatements or frauds, errors or instances of non-compliance as may exist.

6.8 As part of our normal audit procedures, we may request you to provide formal written representations concerning certain information and explanations we have received from you during the course of our audit.

6.9 In order to assist us with a review of your accounts, which constitutes part of our audit, we will request sight of any documents or statements which will be issued with the accounts. We are also entitled to attend all general meetings of the LLP, and to receive notice of all such meetings.

6.10 Once we have issued our report we have no further direct responsibility in relation to the accounts for that financial year. However, we expect that you will inform us of any material event occurring between the date of our report and that of the annual general meeting that may affect the accounts.

6.11 As members you acknowledge and understand your responsibility:

(a) For the preparation of the financial statements in accordance with the applicable financial reporting framework, including where relevant their fair presentation;

(b) For such internal control as the members determine is necessary to enable the preparation of financial statements that are free from material misstatement, whether due to fraud or error; and

(c) To provide us with:

(i) Access to all information of which the members are aware that is relevant to the preparation of the financial statements such as records, documentation and other matters;

(ii) Additional information that we may request from the members for the purposes of the audit; and

(iii) Unrestricted access to persons within the LLP from whom we determine it necessary to obtain audit evidence.

7 Limitation of liability

7.1 You have agreed that our liability as auditors to the partnership will be limited in accordance with sections 532 to 538 of the Companies Act 2006. A separate letter dated insert date sets out the terms of this agreement. Or

7.2 We specifically draw your attention to paragraph XX of our standard terms and conditions which sets out the basis on which we limit our liability to you and to others. You should read this in conjunction with paragraph XX of our standard terms and conditions which excludes liability to third parties. Or

7.3 There are no Third Parties that we have agreed should be entitled to rely on the work done pursuant to this engagement letter.

8 Other Services

8.1 You may request that we provide other services from time to time. If these services exceed £ [insert value], we will issue a separate letter of engagement and scope of work to be performed accordingly.

8.2 Because rules and regulations frequently change you must ask us to confirm any advice already given if a transaction is delayed or a similar transaction is to be undertaken.

9 Agreement of terms

9.1 This letter supersedes any previous engagement letter and applies for accounting periods commencing on or after [insert date]. For periods commencing before this date the previous letter will apply. Once it has been agreed, this letter will remain effective until it is replaced.

9.2 You or we may vary or terminate our authority to act on your behalf at any time without penalty. Notice of variation or termination must be given in writing.

9.3 We shall be grateful if you could confirm your agreement to the terms of this letter by signing the enclosed copy and returning it to us immediately.

9.4 If this letter is not in accordance with your understanding of the scope of our engagement or your circumstances have changed, please let us know.

9.5 This letter should be read in conjunction with the firm's standard terms and conditions.

Yours sincerely

Insert firm name

I/We confirm that I/We have read and understood the contents of this letter and related terms and conditions and agree that it accurately reflects my/our fair understanding of the services that I/We require you to undertake.

Signed .... Date ....

For and on behalf of

Insert LLP name

Appendix 2 – Example written representation

3.13 *The following letter is not intended to be a definitive letter. Representations by members will vary from one LLP to another and from one period to the next. The letter will*

normally be printed on the LLP's letterhead to include relevant statutory information. This letter should be used as a reference only but keeping in mind that every audit is inherently different.

To: [Auditors]

Dear Sirs

The following representations are made on the basis of enquiries of members and staff with relevant knowledge and experience such as we consider necessary in connection with your audit of the LLP's financial statements for the year ended [date]. These enquiries have included inspection of supporting documentation where appropriate. All representations are made to the best of our knowledge and belief.

GENERAL

1. We have fulfilled our responsibilities as members, as set out in the terms of your engagement letter dated [insert date] under the Companies Act 2006, Limited Liability Partnership Acts 2000, Limited Liability Partnership Regulations 2008, Statement of Recommended Practice – Accounting by Limited Liability Partnerships and Companies Act 2006 for preparing financial statements and for being satisfied that they give a true and fair view and for making accurate representations to you.
2. All the transactions undertaken by the LLP have been properly reflected and recorded in the accounting records.
3. All the accounting records have been made available to you for the purpose of your audit. We have provided you with unrestricted access to all appropriate persons within the LLP, and with all other records and related information requested, including minutes of all management and members meetings.
4. The financial statements are free of material misstatements, including omissions.
5. The effects of uncorrected misstatements (as set out in the appendix to this letter) are immaterial both individually and in total.

INTERNAL CONTROL AND FRAUD

6. We acknowledge our responsibility for the design, implementation and maintenance of internal control systems to prevent and detect fraud and error. We have disclosed to you the results of our risk assessment that the financial statements may be misstated as a result of fraud.
7. We have disclosed to you all instances of known or suspected fraud affecting the LLP involving members, management, employees who have a significant role in internal control or others that could have a material effect on the financial statements.
8. We have also disclosed to you all information in relation to allegations of fraud or suspected fraud affecting the LLP's financial statements communicated by current or former employees, analysts, regulators or others.

ASSETS AND LIABILITIES

9. The LLP has satisfactory title to all assets and there are no liens or encumbrances on the LLP's assets, except for those that are disclosed in the notes to the financial statements.

10. All actual liabilities, contingent liabilities and guarantees given to third parties have been recorded or disclosed as appropriate.

11. We have no plans or intentions that may materially alter the carrying value and, where relevant, the fair value measurements or classification of assets and liabilities reflected in the LLP's financial statements.

ACCOUNTING ESTIMATES

12. Significant assumptions used by us in making accounting estimates, including those measured at fair value, are reasonable.

LEGAL CLAIMS

13. We have disclosed to you all claims in connection with litigation that have been, or are expected to be, received and such matters, as appropriate, have been properly accounted for and disclosed in the financial statements.

LAWS AND REGULATIONS

14. We have disclosed to you all known instances of non-compliance or suspected non-compliance with laws and regulations whose effects should be considered when preparing the financial statements.

RELATED PARTIES

15. Related party relationships and transactions have been appropriately accounted for and disclosed in the financial statements. We have disclosed to you all relevant information concerning such relationships and transactions and are not aware of any other matters which require disclosure in order to comply with the requirements of company law or accounting standards.

SUBSEQUENT EVENTS

16. All events subsequent to the date of the financial statements which require adjustment or disclosure have been properly accounted for and disclosed.

GOING CONCERN

17. We believe that the LLPs financial statements should be prepared on a going concern basis on the grounds that current and future sources of funding or support will be more than adequate for the LLP's needs. We have considered a period of 12 months from the date of approval of the financial statements. We believe that no further disclosures relating to the LLP's ability to continue as a going concern need to be made in the financial statements.

We acknowledge our legal responsibilities regarding disclosure of information to you as auditors and confirm that so far as we are aware, there is no relevant audit information needed by you in connection with preparing your audit report of which you are unaware.

Each member has taken all the steps that he/she ought to have taken as a member in order to make himself/herself aware of any relevant audit information and to establish that you are aware of that information.

Yours faithfully

....

DESIGNATED MEMBER

[Date]

Chapter 4

The audit and UK auditing standards

Signposts

- In the broadest terms, an audit involves the collection and evaluation of sufficient and appropriate audit evidence to enable the auditor to express an opinion on the truth and fairness of the LLP's financial statements (see **4.1**).
- Auditors will carry out their work in accordance with International Standards on Auditing (UK and Ireland) and for audits of financial statements for periods commencing on or after 17 June 2016, the International Standards on Auditing (UK and Ireland) become International Standards on Auditing (UK). These standards are issued by the Financial Reporting Council (see **4.2**).
- Audit evidence gathered by the auditor must be both 'sufficient' and 'appropriate'. The term 'sufficient' refers to the quantity of the audit evidence. The term 'appropriate' refers to the quality of the audit evidence (see **4.2**).
- There are broadly six stages in an audit involving planning then assessing risk right through to eventual reporting (see **4.3**).
- Audit planning is a critical aspect of the audit and involves the development of an approach which is not only effective in minimising the risk that material errors will go undetected, but also ensuring the audit is carried out efficiently (see **4.4**).
- An audit team discussion will be held at the planning stage to exchange knowledge and gain an understanding of the client and among other things discuss the susceptibility of the financial statements to material misstatement (see **4.4**).
- At the planning phase, the audit strategy is developed which then leads on to the development of the detailed audit plan (see **4.4**).
- Planning is viewed as a 'continual and iterative process' and it follows that the plan must be continuously updated and amended (where applicable) for any unexpected developments which may arise during the detailed audit (see **4.4**).
- The auditor must obtain an understanding of the LLP and any changes in the LLP's business during the period (see **4.5**).
- It is the members' responsibility to prevent and detect fraud and the auditors will develop procedures which will address their risk assessment that the financial statements contain material misstatement due to fraud, although it is not an auditor's responsibility to detect fraud (see **4.6**).

- Auditors must consider the possibility of management override of internal controls for personal financial gain and, in general, must apply professional scepticism when carrying out an audit (see **4.6**).
- There are other considerations at the planning stage which the auditor must consider including the use of service organisations by the LLP, consideration of laws and regulations and the nature of related parties (see **4.7**).
- An external audit gives a high, but not absolute, level of assurance that the financial statements give a true and fair view and the auditor will apply the concept of materiality to the financial statements (see **4.8**).
- There are two levels of materiality: *financial statement* materiality and *performance* materiality (see **4.8**).
- External auditors may choose to place reliance on an LLP's internal controls and such controls will be documented by the auditor (see **4.9**).
- In developing the audit strategy, the auditor is required to undertake certain procedures to ensure the strategy they develop is appropriate – this is because the audit strategy then leads on to the creation of the detailed audit plan (see **4.10**).
- The audit plan includes the nature, timing and extent of planned risk assessment procedures, further audit procedures at the assertion level and other planned procedures to ensure the audit complies with the UK ISAs (see **4.10**).
- There are various sources from which auditors can obtain their audit evidence to ensure the evidence gathered is both sufficient and appropriate (see **4.11**).
- Third-party and auditor-generated audit evidence is considered the most reliable, although such evidence may be more expensive to obtain (see **4.11**).
- An inherent limitation in an external audit is the use of audit sampling (see **4.12**).
- Sampling offers the auditor the opportunity to obtain the minimum amount of audit evidence which is both sufficient and appropriate to form valid conclusions about the population to which the sample represents (see **4.12**).
- Errors found during audit work are recorded on an 'audit error schedule' or 'summary of unadjusted misstatements' and then assessed as to whether, or not, they are material in the context of the financial statements (see **4.13**).
- Misstatements can be factual misstatements, projected misstatements or judgemental misstatements (see **4.13**).
- The audit file must be reviewed to ensure the audit work carried out is sufficient and this review process should be adequately documented (see **4.14**).
- Unadjusted misstatements must be reviewed at the completion phase as well as undertaking analytical procedures to ensure compliance with the UK ISAs (see **4.15**).
- Once the review process and completion phase is finished, the audit engagement partner can then form their opinion as to whether the financial statements give

a true and fair view and there are a number of opinions which can be expressed depending on whether the auditor considers the financial statements to give a true and fair view or otherwise (see **4.16**).

- Audit working papers must be kept confidential although legislation allows incoming auditors to review the working papers of the outgoing auditors so the incoming auditors can obtain evidence for their audit (eg on opening balances) (see **4.17**).

1 What is an audit?

4.1 The general requirement that the accounts of an LLP are subject to audit has been discussed in Chapter 3. To many, particularly those transferring from a traditional partnership to LLP status, whilst they may be aware of the general concepts of audit, the detail of the audit process may be less familiar. This chapter explains in overall terms what an audit is, and the processes and procedures typically performed by the auditors.

At the most general level, an audit involves the collection and evaluation of sufficient and appropriate audit evidence to enable the audit engagement partner to express an opinion on whether the accounts are prepared, in all material respects, in accordance with the applicable accounting framework and whether they give a true and fair view of the state of the LLP's affairs.

2 UK auditing standards

4.2 The auditors of an LLP are required to carry out their work in accordance with International Standards on Auditing (ISAs) (UK and Ireland) ('auditing standards') which are issued by the Financial Reporting Council. In 2016, the Audit Regulation and Directive was transposed into company law resulting in the standards being revised and reissued. The revised ISAs are effective for audits of financial statements for periods commencing on or after 17 June 2016 and this chapter will consider those ISAs, which have also become ISAs (UK) rather than ISAs (UK and Ireland).

Whilst auditing standards do not dictate the exact nature of the work which auditors should carry out, they do set out both principles and essential procedures which must be applied when carrying out audit work. Individual firms are then able to develop their own methodologies to comply with those auditing standards.

Compliance with auditing standards is usually achieved through the use of an 'audit programme'. An audit programme is a collection of procedures which set out various steps to undertake in order to achieve compliance with the UK auditing standards. Some firms have been criticised in the past by regulatory bodies for relying too heavily on standard audit programmes and not tailoring such programmes to be client-specific.

Whatever methodology the audit firm uses it must ensure that the audit evidence it gathers to support the amounts and disclosures within the LLP's financial statements is both **sufficient** and **appropriate**. 'Sufficient' audit evidence refers to the quantity of the evidence needed and this is affected by the assessment of the risks of material misstatement and the quality of such audit evidence. 'Appropriate' audit evidence refers to the quality of the audit evidence, that is, the relevance and reliability of the evidence in providing support for the conclusions on which the auditor's opinion is based.

At the time of writing the following UK and Ireland auditing standards were in extant:

- ISQC (UK) 1 (Revised June 2016) *Quality Control for Firms that Perform Audits and Reviews of Financial Statements, and Other Assurance and Related Services Engagements*
- ISA (UK) 200 (Revised June 2016) *Overall Objectives of the Independent Auditor and the Conduct of an Audit in Accordance with International Standards on Auditing (UK)*
- ISA (UK) 210 (Revised June 2016) *Agreeing the Terms of Audit Engagements*
- ISA (UK) 220 (Revised June 2016) *Quality Control for an Audit of Financial Statements*
- ISA (UK) 230 (Revised June 2016) *Audit Documentation*
- ISA (UK) 240 (Revised June 2016) *The Auditor's Responsibilities Relating to Fraud in an Audit of Financial Statements*
- ISA (UK) 250A (Revised June 2016) Section A – *Consideration of Laws and Regulations in an Audit of Financial Statements*
- ISA (UK) 250B (Revised June 2016) Section B –*The Auditor's Statutory Right and Duty to Report to Regulators of Public Interest Entities and Regulators of Other Entities in the Financial Sector*
- ISA (UK) 260 (Revised June 2016) *Communication with Those Charged with Governance*
- ISA (UK) 265 *Communicating Deficiencies in Internal Control to Those Charged with Governance and Management*
- ISA (UK) 300 (Revised June 2016) *Planning an Audit of Financial Statements*
- ISA (UK) 315 (Revised June 2016) *Identifying and Assessing the Risks of Material Misstatement Through Understanding of the Entity and Its Environment*
- ISA (UK) 320 (Revised June 2016) *Materiality in Planning and Performing an Audit*
- ISA (UK) 330 (Revised June 2016) *The Auditor's Responses to Assessed Risks*
- ISA (UK) 402 *Audit Considerations Relating to an Entity Using a Service Organisation*
- ISA (UK) 450 (Revised June 2016) *Evaluation of Misstatements Identified During the Audit*
- ISA (UK) 500 *Audit Evidence*
- ISA (UK) 501 *Audit Evidence – Specific Considerations for Selected Items*

- ISA (UK) 505 *External Confirmations*
- ISA (UK) 510 (Revised June 2016) *Initial Audit Engagements – Opening Balances*
- ISA (UK) 520 *Analytical Procedures*
- ISA (UK) 530 *Audit Sampling*
- ISA (UK) 540 (Revised June 2016) *Auditing Accounting Estimates, Including Fair Value Accounting Estimates, and Related Disclosures*
- ISA (UK) 550 *Related Parties*
- ISA (UK) 560 *Subsequent Events*
- ISA (UK) 570 (Revised June 2016) *Going Concern*
- ISA (UK) 580 *Written Representations*
- ISA (UK) 600 (Revised June 2016) *Special Considerations – Audits of Group Financial Statements (Including the Work of Component Auditors)*
- ISA (UK) 610 (Revised June 2016) *Using the Work of Internal Auditors*
- ISA (UK) 620 (Revised June 2016) *Using the Work of an Auditor's Expert*
- ISA (UK) 700 (Revised June 2016) *Forming an Opinion and Reporting on Financial Statements*
- ISA (UK) 701 *Communicating Key Audit Matters in the Independent Auditor's Report*
- ISA (UK) 705 (Revised June 2016) *Modifications to the Opinion in the Independent Auditor's Report*
- ISA (UK) 706 (Revised June 2016) *Emphasis of Matter Paragraphs and Other Matter Paragraphs in the Independent Auditor's Report*
- ISA (UK) 710 *Comparative Information – Corresponding Figures and Comparative Financial Statements*
- ISA (UK) 720 *The Auditor's Responsibilities Relating to Other Information*
- ISA (UK) 800 (Revised) Special Considerations – *Audits of Financial Statements Prepared in Accordance with Special Purpose Frameworks*
- ISA (UK) 805 (Revised) *Special Considerations – Audits of Single Financial Statements and Specific Elements, Accounts or Items of a Financial Statement*

3 The audit process

4.3 Whilst the methodologies of individual audit firms vary, all audits can be analysed broadly into the following stages:

- planning;
- risk assessment;

- developing the audit strategy and audit plan;
- obtaining audit evidence;
- review; and
- reporting.

4 Planning the audit

4.4 Auditors invest a considerable amount of time on each assignment in ensuring that the work is planned, to take full account of the circumstances of the individual client. Planning is essential to developing an approach which is not only effective in minimising the risk that material errors will go undetected (detection risk) and in turn result in the auditor forming the incorrect opinion on the financial statements (audit risk), but sufficient planning also makes the most efficient use of audit staff and client time. Auditing standards contain considerable guidance and requirements with respect to the information the auditors should obtain and the assessments they should make when planning the audit. Standards relating to specific audit planning are found in the 300 series of the UK auditing standards.

The first stage in the planning process is for the auditors to establish the terms on which they are going to act by issuing an engagement letter (see Chapter 3), or to assess whether the provisions of a letter issued in a previous year are still appropriate. Revisions to the letter will be issued where this is considered to be necessary.

Focus

- In respect of recurring engagements, the auditor must review the terms of the engagement letter on an annual basis to ensure they are appropriate and also consider whether the audit client needs to be reminded of the terms of the engagement.

Planning the audit involves the audit team discussion where members of the audit team will discuss the susceptibility of the financial statements to material misstatement (whether due to fraud or error) and exchange knowledge of the client and the matters pertinent to the audit. Key high risk areas of the financial statements are discussed and sensitive issues such as fraud and fraud in relation to related parties are also discussed. In terms of fraud and the audit team meeting, the team must discuss *how* the financial statements **could** be materially misstated due to fraud (for example *how* management ***could*** override internal controls or *how* employees ***could*** manipulate weaknesses in internal controls). The discussion itself is not just about *if* fraud has occurred in the current or previous audits. This is required because the auditor must apply professional scepticism at all times during the course of the audit and set aside all beliefs about previous experiences relating to members' honesty and integrity. The word **could** is in bold type to emphasise that the auditors must be seen to be exercising professional scepticism at all times of the audit and hence it is not enough to consider whether, or not, a fraud has occurred during the year or whether there has been no history of fraud. The auditor must consider how fraud could occur and design procedures around those expectations.

Planning will also involve the development of the audit strategy. The audit strategy sets out the overall direction of the audit and includes consideration of:

- the overall approach to the conduct and management of the audit;
- the approach in organising the nature and timing of expected communications with the LLP;
- the timing and extent of involvement of experts, client personnel and other third parties; and
- direction, supervision and review.

Once the audit strategy has been developed, this leads onto the development of the audit plan. The audit plan is more detailed than the audit strategy and is essentially the means by which the team will gather sufficient appropriate audit evidence to support the amounts, assertions and disclosures in the financial statements by way of specific audit procedures,

The UK auditing standards regard planning as a '*continual and iterative process*'. This means that audit planning is not simply done at the start of an audit and then finished just before the audit fieldwork commences – the audit plan must be continuously updated and amended (where applicable) for any (unexpected) developments which might arise during the course of carrying out the detailed audit work.

5 Understanding the LLP and risk assessment

4.5 At an early stage (more often than not at the planning stage of the audit), the auditors will want to obtain a copy of the members' agreement, find out about the LLP's business, any changes therein and its financial performance during the period, together with any significant transactions or other events which may require specific focus during the audit. In the first year of the auditors' appointment, the amount of information required will be substantially more than in subsequent years, as the auditors seek to build up their understanding of the business and the environment in which the LLP operates which is a mandatory requirement under ISA (UK) 300 and 315. This understanding will not just encompass the LLP's business but will also take into account:

- The appropriateness of the selection and application of accounting policies, including those relating to revenue recognition (see Chapter 7) and the classification of members' interests (see Chapter 5).
- The objectives and strategies of the LLP.
- How the LLP measures and reviews its financial performance.
- The internal controls operated by the LLP, including:
  - its overall control environment (ie the governance and management functions and attitudes thereto within the LLP);
  - its risk assessment processes, so far as they affect the financial statements;
  - the information systems and business processes relevant to financial reporting (including controls over IT systems); and
  - controls operated by the LLP and how they are monitored.

- The regulatory framework within which the LLP operates.
- The structure of the LLP.
- The goods/services provided by the LLP and any other pertinent information considered important and relevant to the audit.

The methods adopted to obtain this information will vary, but could include meetings, telephone conversations and/or use of a questionnaire (for example an internal control questionnaire or an internal control evaluation questionnaire).

The auditors consider the risk of misstatement both at overall financial statement level and at what is termed the *assertion level* for each component of the financial statements (for example completeness, existence, rights and obligations).

6 Fraud

4.6 It is the responsibility of the members of the LLP to take reasonable steps to prevent and detect fraud, and this responsibility is specifically referred to in the statement of members' responsibilities accompanying the accounts. Therefore, whilst the detection of fraud is outside the role of the auditors, in order to assess fully the risk of a material misstatement in the accounts, they are required to identify and assess the risk of material misstatement due to fraud, and evaluate the controls the LLP has in place to mitigate the risk. The inherent weaknesses of auditing mean that despite the audit procedures applied during the course of the audit being effective and gathering sufficient and appropriate audit evidence, even material misstatements (due to fraud) may go unnoticed. It is for this reason that ISA (UK) 240 *The Auditor's Responsibilities Relating to Fraud in an Audit of Financial Statements* outlines the responsibility of the auditor as being that of obtaining **reasonable** (ie not absolute) assurance that the financial statements, taken as a whole, are free from material misstatement, whether caused by fraud or error.

Auditing standards specifically require that the auditors perform procedures to obtain information that they can use to identify and assess the risk that fraud could give rise to a material error in the accounts. There are two types of fraud that the auditors need to consider: fraudulent financial reporting, and the misappropriation of assets. ISA (UK) 240 also regards management override of internal controls as being a significant risk, regardless of the auditor's past experience of the LLP. In this respect, the procedures outlined in paragraph 32 to ISA (UK) 240 must be carried out as a minimum to address this significant risk and are as follows:

(a) Test the appropriateness of journal entries recorded in the general ledger and other adjustments made in the preparation of the financial statements. In designing and performing audit procedures for such tests, the auditor shall:

    (i) make inquiries of individuals involved in the financial reporting process about inappropriate or unusual activity relating to the processing of journal entries and other adjustments;

(ii) select journal entries and other adjustments made at the end of a reporting period; and

(iii) consider the need to test journal entries and other adjustments throughout the period.

(b) Review accounting estimates for biases and evaluate whether the circumstances producing the bias, if any, represent a risk of material misstatement due to fraud. In performing this review, the auditor shall:

(i) evaluate whether the judgments and decisions made by management in making the accounting estimates included in the financial statements, even if they are individually reasonable, indicate a possible bias on the part of the entity's management that may represent a risk of material misstatement due to fraud. If so, the auditor shall re-evaluate the accounting estimates taken as a whole; and

(ii) perform a retrospective review of management judgments and assumptions related to significant accounting estimates reflected in the financial statements of the prior year.

(c) For significant transactions that are outside the normal course of business for the entity, or that otherwise appear to be unusual given the auditor's understanding of the entity and its environment and other information obtained during the audit, the auditor shall evaluate whether the business rationale (or the lack thereof) of the transactions suggest that they may have been entered into to engage in fraudulent financial reporting or to conceal misappropriation of assets.[1]

In respect of fraud, auditors should also consider the susceptibility of material misstatement due to fraud because of management override of internal controls (ie how fraud *could* occur due to management override of controls and keep in mind that ISA (UK) 240 views this as a significant risk, so it cannot be ignored). Employee fraud tends to arise because of a manipulation of weaknesses in internal controls rather than overriding internal controls (overriding of controls tends to be perpetrated by management), so auditors should consider the effectiveness of the LLP's internal control environment and consider how an employee *could* perpetrate a fraud, bearing in mind that no internal control system can be 100% effective against fraud or error (robust systems might mitigate the occurrence of fraud or error, but they would not be able to prevent it in its entirety).

The auditors are required to discuss the risk of fraud with management, including the processes that management have put in place for identifying and responding to the risk of fraud. The auditors are also required to obtain information with respect to actual or suspected fraud. To the extent that a risk of misstatement is identified, specific audit tests are designed to mitigate that risk.

Auditing standards contain a presumption that there is always a risk of fraudulent financial reporting with respect to revenue recognition and, therefore, ordinarily this is an area that the auditors will pay particular attention to. In addition, ISA (UK) 550 *Related Parties* acknowledges that the nature of related party relationships may, in some circumstances,

1 ISA (UK) 240, para 32.

also give rise to higher risks of material misstatement than with unrelated parties and paragraph 12 to ISA (UK) 550 makes a specific requirement for the audit team to consider the susceptibility of the financial statements to material misstatement due to fraud or error that could arise from the LLP's related party relationships and transactions.

7 Other planning considerations

4.7 Auditing standards also require that a number of other specific matters are considered when planning the audit. These include:

- Establishing the extent to which the LLP uses service organisations for processing data, maintaining accounting records, the safe custody of assets such as investments, or initiating transactions on the part of the LLP. Where the activities of the service organisation are considered to be significant, ISA (UK) 402 *Audit Considerations Relating to an Entity Using a Service Organisation* requires the auditors to carry out additional procedures in relation to the information held by the service organisation. The auditors must also obtain an understanding of the services provided by a service organisation and the internal controls present at the service organisation.
- Ascertaining whether there are any laws and regulations which provide the legal framework within which the LLP conducts its business and which are central to its ability to conduct that business. Where such laws and regulations are identified, ISA (UK) 250A (Revised June 2016) *Consideration of Laws and Regulations in an Audit of Financial* Statements requires the auditor to obtain sufficient and appropriate evidence of compliance with those laws and regulations. Auditors are not, however, required to consider all laws and regulations which might be applicable to the LLP, only those where non-compliance might result in the LLP being unable to continue in business. The provisions of some laws and regulations have a direct effect on the LLP's financial statements in that they determine the amounts and associated disclosures. Other laws and regulations must be complied with by management so that the LLP can continue in business but which do not have a direct effect on the LLP's financial statements.
- Ascertaining the nature of related parties (see **9.37–9.42**) and designing procedures to minimise the risk that the accounts will fail to disclose the existence of a material related party transaction. ISA (UK) 550 *Related Parties* requires the auditor to identify, assess and respond to the risks of material misstatement which arise from the LLP's failure to appropriately account for, or disclose, related party relationships, transactions or balances in accordance with the requirements of the financial reporting framework.
- Consideration of the applicability of the going concern assumption (see Chapter 10). The concept of going concern is considered a material issue in all businesses and ISA (UK) 570 (Revised June 2016) *Going Concern* requires the auditor to form a conclusion as to whether management's use of the going concern presumption is appropriate in the LLP's circumstances (in other words whether the LLP has the ability to continue in business for the foreseeable future – ie for at least 12 months from the date the financial statements are authorised for issue and the auditor's report signed).

> **Focus**
>
> - With regards to the final bullet point concerning the going concern presumption – care must be taken to correctly apply the UK version of ISA 570. The mainstream ISA 570 issued by the International Auditing and Assurance Standards Board requires the period of assessment for going concern to be 12 months from the date of the financial statements (ie 12 months from the balance sheet date). ISA (UK) 570 is more onerous in its requirements and requires the assessment to be 12 months from the date of approval of the financial statements.

8 Materiality

4.8 In issuing the auditor's report on a set of accounts, the auditors are not stating that they are absolutely 100% correct, but instead they are saying they have obtained *reasonable assurance* that the financial statements are free from material misstatement. The term 'reasonable assurance' is not absolute assurance, but is a high level of assurance. Materiality is an expression of the relative significance or importance of a particular matter. ISA (UK) 320 (Revised June 2016) *Materiality in Planning and Performing an Audit* says that a misstatement (or multiple misstatements), including omissions, are considered to be material if they, individually or in the aggregate, could reasonably be expected to influence the economic decisions of users taken on the basis of the financial statements.

Materiality is not only considered in the context of the accounts as a whole, but may also be applied in the context of any individual primary statement (profit and loss account and balance sheet) or of individual items included therein. There is no specific mathematical definition of materiality, due to the fact that it has both qualitative and quantitative aspects and audit firms develop their own methodologies for applying the requirements. Often materiality is calculated as ½–1% of turnover, 5–10% of pre-tax profit and 1–2% of gross assets and then an average struck to arrive at a financial statement materiality level (known as the 'averaging method'), however there is no 'one-size-fits-all' where materiality levels or the calculation of such are concerned. Materiality is very much a judgement call on the part of the auditor.

At the beginning of the audit, an indicative level of materiality will be calculated, which is usually based on a percentage of turnover, profit or gross assets or a combination. This serves as a guideline to the auditors to enable them to assess the areas where there is the potential for the greatest risk of material error. Items in the financial statements falling below the calculated materiality figure may be subject to either fewer audit procedures than other areas or, in some cases, no procedures at all.

ISA (UK) 320 includes the concept of *performance* materiality. The idea of performance materiality is that modern day audit techniques are concerned with sampling (ie the auditor will only test a selection of items to obtain reasonable assurance that the financial statements are free from material misstatement). There is always an unavoidable risk that items will go undetected so the idea of performance materiality is to reduce the possibility that the total of all errors which have been found during the audit, together with the undetected errors in the accounts do not exceed overall materiality levels. There is no prescribed calculation in ISA

(UK) 320 to arrive at a materiality, or a performance materiality, level but the application of performance materiality can be illustrated in the following example:

Example – application of performance materiality

An LLP operates in the pharmaceutical industry developing drugs for medical conditions and as such has a highly significant amount of research and development expenditure.

The audit engagement team has planned the audit of the financial statements for the year-ended 30 June 2017. The firm has determined a materiality level for the financial statements as a whole of £90,000 which has been calculated using the traditional 'averaging' method (1% of turnover, 2% of gross assets, 10% of pre-tax profit). Recently there has been a lot of interest by potential investors and initial talks have been entered into by potential investors to purchase the LLP due to its reputation. The potential investors are particularly interested in the results of the audited financial statements as at 30 June 2017.

The LLP's draft financial statements show that capitalised development expenditure has a net book value of £2.5 million which is clearly material to the financial statements. However, the audit engagement partner has emphasised the point that he is aware the members are keen to capitalise as much development expenditure as possible in order to boost the balance sheet and has therefore advised the audit engagement team to apply performance materiality to the development expenditure.

This is because paragraph 18.8H in FRS 102 (September 2015) *The Financial Reporting Standard applicable in the UK and Republic of Ireland*, which the LLP is reporting under, only allows development expenditure which meets the recognition criteria to be capitalised – any expenditure which does not meet the recognition criteria is written off to the profit and loss account as incurred (because it is classed as research expenditure), hence there is a risk of material misstatement within the area of research and development.

Performance materiality is based on professional judgement. There is no guidance in ISA (UK) 320 as to how to calculate it. In the case of the LLP, performance materiality needs to be applied to an area which could influence the economic decisions of the user of the LLP's financial statements (i.e. potential investors). Performance materiality could well be determined as a percentage of financial statement materiality, say, 60%. As a result, a performance materiality of (60% × £90,000) – £90,000 = £36,000 could be set for the audit of research and development expenditure. The auditor could set higher or lower percentages, or even come up with a more complex formula, depending on their professional judgement.

---

9 Assessment of information systems and internal controls

4.9 The LLP's own systems of internal control and recording of accounting information will influence the audit approach. In some circumstances, the auditors may determine that the internal controls which the LLP has in place in a particular area are sufficiently robust to reduce significantly the risk of a material error arising. In these circumstances, the auditors may rely on these controls (having first tested them) to reduce the level of their own work. This is generally known as a compliance approach. Care must be exercised by the auditor when placing reliance on an LLP's internal control systems and where the auditor does place greater reliance on the effectiveness of a control, ISA (UK) 330 (Revised June 2016) *The Auditor's Responses to Assessed Risks* requires the auditor to obtain more persuasive audit evidence.

Irrespective of whether the auditors intend to rely on the LLP's own systems and controls, auditing standards require that they obtain an understanding of the information system, including the related business processes relevant to financial reporting, and of control activities. This usually results in the auditors documenting the key transaction flows of the LLP (eg the sales cycle, the purchases cycle and the payroll cycle etc), together with the internal controls operating over those transaction flows. Some testing will also be carried out to ascertain that the systems operate as described and documented.

Focus

- In practice it is common to undertake detailed tests of control on an LLP's internal control system at least every three years. Limited tests of control on the major cycles are done every year.

Different audit firms will document their understanding of an LLP's systems and controls differently. The most common methods of documenting systems and controls includes:

- *Narrative notes* which consist of a written description of the system showing what occurs in the system at each stage and the controls that operate at each stage.
- *Questionnaires* can consist of internal control questionnaires (ICQs) or internal control evaluation questionnaires (ICEQs). These questionnaires contain a list of questions relevant to the systems and controls; ICQs are used to assess whether controls exist, whereas ICEQs are used to test the effectiveness of the controls.
- *Flowcharts* are graphic illustrations of the internal control system for each cycle of the LLP's business. Lines usually demonstrate the sequence of events and standard symbols are used to signify controls or documents.

10 Audit strategy and audit plan

4.10 Based on the information obtained, the auditors will then develop both an overall strategy as to how the audit work should be scoped, which then allows a detailed plan to be developed, usually in the form of work programmes for each area of the accounts. These programmes will then be used by the staff carrying out the fieldwork to guide them through the performance of that work. The audit strategy and programmes may be updated during the performance of the work, where circumstances are not as envisaged at the time the overall strategy was prepared.

Many audit firms use automated audit software which already includes audit programmes. Whilst such programmes are perfectly acceptable to use, it is important that the auditor ensures they are tailored to be specific to the LLP audit. Many software programmes contain 'generic' audit tests which can sometimes result in a 'tick box' approach being applied by audit firms. The danger in using a tick-box approach is that it may result in audit evidence being obtained which is not sufficient nor appropriate, which is time-consuming and costly. Careful reviews of audit programmes by the audit engagement partner may be necessary (particularly where the LLP is a complex audit) to ensure that the audit programmes are appropriate.

In developing an audit strategy, ISA (UK) 300 (Revised June 2016) *Planning an Audit of Financial Statements* requires the auditor to:

- identify the characteristics of the LLP's engagement which defines its scope;
- establish the reporting objectives so that the auditor can plan the timing of the audit and the communications which will be required;
- consider significant issues relating to the LLP which will direct the audit team's efforts;
- review the work performed on other preliminary engagement activities and the knowledge gained on other engagements performed by the engagement partner for the LLP and consider its relevance; and
- determine the nature, timing and extent of resources required in order to perform the audit engagement.

Once the audit strategy has been developed, the audit plan can then be produced. The audit plan is more detailed than the audit strategy and includes a description of:

- the nature, timing and extent of planned risk assessment procedures;
- the nature, timing and extent of planned further audit procedures at the assertion level; and
- other planned procedures which are required in order that the audit engagement complies with the UK ISAs.

The audit plan is prepared at the start of the engagement so the team is aware of the procedures to be carried out. An important aspect to emphasise where audit planning is concerned is that it does not stop once the audit plan is completed. ISA (UK) 300 recognises that planning is a 'continual and iterative process' and therefore changes to the audit plan may be needed during the detailed audit fieldwork because of issues arising during the course of the audit. This may also include revisions to financial statement and performance materiality. Where changes to the audit plan are required due to issues arising during the audit, such changes must be adequately documented.

Example – changes to an audit plan

During the course of the planning an LLP's audit, the auditor's initial analytical review confirmed that gross profit margins had remained static on the previous year and therefore she devised audit procedures to determine this was the case. During the on-site audit fieldwork, the auditor discovered several purchase invoices that had not been accrued for at the year-end resulting in a significant reduction in the gross profit margins in the year under audit.

Clearly in a situation like this, the original planned audit procedures would have to be changed (resulting in a change to the audit plan) because more work will have to be undertaken to ascertain why the gross profit margins have disproportionately reduced (other than the unaccrued purchase invoices), but also establishing why the internal controls had also not picked up this omission which would also result in creditors being understated as well as costs.

---

11 Obtaining audit evidence

4.11 The evidence which auditors obtain is one of the most crucial aspects of the audit. ISA (UK) 500 *Audit Evidence* says that the evidence obtained by the auditor must be 'sufficient' and 'appropriate'. The term 'sufficient' refers to the quantity of the evidence needed and the evidence is affected by the assessment of the risks of material misstatement and the quality of such evidence. The term 'appropriate' refers to the quality of the audit evidence, that is, the relevance and reliability of the evidence in providing support for the conclusions on which the auditor's opinion is based.

As part of the planning process, the auditors will have determined the sources from which they will obtain their audit evidence. The evidence can come from one of three sources: (1) the LLP itself (for example, work in progress/accrued income calculations), (2) third parties (for example, confirmation of bank balances provided directly to the auditors), or (3) generated by the auditors (for example, the re-performance of a bank reconciliation). The independent nature of an audit means that third-party and auditor-generated evidence are considered to be more reliable, but such evidence is also more expensive to obtain. In planning their work, the auditors will usually seek to obtain a balance of evidence from all sources, but a level of third-party evidence will always be necessary.

ISA (UK) 500 acknowledges that there is more than one way in which the auditors can obtain evidence, and the most appropriate method or methods will be adopted for each item in the accounts. The following are the principal categories:

- *Inspection of records or documents*. This tends to be the most commonly used procedure and involves substantiating amounts in the accounting records by reference to documents. Revenue, for example, will be audited in part by agreement to the related contracts and invoices, together with any proof of delivery of goods or services.

Example – inspection of records or documents

The financial statements of an LLP show the addition of a large number of computers during the year of £80,000 which is very material to the accounts. The audit senior has emailed the purchase ledger clerk and asked for a copy of the invoice to be scanned and sent to the audit firm so that they can verify the rights and obligations assertion relating to this equipment.

The invoice from the supplier could have been altered by the LLP to put the invoice in the name of the LLP. The auditor should have inspected the original invoice whilst carrying out the detailed audit work at the LLP's premises as it is considered that original documents are more reliable than photocopies, scanned copies or copies transmitted by facsimile.

- *Observation and physical inspection.* Whilst, in general, observation tests are of limited application because they are only valid at a point in time, in some circumstances there is no alternative procedure that can be performed. Probably the most common observation test carried out by the auditors is attendance at the stock count of a client where there are material amounts of stock.

Example – observation and inspection

The audit senior has attended the year-end stock count of an LLP and is observing a team of counters checking the quantities and pricing of stock.

While errors or omissions may not be made when the auditor is in attendance at the stock count, the procedures adopted by management may not be followed in their entirety once the auditor has left.

- *Inquiry and confirmation.* This covers a wide range of possible tests, from simply seeking clarification from the LLP's staff of something within the accounting records to requesting third-party confirmation of items such as bank or sales ledger balances.

Example – inquiry and confirmation

As part of the audit process, the audit senior has written to the LLP's bank and ask for a bank audit letter (sometimes called a 'bank confirmation letter' or 'bank certificate') at the balance sheet date to confirm the balances per each bank account operated by the LLP during the financial year.

The bank audit letter is external confirmation from the bank (hence third party) and is more reliable than internally-generated evidence provided by the LLP.

- *Recalculation and re-performance.* Re-performance of calculations to check their mathematical accuracy, for example, depreciation calculations or testing ageing of accounts receivables.

Example – recalculation

The accounting policy for depreciation of assets in an LLP is to depreciate on a pro-rata basis only in the year that the asset is acquired and disposed. The LLP's year-end is 31 March 2017 and on 1 July 2016 an item of machinery was purchased.

In this example, the auditor will be checking that the accounting policy in respect of depreciation has been correctly calculated by recalculating the depreciation charge based on 9/12 of a full year's depreciation charge.

Example – reperformance

The audit senior is auditing an LLP's payroll for the year and is checking that the year-end PAYE and NIC liability is fairly stated. This can be done by calculating the amount of PAYE and NIC for the entire year, deducting the payments made to HMRC during the year as well as any deductions from PAYE/NIC that the LLP is eligible to claim (such as employment allowance). This will help to identify any potential over- or under-payments of taxes during the year or at the year-end. It will also offer comfort to the auditor if their reperformance of the PAYE/NIC control account agrees to the year-end financial statements.

- *Analytical procedures*. The analysis of the relationships between amounts included within the accounts, either within the same period, or between comparable amounts from different periods or, in some circumstances, industry statistics. In carrying out analytical procedures, the auditors will initially develop their own estimate of the figures they expect to see, compare this estimate with the actual outcome, obtain an explanation for any differences, and then corroborate that explanation by reference to other information available from the LLP.

Example – analytical procedures

The audit senior has undertaken an analytical review of an LLP's profit and loss account. He has noticed that gross profit margins in 2017 were 40% and in 2016 were 55%.

The fluctuation in gross profit margins would need to be investigated by the audit senior to ensure that they are, in fact, correct as gross margins usually (although not always) are expected to remain fairly consistent from one reporting period to the next.

---

12 Sampling

4.12 Auditors are required to obtain reasonable, but not absolute, assurance as to the amounts included within the accounts. As a result of both this requirement and the need for efficiency, audit evidence is usually obtained on the basis of sample testing which is dealt with in ISA (UK) 530 *Audit Sampling*. Some audit firms have developed elaborate statistical models to enable them to select their samples whereas other firms take a more judgemental approach. Irrespective of the precise methods adopted for ascertaining the sample to be tested, there are some general principles to which the auditors will always adhere:

- Items are selected in such a way as to give a reasonable expectation that they are representative of the total population. For example, it would be inappropriate to test sales by only looking at transactions in one month. Where an LLP has more than one business stream, samples will need to be selected so that, as a minimum, all material types of business are covered.
- Selection must be made without any conscious bias – all items should have an equal chance of being selected. Items should not be selected for sampling simply because they are easy to locate.
- Where possible, the population to be tested should be stratified. A small number of high-value items covering a relatively large proportion of the population will usually be the most efficient approach.
- Specific key items should be tested – in particular, those which are particularly prone to error or misstatement – for example, all debts over a certain age.

The use of sampling methods means that auditors will not usually test all the information available to them because this would be both impractical and uneconomical. However, auditors may well deem 100% selection to be appropriate when there are a small number of high value items which make up a population, or when there is a significant risk of material misstatement and other audit procedures will not provide sufficient appropriate audit evidence.

Sampling offers the auditor the opportunity to obtain the minimum amount of audit evidence which is both sufficient and appropriate in order to form valid conclusions on the population. In addition, the use of sampling reduces the risk of 'over-auditing' in certain areas resulting in a much more efficient review of the working papers at the review stage of the audit.

13 Errors found during audit work

4.13 Where errors are found by the auditors during the course of their work, these will be recorded within the audit working papers on an 'audit error schedule' or an 'uncorrected misstatements schedule' and assessed as to whether or not they are material in the context of the accounts. In making this assessment, both the effect of individual errors and the cumulative effect of items which are essentially immaterial will be considered and they are combined to see if the cumulative effect of all the immaterial misstatements become material in aggregate. ISA (UK) 450 *Evaluations of Misstatements Identified During the Audit* requires the auditors to evaluate the effect of identified misstatements on the audit as well as evaluate the effect of uncorrected misstatements (if any) on the financial statements. The auditors will discuss the errors with the members, and request that the accounts be amended to deal with those which are, in their opinion, material. The members may choose to process all amendments but, where they decide that this is not necessary, the written representation given to the auditors (see **3.6**) will need to explain the reasons for non-adjustment – namely that, in the opinion of the members, they are not considered to affect the overall truth and fairness of the accounts due to the uncorrected misstatements being immaterial.

Where material misstatements are not corrected by the members, this will result in the auditor's qualifying their audit opinion accordingly.

In terms of misstatements, they can be either 'factual', 'projected' or 'judgemental'. *Factual* misstatements are those where there is no doubt and for which documentation is available. *Projected* errors are the auditor's best estimate of misstatements in populations usually derived from sampling. *Judgemental* misstatements are differences arising from the judgements of management concerning accounting estimates.

Example – audit sampling and error projection

The auditors of an LLP are testing sales invoices. The population of sales invoices amounted to £100,000 and the values of the invoices in the sample amounted to £35,000. The following are the results of the sample:

1. The audit senior tested all material items in the sample which amounted to £20,000 and included an error of £1,000. As the audit senior has tested all material items in the sample the error will not be reproduced in the remainder of the population and in this respect the likely error from the sample is limited to £1,000.
2. The audit senior tested a number of other invoices amounting to £15,000 and found an error of £500. In contrast to the testing in 1 above, this error could be reproduced in the sample because both the population and the sample are limited to the remaining non-material items. The 'projected' error by extrapolation will be the error discovered (£500) × the remaining population of (£100,000 – £20,000) £80,000/the sample £15,000 which is £2,667.

The total projected error is £1,000 + £2,667 = £3,667. If the members decide to correct the 'actual' adjustments which are £1,000 found in 1 and £500 in 2 hence £1,500, the projected error will be £2,167. This method is commonly referred to as the 'ratio' method.

If the above samples had not been split into two elements (material and non-material items), the projected error would be found by extrapolating over the total population. This would have increased the errors discovered because the errors would have been calculated as £1,500 x the population of £100,000/the sample of £35,000 = £4,286.

Example – the difference method

The difference method should be used where the error does not have a direct relationship to the monetary value of the item. It is relatively constant for all items, and so will increase in proportion to the number of items in the population. It is calculated as follows:

$$\textit{Error found in the sample} \times \frac{\textit{Number of items in the population}}{\textit{Number of items in the sample}} = \textit{Most likely error in population}$$

During the course of the control tests to ensure all goods despatched are invoiced, the auditor has noted the following deviations:

Number of despatch notes not found	1
Number of despatch notes without invoices	3
Authorised cancellations	(1)
Actual deviations	3

Deviation rate = 3/100 = 0.33

The conclusion is that despatches are being invoiced satisfactorily as the error rate in the sample is acceptably low.

---

14 Review

4.14 ISA (UK) 230 *Audit Documentation* requires that all working papers be reviewed by a member of the team who is more experienced than the preparer and is a basic quality control requirement of ISA (UK) 220 *Quality Control for an Audit of Financial Statements*. Reviewing the audit file not only ensures that the work carried out is sufficient to enable an audit opinion to be expressed, but also ensures that those not involved in the day-to-day work (typically the manager and partner) are aware of all significant issues affecting the LLP and its accounts. The audit engagement partner who will sign the auditor's report is not necessarily required to review all working papers but, at a minimum, the review must cover critical areas of judgement, significant risks and such other areas as they consider to be of importance.

The review process should be adequately documented to ensure there is evidence on file that the audit working papers have been reviewed by the audit engagement partner. This can be done either by way of initialling the working papers or having a separate schedule documenting the overall review process. Some 'paperless' audit systems will not allow the audit to be finalised unless there has been a review of the working papers undertaken.

15 Completion of the audit

4.15 The completion stage of the audit is crucially important because it is at this stage that the audit engagement partner reviews the evidence obtained with a view to forming their opinion as to whether the LLP financial statements give a true and fair view. The audit engagement partner must review the schedule of unadjusted misstatements to comply with the provisions in ISA (UK) 450 and establish the impact of the unadjusted misstatements. This evaluation will be done in conjunction with the materiality levels to determine if the unadjusted misstatements are material both individually and in aggregate.

ISA (UK) 520 *Analytical Procedures* requires the auditor to perform analytical procedures near the end of the audit to assist the auditor in forming an overall conclusion as to whether the financial statements are consistent with the auditor's understanding of the entity. Such procedures will not be markedly different from those applied at the planning stage (such as ratio analysis and comparisons with prior year financial statements). Undertaking analytical procedures at the end of the audit will provide the auditor with the information needed to explain any unusual trends, fluctuations or relationships within the LLP's financial statements.

In addition to ensuring that all the audit work has been completed satisfactorily, there are a number of other procedures which the auditors are required to carry out prior to the auditor issuing the auditor's report. These will include the following:

- Discussing with the members the extent to which there have been any events, subsequent to the completion of their fieldwork and through to the date of the auditor's report, which provide additional evidence as to any of the amounts included within the accounts or which should be disclosed in the accounts. This is a requirement of ISA (UK) 560 *Subsequent Events* which requires the auditor to perform procedures to obtain sufficient appropriate audit evidence that all events which have occurred between the balance sheet date and the auditor's report that either require adjustment or additional disclosure within the LLP's financial statements have been identified.
- Ascertaining whether there have been any changes in circumstances which might affect the members' assessment of whether the LLP is a going concern. ISA (UK) 570 *Going Concern* requires that the auditor remains alert throughout the course of the audit for any events or conditions which may cast doubt on the LLP's ability to continue as a going concern. The concept of going concern is discussed in more detail in Chapter 10.
- Obtaining written representations from the members. ISA (UK) 580 *Written Representations* requires the auditor to consider the matters to be included within the members' written representation and ISA (UK) 580 requires the representation to be dated as near as possible to, but not after, the date of the auditor's report. Written representations are considered to be audit evidence, but should complement existing audit evidence – in other words they cannot be regarded as sufficient and appropriate audit evidence on their own, primarily because they are internally-generated by the LLP. An illustrative written representation letter is shown in Appendix 2 to Chapter 3.

16 The auditor's opinion

4.16 Chapter 3 sets out the general requirement that an auditor's report should contain the auditor's opinion as to whether or not the accounts give a true and fair view. A variety of circumstances may lead to the auditor expressing a qualified 'except for', adverse or disclaimer of opinion. Where the auditors have not been able to obtain all of the information they require ('limitation of scope' or 'insufficient evidence'), or they disagree with the accounting treatment adopted by an LLP or disclosure (or non-disclosure) of an item in the accounts, a qualified audit opinion is expressed. The qualification can take a number of forms:

- *'Except for'*. Where the auditors have been unable to obtain sufficient and appropriate audit evidence with respect to one or more items, but where they are satisfied with the evidence available in all other areas. This form of opinion is also used where the auditors disagree with the accounting treatment or disclosure (or non-disclosure) in relation to an item in the accounts.
- *Disclaimer.* When the possible effect of a limitation in scope is so material and/or pervasive that the auditors have not been able to obtain sufficient appropriate evidence to enable them to form an opinion on the accounts. This can usually occur where the accounting records have been destroyed and the financial statements re-constructed.
- *Adverse opinion*. Where the auditors consider that the matter with which they disagree is so material and pervasive that the accounts are misleading. In these circumstances, the auditor's opinion will state that the accounts do not give a true and fair view.

In certain circumstances, there may be uncertainties surrounding an issue concerning the accounts, where the effect of the possible range of outcomes could be material. In these circumstances, where the auditors consider that this is a matter to which attention should be drawn, the auditors will make reference to the existence of the issue in their report by way of an 'emphasis of matter' paragraph, but this does not constitute a qualification of the auditor's opinion. This could arise, for example, where the LLP's corresponding figures have been restated. An emphasis of matter paragraph is cross-referenced to the relevant disclosure note in the LLPs financial statements and always contains a phrase along the lines of 'Without qualifying our opinion …'. This is to highlight to the user of the LLP's accounts the fact that an emphasis of matter paragraph is not a qualified opinion so as to avoid any misunderstanding.

17 Audit working papers

4.17 The auditors will record the results of the work performed on working papers which may be manual, electronic, or a combination of both. The auditors are under a professional obligation to safeguard the confidential nature of the working papers and they will not usually allow access to them by any third party, including the members of the LLP. Audit working papers are the crucial content of an audit file and record the work done and conclusions reached in order to allow the audit engagement partner to form their opinion as to whether the LLP's financial statements give a true and fair view.

However, legislation in the UK requires that, where there is a change in auditors, the new auditors may access the predecessor auditor's working papers for the immediately preceding financial period. Where such a request is received, the previous auditors are under a legal obligation to permit access. The outgoing auditors may also charge the LLP for the reasonable costs of allowing the incoming auditors access to the working papers.

ISQC (UK) 1 *Quality Control for Firms that Perform Audits and Reviews of Financial Statements, and Other Assurance and Related Services Engagements* suggests that the assembly of the audit file and working papers should be done on a timely basis. ISQC (UK) 1 suggests a time limit of not more than 60 days after the date of the auditor's report.

Chapter summary

- An audit involves the collection and evaluation of sufficient and appropriate audit evidence to enable the auditor to express an opinion on whether the accounts give a true and fair of the state of the LLP's financial affairs.
- Auditing standards in the UK were revised as part of the transposition of the Audit Regulation and Directive into legislation. The revised ISAs (UK) are effective for audits of financial statements for periods commencing on or after 17 June 2016. Prior to the revisions, the ISAs were referred to as ISAs (UK and Ireland).
- The audit process can be analysed into six broad stages from planning through to reporting.
- Planning is viewed as a crucial aspect of the audit process and will also involve agreeing the terms of the engagement with the LLP or reviewing existing terms to ensure they are appropriate and up-to-date.
- Risk assessment processes feature heavily in audit and include the use of various techniques (such as internal control questionnaires) in assessing where the risk of material misstatement may occur.
- While the detection of fraud is not the responsibility of the auditor, the procedures adopted by the auditor may serve to detect that fraud has occurred. Auditors are mandated to apply professional scepticism during the course of their work.
- Auditors will not give 100% assurance that the financial statements are free from material misstatement whether caused by fraud or error. Instead the auditor's report will provide reasonable assurance within the context of materiality.
- Auditors may rely on an LLP's internal control to provide audit evidence; although where reliance is placed on such controls, ISA (UK) 330 would require the auditor to obtain more persuasive audit evidence.
- At the planning phase the audit strategy is developed and this then leads on to the development of the audit plan, which is more detailed than the audit strategy.
- Audit planning is viewed as a continual and iterative process; and changes to the audit plan should be made where considered necessary during the execution of the audit fieldwork (for example where audit evidence contradicts the auditor's understanding).
- Auditors will use sampling techniques to gather evidence, rather than sample every item in a population.
- Errors found during the course of the audit will be accumulated on an 'audit error schedule' or 'summary of unadjusted errors' schedule. These errors will then be considered in isolation and in combination to judge whether they are material.
- The audit engagement partner should review the audit documentation obtained during the course of the audit (particularly audit documentation relating to material areas) in forming their opinion.
- The audit opinion can be unqualified, qualified 'except for', adverse or disclaimer.
- Emphasis of matter paragraphs are not a form of qualified audit opinion.

Chapter 5

Accounting for members' interests and remuneration – principles

Signposts

- Section 22 *Liabilities and Equity* in FRS 102 *The Financial Reporting Standard applicable in the UK and Republic of Ireland* (September 2015) deals with the issue of financial instruments which causes some difficulty where LLPs are concerned (see **5.1**).
- Puttable instruments increase the complexity for LLPs although these are not as common (see **5.1**).
- According to Section 22, financial instruments are either 'debt' or 'equity' depending on the substance of the transaction (see **5.2**).
- Members of an LLP have two sorts of rights: rights which the members have in respect of amounts subscribed or contributed to the LLP and rights to remuneration either by way of salary arrangement or profit share (see **5.2**).
- Accounting for members' capital as either debt or equity depends on whether the LLP has the unconditional right to withhold payment to members (see **5.3**).
- The ways in which members of an LLP are remunerated will vary between LLPs but will reflect the fact that the members are in the position of both owning and working in the LLP (see **5.4**).
- 'Members remuneration charged as an expense' must be shown immediately after 'Profit or loss for the financial year before members' remuneration and profit shares' according to the SORP (see **5.5**).
- Unpaid profits for the year which the LLP has the unconditional right to withhold at the balance sheet date are treated as available for discretionary division among members (see **5.6**).
- The SORP requires disclosure of the way in which each type of remuneration has been determined and accounted for (see **5.6**).
- Members' interests can be shown as three types of balance in the balance sheet (see **5.7**).
- The puttable exception can be difficult for LLPs to apply and the SORP contains some additional guidance (see **5.8**).

- Members' balances are treated as equity only if the LLP has the unconditional right to withhold them from the member (or if they have been paid, the LLP has the unconditional right to reclaim them) (see **5.9**).
- Profit which forms part of 'Profit available for discretionary distribution among members' in the profit and loss account is treated as equity (see **5.10**).
- The SORP requires the financial statements of an LLP to include a comprehensive statement of components of members' interests and movements during the year (see **5.11**).
- If the LLP is required to produce a cash flow statement under Section 7 *Statement of Cash Flows* of FRS 102, the SORP requires separate disclosure of transactions with members (and former members) from transactions with non-members (see **5.12**).
- It is fairly common practice for a member of an LLP to borrow in order to fund their initial capital requirements and may not necessarily require disclosure in the LLP financial statements (see **5.13**).
- There are a number of additional disclosures relating to members' remuneration that the Regulations and the SORP require in the notes to the financial statements (see **5.14**).
- The members' report should include details of the policies adopted by the LLP with regards to capital maintenance including a discussion of the policies adopted in dealing with members' drawings (see **5.15**).
- The LLPs accounting records will need to contain sufficient detail to be able to ascertain the financial relationship between each member and the LLP (see **5.16**).

1 Introduction

5.1 The area that has probably given rise to the most practical difficulties for LLPs where FRS 102 *The Financial Reporting Standard applicable in the UK and Republic of Ireland* is concerned is the application of Section 22 *Liabilities and Equity*. The definition of financial instruments is so widely drawn that the various rights that members have to participate in an LLP, whether by way of capital or sharing of profits, fall within the requirements of this section. However, as Section 22 only applies for accounting periods commencing on or after 1 January 2015 (with early adoption permissible) or 1 January 2016, depending on whether the LLP is small, (and prior to new UK GAAP, FRS 25 *Financial instruments: Presentation* only previously applied for periods beginning on or after 1 January 2005), members' agreements prepared before these standards became applicable are in many cases difficult to interpret in the light of the very precise definitions contained in them. The application of the principles of Section 22 to LLPs is considered at some length in the SORP.

The SORP also considers another level of complexity, albeit in practice one that is unlikely to apply to many LLPs, which relates to puttable instruments and which is considered further at **5.8**.

This Chapter considers the principles of Section 22 as they apply to LLPs, and some of the practical implications are considered in the following chapter.

2 Members' interests as financial instruments

5.2 Section 22 of FRS 102 (September 2015) requires, amongst other things, that financial instruments be classified as either liabilities or equity (the term used for residual interests), by reference to substance rather than legal form. The term 'substance over form' is taken to mean the commercial reality of the transaction. The definition of equity is very tightly drawn and, unless an entity has an unconditional right to withhold payment to an instrument holder, unpaid amounts are classed as a liability and related returns as an expense. Other than in the limited circumstances of what are termed 'puttable instruments', which are considered further below, if an entity (including an LLP) cannot avoid paying an amount to a third party, it has a liability.

The rights that a member has in respect of its relationship with an LLP (referred to in the SORP as 'participation rights') fall into two types each requiring separate analysis. There are the rights which the members have in respect of amounts they have subscribed or otherwise contributed to the LLP, and their rights to remuneration, whether through salary-type arrangements or profit share.

Whether each right represents either a liability or equity will determine where it is included within the LLP's accounts.

The implications for LLPs are, therefore, wide-ranging, and each LLP needs to examine its members' agreement very carefully to determine the relevant accounting treatments.

3 Members' capital

5.3 In the majority of LLPs, members will be required to contribute capital, although in practice there is wide variation as to how this is achieved. The contribution of capital can occur both at the stage someone initially becomes a member and at subsequent dates.

Capital may be contributed either by way of a cash payment by the member or through an arrangement whereby a member agrees to 'capitalise' part of their profit allocation for the year. The latter might typically happen on initial admission, when it might be agreed that the member could reach their capital requirement over a number of years.

Unlike a limited company, an LLP is able to repay to the members any of its capital or convert it to debt without any legal restrictions, and the terms and conditions attaching to members' capital will be determined by the members' agreement. Whilst this appears to create greater flexibility, in practice it is probable that restrictions will exist as a result of external requirements placed on the LLP to maintain a certain level of capital (for example, by banks and the Financial Conduct Authority). LLPs repaying capital will also need to be aware of the risk of this being viewed as a preference over creditors, in the event of the LLP subsequently running into financial difficulties and becoming insolvent.

The accounting classification of members' capital between equity and debt depends on whether the LLP has the unconditional right to withhold repayment to the members. Where the members' agreement entitles a member to the return of capital on retirement from the LLP, the capital is classified as a debt due to members (ie a liability), other than in those cases where the requirements in respect of puttable instruments are met (see below). This is because 'debt' would be considered to be a 'financial liability' and a financial liability is any liability which is:

- A contractual obligation to:
  - deliver cash or another financial asset to another entity; or
  - exchange financial assets/financial liabilities with another entity under conditions which are deemed to be potentially unfavourable to the entity; or
- A contract that will, or might be, settled in the entity's own equity instruments and:
  - under which the entity is, or may be, obliged to deliver a variable number of the entity's own equity instruments; or
  - which will, or may be, settled other than by the exchange of a fixed amount of cash or another financial asset for a fixed number of the entity's own equity instruments. However, in this respect, the entity's own equity instruments do not include instruments which are themselves contracts for the future receipt or delivery of the entity's own equity instruments.

Where there is no requirement to repay capital to members, it will be treated as equity. The terms attaching to capital have wider implications than purely accounting. Where the LLP has the right to refuse capital payments that reduce total capital below a minimum level, this increases the rights of the LLP relative to the individual members. If, for example, the business faced difficult times and an outflow of members, the right of the LLP to hold a minimum level of capital would reduce the extent to which a withdrawal of the firm's working capital would compound the effect of the loss of key members.

In some circumstances, members may be entitled to receive interest on their capital. In determining the accounting treatment of any such interest, the requirements of Section 22 are again relevant. On initial recognition of the capital, it is also necessary to consider any related cash outflows and the extent to which they are at the discretion of the LLP. In circumstances where the LLP has no requirement to repay capital, but there is mandatory interest payable on that capital, it will represent what is termed a compound financial instrument in Section 22. In such cases the debt element (interest) is calculated first, by reference to the net present value of the cash flows and any excess of the capital over that amount will be classed as equity. In a number of cases the debt element will be equal to the amount of the capital, resulting in the capital being classified as a liability in its entirety.

Example – interest paid to members and capital repaid at the discretion of the LLP

The constitution of Westhead LLP requires that its members subscribe capital to the LLP on admission to the partnership. Repayments of this capital amount are made to the outgoing member on retirement and this is subject to the LLP passing a resolution prior to any capital being repaid. If a resolution is not passed, the LLP has the right to retain the capital indefinitely. The terms of the members' agreement also make provision for the member to receive a market rate of interest on all capital which they have subscribed.

In this example, the LLP must pass a positive resolution in order to repay capital amounts to outgoing members and where no positive resolution is passed, the LLP has the ability to retain the capital indefinitely. Notwithstanding this latter possibility, the LLP still has an obligation to pay the subscriber interest on that capital at market rates. As a consequence, Section 22 of FRS 102 would require a liability to be recognised in the LLP's financial statement as a member subscribes to the partnership which reflects the present value of the minimum non-discretionary cash flows (the interest). Because the return is at a market rate at the time the member subscribes the capital, the entire capital will fall to be treated as a liability.

---

4 The nature of members' remuneration

5.4 The way in which members are remunerated will vary between LLPs but will reflect the fact that the members are in the position of both owning the LLP and, usually, working within it. In a company environment the distinction between the rewards a director receives in his or her capacity as a shareholder (ie by virtue of ownership) (dividends) and those received for services provided (directors' remuneration) are more readily distinguished, but within an LLP the distinction between the two is frequently blurred. The accounting treatment and presentation of amounts payable to members is primarily not determined by whether the payments are rewards for working in the LLP or ownership thereof, but by whether or not the LLP has discretion over payment of the amounts.

Members may be rewarded for their involvement with the LLP through one or more of the following:

- *Salaried remuneration.* Changes to the tax legislation from 6 April 2014 effectively mean that some members of an LLP will not be treated as self-employed, but are now taxed as if they are employees (often referred to as 'disguised remuneration') subject to meeting the following criteria:

  Condition A: It is reasonable to expect that at least 80% of the members' pay is fixed, or if variable, then without reference to, or in practice unaffected by, the LLP's profit or loss.

  Condition B: The member has no significant influence over the affairs of the LLP.

  Condition C: The members' contribution to the LLP is less than 25% of the disguised salary.

- *Fixed share.* Members may be 'guaranteed' a certain amount of remuneration each year either within the membership agreement or through individual arrangements between the LLP and the member. This amount will be paid to them irrespective of the level of profits made by the LLP.
- *Share in residual profit.* Members are awarded a share of the profit made by the LLP, after the payment of any salaried remuneration and fixed shares. The basis of allocation will vary but will typically be based on a formula linked to factors such as seniority and the capital introduced by the member. Often, members will be entitled to a fixed amount, as well as a share in residual profit.
- *Drawings.* While salaried remuneration, fixed shares and residual shares refer to the member's entitlement to profit, drawings refer to the cash payments received in respect of that entitlement. Depending on the terms of the members' agreement, drawings may be paid in respect of profit to which the member is already entitled, or may be paid in advance of the division of profit to the member. Whether or not any drawings paid in excess of profit allocation are to be repaid to the LLP will again depend upon the terms of the membership agreement.

5 Accounting for members' remuneration

5.5 The SORP's treatment of members' remuneration and profit share, and the related balance sheet items, reflects the presentation requirements of Section 22 of FRS 102 and whether the participation rights in relation to profits of the LLP are a liability or equity. This assessment should be made independently of the assessment in respect of capital. Those rights that are a liability will be treated as an expense in the current period's profit and loss account; those that are equity will be treated as an addition to the reserves of the LLP.

The provisions in FRS 102 allow entities a choice of whether to present total comprehensive income for the period in one statement (being the 'statement of comprehensive income') or, alternatively, in two statements (being an 'income statement' which is the profit and loss account and a 'statement of comprehensive income'). The LLP Regulations require that the profit and loss account discloses a total for 'Profit or loss for the financial year before members' remuneration and profit shares'. Members' remuneration charged as an expense should be shown immediately after this, with the remainder being profit or loss available for discretionary division among members.

Paragraph 51 of the SORP requires the following disclosure to be made on the face of the profit and loss account.

Profit or loss for the financial year before members' remuneration and profit shares	X
Members' remuneration charged as an expense	(X)
Profit or loss for the financial year available for discretionary division among members	X[1]

1 LLP SORP, para 51.

In determining the amount which is charged as an expense, both the amounts payable to the member and any associated employment costs should be included.

6 Identifying members' remuneration charged as an expense

5.6 In determining whether amounts paid to members during an accounting period from that period's profit should be treated as an expense, the SORP considers whether the LLP has the unconditional right to repayment of these amounts from the members at the balance sheet date. If it does not, the amounts are treated as an expense.

For profit that has not yet been paid to members at the year end, the SORP considers whether the LLP has the unconditional right to withhold those amounts from members at the balance sheet date. If it does not, the amounts are again treated as an expense. It is in this area that particular care is needed when analysing the members' agreement, in order to determine whether there is an automatic division of profit or whether further action is required by the LLP before the members are entitled to receive those profits.

It is also important that the decision to divide profits, which is the event that creates the obligation to pay those profits to the members, is distinguished from the arrangements for profit sharing. A provision in the members' agreement that sets out the profit shares of members does not of itself constitute an agreement for the sharing of profits.

Unpaid profits for the year that the LLP has the unconditional right to withhold at the balance sheet date are treated as available for discretionary division among members.

In practical terms, remuneration charged as an expense comprises the following:

- *Drawings made against current year profit, of which the LLP does not have the unconditional right to demand repayment at the year end.* This will include salaried remuneration and fixed profit shares. Where the members' agreement stipulates that payments on account of residual profit cannot be reclaimed, except to the extent amounts paid exceed the member's profit division for the year, payments of residual profit made in the year are also treated as an expense.
- *Undrawn profit, which the LLP does not have the unconditional right to withhold from the members at the year end.* This will include, for example, profit-related bonuses to which members are entitled, either through a contract with the LLP or the members' agreement. All undrawn profit will be treated as an expense if, for example, the members' agreement requires automatic division of those profits.

Profit available for discretionary division among members comprises the following:

- *Drawings made from current year profit, of which the LLP has the unconditional right to demand repayment at the year end.* This might occur where payments on account of residual profit are made, and the members' agreement stipulates that no residual profit is divided among the members until some process of post year end approval has taken place.

- *Undrawn profit, which the LLP has the unconditional right to withhold from the members at the year end.* This will relate to undrawn residual profit, the division of which is subject to post year end approval.

The following table, reproduced from paragraph 54 of the SORP, summarises the treatment of members' remuneration:

Nature of element of member's remuneration	Treat as
Remuneration that is paid under an employment contract	Expense, described as 'Members' remuneration charged as an expense', and deducted after arriving at 'Profit for the financial year before members' remuneration and profit shares'
Other payments, arising from components of members' participation rights in the profits for the year that give rise to liabilities in accordance with section 22 of FRS 102, such as mandatory interest payments	
Automatic division of profits	
Any share of profits arising from a division of profits that is discretionary on the part of the LLP (ie, where the decision to divide the profits is taken after the profits have been made)	Allocation of profit[2]

When profit available for discretionary division among members is subsequently divided, there is no impact on the profit and loss account, and the movement is reflected in the reconciliation of movements in members' interests, of which an example is provided at **5.11**. The balance sheet treatment of amounts paid and payable to members and of undivided profit is explained at **5.15**.

For a large proportion of LLPs, the remuneration of members will comprise both an expense element and an allocation of profits, which will need to be separately recorded and accounted for.

In addition to impacting its presentation in the profit and loss account and balance sheet, the extent to which members receive remuneration that falls to be treated as an expense affects the valuation of any work in progress. Remuneration charged as an expense will need to be included within the calculation of work in progress whereas discretionary profit allocation will be excluded. Accounting for work in progress is considered in more detail in **7.7**.

The SORP requires disclosure of the way in which each type of remuneration has been determined and accounted for and it may be most appropriate to include this within the accounting policy note.

2 LLP SORP, para 54.

7 The composition of members' interests

5.7 Within the balance sheet, amounts relating to the interaction of the LLP with its members can give rise to three types of balance:

- *Amounts due from members.* Amounts which are debts owed by the members to the LLP, for example, drawings paid in excess of profit entitlement.
- *Loans and other debts due to members.* Amounts which are liabilities owed by the LLP to the members, for example, undrawn profit allocations and capital that is classed as a liability because the LLP cannot avoid repayment.
- *Members' other interests (equity).* Includes only those amounts that the LLP has the unconditional right to withhold from the members, for example, undistributed profits that the LLP has the right to retain, capital introduced by members whose repayment is subject to approval, and other reserves, for example revaluation reserves.

The SORP requires 'Loans and other debts due to members' and 'Members' other interests' to be disclosed separately on the face of the balance sheet. 'Loans and other debts due to members' and 'Members capital' should be included in balance sheet item J to the extent that they are classified as a liability. 'Members' capital', 'Revaluation reserve' and 'Other reserves' are classified in equity (balance sheet item K) to the extent that they are classified as equity and the SORP also requires separate disclosure of these on the face of the balance sheet. Equity cannot include members' capital which is classified as a liability to conform to the requirements in Section 22 of FRS 102. The consequence of this is that some LLPs will classify all capital as a financial liability in cases where individual members have the right to demand repayment of such balances (such as when they retire) and when the LLP does not have the unconditional right to refuse such repayment (except where the conditions for the puttables exception are met).

8 Puttable instruments

5.8 Section 22 of FRS 102 provides additional guidance in respect of a *puttable instrument.* A 'puttable instrument' is a financial instrument which gives the holder of the instrument the right to sell that instrument back to the issuer for cash or for another financial asset. Alternatively, it may be redeemed or repurchased by the issuer on the occurrence of an uncertain future event or on the death or retirement of the holder of the puttable instrument.

For LLPs, there are certain situations when the classification of a financial instrument will meet the definition of a financial liability, but will instead fall to be classified as equity if the conditions are met. Paragraph 22.4 of FRS 102 is drafted in such a way that it applies to individual classes of financial instrument. The overall structure of an LLP may consist of one, or more, classes of financial instrument.

Example – different classes of financial instrument

Whitaker LLP (Whitaker) requires members to subscribe to capital on admission to the partnership. In addition, Whitaker also requires its members to make loans to the LLP as and when required. These loans are separate financial instruments from capital subscriptions.

In this example, Whitaker will have two classes of financial instrument (the capital subscriptions and the loans from the members).

There are certain criteria which have to be met if a puttable instrument is to be classed as equity:

- The instrument entitles the holder to a pro-rata share of the entity's net assets in the event of the entity's liquidation (net assets being the assets which remain after all liabilities have been deducted).
- The instrument is in a class of instruments which are subordinate to all other classes of instruments.
- All the financial instruments in the subordinate class have identical features.
- With the exception of the contractual obligation for the issuer to repurchase or redeem the instrument for cash or another financial asset, there are no other contractual obligations to deliver cash or another financial asset to another entity, or to exchange financial assets or financial liabilities under conditions which are potentially unfavourable to the entity and the contract is not one which will, or may be, settled in the entity's own equity instruments.
- The total amount of expected cash flows which are attributable to the instrument over the life of the instrument are based substantially on the profit or loss, the change in the recognised net assets or the change in the fair value of the recognised and unrecognised net assets of the entity over the life of the instrument.

The second requirement in the criteria above is that the class of instruments is subordinate to all other instruments of the issuer. Therefore, to conform with paragraph 22.4 of FRS 102, where members' interests comprise of more than one class of instrument, equity classification under the puttables exception is only eligible for the class of instrument which is subordinate to all others.

An LLP will typically have at least two individual classes of financial instruments – capital and profit share. Each financial instrument may have more than one component (for example, fixed and variable profit shares). The arrangement in most LLPs mean that the residual interest in the LLP will usually be members' capital. However, this will be applied differently in two sets of circumstances – first, if the residual interest may be 'put' on the LLP (ie redeemed at the option of the member without liquidation of the LLP) and, secondly, where it may be put only on the liquidation of the LLP. In the former, only the whole instrument can be reclassified; in the latter, it is possible to reclassify a component of the instrument. These circumstances are discussed further in Chapter 6.

When a puttable financial instrument obliges the entity to make payments to the holder of the instrument before liquidation, the instrument is classified as a liability (this can be the case where the LLP is required to make mandatory interest or other non-discretionary payments to the holder of the instrument). This treatment is appropriate because of the requirement in paragraph 22.4(iv) of FRS 102 which says that 'apart from the contractual obligation for the issuer to repurchase or redeem the instrument for cash or another financial asset, the instrument does not include any contractual obligation to deliver cash or another financial asset to another entity…'. If the LLP is required to make mandatory interest or other non-discretionary payments to the holder, the instrument will fail to meet the criteria in paragraph 22.4. There is no equivalent restriction for instruments which are only redeemable on liquidation.

Another issue which needs to be carefully considered by LLPs is the distinction between those transactions between the members and the LLP which are undertaken in the members' role as owners and non-owners. Paragraph 42C to the SORP contains an example of a profit or loss sharing arrangement whereby profit or loss is allocated to the instrument holders on the basis of services rendered or business generated during the current and previous years. The SORP acknowledges that these arrangements are transactions with instrument holders in their capacity as non-owners and should not be considered when assessing the features listed in paragraph 22.4 of FRS 102. Conversely, the SORP acknowledges that profit or loss sharing arrangements which allocate profit or loss to instrument holders based on the nominal amount of their instruments relative to others in the class may represent transactions with the instrument holders in their role as owners and hence should be considered having reference to the provisions in paragraph 34 of the SORP.

The puttable exception can be quite complicated to apply and the SORP contains some additional guidance in Appendix 2.

9 Presentation of members' interests within the accounts

5.9 Members' balances are treated as equity only if the LLP has the unconditional right to withhold them from the member (or, in the case of amounts that have been paid to members, if the LLP has the unconditional right to reclaim them). Otherwise they are treated as a liability due to the member. Under the SORP, all members' balances in the LLP, whether equity or a liability, are shown within 'net assets attributable to members', on the 'bottom half' of the balance sheet (statement of financial position). This treatment differs from a company balance sheet, where only equity balances are included in the bottom half of the balance sheet and all liabilities are shown in the top half as a deduction from net assets. As a consequence, any LLP which has zero equity (because, for example, all capital must be returned and all profits are automatically divided) does not present a balance sheet that totals zero but one that shows the net assets attributable to members. The presentation of members' interests is further illustrated in the example accounts in Appendices 1 and 2 in this book.

In an LLP, 'net assets attributable to members' can only include members' balances in the LLP, and, unless the member has the legal right to offset amounts he owes the LLP against amounts it owes him, they must be presented separately, with amounts owed by the member being disclosed within debtors in the top half of the balance sheet.

The SORP also requires that total members' interests be presented in the accounts by showing the sum of amounts due from members, amounts due to members and members' other interests as a memorandum item on the balance sheet. This is also illustrated in the example accounts.

The presentation of amounts within 'net assets attributable to members' in an LLP also differs from the presentation of partners' balances that is normally adopted in a general partnership. In a general partnership, balances would normally be categorised by their purpose (capital, current, taxation, etc). In an LLP, they are first categorised by whether they are equity or debt, and then subcategorised between capital and other amounts. For example, in an LLP there is no difference in disclosure between current account balances and taxation balances that are payable to or on behalf of, members; both are included within 'loans and other debts due to members – other amounts'.

10 Classification of profit in the balance sheet

5.10 The balance sheet treatment of profits follows the treatment in the profit and loss account, which is explained at **5.6**.

Profit which forms part of 'profit available for discretionary distribution among members' in the profit and loss account should be treated as equity. To the extent that drawings have been made against profit that is included within equity (which is the case where the LLP has the unconditional right to reclaim drawings), these drawings are shown as 'other debts due from members' within debtors.

Members' remuneration charged as an expense represents profit that the LLP does not have the unconditional right to withhold from the members, and, to the extent it has not been drawn, is presented as a liability due to members in the balance sheet. Where profit that was available for discretionary distribution at the end of the previous year has been divided among the members in the current year, but has not yet been paid, this is also presented as a liability.

The policy for division of profit can significantly impact the shape of an LLP's balance sheet, as demonstrated in the example below.

Example – division of profit

Members' capital is 100, and members are entitled to have this repaid when they leave.

The LLP has made 350 units of profit for the year, of which 250 have been drawn in the year and 100 remain undrawn.

- In LLP A, all profit is automatically divided (ie the LLP does not have the unconditional right to withhold any profit made from the members), and the undrawn profit of 100 units is presented within loans and other debts due to members.

- In LLP B, drawn profit is divided and cannot be reclaimed by the firm, but the division of undrawn profit is subject to post year end approval. The undrawn profit of 100 units is presented within equity.
- In LLP C, division of all profit is subject to post year end approval. All 350 units of profit are presented within equity and the 250 units that have been drawn are presented as 'amounts due from members'.

Members' capital is presented within 'loans and other debts due to members', as it is a liability rather than 'equity'.

	A	B	C
Cash	200	200	200
Trade debtors	100	100	100
Amounts due from members	–	–	250
Trade creditors	(100)	(100)	(100)
Net assets attributable to members	200	200	450
Loans and other debt due to members			
Members' capital classified as a liability	100	100	100
Other amounts	100	–	–
	200	100	100
Members' other interests			
Members' other interests – other reserves classified as equity	–	100	350
	200	200	450
Total members' interests			
Amounts due from members	–	–	(250)
Loans and other debts due to members	200	100	100
Members' other interests	–	100	350
	200	200	200

11 Reconciliation of movement in members' interests

5.11 FRS 102 at paragraph 4.12 requires certain disclosures to be made which relate to an entity's share capital and reserves. For those entities which do not have share capital (such as an LLP), equivalent information is required to be disclosed which shown the movement in the period for each category of equity, and the rights, preferences and restrictions attaching to each category of equity.

To meet this requirement, the SORP requires the accounts of the LLP to include a comprehensive statement of the components of members' interests and movements during the year. An example is provided on page 95.

	EQUITY Members' other interests				**DEBT Loans and other debts due to members less any amounts due from members in debtors**			**TOTAL MEMBERS' INTERESTS**
	Members' capital (classified as equity)	**Revaluation reserve**	**Other reserves**	**Total**	**Members' capital (classified as debt)**	**Other amounts**	**Total**	**Total 2XX1**
Amounts due to members						X	X	
Amounts due from members						(X)	(X)	
Balance at [start of the period]	X	X	X	X	X	X	X	X
Members' remuneration charged as an expense, including employment and retirement benefit costs						X	X	X
Profit/(loss) for the financial year available for discretionary division among members			X	X				X
Members' interests after profit/(loss) for the year	X	X	X	X	X	X	X	X
Other divisions of profits/(losses)			(X)	(X)		X	X	-
Surplus arising on revaluation of fixed assets		X		X				X
Introduced by members	X			X	X		X	X
Repayments of capital	(X)			(X)	(X)		(X)	(X)
Repayment of debt (including members' capital classified as a liability)					(X)		(X)	(X)
Drawings						(X)	(X)	(X)
Other movements	X	X	X	X	X		X	X
Amounts due to members					X	X	X	
Amounts due from members						(X)	(X)	
Balance at [end of period]	X	X	X	X		X	X	X

Small LLPs reporting under the provisions of FRS 102, Section 1A *Small Entities* need not present the reconciliation of the movement in members' other interests. However, in some cases, a small LLP will present the reconciliation in order that the financial statements give a true and fair view. To maintain consistency with the requirements for small companies (which are not required to produce a statement of changes in equity), the SORP instead encourages the reconciliation of members' other interests, rather than mandates it.

Focus

A point worthy of note is that the 2017 SORP does not require an LLP to prepare a statement of changes in equity if the LLP has no equity. Where the LLP does not present such a statement because it has no equity and the statement of changes in equity is not replaced as a primary statement by a reconciliation of members' interests, the SORP requires a statement to be made on the face of one of the other primary statements or within the notes to the accounts that the LLP does not have any equity and hence a statement of changes in equity is not presented.

12 Members' interests in the cash flow statement

5.12 Where an LLP falls within the scope of Section 7 *Statement of Cash Flows*, it will be required to prepare a cash flow statement. Section 7 is notably different than under previous GAAP in FRS 1 *Cash flow statements (revised 1996)* and requires a cash flow statement which analyses cash flows during the period between:

- operating activities;
- investing activities; and
- financing activities.

Operating activities are the principal day-to-day revenue-producing activities of the LLP which do not fall to be classed as investing or financing activities. This category is essentially the 'default' category.

Investing activities are the acquisition and disposal of long-term assets and other investments not included in cash equivalents. For example, investing activities would represent cash payments used by the LLP to purchase a fixed asset or show the disposal proceeds from the sale of a fixed asset.

Financing activities are activities which result in changes to the contributed equity and borrowing structure of the LLP. An example could be where the LLP has taken out a loan and the proceeds from the loan would be shown within financing activities.

Paragraph 74A of the 2014 SORP considers the presentation of cash flows with members (and former members) and summarises these as follows:

Nature of transaction	Classification of cash flows
Remuneration that is paid under an employment contract	Operating cash flow
Other remuneration (discretionary or non-discretionary) for services provided	Operating cash flow
Post-retirement payments to former members	Operating cash flow
Capital introduced by members (classified as equity or liability)	Financing cash flow
Repayment of capital or debt to members	Financing cash flow
Payments to members that represent a return on amounts subscribed or otherwise contributed	Financing cash flow[3]

The SORP requires separate disclosure of transactions with members (and former members) from transactions with non-members. This is to assist with an understanding of the LLPs ability to generate cash flows, and the needs of the LLP to utilise those cash flows.

13 Borrowings of members

5.13 It is not uncommon for the members of an LLP to borrow in order to fund at least their initial capital requirements. These arrangements frequently involve the LLP entering into a guarantee, indemnity or similar arrangement with the provider of the funding.

The fact that the members' interests have been funded by way of borrowings is not of itself something which requires disclosure in the accounts. Instead it is necessary to look at the extent of the LLP's obligation to the provider of finance and how this should be treated.

It would be unusual to include a provision in the accounts for the amount of any such loan. FRS 102 at Section 21 *Provisions and Contingencies* (see **9.2**) would only require a provision to be recognised when the LLP had a legal or constructive obligation to repay the loan and the requirement for repayment was probable at the year end and the amount of the repayment could be reliably measured. Circumstances where this might arise include the death or early retirement through ill-health of a member. In determining the amount of any provision, the LLP should take into account the extent to which it is legally entitled to offset the liability against the capital interests and other debts due to the member. In addition, in certain circumstances, such as the death of a member, the repayment may be covered by insurance.

3 LLP SORP, para 74A.

Where it is unlikely that the guarantee or indemnity will be called, its existence should, nevertheless, be disclosed as a contingent liability in the notes to the accounts to comply with the provisions in Section 21 of FRS 102, unless the possibility of it being called upon is remote.

14 Members' remuneration disclosures

5.14 In addition to the requirement to disclose members' remuneration charged as an expense separately on the face of the profit and loss account, the Regulations and the SORP require a number of additional disclosures to be made in the notes to the accounts.

With the exception of micro-entity LLPs reporting under FRS 105 *The Financial Reporting Standard applicable to the Micro-entities Regime*, all LLPs, including small LLPs must disclose the average number of members during the year in a note to the accounts. This is a new requirement for small LLPs who would not have previously made such a disclosure. An LLP will do this by dividing the total number of members of the LLP for each month (or part thereof) in the financial year by the number of months in the financial year and round the result to the nearest whole number. Whilst not required by either the Regulations or the SORP, the members may wish to include details of average members' remuneration. Where this option is taken, the SORP states that it should be calculated by reference to the disclosed average number of members and the amount of 'profit before members' remuneration and profit shares' shown in the profit and loss account.

Where there are factors which distort the amount of profit attributable to members in the year (for example, adjustments to retirement benefits), the members are allowed to disclose an adjusted average members' remuneration, provided that a reconciliation between the basic and adjusted calculations is provided.

For large and medium-sized LLPs, where the profit of the LLP before members' remuneration and profit shares is greater than £200,000, the notes to the accounts are required to disclose the remuneration of the member with the highest entitlement to profit. As well as entitlements from the LLP, this will also include any amounts paid to the member by a subsidiary undertaking or other third party. The SORP does not specify how the amount should be calculated, although those LLPs that have arrangements whereby some profits will only be allocated in subsequent periods will need to consider which profits are included within the remuneration figure. In these circumstances, it could be either the share of the profit for the period that was agreed after the period end or the amounts allocated in the reporting period relating to profits made in earlier periods. The SORP requires that the method of calculation should be disclosed, and that a consistent policy should be applied year on year. The 'highest paid' member does not have to be named.

Where it is considered that it will assist an understanding of the financial performance of the LLP, the SORP recommends that members' remuneration charged as an expense should be further analysed within the notes to the financial statements, for example, between that which is paid under a contract of employment and that which relates to amounts arising from participation rights that give rise to a liability.

15 Disclosure of members' balances

5.15 The extent to which members' balances should be disclosed as equity or as 'loans and other debts due to members' is discussed above.

The Regulations require separate disclosure of the aggregate amount of money advanced by the members by way of loan, the aggregate amount of money owed to members in respect of profits and any other amounts. To the extent that this information is not ascertainable from the reconciliation of movements in members' interests, additional disclosure should be made. The total amount due after more than one year should also separately be disclosed.

In addition, the SORP requires that the notes to the accounts disclose where amounts due to members would rank on a winding up in relation to other unsecured creditors. In the absence of any agreement to the contrary, amounts due to members will rank equally with other creditors. However, in the absence of any subordination, the LLP may find it difficult to obtain credit from third parties, particularly banks. It is not unusual, therefore, for an LLP to subordinate all or part of the debt due to the members to other creditors in the event of a winding up.

Focus

- When the CCAB last consulted on changes to the SORP, some respondents commented that they felt that the disclosures concerning how loans and other debts due to members rank in relation to other unsecured creditors were onerous and overly burdensome in comparison to financial reporting by other types of entities.
- LLPs do not have any of the capital maintenance provisions which apply to companies and therefore the CCAB believes that these disclosures are necessary to give a true and fair view, regardless of the size of the LLP. Notwithstanding the fact that Section 1A of FRS 102 does not require such disclosure, the SORP mandates a small LLP to make the disclosure in order to give a true and fair view.

The members' report should include details of the policies adopted by the LLP with respect to capital maintenance. This includes a discussion of the policies adopted in dealing with members' drawings and how these are managed when they come into conflict with the cash requirements of the LLP.

The policy under which members make contributions of equity or debt to the LLP and the terms of their repayment should be disclosed. The members' report must also include details of equity which has been converted to debt (and vice versa) both within the year and for the period from the year end up until the date the accounts are approved.

16 Accounting records

5.16 While the published LLP accounts will only show members' interests at an aggregated level, the accounting records maintained with respect to members' interests will need to contain sufficient detail to be able to ascertain the financial relationship between each member and the LLP. They will, therefore, need to include details of the capital introduced by the member, profits allocated, and any salaries paid and drawings made.

Chapter summary

- Financial instruments should be classified as either liabilities or equity and should also reflect the substance of the transaction, rather than legal form.
- The accounting classification of members' capital between equity and debt will depend on whether the LLP has the unconditional right to withhold repayment to the members.
- The accounting treatment and presentation of amounts payable to members is primarily not determined by whether the payments are rewards for working in the LLP or ownership of the LLP but by whether or not the LLP has discretion over payment of the amounts.
- The SORP's treatment of members' remuneration and profit share reflects the presentation requirements of Section 22 of FRS 102.
- Paragraph 22.4 of FRS 102 is drafted in such a way that it applies to individual classes of financial instrument. The overall structure of an LLP may consist of one, or more, classes of financial instrument.
- Members' balances are only treated as equity only if the LLP has the unconditional right to withhold them from the members, otherwise they are treated as a liability.
- Small LLPs are encouraged to present a reconciliation of members' other interests.
- Paragraph 74A of the SORP considers the presentation of cash flows with members and former members.
- In addition to the requirement to disclose members' remuneration charged as an expense separately on the face of the profit and loss account, the Regulations and the SORP require a number of additional disclosures within the notes to the accounts.
- With the exception of micro-entity LLPs, all LLPs are required to disclose the average number of employees during the year.
- The members' report should include details of the policies adopted by the LLP with respect to capital maintenance.
- The accounting records maintained by the LLP should contain sufficient detail to be able to ascertain the financial relationship between each member and the LLP.

Chapter 6

Accounting for members' interests and remuneration – practical considerations

Signposts

- Appendix 2 of the SORP contains a number of examples which seek to assist in determining when members' participation rights are equity and when they are debt (see **6.1**).
- This chapter considers some practical examples to help highlight how the split between debt and equity works (see **6.2–6.8**).
- The SORP does not address accounting for losses by LLPs as the ways in which losses are addressed vary among LLPs (see **6.9**).
- In some cases the life of an LLP may be deliberately short as it may only have been created for a specific purpose and hence when the project is complete it may be liquidated (see **6.10**).

1 Introduction

6.1 **Chapter 5** considered the principles of accounting for members' interests and remuneration as a consequence of the application of Section 22 *Liabilities and Equity* in FRS 102 (September 2015) *The Financial Reporting Standard applicable in the UK and Republic of Ireland*. This chapter considers some of the implications of applying those principles to the varied ways in which an LLP might choose to operate so far as members' capital and profit shares are concerned.

Appendix 2 of the SORP contains a number of examples that seek to assist in determining when members' participation rights are equity and when they are debt.

2 Assumptions used in the examples

6.2 In the following examples, unless otherwise stated, the basic information in respect of 2XX1 is as follows:

- number of members = 10;
- capital subscribed by each member = £10,000;

- profit made in the year = £1,000,000; and
- drawings paid to members = £700,000.

3 Capital and profits both treated as equity

6.3

Relevant conditions contained in the members' agreement

On retirement, capital is not returned to the outgoing member unless agreed by a majority of members.

The decision to divide profit requires agreement of a majority of members. The decision to divide all profits of the year is taken after the year end.

Analysis

The LLP does not have an obligation to return capital or distribute profits to its members.

Accounting treatment

Capital of £100,000 is shown in equity on the balance sheet.

Profits of £1,000,000 are shown as retained profit for the year available for discretionary division among members in the profit and loss account and as part of equity within other members' interests.

Drawings of £700,000 are included within debtors.

Treatment of profit available for discretionary division in subsequent year

Following the year-end, the members agreed to divide the £1,000,000. The undrawn £300,000 is paid.

Profit for the year 2XX2 is £1,200,000 and drawings in respect of that year are £800,000.

Total drawings shown in the reconciliation of members' interests will be £1,100,000 (£300,000 + £800,000). £800,000 will also be included within debtors on the balance sheet.

Presentation in reconciliation of members' interests

	EQUITY			DEBT	Total Members' Interests	Total Members' Interests
	Members' Other Interests			Loans and other debts due to members less any amounts due from members in debtors	2XX2	2XX1
	Members' Capital (Classified as equity)	Other Reserves	Total			
	£	£	£	£	£	£
Amounts due to members				-		
Amounts due from members				(700,000)		
Balance at	100,000	1,000,000*	1,100,000	(700,000)	400,000	XXXXXX
start of the period 2XX2						
Profit for the financial year available for discretionary division among members		1,200,000	1,200,000		1,200,000	1,000,000
Members' interests after profit for the year	100,000	2,200,000	2,300,000	(700,000)	1,600,000	XXXXXX
Other divisions of profits/ losses		(1,000,000)	(1,000,000)	1,000,000		
Drawings				(1,100,000)	(1,100,000)	(700,000)
Amounts due to members				-		
Amounts due from members				(800,000)		
Balance at end of 2XX2	100,000	1,200,000	1,300,000	(800,000)	500,000	XXXXXX

*assumes no amounts other than the profit and drawings for the previous period.

Part of profits are divided during the year

The members agree to divide £600,000 during the year and the division of the remaining £400,000 is agreed after the year.

Accounting treatment of profits

Profits of £1,000,000 are shown as retained profit for the year, available for discretionary division among members in the profit and loss account and as part of equity within other members' interests.

Drawings of £100,000 (£700,000 – £600,000) are shown in debtors.

Presentation in reconciliation of members' interests

	EQUITY Members' Other Interests			DEBT	Total Members' Interests 2XX1	Total Members' Interests 2XX0
	Members' Capital (Classified as equity)	Other Reserves	Total	Loans and other debts due to members less any amounts due from members in debtors		
	£	£	£	£	£	£
Amounts due to members				XXXXXXX		
Amounts due from members				XXXXXXX		
Balance at start of the 2XX1	100,000	XXXXXX	XXXXXX	XXXXXX	XXXXX	XXXXX
Profit for the financial year available for discretionary division among members		1,000,000	1,000,000		1,000,000	XXXXX
Members' interests after profit for the year	100,000	1,000,000	1,100,000	XXXXXX	XXXXXX	XXXXXX
Other divisions of profits/ losses		(600,000)	(600,000)	600,000		
Drawings				(700,000)	(700,000)	XXXXXX
Amounts due to members				XXXXXX	XXXXXX	XXXXXX
Amounts due from members				(100,000)	(100,000)	XXXXXX
Balance at end of 2XX1	100,000	400,000	500,000	XXXXXX	XXXXXX	XXXXXX

4 Capital and profits both treated as liabilities

6.4

Relevant conditions contained in the members' agreement

On retirement, capital must be returned to the retiring member.

Profits are automatically divided equally between all members.

Analysis

The LLP has an obligation to return capital and distribute profits to its members.

Accounting treatment

Capital of £100,000 is shown as a liability on the balance sheet (members' capital classified as debt). In the reconciliation of members' interests, it is included within loans and other debts due to members.

Profits of £1,000,000 are shown as members' remuneration charged as an expense in the profit and loss account, and the profit available for discretionary division is nil.

The undrawn element of profit (£300,000) is included within loans and other debts due to members.

5 Capital is equity and profits are part equity and part liability

6.5

Relevant conditions contained in the members' agreement

On retirement, capital is not returned unless agreed by a majority of members.

25% of profits are divided automatically, the decision to divide the remainder requires the agreement of all members.

Analysis

The LLP has no obligation to return capital.

The LLP has an obligation to pay 25% of profits.

The LLP has no obligation to pay 75% of profits.

Accounting treatment

Capital of £100,000 is shown in equity on the balance sheet.

£250,000 is shown as members' remuneration, charged as an expense in the profit and loss account, and the retained profit available for discretionary division among members is £750,000.

Drawings of £450,000 (£700,000 – £250,000) are included within debtors.

6 Requirement to keep minimum level of capital

6.6

Relevant conditions contained in the members' agreement

On retirement, capital must be returned to the retiring member unless the amount falls below £90,000.

Analysis

The LLP has no obligation to return capital to the extent that total capital is £90,000 or less.

Accounting treatment

Capital of £90,000 is shown in equity on the balance sheet.

Capital of £10,000 is shown as a liability on the balance sheet (members' capital classified as debt).

7 Interest on capital

6.7 Capital is a liability

Relevant conditions contained in the members' agreement

On retirement, capital must be returned to the retiring member.

Members are entitled to interest on capital at 5% per annum.

Decision to divide profit requires agreement of a majority of members.

Analysis

The LLP has an obligation to return capital and pay interest thereon.

The LLP does not have an obligation to distribute profits to members.

Accounting treatment

Capital of £100,000 is shown as a liability on the balance sheet (members' capital classified as debt).

Interest of £5,000 is charged in the profit and loss account within members' remuneration charged as an expense.

To the extent the interest is unpaid, it is included within loans and other debts due to members.

Profits of £999,995 are shown as profit available for discretionary division among members.

Drawings of £700,000 are included within debtors.

Capital is 'equity'

Relevant conditions contained in the members' agreement

On retirement, capital is not returned unless agreed by a majority of members.

Members are entitled to interest at 5% per annum.

Decision to divide profit requires agreement of a majority of members.

Analysis

Whilst the LLP has no obligation to repay capital, it does have an obligation to pay interest. In accordance with the requirements of Section 22 in FRS 102 (September 2015), such an arrangement is regarded as a compound financial instrument requiring a 'split' approach to accounting. This means that the instrument is 'split' between its debt component and its equity component.

The LLP does not have an obligation to distribute profits to members.

Accounting treatment

Section 22 requires that the debt portion of the instrument be valued first, and this is done by calculating the present value of the future committed cash flows. In this example, that would be £5,000 at 5% in perpetuity, resulting in a discounted cash flow of £100,000. Therefore, all of the members' capital will be shown as a liability in the balance sheet. Had the future cash flows been less than £100,000, the lesser amount would have been recorded as a liability and the difference between that amount and £100,000 as equity. Were the cash flows to have exceeded £100,000, then a liability would have been recognised but restricted to the proceeds received by the LLP, namely £100,000.

8 Capital requirements met through profit share

6.8

Relevant conditions contained in the members' agreement

On retirement, capital is not returned unless agreed by a majority of members.

New members are not required to introduce capital in cash, but can accumulate it from their profit share in equal amounts in the first five years of membership.

Profits are automatically divided equally between all members.

In this example, it is assumed that an 11th member joins in the year.

Analysis

The LLP does not have an obligation to return capital.

The LLP does have an obligation to distribute profits to members.

New members' capital accumulated from profits is accounted for as a transfer within members' interests.

Accounting treatment

Capital of £102,000 is shown in equity on the balance sheet ((£10,000/5) + £100,000).

Profits of £1,000,000 are shown as members' remuneration charged as an expense in the profit and loss account, and the retained profit is nil.

The capital accumulated from profits (£2,000) is shown within the reconciliation of members' interests.

Presentation in reconciliation of members' interests

	EQUITY Members' Other Interests			DEBT	Total	Total
	Members' Capital (Classified as equity)	Other Reserves	Total	Loans and other debts due to members less any amounts due from members in debtors	2XX1	2XX0
	£	£	£	£	£	£
Amounts due to members				XXXXXXX		
Amounts due from members				XXXXXXX		
Balance at start of 2XX1	100,000	XXXXXX	XXXXXX	XXXXXX	XXXXXX	XXXXXX
Members' remuneration charged as an expense, including employment and retirement benefit costs				1,000,000	1,000,000	XXXXXX
Members' interests after profit for the year	100,000	XXXXXXX	XXXXXXX	XXXXXXX	XXXXXX	XXXXXX
Capital introduced by members	2,000			(2,000)	-	XXXXXX
Drawings				(700,000)	(700,000)	XXXXX
Amounts due to members				XXXXXX		
Amounts due from members				XXXXXX		
Balance at end of 2XX1	102,000	XXXXXX	XXXXXX	XXXXXX	XXXXXX	XXXXXX

9 Losses

6.9

The SORP does not address accounting for losses made by LLPs, as the ways in which these are addressed within members' agreements are varied. It is, however, usual for the provisions in respect of losses to be different to those in respect of profits – ie there is often no requirement for members to contribute to losses in the same way they share in profits.

Example 1 – Profits of subsequent periods reduced by past losses (profits are equity)

Relevant conditions contained in the members' agreement

On retirement, capital must be returned to the retiring member.

Decision to divide profit requires agreement of a majority of members.

Members are not required to contribute to losses.

In 2XX0 (the LLP's first year of trading), the LLP makes a loss of £300,000, and drawings were £600,000.

In 2XX1, the LLP makes a profit of £1,000,000, and drawings are £700,000.

In 2XX2, the LLP makes a profit of £1,200,000, and drawings are £800,000.

The remaining undrawn profits from 2XX1 are also paid (£300,000).

Capital remains unchanged throughout at £100,000.

Analysis

The LLP has an obligation to return capital.

The members have no obligation to contribute to losses.

Profits are included within profits available for discretionary division among members in the profit and loss account and equity in the balance sheet.

Accounting treatment

Capital of £100,000 is shown as a liability on the balance sheet (members' capital classified as debt).

In 2XX0:

- A loss of £300,000 is recorded in the profit and loss account (loss available for discretionary division among members). This amount is included within members' other interests on the balance sheet.
- Drawings of £600,000 are included within debtors.

In 2XX1:

- A profit of £1,000,000 is recorded in the profit and loss account (profit available for discretionary division among members). This amount is also included within members' other interests on the balance sheet.
- Drawings of £700,000 are included within debtors.

In 2XX2:

- A profit of £1,200,000 is recorded in the profit and loss account (profit available for discretionary division among members). This amount is also included within members' other interests on the balance sheet.
- The decision to divide the profits of the previous year is reflected within the reconciliation of members' interests, but also takes account of the requirement to make good past losses. A division of £700,000 is therefore reflected.
- Drawings of £800,000 are included within debtors.

Presentation in reconciliation of members' interests

	EQUITY		**DEBT**	Total
	Members' Other Interests		Loans and other debts due to members less any amounts due from members in debtors	2XX0
	Other Reserves	Total		
	£	£	£	£
Balance at start of 2XX0	-	-	-	-
Loss for the financial year available for discretionary division among members	(300,000)	(300,000)	-	(300,000)
Members' interests after profit/(loss) for the year	(300,000)	(300,000)	-	(300,000)
Introduced by members			100,000	100,000
Drawings			(600,000)	(600,000)
Amounts due to members	(300,000)	(300,000)	100,000	

	EQUITY		**DEBT**	Total
	Members' Other Interests		Loans and other debts due to members less any amounts due from members in debtors	2XX0
	Other Reserves	Total		
Amounts due from members			(600,000)	
Balance at end of 2XX0	(300,000)	(300,000)	(500,000)	(800,000)

	EQUITY		**DEBT**	Total	Total
	Members' Other Interests		Loans and other debts due to members less any amounts due from members in debtors	2XX1	2XX0
	Other Reserves	Total			
	£	£	£	£	£
Amounts due to members			100,000		
Amounts due from members			(600,000)		
Balance at start of 2XX1	(300,000)	(300,000)	(500,000)	(800,000)	-
Profit/(loss) for the financial year available for discretionary division among members	1,000,000	1,000,000		1,000,000	(300,000)
Members' interests after profit/(loss) for the year	700,000	700,000	(500,000)	200,000	(300,000)
Introduced by members		-	-	-	100,000
Drawings			(700,000)	(700,000)	(600,000)
Amounts due to members			100,000		
Amounts due from members			(1,300,000)		
Balance at end of 2XX1	700,000	700,000	(1,200,000)	(500,000)	(500,000)

	EQUITY		**DEBT**	Total	Total
	Members' Other Interests		Loans and other debts due to members less any amounts due from members in debtors	2XX2	2XX1
	Other Reserves	Total			
	£	£	£	£	£
Amounts due to members			100,000		
Amounts due from members			(1,300,000)		
Balance at start of 2XX2	700,000	700,000	(1,200,000)	(500,000)	(800,000)
Profit for the financial year available for discretionary division among members	1,200,000	1,200,000		1,200,000	1,000,000
Members' interests after profit/(loss) for the year	1,900,000	1,900,000	(1,200,000)	700,000	200,000
Other divisions of profits/losses	(700,000)	(700,000)	700,000		
Drawings			(800,000)	(800,000)	(700,000)
Amounts due to members			100,000		
Amounts due from members			(1,400,000)		
Balance at end of 2XX2	1,200,000	1,200,000	(1,300,000)	(100,000)	(500,000)

It should be noted that, in practice, the members' agreement may include clauses with respect to the adjustment of future drawings to take account of past losses. Careful analysis of the members' agreement will, therefore, always be required.

Example 2 – Profits of subsequent periods reduced by past losses (profits are liabilities)

Relevant conditions contained in the members' agreement

On retirement, capital must be returned to the retiring member.

All profits are divided automatically.

Members are not required to contribute to losses.

In Year 1 (the LLP's first year of trading), the LLP makes a loss of £300,000, and drawings are £600,000.

In Year 2, the LLP makes a profit of £1,000,000, and drawings are £700,000.

Capital remains unchanged throughout at £100,000.

Analysis

The LLP has an obligation to return capital.

The members have no obligation to contribute to losses.

Profits are a liability to the extent they exceed past losses.

Accounting treatment

In Year 1:

- Members' remuneration charged as an expense is zero, and the LLP records a loss available for discretionary division of £300,000. This amount is included within members' other interests in the balance sheet.
- Drawings of £600,000 are included within debtors. However, careful consideration is required as to whether such a debtor will be recovered from future profits and whether a provision should be made against it (keeping in mind that assets should not be stated at any more than their recoverable amount).

In Year 2:

- Members' remuneration charged as an expense is £700,000 (£1,000,000 – £300,000). The LLP records a profit of £300,000 available for discretionary division, which is included within members' other interests in the balance sheet.

Presentation in reconciliation of members' interests

	EQUITY		DEBT	Total
	Members' Other Interests		Loans and other debts due to members less any amounts due from members in debtors	Year 1
	Other Reserves	Total		
	£	£	£	£
Balance at start of Year 1	-	-	-	-
Members' remuneration charged as an expense, including employment and retirement benefit costs			-	-
Loss for the financial year available for discretionary division among members	(300,000)	(300,000)		(300,000)
Members' interests after profit/(loss) for the year	(300,000)	(300,000)	-	(300,000)
Introduced by members			100,000	100,000
Drawings			(600,000)	(600,000)
Amounts due to members			100,000	
Amounts due from members			(600,000)	
Balance at end of Year 1	(300,000)	(300,000)	(500,000)	(800,000)

	EQUITY		**DEBT**	Total	Total
	Members' Other Interests		Loans and other debts due to members less any amounts due from members in debtors	Year 2	Year 1
	Other Reserves	Total			
	£	£	£	£	£
Amounts due to members			100,000		
Amounts due from members			(600,000)		
Balance at start of Year 2	(300,000)	(300,000)	(500,000)	(800,000)	-
Members' remuneration charged as an expense, including employment and retirement benefit costs			700,000	700,000	-
Profit for the financial year available for discretionary division among members	300,000	300,000		300,000	(300,000)
Members' interests after profit/(loss) for the year	-	-	200,000	200,000	(300,000)
Introduced by members		-	-	-	100,000
Drawings			(700,000)	(700,000)	(600,000)
Amounts due to members			100,000		
Amounts due from members			(600,000)		
Balance at end of Year 2	-	-	(500,000)	(500,000)	(500,000)

Example 3 – Member has obligation to make good losses

Relevant conditions contained in the members' agreement

All profits are divided automatically.

Members are required to contribute to losses.

Analysis

The members have an obligation to contribute to losses.

Accounting treatment

The profit and loss account reflects the obligation of the members to contribute to the losses of the LLP. This should be included in the line 'Members' remuneration charged as an expense', although 'Members' obligations in respect of losses' might be a more appropriate wording.

An equivalent amount will also be included on the balance sheet within amounts due from members. Consideration will need to be given as to whether such amounts are recoverable and, where they are not, provision should be made so they are carried at recoverable amount.

---

10 Limited life LLP

6.10 LLPs are often used as the vehicle to carry out a specific project – for example, development of a property. Such LLPs may then be liquidated once the project is complete.

Careful analysis of the arrangements is required to determine the appropriate accounting treatment of the interactions with members, particularly in respect of capital. The provisions contained in paragraph 22.4 of FRS 102 (September 2015) relating to puttable instruments may well have an effect on the determination of whether that capital is debt or equity. For example, it is not unusual in these circumstances for a members' agreement to include a clause that requires capital to be returned to members, but only upon the liquidation of the LLP. Whilst this might at first sight appear to be a liability, because of an unavoidable obligation to return cash to members, the provisions contained in paragraph 22.4 of FRS 102 (September 2015) may result in a different position, as it sees obligations arising only on liquidation as circumstances that are indicative of a residual interest. Where all of the conditions are met, the capital would be classified as equity.

Chapter summary

- Appendix 2 of the SORP contains some useful worked examples which will help preparers of financial statements to determine when members' participation rights are to be classed as debt or equity.
- The members' agreement should be carefully scrutinised to ensure the correct accounting treatment is applied, particularly where LLPs may have an obligation to repay capital.
- Some LLPs will only have a limited lifespan as they may only be used to carry out a specific project. In these situations, careful analysis of the arrangements in the members' agreement is needed to ensure appropriate accounting treatment; particularly in respect of capital.

Chapter 7

Revenue recognition and work in progress

Signposts

- The timing of revenue recognition is critical for many LLP's – particularly professional services as the turnover figure is the key driver of profit on which members' will be taxed (see **7.1**).
- Section 23 *Revenue* in FRS 102 *The Financial Reporting Standard applicable in the UK and Republic of Ireland* differentiates between the sale of goods, rendering of services as well as revenue from interest, royalties and dividends (see **7.2**).
- Section 23 uses the 'stage of completion' method as a means of establishing the amount of revenue to be recognised in a service/construction contract (see **7.2**).
- Service contracts will need to be scrutinised carefully and their terms understood in determining the extent to which revenue should be recognised in an accounting period (see **7.3**).
- Progress payments/advance payments received by the LLP are not revenue because they do not reflect the work performed (see **7.3**).
- The value attributable to the amount of revenue under a service contract is determined with reference to how much can be charged for the work that is being performed (see **7.4**).
- Revenue recognised in respect of work performed but not yet billed is included in turnover and accrued within debtors (or 'amounts recoverable on contracts') (see **7.5**).
- If work has been carried out but the criteria in Section 23 has not been met, work in progress is recognised (see **7.6**).
- Work in progress has to be valued at the lower of cost and estimated selling price, less costs to complete and sell (see **7.7**).
- Various methods of valuing work in progress are used by professional firms, but whichever method is used, the firm will need to determine the amount of overheads to be included in work in progress (see **7.8**).
- A simple method which can be justified and reasonable when valuing work in progress and one which is consistently applied should normally be adequate (see **7.8**).

- Professional judgement needs to be applied to contracts which are undertaken on a contingent fee basis where the work is incomplete at the reporting date (see **7.9**).
- Whilst it is fairly uncommon for LLPs to operate in the construction industry, Section 23 to FRS 102 does contain guidance on the accounting for construction contracts and revenue recognition within a construction contract (see **7.10 and 7.11**).

1 Section 23 *Revenue*

7.1 FRS 102 *The Financial Reporting Standard applicable in the UK and Republic of Ireland* at Section 23 *Revenue* is the section which deals with the principles involved in revenue recognition. The timing of revenue recognition is critical for many LLPs – particularly professional practices – and this can have a direct tax consequence on the members because the turnover figure (being the headline figure in the accounts) is the key driver of profit on which members will be taxed. The importance of correctly recognising an appropriate amount of turnover at the correct time cannot be over-emphasised. The wording in Section 23 of FRS 102 is not the same as that contained in previous UK GAAP (UITF 40 and Application Note G to FRS 5 *Reporting the substance of transactions*) and therefore care must be taken by LLPs in ensuring that the provisions in Section 23 are applied correctly to avoid any contentious issues either with other members of the LLP or with HM Revenue and Customs.

Focus

- FRS 102 may be updated in the future to incorporate the provisions of IFRS 15 *Revenue from Contracts with Customers*. At the time of writing, the Financial Reporting Council (FRC) had indicated that they intended to update Section 23 to improve the separation of contracts for the purposes of recognising and measuring revenue so that it is similar to IFRS 15. These amendments were proposed in September 2016 as part of the FRC's triennial revenue of FRS 102 and were planned to be effective for accounting periods starting on or after 1 January 2019 (with early-adoption permissible). Exposure Drafts of the FRC's intentions as part of the triennial review of FRS 102 are expected to be published in the first quarter of 2017.

2 The principles of revenue recognition

7.2 Section 23 differentiates between revenue which arises from the sale of goods and that which arises from the provision of services. It also deals with revenue which arises in a construction contract as well as revenue which arises from the use by others of assets which generate interest, royalties and dividends to the LLP. Whilst LLPs are often service organisations, this chapter does take a look at the concept of construction contract accounting because such provisions are incorporated within Section 23. In recognition that it is relatively uncommon for LLP's to operate in a construction environment, this particular concept is considered at the end of this chapter.

The underlying principle of Section 23 is that revenue should be recognised when, and to the extent that, an entity has earned the right to payment through a performance-related condition. A *performance-related condition* is defined as '*a condition that requires the performance of a particular level of service or units of output to be delivered, with payment of, or entitlement to, the resources conditional on that performance*'. When dealing with the sale of goods, in most cases a performance-related condition will equate to the delivery of the relevant goods, and hence Section 23 will be relatively easy to apply. However, when dealing with service contracts, the principles can be more difficult to interpret and, under old UK GAAP when Application Note G to FRS 5 and UITF 40 were first issued, many LLPs found that their revenue was being recognised earlier than may previously have been the case. Similar principles are included in Section 23 and thus the remainder of this chapter, therefore, concentrates on accounting for revenue from the rendering of services and revenue in a construction contract.

It can be somewhat problematic for LLPs to decipher the amount of revenue receivable in a service contract at the end of a reporting period. Paragraph 23.14 to FRS 102 says that if the outcome of a transaction which involves the rendering of services can be estimated reliably (ie whether it is a profit- or loss-making contract) then revenue is recognised having reference to the *stage of completion* of the transaction at the end of the reporting period. The stage of completion is often a best estimate and judgement will always be a crucial aspect of arriving at this estimate. In some cases, particularly in construction contracts, professional valuations might need to be obtained to accurately ascertain the stage of completion. For the purposes of Section 23, the outcome of a transaction can be reliably estimated if all of the following conditions can be met:

- the amount of revenue to be recognised can be measured reliably;
- it is probable (ie more likely than not) that cash, or other forms of assets, directly attributable to the transaction will flow to the entity;
- the stage of completion of the transaction can be reliably measured; and
- the costs which have been incurred, and which will need to be incurred to complete the transaction, can also be reliably measured.

When an LLP is undertaking a contract on behalf of a customer/client which involves the rendering of services the LLP must determine the stage of completion which will result in a reliable measure of the work performed. Paragraph 23.22 outlines three possible methods that an LLP might use as follows:

- the proportion that costs incurred for work performed as at the reporting date to the estimated total costs (which must exclude any costs which relate to future activity);
- surveys of the work performed; and
- completion of a proportion of the contract or completion of a physical proportion of the contract.

Example – progress payment from a customer

An LLP is undertaking a large project for its customer in developing a bespoke database management system. The work is scheduled to take two years and the LLP has received an advanced payment from its customer to cover initial costs. The financial accountant has credited the advance to turnover.

Advances received from a customer should not be reflected within turnover because they do not reflect the work performed (this also applies to any progress payments received from a customer). The financial accountant should credit the advance to a 'contract account' within the nominal ledger and only recognise revenue in accordance with paragraphs 23.14–23.16 (paragraphs 23.17–23.20 for construction contracts).

To the extent, therefore, that a service organisation has performed work and the fee is not conditional on a future event outside the entity's control, this will normally represent earned income. As a result, unbilled amounts should be accrued at selling price and be recognised as revenue within the LLP's profit and loss account.

If the outcome of a service contract **cannot** be reliably estimated, the LLP must recognise revenue to the extent of the expenses recognised which are recoverable.

If services are performed by an indeterminate number of acts over a specified period, the LLP must recognise revenue on a straight-line basis over that specified period. There may be occasions when the members regard another alternative measurement method as being more representative of the stage of completion and in such cases the LLP can use an alternative method than the straight-line method.

3 Analysing contracts

7.3 In determining the extent to which revenue needs to be recognised in an accounting period, the contracts in progress at the year-end need to be analysed and their terms understood. Many contracts will stipulate when fees on account are to be raised but these may not correlate with the principles of revenue recognition (indeed paragraph 23.22 refers to progress payments and advances which have been received by customers/clients often do not reflect the work performed and so care needs to be taken with such payments/advances to ensure correct accounting treatment). Some contracts, because of their size or complexity, may need to be considered individually. In other cases, examination of a single contract may show it to have a number of individually identifiable phases and each of those phases may need to be accounted for separately. More commonly, however, there will be a number of contracts to provide a similar type of service which should be considered together.

In general, achieving the right to payment on a service contract will be related directly to a performance-related condition. As such, revenue should ordinarily be recognised in proportion to the extent of progress on the contract. In most cases, the extent of contract activity can be determined by comparing the amount of time spent or costs incurred in providing the service up to the date of the accounts to the total time or costs that it is expected will be spent or incurred in delivering the service.

Example – completion of a self-assessment income tax return

Consider the position of a tax accountant who is halfway through completing a client's tax return at the accountant's financial year-end. Whilst it could be argued that a half-completed tax return is of little practical use, it can also be assumed that the computation will be completed and, by extension, that the accountant will complete all of the tax returns that he is working on at his year end, particularly if the year-end date is 31 January. Section 23 requires that the principles in paragraph 23.14 should be applied in accounting for this contract. The accountant would therefore recognise 50% of the income from the individual contract, and then apply similar calculations to all other contracts.

Not all contracts will be so straightforward and contract terms need to be examined carefully to identify specific circumstances, such as identifiable milestones or contingent fee arrangements, which affect how the associated revenue should be calculated.

Where a contract has identifiable milestones, revenue will be recognised dependent on the milestones that have already been reached and the extent of progress towards the next milestone.

Where there is a contingent fee arrangement and the contingency is outside the control of the LLP, no revenue should be recognised until the contingent event occurs.

Example – law firm operating on a 'no win, no fee' basis

A law firm is acting for a client under a 'no win, no fee' arrangement. The case has been ongoing for several months and the year-end financial statements are about to be completed. The bookkeeper is unsure as to whether any revenue should be recognised in this case and the trial is not listed to be heard in court for three months'.

In this case the outcome of the trial is outside the control of the law firm. As a result, no revenue should be recognised until the case has been won (if the law firm does, indeed, win) because it is only at that stage that the law firm has a right to consideration.

Even where the contingency is resolved after the financial period end, but before the accounts are approved, no revenue should be recognised in the period. The accounting treatment of work in progress in such circumstances is considered further at **7.9**.

4 Determining the value of revenue

7.4 The value attributable to the recognised proportion of revenue under a service contract is determined with reference as to how much can be charged for the work that is being performed. This will usually be stipulated in the contract, either in the form of a lump sum amount, an hourly rate, or a combination of the two.

Where fees are charged to the client with reference to time spent at an hourly rate, staff members will normally be required to record details of how much time they have spent on different tasks and clients in some form of time recording system. In such situations, firms often calculate accrued income by starting with unbilled time as stated in their time recording systems, valued at standard hourly rates. This will then be adjusted for amounts that are not expected to be fully recoverable, either on a case-by-case basis, or by applying a percentage that reflects past experience of actual recoveries compared to cost.

For certain types of service, contracts may stipulate two different fees dependent upon the outcome of a future event. Revenue should only be recognised based on the value the LLP is certain to get – usually the lowest.

Example – fee outcome depending on a contingent event

A law firm has a contract to advise Company A on the acquisition of Company B. The fees agreed with Company A are that, if the transaction is successful, the law firm will bill £125,000 and, if it is unsuccessful, the fee will be £75,000.

At the year end, it is estimated that 60% of the services have been provided, and so the appropriate level of revenue to be included in the accounts would be £45,000 (60% of £75,000).

---

5 Accounting entries

7.5 Where an entity recognises revenue in respect of work that has been performed but not yet billed, this amount is included in turnover and also as accrued income within debtors. The cost of performing the work should not be carried forward within work in progress, but should be recognised as a cost in the profit and loss account. The double-entry is as follows:

Dr Debtors (amounts recoverable on contracts)	£X
Cr Revenue	£X

Where invoices have been raised which exceed the amount of revenue that can be recognised, the excess should not be included in the profit and loss account but as deferred income within creditors (usually as creditors falling due within one year). If the amounts have been paid, then they should be disclosed within creditors as 'payments received on account'.

6 Work in progress

7.6 Where an LLP has carried out work but has not yet met the criteria to recognise revenue in paragraph 23.14 of FRS 102, work in progress should be recognised.

Work in progress is an example of the 'matching' concept of accounting. If costs have been incurred to produce goods or services in one period and the related revenue will not arise until a later period, then the costs are deferred and released in the period that the revenue arises so that the two 'match' each other. Costs should only be deferred to the extent that they are expected to be recovered against future revenue, and so work in progress is recognised at the lower of cost and estimated selling price less costs to complete and sell (ie the amount that will be received net of any further costs to be incurred in the process).

7 Determining the cost of work in progress

7.7 As noted at **7.6**, work in progress has to be included in the balance sheet at the lower of cost and estimated selling price less costs to complete and sell (this used to be referred to as the 'lower of cost and net realisable value' in previous UK GAAP). Section 13 *Inventories* deals with goods in the process of production insofar as work in progress is concerned (but not work in progress arising under construction contracts, which is dealt with under Section 23 of FRS 102). Section 13 says that *cost* does not just include materials (which is unlikely to be relevant to the majority of LLPs) but also direct labour and overheads.

Direct labour should include the cost of those employees who have been directly involved in the provision of the related service. The employees' cost should include not only their wages or salaries, but also other employment costs, such as national insurance contributions and pensions. Where members' time is included within work in progress, it should be valued to the extent that it is charged as an expense in the profit and loss account (see Chapter 5). Amounts received by members, by way of allocation of profits available for division amongst members, should be excluded from the valuation of work in progress.

When valuing work in progress, account should be taken of all 'direct' overheads. Other overheads should only be included in work in progress to the extent that they are incurred in the provision of the related service. Costs such as administrative overheads and selling expenses must not be included in the cost of work in progress.

Overheads should be allocated to work in progress on the basis of the LLP's normal level of activity. Overhead costs which are the result of inefficiencies, such as the effect of abnormal changes in procedures, should not be included in the valuation.

Irrespective of whether the time input by a member is included within work in progress, the general accounting requirement to match costs and revenues means that any overhead related to the member's time should be included in the valuation.

The above principles will also apply to any stock produced by an LLP involved in manufacturing or production.

8 Valuing work in progress in practice

7.8 In calculating the cost of work in progress, some professional services firms take the value of unbilled fee-earner time at charge-out rates as a starting point, and then reduce this value by the gross profit element included within the charge-out rates. Others build up an hourly cost for each fee-earner from their salary and related costs plus an allocation of overheads.

Whichever method is used, the firm will need to determine the amount of overheads to be included in work in progress (or to be deducted in arriving at gross profit). Particular problems may arise when trying to deal with areas such as central management overheads. Salaries for this area may well include an element of either direct provision of service or the supervision of service delivery, as well as administration. Central costs should be apportioned between direct and indirect costs on a reasonable basis and this should then be consistently applied.

Where an hourly cost is calculated for each fee-earner, further complications can arise in allocating the overheads between fee-earners. The most usual approach is an allocation which is in proportion to direct labour costs.

In practice, a complicated method of calculating the cost of work in progress is often unnecessary, and a simple method, which can be justified as reasonable and is consistently applied, should normally be adequate.

For most firms, a significant part of the standard 'selling price' relates to recovery of indirect costs and profit. As a result, unless the work is subject to an unsettled contingency, which will potentially cause it to be heavily discounted, or no charge to be made for it, it is relatively unusual for further provision against the cost of work in progress to be necessary.

9 Work in progress and contingent fee arrangements

7.9 One area that has given rise to particular debate is contracts undertaken on a contingent fee basis where the work is incomplete at the reporting date.

Where a contract contains a specific deliverable which is much more significant than any other, the LLP must delay the recognition of revenue until that significant deliverable is completed. In such a situation it may be the case that no revenue is recognised, but this should not preclude the LLP from recognising the costs incurred on the contract up to the reporting date as work in progress.

Contingent fee arrangements will normally be accounted for under the provisions laid down in paragraphs 23.14 to 24.16 of FRS 102. Under previous UK GAAP it was acceptable to either expense the cost of the work performed as incurred, or to recognise the costs of work performed as work in progress at the period end (which were subject to the usual considerations relating to recoverability). Where an LLP has always recognised work in progress, the requirements in Section 23 will not result in any difference from what was the case under previous UK GAAP.

10 Construction contracts

7.10 Whilst it is fairly uncommon for LLPs to operate in the construction sector, it is worth noting that Section 23 incorporates the guidance for construction contracts and recognises that construction contracts themselves may pose a particular accounting issue in that such contracts may well span more than one (if not several, in some cases) accounting periods. Construction contracts are dealt with in paragraphs 23.17 to 23.20 of FRS 102 and regard must also be had to the 'percentage of completion method' dealt with in paragraphs 23.21 to 23.27.

The principles involved where construction contracts and Section 23 are concerned are fairly similar. Revenue and costs in a construction contract are recognised by reference to the stage of completion of the contract activity at the reporting date.

Section 23 is usually applied separately to each construction contract but there may be occasions when the section will have to be applied to those components of a contract which are separately identifiable in a single contract, or to a group of contracts together so as to reflect the substance of a contract or a group of contracts.

Example – one contract treated as separate contracts

Cory Construction LLP has been awarded a construction contract which requires the construction of several retail units on new retail park in a vibrant city centre location in the UK. Whilst the contract is a single contract in itself, the contractor invited separate proposals for each unit which have all been separately negotiated and the costs and revenues associated with each unit can be identified.

For the purposes of Section 23, if a construction contract covers a number of contracts, the construction of each asset (in this case each retail unit) is treated as a separate construction contract. This occurs when:

- separate proposals have been submitted for each asset (in this case each retail unit);
- each asset has been the subject of separate negotiation. Both the contractor and the customer are able to accept, or reject, a specific part of the contract relating to an individual asset; and
- both the costs and the revenues associated with each asset can be identified.

Example – group of contracts treated as a single contract

Cory Construction LLP has tendered for three contracts with a well-known supermarket. The contract is to build a supermarket in a local town centre with a petrol station and car park all on the same location. Separate contracts are available for all three projects but they are only going to be awarded to one contractor and with an overall profit margin and hence are being negotiated effectively as a single package. All three projects have to be completed on the same date so that the supermarket can open as scheduled.

Paragraph 23.20 to FRS 102 requires a group of contracts to be treated as a single construction contract when the following conditions are met:

- the group of contracts are all negotiated as a single package;

- the contracts are so closely interrelated that they are essentially part of a single project and have an overall profit margin; and
- the contracts are undertaken concurrently or in a continuous sequence.

---

11 Accounting for a construction contract

7.11 Construction contract accounting can become very complicated in some cases. Section 23 requires the 'percentage of completion method' to be applied where construction contracts are concerned. Any estimates of revenue and costs are reviewed by the LLP as the contract progresses.

If a contract is profit-making, the LLP must recognise revenue by reference to the stage of completion together with a similar percentage for revenue.

Example – profit-making contract

Cory Construction LLP has been awarded a contract amounting to £100,000 which is expected to make a profit at the end of the contract of £30,000. At the balance sheet date, the valuation agent confirmed the contract was 40% complete.

As the contract is expected to yield a profit of £30,000, Cory Construction LLP will recognise 40% of revenue and 40% of costs to date. Hence the profit and loss account extracts will be as follows:

Turnover	(£100,000 × 40%)	£40,000
Cost of sales	(£70,000 × 40%)	£28,000
Gross profit		£12,000 (or 40% × £30,000)

There may be occasions when a contract is loss-making. In such cases, paragraph 23.26 says that the expected loss must be recognised immediately with a corresponding provision for an onerous contract.

Example – loss-making contract

Cory Construction LLP has a contract which is expected to make a loss of £1,000. The finance director has calculated that the amount of the contract revenue to be recognised is £800.

The profit and loss account will recognise revenue of £800. The loss is estimated to be £1,000 and must be recognised immediately to comply with the provisions in paragraph 23.26. Hence cost of sales will be £1,800 to generate the required loss (in other words, cost of sales is essentially a balancing figure).

It may not be possible at the reporting date to assess whether a contract will be profit- or loss-making and in these situations the provisions in paragraph 23.25 (a) and (b) will become relevant. Nil profit is recognised in profit or loss when the outcome of a construction contract cannot be reliably estimated and this is achieved by recognising revenue to the extent of costs incurred that it is probable will be recoverable.

Example – uncertainty in a contract

Cory Construction LLP enters into a two-year contract. At the reporting date, the project manager is unable to ascertain whether the contract will yield a profit or a loss. Costs incurred up to the reporting date are £10,000.

As the outcome of the contract cannot be estimated reliably, the amount of turnover to be recognised in the LLP's financial statements is the same as costs incurred, resulting in no profit being taken, hence:

Dr Debtors (Amounts recoverable on contract)	£10,000
Cr Revenue	£10,000

Chapter summary

- FRS 102 deals with revenue recognition in Section 23 *Revenue* and the timing of revenue recognition is a critical factor as it can (and often does) have direct tax consequences.
- The general principle is that revenue should be recognised when the LLP has a right to receive economic benefit in return for goods and/or services provided.
- Section 23 outlines five criteria which must be met for revenue recognition in respect of the sale of goods and four criteria in respect of the rendering of services.
- Contracts may need to be analysed on a case-by-case basis and their terms understood to ensure revenue is recognised appropriately.
- Professional firms often use various methods of charging fees to clients and these are usually recorded in a form of time recording system.
- Work in progress should be valued at the lower of cost and estimated selling price less costs to complete and sell.
- There does not have to be complicated methods of valuing work in progress amounts; indeed a simple method which can be justified as reasonable and which is consistently applied should normally suffice.
- Contingent fee arrangements are usually accounted for under the provisions of paragraphs 23.14 to 23.16 of FRS 102.
- Section 23 in FRS 102 also deals with construction contracts and whilst it is relatively uncommon for construction companies to operate as LLP's, the principles in this particular section of FRS 102 may well apply to an LLP.

Chapter 8

Taxation

Signposts

- Whilst this chapter deals primarily with taxation, it aims only to give a brief overview and should not be regarded as comprehensive advice (see **8.1**).
- LLPs are partnerships in a 'corporate wrapper' and its member are subject to tax directly on their share of the LLPs profit, including a share of any investment income earned by the LLP and on the proceeds from any capital assets (see **8.2**).
- A 'representative member' must sign the LLP tax return and confirm that the information in the tax return is complete. There are penalties applied by HMRC to each separate member for late returns (see **8.2**).
- The taxation and NI position of salaried members of an LLP is complex (see **8.3**).
- The Finance Act 2014 introduced anti-avoidance provisions designed to prevent tax loss in situations where employment is disguised through an LLP (see **8.4**).
- Each member is required to settle his or her tax liability by making two payments on account and a final balancing payment (see **8.5**).
- Setting funds aside in a tax reserve should help to avoid any additional cash flow difficulties, but tax reserve funds will form part of the members' funds available for distribution to creditors in the invent of insolvency (see **8.6**).
- The starting point for assessing taxable profits will be the profit as per the annual accounts which are prepared using Generally Accepted Accounting Practice (see **8.7**).
- Tax legislation does not recognise annuities as being an allowable expense for profits for the purposes of tax (see **8.8**).
- HMRC will generally allow a tax deduction to be claimed for provisions which are made in accordance with Section 21 of FRS 102 *Provisions and Contingencies* (see **8.9**).
- If an LLP borrows money for the purposes of its trade, any interest is likely to be allowable for the purposes of tax as an expense through the profit and loss account (see **8.10**).
- Proceeds from the disposal of an asset must be reported on the LLP's tax return. The associated capital gain is calculated on the capital gains tax pages of the member's tax return and not collectively on the partnership return (see **8.11**).

1 Introduction

8.1 Whilst this book deals principally with accounting requirements, the taxation of LLPs and its members cannot be entirely ignored. This chapter aims only to give a brief overview of the taxation of LLPs and will cover some areas where the taxation treatment may differ from the accounts. It should not be regarded as comprehensive advice, and reference should be had to taxation specialists where appropriate.

2 Basic tax principles and compliance procedures

8.2 An LLP is not in itself subject to tax but is, as described by HM Revenue & Customs (HMRC), a 'transparent' entity, which means that, unless certain circumstances apply, such as that the LLP is being wound up, the LLP is 'looked through' and its members are subject to tax. In effect, LLPs are partnerships in a corporate wrapper. Each member will be taxed directly on his share of the LLP's profits, including a share of any investment income earned by the LLP and on the proceeds received from any capital assets. If the LLP is trading, members are also currently liable to Class 2 and Class 4 national insurance (NI) contributions.

Despite the fact that the LLP is not itself liable to tax, as for a general partnership, it must complete a tax return for each fiscal year. Fiscal years run from 6 April in one year to 5 April in the following year. There are special rules that apply if there is no accounting period ending in the tax year but, in general, the tax return will include the results for the accounting period ended within the fiscal year. For example, if an LLP has a 30 June year end, the 2015/16 return (covering the period 6 April 2015 to 5 April 2016) would include results for the accounting period ended 30 June 2015. Investment income which has been taxed at source, proceeds from the disposal of capital assets, and charges on income are, however, included in the tax return on the basis of the fiscal year in which they arose.

In addition to the general requirement to retain accounting records discussed in Chapter 2, the LLP must also maintain any additional records relating to the tax position for five years and ten months following the end of the tax year in which the accounting period ended.

HMRC may in principle require any member of the LLP to file an LLP tax return but in practice the notice will normally be served on a 'representative member' either selected by HMRC or nominated by the members. The representative member must sign the return to confirm that the information shown thereon is correct and complete. Although it is the representative member who is responsible for filing the return, where the return is filed late and penalties become payable, those penalties are exigible from each member separately. The following penalties may be applied by HMRC *to each member separately* for 2010/11 onwards (FA 2009, Sch 55):

- Return up to three months late – £100 fixed penalty.
- More than three months late – £10 per day (up to 90 days (maximum £900) payable only if HMRC give notice of the penalty and the notice specifies the date from which the penalty is payable).

- More than six months late – the greater of 5% of tax liability and £300.
- More than 12 months late – greater of relevant percentage of liability shown by the return and £300. The relevant percentage may be as much as 200% in some special cases.
- Incorrect LLP return – up to 100% of the tax lost. The penalty may in some special cases be as much as 200% of the tax liability.
- Failure to keep and maintain records – £3,000.

Whilst certain penalties may sometimes be negotiated with HMRC, the penalties for late submission of a return are mandatory and can in aggregate be substantial depending upon the size of the firm. Although late filing penalties are exigible from members separately it is only the representative member who has any right of appeal against these penalties, in which case the appeal is treated as a composite appeal made on behalf of all relevant members. Thus, although the LLP return notice is issued only to the 'representative member', all members have a very clear interest in ensuring that the representative member fulfils his or her statutory obligations in a timely fashion.

The tax return must be filed with HMRC by 31 January following the end of the fiscal year if this is done electronically, or 31 October if on paper. For example, the 2015/16 return must be filed by 31 January 2017 if it is being filed electronically, and otherwise it should be filed by 31 October 2016.

Following completion of the LLP return, the firm should provide each member with a member's statement, showing their share of income as reported on that return. Each member is then responsible for including this income on his or her personal tax return.

It may sometimes happen that a member disagrees with the amount of taxable profit allocated to him or her on the LLP tax return. The question then arises whether the profit share shown on the LLP return is conclusive as regards the member or whether the member is entitled to enter a different figure on his or her personal return. Obiter dicta in *Self v HMRC* [2009] UKFTT 78(TC) suggest that the proper course is for the member to include on the personal return the amount which is believed to be correct and to explain in the 'white space' any discrepancy with the LLP return.

3 Salaried members

8.3 The taxation and NI position of salaried members of an LLP is complex.

HMRC have historically taken the view that all those who are registered as members at Companies House as members of an LLP fall to be treated for tax purposes as self-employed and not as employees of the LLP. This, despite the fact that Limited Liability Partnerships Act 2000 (LLPA 2000) clearly allows for employee members, which would imply that in some circumstances members are capable of being employees of the LLP, which may appear to be at odds with HMRC's interpretation.

The employment law case of *Tiffin v Aldridge* (2012) 2 All ER 1113 also confirmed that an LLP member could be an 'employee' of the LLP, albeit the claimant in the case was, on the facts, held to be a 'partner (member)'.

Nonetheless, it appears to be the case that the normal case law tests determining whether a person is an employee which would apply, for example, in the case of a salaried member of a general partnership, have no relevance to membership of an LLP: for tax purposes a member of an LLP is treated as self-employed, unless the special rules described below are in point.

Where members of an LLP are treated as partners, not employees, the self-employed (Class 2 and Class 4) rates of NI will currently apply.

4 Disguised employment

8.4 The Finance Act 2014 introduced rules (effective from 6 April 2014) to prevent tax loss in situations where employment is disguised through limited liability partnerships. Broadly, the changes affect LLP members who work for LLPs on terms that HMRC view as 'tantamount to employment' (ie disguised employment). They will primarily affect LLP members who have a fixed share of profit.

The rules only apply to individuals that are members of LLPs, and to fall within the rules they have to satisfy three conditions (A–C) as follows: if any of the conditions are not fulfilled the new rules do not apply and the individual will not be treated as an employee.

Condition A is that there are 'relevant arrangements' in place for the individual to perform services as a member of the LLP. 'Relevant arrangements' means arrangements under which amounts are to be, or may be, payable by the LLP in respect of the individual's performance of services for the partnership in his capacity as a member of the partnership. The condition will be met if it is reasonable to expect that at least 80% of the total amount payable by the LLP in respect of the individual's performance during the relevant period of services for the partnership in the individual's capacity as a member of the partnership, will be disguised salary.

An amount will be treated as 'disguised salary' if it:

- is fixed;
- is variable, but is varied without reference to the overall amount of the profits or losses of the LLP; or
- is not, in practice, affected by the overall amount of those profits or losses.

In many cases, this condition will not be fulfilled as partners in an LLP will be remunerated by reference to the overall profits available.

Condition B is that the person concerned does not have significant influence over the affairs of the partnership.

Condition C is that the person's partnership capital is less than 25% of the amount which is reasonably expected to be disguised salary for the tax year. In other words, to avoid being treated as an employee under this test the person concerned has to have at stake capital of at least one quarter of their partnership income. The partnership capital is determined on 6 April 2014 or at the date of appointment of the partner and then at the beginning of each subsequent tax year or whenever the partnership sharing arrangements change.

If a person satisfies all three conditions above, then that person is taxed as if they were an employee of the partnership for all tax purposes, although their wider legal status as a member of the LLP is not changed. In other words, this is purely a tax measure.

Under the rules, as outlined above, a salaried member will be deemed to be employed by their LLP for tax and NICs purposes. In these circumstances, the LLP will be liable to deduct and pay tax and NICs on any amount paid to the salaried member as if it were employment income for tax and employed earners' earnings for NICs. The LLP will be the secondary contributor for NICs, and will be responsible for paying NICs on earnings and benefits.

5 Timing of tax payments

8.5 Each member is required to settle his or her tax liability by making two payments on account and a final balancing payment. The payments on account fall due for payment on the 31 January during the fiscal year and the 31 July following the end of the fiscal year. Each payment on account is based upon 50% of the previous year's liability to income tax and Class 4 NI contributions. The final balancing payment falls due for payment on 31 January following the end of the fiscal year.

Example– payment of taxes

For the fiscal year 2015/16, tax will fall due for payment as follows:

1st payment on account	31 January 2016
2nd payment on account	31 July 2016
Balancing payment	31 January 2017*

* The 1st payment on account in respect of the 2016/17 year will also be due for payment on this date.

Class 2 and Class 4 NI contributions are paid at the same time as the tax liability.

6 Providing for tax in the accounts

8.6 There is no requirement for an LLP to make provision for tax in its accounts. However, many firms choose to set aside a separate tax reserve and a separate tax fund, to ensure that profits are not over-distributed and that members can pay their tax liabilities. There is no requirement to make separate disclosure of the tax reserves, as the LLP is effectively merely holding back profits and in due course acting as agent in making tax payments on behalf of the members.

The basis of reserving for tax will differ depending upon various factors, primarily the general attitude of members to setting aside funds. Perhaps the most common basis is to reserve on the assumption that all of the members will retire on the balance sheet date, setting aside tax on all profits earned to that date and allowing relief for any overlap profit. It may alternatively be considered appropriate to set aside funds which are sufficient to cover tax payments falling due over the course of the following 12 months.

The timing of tax payments means that, if profits fall and members have not themselves been sufficiently disciplined to set aside from drawings funds to pay tax, members can often find that they are required to pay tax on an earlier year's higher profits from reduced current year drawings. Setting aside funds in tax reserves should help avoid these additional cash flow difficulties. It should be borne in mind that, in the event that the firm is insolvent and required to pay its creditors, any tax reserve funds will form part of the members' funds available for distribution to creditors. For this reason, some firms may prefer to keep their tax reserve funds outside the LLP using a 'tax trust account'.

7 Profits subject to tax

8.7 The starting point for assessing taxable profits will be the profit as shown in the annual accounts. LLPs are not permitted to use the cash basis for calculating taxable income, and must prepare accounts for *tax purposes* using Generally Accepted Accounting Practice (either UK GAAP or EU-adopted IFRS) principles. The members of an LLP may agree to retain some profit (or losses) in the LLP and allocate to the members an amount which is different from the total profit or loss for the financial year (see Chapter 5). For tax purposes, however, the members will be subject to tax on all profits arising regardless of whether all of those profits have been allocated to them.

The total amount of profit, as adjusted for tax purposes (see below), is divided between the members in accordance with their arrangements for profit sharing and it is this amount that is subject to tax. If the firm holds unallocated profits, a member may be subject to tax on a sum far greater than the amount which has actually been allocated to him. The LLP will need to establish a mechanism (such as equalisation adjustments in tax reserves) to deal with this situation.

Whilst taxable profits will be based upon the profit shown in the accounts, tax legislation provides for certain adjustments to be made before the taxable profit can be established. For example, depreciation is not an allowable deduction for tax purposes, although relief is given for the purchase of some fixed assets by way of capital allowances.

Complications can arise where an LLP incurs a loss. As part of the firm's liability protection for members, many LLPs will have provisions which ensure that the loss is kept within the LLP and is not, for accounting and legal purposes, allocated to the members. However, when submitting the tax return for the LLP, it will be necessary to allocate the tax loss to members.

In the case of trading LLPs, losses may be restricted. The total sideways loss relief that an LLP member can claim, in respect of their share of the LLP's trading losses for any tax year, is restricted to the member's capital contribution as at the end of the tax year less the total sideways loss reliefs previously given at any time in respect of losses from the same trade. From 6 April 2013, a cap applies to certain previously unlimited income tax reliefs that may be deducted from income. The cap is set at £50,000 or 25% of income, whichever is greater.

In the case of a non-active LLP member, losses sustained on or after 2 March 2007 are subject to a £25,000 annual limit. Non-active for this purpose means a partner who does not spend on average at least ten hours per week personally engaged in trading activities. Capital contributions made by a non-active partner on or after 2 March 2007 do not count if the main purpose, or one of the main purposes, for contributing them was for the partner to claim sideways loss relief.

8 Retirement benefits and annuities

8.8 As discussed in Chapter 9, the SORP requires an LLP to provide for the present value of the best estimate of the expected liability for future payments to current and former members.

The amounts charged in the accounts can be significant. For this reason, in some cases the remaining partners take on the commitment to pay the annuity to the retiring partner, so that the LLP accounts are not affected.

Tax legislation does not, however, recognise annuities as being an allowable expense from profits for tax purposes. Whether the annuity is paid by the LLP or by the members, relief is given as a charge on income against each member's overall tax liability as and when the annuity is paid. Basic rate tax relief (currently 20%) is given at source on the payment of the annuity to the former member (ie members make the payment net of basic rate tax unless there is a corporate member). If the members are higher rate taxpayers, they may then make a claim on their personal tax return for relief from the remainder of the tax. The amount of the annuity paid in the *fiscal year* is disclosed on the LLP return and on each member's statement. The member must declare the charge on income on the personal section of his tax return and not on the partnership pages relating to the LLP.

Whilst the members eventually receive full tax relief for the annuity, the relief is given over the life of the annuity rather than when a provision is made in the accounts.

9 Other provisions

8.9 Annuities (and pensions) are perhaps the exception to the general rule for allowing provisions for tax purposes. HMRC will generally allow a tax deduction to be claimed for provisions that are made in accordance with FRS 102, Section 21 *Provisions and Contingencies* (see Chapter 9).

10 Members' borrowings

8.10 An LLP may borrow funds itself or require its members to contribute capital for which they may need to borrow funds from a bank. If the LLP borrows money for the purposes of its trade, any interest is likely to be allowable for tax purposes as an expense through the profit and loss account. Interest on members' personal loans to introduce capital will not be an expense in the profit and loss account but members can, in general, obtain tax relief for the interest paid through their personal tax returns. However, an important exception to this rule is for members of investment LLPs and property investment LLPs, where no relief is available on members' loans to provide capital.

Where capital is withdrawn from the LLP, this will be treated as reducing the amount of capital invested and, therefore, tax relief will not be available on the proportion of the loan interest relating to the withdrawn funds. In order to show a clear trail of capital invested in the LLP, it is recommended that separate records of capital and current accounts are maintained within the LLP, so that profits can be withdrawn without affecting tax relief on borrowings for the firm's capital.

Where members have mortgages or other borrowings which do not attract any interest tax relief, it may be possible to arrange for the borrowing to be taken out in respect of LLP capital and therefore obtain tax relief. This is known as capital recycling, and it is imperative that any recycling is carried out in a strict order and that the transactions are completed and are not mere book entries.

Care must be taken with any capital recycling, particularly in light of the case of *Lancaster v Revenue and Customs Commissioners* [2009] UKFTT (TC), in which interest relief was denied on borrowing to fund a partnership. Advice from a specialist tax adviser should be sought to ensure that any recycling is not caught by this case.

11 Capital gains tax

8.11 The assets of an LLP are treated for tax purposes as owned by the members. Whilst members may own the assets in differing ratios to their income sharing arrangements, in the absence of a separate agreement, any proceeds from the disposal of an asset would be taxed on the members in these same profit sharing ratios.

The proceeds from the disposal of an asset must be reported on the LLP's tax return. However, the gain is calculated on the capital gains tax pages of the member's tax return and not collectively on the partnership return. Where the LLP is carrying on a trading activity, a gain arising on the disposal of a member's share of the firm may be eligible for entrepreneur's relief. The conditions for entrepreneur's relief are tightly drawn but, provided the conditions are met, the net gains will be charged to capital gains tax at a rate of 10%. From 6 April 2011 there is a lifetime limit of £10 million for gains subject to entrepreneur's relief.

Where there has been a revaluation of the firm's assets, followed by a subsequent change in the asset sharing ratios, complications arise because each change in the asset sharing ratios amounts to a disposal by those members reducing their share of the asset, and an acquisition by those increasing their share. This can require complex capital gains tax records to be maintained and the performance of involved computations.

Chapter summary

- An LLP itself is not subject to tax; instead the LLP is 'looked through' and its members are subject to tax.
- LLPs are partnerships in a corporate wrapper.
- Penalties and interest can be (and often are) levied by HMRC in the event of a late return and while some penalties can sometimes be negotiated, penalties for late submissions of a tax return are mandatory and can be substantial depending on the size of the firm.
- The tax and NI positions of salaried members of an LLP are complex and an LLP member could be an employee of the LLP.
- There are rules introduced in Finance Act 2014 in respect of disguised employment which only apply to individuals which are members of LLPs. If Conditions A to C are not fulfilled the rules will not apply and the individual will not be treated as an employee.
- Each member of an LLP is required to settle his or her tax liability by making two payments on account together with a final balancing payment.
- While there is no requirement to make provision in an LLP's accounts, some firms choose to set aside a separate tax reserve and a separate tax fund to ensure that profits are not over-distributed and thus allowing members to be able to pay their tax liabilities as they fall due.
- The starting point to arrive at profits subject to tax will be the profit as per the LLP's annual accounts. The LLPs accounts must be prepared under GAAP principles.
- In respect of retirement benefits and annuities, the LLP SORP requires the LLP to provide for the present value of the best estimate of the expected liability for future payments to current and former members. The amounts charged in the accounts may be significant and in some cases the remaining partners take on the commitment to pay the annuity to the retiring partner so the accounts are not affected.
- If an LLP borrows money for the purposes of its trade, the interest is likely to be an allowable expense via the profit and loss account. However, interest on members' personal loans to introduce capital will not be an expense in the profit and loss account, although members can, usually, obtain tax relief for the interest paid through their personal tax returns (with the exception of members of investment

LLPs and property investment LLPs, where no relief is available on members' loans to provide capital).

- The assets of an LLP are treated for tax purposes as owned by the members. Proceeds from disposal of assets are reported on the LLP's tax return; however, the gain is calculated on the capital gains tax pages of the member's tax return and not collectively on the partnership return.

Chapter 9

Other accounting standards

Signposts

- There are certain sections within FRS 102 (September 2015) *The Financial Reporting Standard applicable in the UK and Republic of Ireland* which may affect the financial statements of an LLP (see **9.1**).
- The term 'provision' can mean two fundamentally different things in accounting and it is crucial that LLPs make the correct distinction between the two (see **9.2**).
- Care must be taken to ensure that a provision in the context of Section 21 *Provisions and Contingencies* meets the three specific recognition criteria (see **9.3**).
- Provisions should not be made for future repairs and maintenance expenditure, however provisions for dilapidations may be made if the recognition and measurement criteria are met (see **9.5**).
- The time value of money should be taken into consideration for a provision if it is material (se **9.6**).
- Provisions for future operating losses should not be made (see **9.7**).
- Provisions should be made for obligations under an onerous contract but should not be made where the contract has merely turned out to be less profitable than originally anticipated (see **9.8**).
- Strict conditions have to be met in order to make a provision for restructuring costs (see **9.9**).
- Amounts in respect of 'reimbursements' should only be provided for in the financial statements if their receipt is 'virtually certain' (see **9.10**).
- Retirement benefits are one of the most complex issues for LLPs (see **9.11**).
- Defined contribution pension plans are fairly straightforward to account for, but defined benefit pension plans are far more complex (see **9.11**).
- Annuities may be payable to members and can either be 'predetermined' or 'profit-dependent' and a combination of these can be possible (see **9.12**).
- The SORP requires the principles of Section 11 *Basic Financial Instruments*, Section 12 *Other Financial Instruments Issues* and Section 21 *Provisions and Contingencies* of FRS 102 to be applied in accounting for retirement benefits (see **9.12**).

- There are times when an annuity will meet the definition of an insurance contract and be subject to the accounting requirements in FRS 103 *Insurance Contracts* (see **9.12**).
- The SORP recognises that in practice any obligations to make post-retirement benefits to members will often to be set out in the members' agreement and reflect significant mortality risk. On transition to new UK GAAP, the obligations will fall under the provisions in FRS 103 although the LLP will still be allowed to continue with its previous accounting policies (see **9.12**).
- A flowchart is reproduced in this chapter which gives guidance on how to determine which guidance applies to a particular obligation (see **9.12**).
- Liabilities in respect of post-retirement benefits are recognised on the expectations of the probable date the member will cease to be a member and the amounts likely to be payable to him/her from that date (see **9.13**).
- Amounts recognised in the profit and loss account relating to current members are included within 'Members' remuneration charged as an expense' (see **9.14**).
- Changes in the liability for former members are recognised within the relevant profit and loss heading (but not in 'Members' remuneration charged as an expense') (see **9.14**).
- Investments made to meet the requirements to fund retirements in the near future should be separately identified in the notes to the LLP financial statements (see **9.15**).
- On conversion to an LLP, the relationship between the LLP and any predecessor entity has to be carefully considered (see **9.16**).
- Tangible fixed assets are recognised when it is probable that future economic benefits will flow to the LLP and the cost of the asset can be reliably measured. Cost can comprise of several parts (see **9.17** and **9.18**).
- Subsequent expenditure on a tangible asset should only be capitalised if it enhances the performance of the asset in excess of its previous capabilities (see **9.19**).
- Tangible fixed assets can be carried under the 'cost model' or be subsequently revalued, although the revaluation model is prohibited for micro-entity LLPs reporting under FRS 105 *The Financial Reporting Standard applicable to the Micro-entities Regime* (see **9.20**).
- Tangible fixed assets must be depreciated over their expected useful lives – although land is typically not depreciated as land has an indefinite useful life (see **9.21**).
- Assets are impaired when their carrying amount falls below a recoverable amount and there are various indicators of impairment (see **9.22** and **9.23**).
- The 'recoverable amount' of an asset is the higher of its fair value less costs to sell and value in use (see **9.24**).

- Impairment losses in respect of a cash-generating unit are allocated in a specific order (see **9.29**).
- There are specific additional requirements in FRS 102 relating to the impairment of goodwill (see **9.30**).
- Assets subject to leasing are classified as either an 'operating' lease or a 'finance' lease and the correct classification is critical as the accounting methods for both are significantly different (see **9.31–9.33**).
- Events which take place after the date of the financial statements but before the financial statements are authorised for issue should be considered as to whether they are 'adjusting' or 'non-adjusting events' (see **9.34–9.36**).
- Related party transactions are considered in both legislation and in Section 33 *Related Party Disclosures* of FRS 102 (see **9.37–9.38**).
- A transaction is entered into with a related party when the LLP provides goods, services or incurs obligations with a related party regardless of whether a price is charged or not (see **9.40**).
- There are certain disclosure exemptions from disclosing transactions with related parties and further exemptions applicable to small LLPs (see **9.41**).
- In respect of related party transactions which have to be disclosed, there are detailed disclosures which need to be made to ensure the user understands that the financial statements do include the effects of related party transactions (see **9.42**).
- Small entities reporting under Section 1A *Small Entities* of FRS 102 need only disclose material related party transactions that have not been concluded under normal market conditions (see **9.43**).

1 Introduction

9.1 An important concept in the world of financial reporting is that financial statements have to be prepared using Generally Accepted Accounting Practice (GAAP). The use of accounting standards enables financial statements to give a 'true and fair view'. The true and fair concept has been enshrined into legislation for many years, although it has never been defined in the context of the law. In addition to GAAP, Limited Liability Partnerships (LLPs) prepare accounts in accordance with legislation and the Statement of Recommended Practice (SORP) – Accounting by Limited Liability Partnerships. However, in addition to the SORP, there are a number of other sections of FRS 102 (September 2015) *The Financial Reporting Standard applicable in the UK and Republic of Ireland* which may be particularly relevant to LLPs. These are as follows:

- Section 21 Provisions and Contingencies.
- Section 28 Employee Benefits.
- Section 17 Property, Plant and Equipment.
- Section 27 Impairment of Assets.

- Section 20 Leases.
- Section 32 Events after the End of the Reporting Period.
- Section 33 Related Party Disclosures.

The main provisions of each of the above, as they are likely to affect LLPs, are discussed below. However, this chapter does not cover all aspects of the sections of FRS 102 (September 2015) that might be relevant to the circumstances of any particular LLP, and reference should be made to the detail of the section as considered appropriate.

Focus

- The Financial Reporting Council have issued some Staff Education Notes which aim to illustrate how various complex issues in certain sections of FRS 102 work. The Staff Education Notes are not designed to be substitutes for the official standard and can be downloaded, free of charge, from www.frc.org.uk.

Provisions and contingencies

2 Use of the term 'provisions'

9.2 The term 'provision' can mean two fundamentally different things in financial reporting and it is important that LLPs correctly distinguish between the two. A provision is defined in the Glossary to FRS 102 as a liability of uncertain timing or amount. However, a provision can also be an adjustment to the carrying value of an item within the financial statements.

Example – a provision for a liability

An LLP is currently defending itself in a court case against one of its clients who is claiming damages for loss of earnings. The legal advisers acting for the LLP have advised that it is unlikely the LLP will be successful in its defence and have given an estimate of damages to be £20,000 which will be due for payment in the next accounting period.

In this example, the damages meet the definition of a 'provision for a liability' and must be included as such within the financial statements at the reporting date regardless of the fact that the payment is going to be made in the subsequent accounting period. This is because the conditions giving rise to the legal claim were in existence at the reporting date (ie the LLP has an obligation at the reporting date as a result of a past event).

Example – a provision against a carrying amount

An LLP has trade debtors in its balance sheet as at 31 December 2017 amounting to £100,000. The finance director has estimated (based on past practice and experience) that it is likely 5% of these debtors will fail to pay and therefore makes a provision equalling 5% of the trade debtors.

The finance director's write-down of debtors is known as a bad debt 'provision' rather than as a provision for a liability as in the example above. This provision for bad debts reduces the carrying value of the trade debtors at 31 December 2017 to recoverable amount.

It can be noted, therefore, that the term 'provision' can be taken to mean different things in the world of accountancy. In the first example the LLP was making a provision for a liability, whereas in the section example, the LLP was making a provision for a bad debt. Other provisions can include a provision for slow-moving or obsolete stock or a provision for depreciation. Such accounting adjustments are not covered by the requirements of Section 21.

3 The principles of Section 21 *Provisions and Contingencies*

9.3 The issue of provisions and contingencies has been a controversial one over the years as they have historically lent themselves to a whole host of accounting manipulations. Prior to the issuance of accounting standards in this area (namely SSAP 18 *Accounting for contingencies* which was superseded by FRS 12 *Provisions, contingent liabilities and contingent assets* that effectively became Section 21 in FRS 102) there was no guidance for entities which dealt with the definition, recognition, measurement, use and presentation of provisions and hence reporting entities were frequently exploiting this loophole by creating provisions, under the guise of prudence, in one accounting period, only to release them in the next accounting period, primarily for the purpose of profit manipulation.

In years when profits were high, management would create a provision to reduce profit to an acceptable level and then in succeeding years, management would write-down this provision to manipulate profit (ie management would focus on the profit line and then work upwards).

The creation and reversal of artificial provisions became known as 'big bath accounting' or 'big bath provisions' and it was this practice that eventually led to accounting standards being introduced to put a stop to entities manipulating the financial statements.

Before an LLP can recognise a provision within its accounts, it must be able to satisfy each of the three criteria set out in FRS 102, paragraph 21.4 (a) to (c) in Section 21:

- the LLP must have an obligation at its reporting date as a result of a past event;
- it must be **probable** (ie more likely than not) that the LLP will transfer economic benefits (ie pay cash) to settle the obligation; and
- a reliable estimate can be made of the amount involved.

Example – uncertain obligation

Limefields LLP is a city centre firm of surveyors which has been established for several years. One of its clients has instigated legal proceedings on the grounds of negligent advice. The senior partner is refuting the claim on the basis that the client failed to supply accurate and timely information. The LLP has instructed its law firm to defend the legal action and at the year-end the law firm had incurred legal costs of £5,000 and it is likely that further costs are in the region of £10,000 after the hearing. The LLP is considering whether to make a provision in the company's financial statements for £10,000 in the event that they lose the case. The lawyers have confirmed that they are unable to establish whether the LLP will be successful in the claim and the Barrister who has been engaged on the claim has confirmed that in her experience the claim could go either way.

The criteria in paragraph 21.4(b) says that it must be **probable** (ie more likely than not) that the LLP will be required to transfer economic benefits in settlement. Limefields LLP legal advisers have confirmed that they cannot be certain whether, or not, the LLP will win the case and therefore a provision cannot be made within the financial statements because all three criteria cannot be met. As a result, disclosure as a contingent liability should be made within the financial statements.

---

4 Constructive obligation

9.4 A constructive obligation arises where, through custom and practice, the LLP has created a valid expectation on the part of a third party that the LLP will satisfy its obligation. Constructive obligations can be very subjective and are not as 'clear cut' as a legal obligation as can be seen in the following example.

Example – constructive obligation

Scanlon Scanning LLP is a very successful document management bureau. They offer a range of products and services to handle customers' document management in the modern age of becoming 'paperless'. They supply scanning equipment to customers and associated software on-site so that their customer can scan paperwork into electronic files and then send the paper files to their storage department where these files are held in secure units. In addition, Scanlon Scanning offers routine upgrades to their customers and on-site maintenance and support for both their software and scanning equipment.

The LLP has been operating successfully for over 30 years and was originally set up by husband and wife, Les and Lisa. As the company grew over the years, Les and Lisa remain as designated members and have a management team in place to deal with the day-to-day routine running of the business. The members introduced a bonus system 11 years ago for management and staff which calculates bonuses using a pre-determined formula on profits.

At a meeting of the members on 27 March 2018 it was confirmed that initial indications suggested that the profit target had been hit and there was going to be a large excess over this target because the LLP had been awarded additional significant contracts in the year.

The members agreed that a bonus to management would be provided once the actual figures were confirmed which the accountancy firm have indicated will be around the middle of May 2018.

The final figures were agreed on 15 May 2018 for the year-ended 31 March 2018 and a bonus was accrued in the financial statements.

The question here relates to whether the bonus *should* have been accrued in the 31 March 2018 financial statements or if it should have been provided for in the 31 March 2019 financial statements when it was actually paid.

The designated members, Les and Lisa, introduced the bonus scheme 11 years ago which has not changed and over the years the practice of the LLP has been to pay a bonus based on profit targets. Over the years, management have 'expected' this bonus to be paid because the benchmark has been reached and this has then created a constructive obligation on the part of the LLP. Paragraph 21.6 to FRS 102 confirms that such an obligation means that the LLP has no realistic alternative to settling the obligation and therefore such a constructive obligation can be recognised as a provision within the LLP's financial statements as at 31 March 2018.

Where the obligation to pay only becomes apparent *after* the balance sheet date, but it clearly arises as the result of an event before that date, a provision should be recognised. For example, an unexpected legal claim might be received after the balance sheet date in respect of damage alleged to have occurred before that date. In these circumstances, a provision would be recognised, but it would not be acceptable to create a general provision for possible legal claims arising from work performed. The latter has historically been an approach adopted particularly by professional practices to take account of potential professional indemnity claims. Such provisions are not permitted in the accounts of the LLP, but the members could decide to make an allowance for such possible claims prior to determining the profits available for distribution.

5 Repairs and maintenance expenditure

9.5 Future repairs and maintenance do not relate to present obligations of the LLP arising as a result of a past event. Accordingly, no provision should be made for them, even in the circumstances where legislation might require regular maintenance in order for the asset to continue to be used in the business.

The one exception to this general rule is where an asset is held under a lease, and the lease term includes a requirement for the asset to be made good at whatever stage of the lease it is returned to the lessor. In these circumstances, there is both a legal obligation and a past event (the signing of the lease). Such terms are particularly common in the case of property leases, where provision is often required for the future cost of dilapidations.

In the property lease situation, having determined that there is an obligation under the terms of the lease, the LLP must then ascertain whether it is probable that there will be an economic transfer of benefits to settle the obligation. This may arise because the LLP has made the decision to vacate the property and move elsewhere, or perhaps as a consequence of a landlord break clause within the terms of the lease which the members have reason to believe will be activated. Once this criteria has been satisfied, then the potential dilapidations payable must be estimated. In such circumstances, it may be appropriate for the members to instruct a qualified property expert, such as a surveyor. Having quantified the obligation, the charge to the profit and loss account should then be spread, on an appropriate basis, across the periods between when the three criteria in Section 21 were satisfied and when the LLP is likely to vacate the property. Where the LLP has more than one property, it should have a consistent accounting policy across all of its properties.

6 Time value of money

9.6 It might be the case that the effect of the time value of money (when discounting provisions to present day values) becomes material. Where the time value of money is material, Section 21 requires the amount of the provision to be the present value of the amount expected to be required to settle the obligation. The LLP must use a pre-tax discount rate (or rates) which reflect(s) current market assessments of the time value of money and risks specific to the liability. The likelihood is that the vast majority of provisions will not require discounting to present day values, but if they do require discounting then the risks which are specific to the liability must be reflected in either the discount rate or in the estimation of the amounts required to settle the obligation – the important part in this respect is that it cannot be both.

7 Future operating losses

9.7 Paragraph 21.11B prohibits provisions being made for future operating losses. This is because there is no past event which puts an obligation on the part of the LLP to incur costs or pay out resources and hence they do not meet the definition of a liability. In addition, future operating losses relate to an activity which will continue and are therefore presumed to be avoidable and so no present obligation exists.

Example – future operating losses interacting with impairment

An LLP has a division which has made a loss in the year and the budgets suggest they are going to make future operating losses due to constraints in the marketplace.

Where an entity is expected to incur future losses this is an indication that an impairment review should be carried out on the appropriate division in accordance with Section 27 *Impairment of Assets*. The impairment review would determine whether those assets have suffered an impairment and hence need writing down to recoverable amount. In addition, future operating losses may be indicative that the entity has one, or more, onerous contracts.

---

8 Onerous contracts

9.8 An onerous contract is defined in the Glossary to FRS 102 as:

> 'A contract in which the unavoidable costs of meeting the obligations under the contract exceed the economic benefits expected to be received under it.'

Paragraph 21.11A of FRS 102 briefly deals with onerous contracts and cross-refers to Example 2 in the Appendix to Section 21. Provision should be made for the obligations under such a contract. Provision should not, however, be made where the contract has merely turned out to be less profitable than originally envisaged. In these circumstances, the effect on the carrying value of other related assets might, however, need to be considered.

One of the most common types of onerous contract is the lease on a vacated property. In these cases, provision should be made in the accounts, calculated by reference to the likely future rentals to be paid less any rent that can be obtained from subletting the property (sublet income should only be deducted provided that, by the balance sheet date, either the property has been formally sublet or the LLP is actively marketing the property). The provision should also include the other costs associated with the property, such as rates.

Example – an onerous contract

An LLP provides consulting services in respect of pensions and other post-employment benefits and has entered into a lease with an unconnected third party to rent its offices for a five-year period with no break clauses or early cancellation. In year three, due to unprecedented demand for the LLP's services, additional staff have been recruited and the LLP has now outgrown its current offices. The members have sourced larger premises which can house its current and additional staff.

The landlord of the property which is being vacated has refused to allow the property to be sublet and is refusing to allow the company to break out of the lease early. This is representative of an onerous contract – a property lease which has been abandoned by the LLP and which cannot be sublet and the LLP expects to receive no further benefit from the lease but it is still committed to pay the landlord rentals in order to conform to the terms of the original lease.

A provision for future rentals will be recognised and measured in the same way as any other sort of provision.

---

9 Restructuring costs

9.9 In terms of restructuring, this issue is covered in paragraph 21.11C in FRS 102. However, care must be taken when making a provision for restructuring costs because there are strict conditions that have to be met. Essentially, a constructive obligation will only arise in respect of restructuring costs when the entity:

- has drawn up a detailed and formal plan for the restructuring which identifies at least:
  - the business (or part thereof) which is going to be affected;
  - the principal locations which will be affected;
  - compensation for their services which are to be terminated;
  - the costs that will be incurred; and
  - when the restructuring is going to be instigated; and
- has created a valid expectation in the mind-sets of those which will be affected that it will carry out the restructuring either by commencing the restructuring exercise or announcing the plan's main features.

If the above criteria can be met in respect of a restructuring exercise at the balance sheet date, the LLP can recognise a provision to carry out the restructuring.

The decision by the members to go ahead with their plan will not, of itself, be sufficient to constitute a constructive obligation; there must be a valid expectation on the part of those affected that it will take place. This will be indicated either by the LLP having started to implement the plan, or by having announced its main features to those who are affected by it and this is required in order to comply with paragraph 21.11C (b) in FRS 102.

Only amounts which directly relate to the restructuring exercise should be provided for in the LLP's accounts and which are no associated with the ongoing activities of the entity.

10 Reimbursement of amounts included within provisions

9.10 In certain circumstances, the risk reflected by the provision might be offset by arrangements for reimbursement, for example through an insurance policy. The reimbursement may be recognised in the accounts when it is *virtually certain* that it will be received upon the settlement of the provision (FRS 102 paragraph 21.13). When the reimbursement becomes virtually certain it is not classified as a contingent asset and should then be recognised in the balance sheet as a separate asset and not offset against the related liability. In the profit and loss account, however, the expected income should be netted against the charge arising as a consequence of the provision.

Example – incorrect treatment of a reimbursement

An LLP operates as an accountancy and taxation firm with a year-end of 31 October 2017. The firm has recently been sued by one of its clients for the negligent preparation of a corporation tax return. The firm has received confirmation from its Professional Indemnity Insurers that the insurance company will refund part of the obligation and has provided this confirmation in writing on 30 September 2017. The accountant preparing the firm's financial statements for the year-ended 31 October 2017 has made the following journal entries to incorporate the insurance reimbursement into the LLP's financial statements:

Dr Provisions for liabilities	£X
Cr Claims account	£X

The original provision was posted to the claims account in the profit and loss account and hence the claims account is presented net, as is the liability representing the provision in the LLP's balance sheet.

The treatment by the accountant preparing the LLP's financial statements is in contravention of paragraph 21.9 in FRS 102. The reimbursement debtor should be presented in the balance sheet as an asset and must not be offset against the provision. However, in the profit and loss account the expense relating to a provision may be presented net of the amount recognised for a reimbursement.

Employee benefits: retirement benefits

The accounting treatment of retirement benefits within LLPs is probably one of the more complex areas.

11 Retirement benefits of employees

9.11 Where retirement benefits are provided to employees under an occupational pension plan, this will most probably be through one of two types of plan:

- *Defined contribution plan (often called a money purchase plan).* In this type of plan, the employee and/or the employer pays regular contributions fixed as an amount or percentage of pay and neither party has an obligation to pay further contributions if the plan has insufficient assets to pay all employee benefits relating to employee service in the current and prior periods. Individual benefits are determined by reference to the contributions paid into the plan in respect of the employee; hence the term 'defined contribution' essentially means the amount of post-employment benefits the employee will receive will be defined by the amount of the contributions the fund has received in respect of that employee.
- *Defined benefit plan* (also called a *final salary plan).* This is a plan where normally the rules specify the benefits to be paid (usually based on the employee's average or final pay) and the plan is financed accordingly. As actuarial and investment risk are borne, in substance, on the entity the LLP does have an obligation to pay further contributions into the plan if the plan has insufficient assets to pay all employee benefits relating to employee service in the current and prior periods.

Accounting for the provision of benefits under defined contribution plans is reasonably straightforward: the employer's cost recorded in the profit and loss account comprises the contributions payable.

Where an employing LLP makes contributions to the personal pension plans of individuals, these contributions are also accounted for as they are paid.

For a defined benefit plan, the situation is far more complex, because the benefits to be paid are dependent on future events, such as the average or final pay of the employee and the remaining lifetime of both the active and pensioner members of the plan.

LLPs are required to account for any defined benefit pension plans in accordance with Section 28 *Employee Benefits* of FRS 102.

In summary, Section 28 requires the following:

- Plan assets to be valued at fair value at the LLP's balance sheet date.
- The plan liabilities to be valued using the projected unit credit method discounted using a high quality corporate bond rate.
- The net pension asset or deficit to be shown separately on the balance sheet. Whilst a liability will nearly always be included, a surplus is only included to the extent that the employer will benefit either as a result of reduced contributions or refunds from the plan.
- The profit and loss charge is analysed between:
  - Amounts included within operating costs:
    - (i) current service costs;
    - (ii) past service costs;
    - (iii) any previously unrecognised surplus deducted from past service costs;
    - (iv) gains or losses on settlements and curtailments; and
    - (v) any previously unrecognised surplus deducted from the settlement or curtailment of losses.
  - Amounts included within financing costs:
    - (i) net interest on the net defined benefit liability during the period.

Actuarial gains and losses are accounted for through the statement of changes in equity.

Focus

- If the LLP has introduced a defined benefit pension plan, or an existing plan's benefits have changed in the current period, the LLP increases or decreases its net defined benefit liability to reflect the change, with the change being recognised in profit or loss.

There is also a significant level of disclosure required in the notes to the accounts, including information about the underlying actuarial assumptions.

Conversion to LLP and, therefore, the adoption of Section 28 causes a number of LLPs a very specific problem not found in similar situations for companies. Where there is a deficit recognised on the 'top' half of the balance sheet, an equivalent amount needs to be recorded within the 'reserves' side of the balance sheet. In the corporate model this is straightforward and is deducted from the profit and loss reserve. However, LLPs do not accumulate a profit and loss reserve in the same way that traditional companies do and all previous profits may well have been distributed. Many LLPs have solved the problem by creating an additional category within members' interests.

The requirements of Section 28 are onerous and forward planning is essential on the part of both those preparing the accounts and those carrying out the audit. Much of the information will probably need to be produced by the actuaries to the pension scheme who will also need reasonable notice of what information is required as it can take some time for the actuaries to complete their work.

There are a number of factors which need to be considered which include:

- The LLP and its pension plan may have different year ends. The consequences of this are that it will not be possible to rely on the plan's accounts to ascertain asset values and the actuarial information may well also need to be prepared to a different date.
- Access may be required by the auditors to the plan's records in order to carry out procedures on movements since the last set of audited accounts. Where the trustees will not permit this or it is considered more efficient, it may be necessary to involve the auditors of the pension plan.
- The actuarial method required by Section 28 may differ from that used by the actuaries when determining the funding rate of the plan and could result in the need for two different valuations.
- There will be additional costs for both preparing the actuarial information and the audit of the disclosures.

12 Retirement benefits of members

9.12 Where members have an employment contract (see Chapter 5) and have retirement benefits which are awarded based on the remuneration received under those contracts, those benefits should be accounted for in the same way as for employees (see above).

Other retirement benefits payable to members in the future (often referred to as annuities) will usually be of one of the following:

- *Predetermined.* An amount which is fixed at the time of retirement (annuity). This may, for example, be by reference to the profits earned in the last year of membership. Alternatively, it could be a fixed sum, which may be index-linked or linked to some other measure which is independent of the profits of the LLP.
- *Profit-dependent.* An amount which effectively results in the member continuing to receive a share in the profits of the LLP post retirement. There are a wide range of methods used for providing profit-dependent benefits and these may include arrangements whereby the LLP has to achieve a certain level of profits before any payment is made. In addition, a maximum level of benefit payable may be imposed either by reference to a percentage of profits or monetary amount.

A combination of the two types of benefit is also possible. For example, a retiring member may be entitled to a lump sum payment based on a factor such as past profits and an additional amount in future years based on the profits of the LLP. The period of time for which the benefit will be paid may also vary.

Details of the retirement benefits of members will usually be found in the members' agreement. This will require careful review to ensure that all benefits have been identified and correctly accounted for. The members' agreement may not, however, contain all details of retirement benefits and a constructive obligation may have arisen as a result of either custom and practice or discussions held with individual members. These will also need to be considered when determining the accounting treatment of members' retirement benefits.

The SORP requires that the principles of Section 11 *Basic Financial Instruments*, Section 12 *Other Financial Instruments Issues* and Section 21 *Provisions and Contingencies* be applied to the accounting for retirement benefits of members.

An annuity would meet the definition of a financial liability under Section 11 or Section 12 of FRS 102 if there is a contractual obligation for the LLP to deliver cash or a financial asset to a member. Annuities will more than likely be subject to uncertainties, for example where payments depend on future profits or significant mortality risk exists. The important factor in this respect is establishing whether the liability is, or is not, an unconditional contractual liability. Unconditional contractual liabilities meet the definition of a financial liability and are, therefore, excluded from the scope of Section 21. An annuity will meet the definition of an insurance contract (and hence be subjected to the provisions in FRS 103 *Insurance Contracts*) if the LLP accepts significant insurance risk (usually mortality risk) and this will apply should the amount payable by the LLP be significantly affected by how long the former member lives. When an annuity is an unconditional contractual obligation for the LLP to deliver cash or a financial asset to a member, and the LLP has not accepted significant insurance risk this will mean the annuity meets the definition of a financial liability and thus fall under the scope of Section 11 or Section 12 of FRS 102 (paragraph 11.9 of FRS 102 outlines the conditions that must be met for such a financial liability to fall within the scope of Section 11). In instances where the conditions are not met, the financial liability is accounted for in accordance with Section 12.

In relation to profit-dependent annuity payments, these will not meet the conditions outlined in paragraph 11.9 and when such annuity payments arise they are to be accounted for either in accordance with FRS 103 (where the payments expose the LLP to significant insurance risk) or in accordance with Section 12 of FRS 102 (where they do not expose the LLP to significant insurance risk).

The SORP at paragraph 80B recognises that in practice any obligations to make post-retirement benefits to members will often be set out in the members' agreement and reflect significant mortality risk. Where this is the case for an LLP, it is likely that the LLP will historically have accounted for the obligations as provisions under the previous FRS 12 *Provisions, contingent liabilities and contingent assets*. On transition to new UK GAAP, the obligations will fall under the provisions in FRS 103 but the LLP will be allowed to continue its previous accounting policies.

Applying the principles of Section 21 means that an annuity should be recognised once the member has an actual or constructive right to receive it, and the LLP has no discretion to withhold payment.

It is most usually the case that the rights to receive an annuity arise over time (ie whilst the member continues to be a member of the LLP) and it follows, therefore, that the liability should be accrued over that period, building up a liability through to the time of retirement.

In many cases the member may only obtain absolute entitlement to an annuity on reaching a specific milestone, for example achieving a specified number of years' service. Even in these circumstances, because the LLP cannot avoid the liability that is accruing in the period through to reaching entitlement, the liability should be built up over the total period of service. Members who choose to leave before reaching the milestone will not be entitled to an annuity.

In certain situations, however, the members may formally agree that, rather than the obligation to the retiring member becoming a liability of the LLP, they instead agree amongst themselves to discharge the obligation out of their profit allocations. As this is a transaction amongst the members, rather than between the LLP and its members, the amounts paid to the retired members are not included within the accounts of the LLP.

Paragraph 76B of the SORP contains a flowchart which is reproduced below which gives guidance on how to determine which guidance applies to a particular obligation:

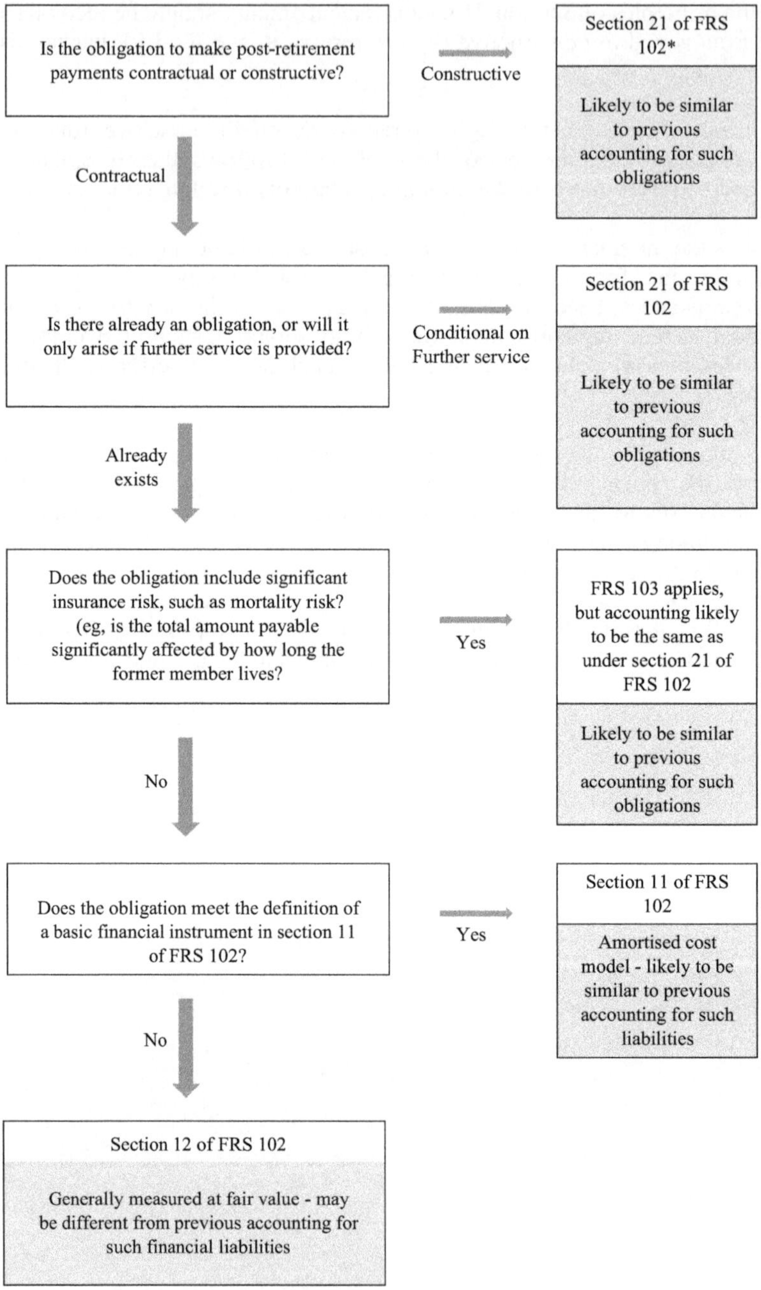

* unless the obligation of certain timing and amount, in which case the general provisions of the Companies Act/GAAP apply.[1]

1 LLP SORP, para 76B.

13 Calculation of the provision

9.13 To the extent that the liability falls within the scope of Section 21 of FRS 102, the liability that is recognised in the accounts should be based on the expectations, as at the balance sheet date, of:

- the probable date the member will cease to be a member; and
- the amounts likely to be payable to him or her from that date.

LLPs with profit-dependent retirement benefit plans will have to make an assessment of their future profits in order to determine the level of provision. Whilst there will have to be a certain amount of subjectivity attached to these estimates it should be possible for the LLP to determine the range of potential outcomes from which a provision could be calculated.

In determining the value of the liability for members' retirement benefits it will often be appropriate to use the principles of Section 28 *Employee Benefits* and therefore to seek the advice of an actuary who will be able to provide details of factors that should be taken into account, such as life expectancy. Where it is probable that such additional input will be required, in a similar way to obtaining Section 28 information for the LLP's accounts, the actuary will need to be contacted well in advance of preparing the accounts and the auditors will also need to be made aware of the need for their involvement.

The liability may need to be recalculated on an annual basis to take account of changes in membership, eligibility for post-retirement payments, financial estimates and actuarial assumptions.

Where the LLP have offered post-retirement payments consistently to previous members at the point of, but not prior to, retirement this could build an expectation in the mind-sets of all members that they will be offered this benefit at the point of retirement. This constructive obligation would then give rise to earlier recognition of the liability rather than recognising the liability at the point of retirement. In the absence of a formal plan, arrangements to provide post-retirement benefits can arise from the actions of the LLP.

14 Presentation of members' retirement benefits

9.14 The amounts that are recognised in the profit and loss account (or statement of comprehensive income) with respect to current members should be included within 'Members' remuneration charged as an expense'. The change in liability in respect of former members, however, should not be included within 'Members' remuneration charged as an expense' but within the relevant profit and loss heading, for example 'Administration expenses'.

The liability with respect to current members should be included within 'Loans and other debts due to members' and be described separately where the amount is material. In the year a member retires, the liability should be transferred and included within the balances in respect of former members.

The liability in the balance sheet with respect to former members should be described as 'Post-retirement payments to former members' and be included either within 'Provisions for liabilities' or 'Creditors', dependent upon the circumstances.

Where former members are awarded amounts with respect to past service after their retirement date, this should be recognised in full in the profit and loss account at the time the award is made.

When the LLP discounts liabilities to present day values (to reflect the time value of money) the unwinding of the discount should be presented next to the interest cost line in the profit and loss account (or statement of comprehensive income) to the extent that it relates to former members. Where the unwinding of the discount relates to current members, it should be included in 'Members' remuneration charged as an expense'.

The LLP should disclose the accounting policy adopted with respect to retirement benefits.

15 Investments held to fund future retirement benefits

9.15 Whilst the amounts involved mean that LLPs are unlikely to make investments of a size that will cover the liability shown in the accounts, they may, for example, make investments to meet requirements to fund retirements in the near future. Any such investments should be included on the balance sheet as investments, but their purpose should be separately identified in the notes.

16 Specific issues on conversion to an LLP

9.16 The relationship between the LLP and any predecessor entity will need to be carefully considered. The LLP may assume responsibility for the retirement benefits of a predecessor partnership or other organisation and, in these circumstances, where a legal or constructive obligation exists to pay those amounts, it should be recognised as a provision in the accounts of the LLP.

More commonly, on transition, the predecessor entity may transfer those liabilities to a third party (for example, an insurance company). In these circumstances the former partners or directors may only have recourse to the LLP in the event of the failure of that third party. To the extent that there has been no default and none is probable, the existence of the right of recourse should be disclosed as a contingent liability in the accounts.

Property, plant and equipment

17 Tangible fixed assets

9.17 Section 17 *Property, Plant and Equipment* deals with the accounting and disclosure requirements for all tangible fixed assets, with the exception of those that are categorised as investment properties carried at fair value, which are subject to the provisions of Section 16 *Investment Property*. A tangible fixed asset can only be recognised on an LLP's balance sheet (statement of financial position) when it is probable (ie more likely than not) that future economic benefits associated with the asset will flow to the entity and the cost of the asset can be measured reliably.

18 The 'cost' of a tangible fixed asset

9.18 Section 17 deals with the issues relating to tangible fixed assets. The section requires that tangible fixed assets should first be recorded at cost although after initial recognition at cost they can be subsequently revalued (although micro-entity LLPs reporting under FRS 105 cannot subject fixed assets to revaluation – see Chapter 14). Costs which may be capitalised are those that are incremental and would have been avoided only if the asset had not been constructed or acquired. The costs which can be considered for capitalisation are as follows:

- The purchase price including legal and brokerage fees. The cost price should be net of any discounts or rebates.
- Costs which are directly attributable in bringing the asset to the location and condition necessary for it to be used in the manner in which the members intend. This could include the labour costs of employees which are directly attributable to the construction of (say) an architectural practice that chooses to design its own property which may include the time of the staff directly involved in the design project.
- Stamp duty, import duties, non-refundable purchase tax; site preparation and clearance costs; initial delivery and handling costs; and installation costs.
- Where the application of Section 21 (see **9.2–9.10** above) means that a provision is required for the dismantling of an asset and/or restoration of a site at the end of its useful economic life, the estimated cost of dismantling should be included as part of the cost of the asset. For example, if an LLP leases a property and installs partitioning, but the terms of the lease state that this must be removed at the end of the lease, the cost of the partitioning included within fixed assets should also include the estimated cost to dismantle it.

The cost of an asset can include interest on borrowings used to finance the production of that asset, to the extent that those costs arise during the period of production (Section 25 *Borrowing Costs* in FRS 102 deals with these issues). Capitalisation of finance costs is an optional policy (which is not available to micro-entity LLP's reporting under FRS 105), but if the LLP chooses to capitalise finance costs it must do so for all fixed assets where finance costs are a material element of the cost. The interest that may be capitalised should relate only to borrowings that would have been avoided if there had been no expenditure on the asset. This does not mean, however, that there needs to be a separately identifiable loan. The funds could arise from using existing cash which could otherwise have been used to repay existing borrowing or from the extended use of existing facilities. Borrowing costs can only be capitalised in respect of 'qualifying assets'. The Glossary to FRS 102 defines a 'qualifying asset' as one which takes a substantial period of time to get ready for its intended use or sale. It is generally taken to mean that a 'substantial period of time' means more than 12 months.

19 Maintenance expenditure versus enhancement

9.19 Subsequent expenditure, which is necessary to ensure that the fixed asset can continue to operate at the same level, should be charged to the profit and loss account as it is incurred. Subsequent expenditure should only be capitalised where it enhances the performance of the fixed asset in excess of its previous capabilities, for example by increasing its life or capacity. If a fixed asset comprises distinct, different components and these are depreciated at different rates (ie the LLP uses 'component accounting'), expenditure to restore 'worn out' parts of the asset can be capitalised.

Example – subsequent expenditure

An LLP owns a light aircraft which it uses in its business and is required, by law, to be overhauled every three years. If the major overhaul does not take place, the aircraft is grounded and cannot be flown.

The LLP must reflect the need to undertake the overhaul or inspection by depreciating an amount of the asset that is equivalent to the expected inspection or overhaul cost over the period until the next inspection or overhaul. Therefore, the cost of the inspection or overhaul is capitalised when incurred because it restores the economic benefits of the aircraft and the carrying amount representing the cost of the benefits consumed is removed from the balance sheet.

---

20 Revaluation

9.20 Tangible fixed assets may be revalued, but where an LLP adopts a policy of revaluation all assets within the same class must be revalued (ie the LLP cannot 'cherry pick' which assets it wants to revalue within a certain class) in order to comply with paragraph 17.15. The classes of fixed asset defined by the regulations are very broad, for example land and buildings; plant and machinery; and fixtures, fittings, tools and equipment. An LLP could adopt a narrower class so long as this is reasonable; for example it is commonplace for an LLP to classify motor vehicles as a separate category of fixed asset. In practice, it is rare that assets other than property are subject to revaluation.

Focus

- A micro-entity LLP that is reporting under FRS 105 is not allowed to use the revaluation model; only the historic cost model is permitted. See Chapter 14.

The decision to revalue a class of assets is one which should only be entered into after careful consideration, as there can be significant costs associated with complying with the requirements contained in paragraph 17.15B. Paragraph 17.15B requires revaluation exercises are carried out with **sufficient regularity** so as to ensure that the carrying amount of the revalued asset(s) is not materially different from that which would be determined using fair value at the end of the year-/period-end.

Focus

- The revaluation frequency is notably different under FRS 102 than was the case under FRS 15 *Tangible fixed assets*. Under FRS 15, revaluations had to be obtained at least every five years, with valuations in the intervening years where there had been a material change in value. Under FRS 102, more professional judgement will be required to ensure that valuations are obtained with sufficient regularity to ensure the carrying value of the revalued asset(s) is not materially different than its fair value.

Paragraph 17.15C of FRS 102 acknowledges that the fair value of land and buildings (note land and buildings are separately accounted for in FRS 102) is usually derived from market-based evidence by appraisal and this is usually carried out by professionally-qualified valuers (ie chartered surveyors). In rarer occasions, if the LLP subjects items of plant and equipment to fair value, market values are usually established through appraisal.

If the LLP owns an item of property, plant and equipment which is considered to be of a 'specialised nature' – ie the item is rarely sold (except as part of a continuing business), and this item of property, plant and equipment has been subjected to the revaluation model, then the LLP may need to estimate fair value using an income or a depreciated replacement cost approach to conform with the requirements of FRS 102.

21 Depreciation

9.21 The general principle is that tangible fixed assets should be depreciated to their recoverable amount over their useful expected life. Paragraph 17.16 states that in the event that major components of an item of property, plant and equipment have significantly different patterns of consumption of economic benefits, then component depreciation is appropriate. This is where the LLP will allocate the initial cost of the asset to its major components and then depreciate each component separately over its useful life. A typical example would be land and buildings which have to be separately accounted for under FRS 102 (paragraph 17.8). The land generally has an indefinite life and is therefore not depreciated, but buildings are considered to have a finite life and must be depreciated accordingly.

Example – component depreciation

An LLP owns a furnace which requires relining on a five-year cycle.

In accordance with paragraph 17.16, for depreciation purposes the LLP may account separately for the major components (the furnace lining) which have a substantially different useful economic lives from the rest of the asset. In this example, the furnace lining will be depreciated over its useful life of five years so that the depreciation profile of the whole asset more accurately reflects the actual consumption of the asset's economic benefits.

Section 17 to FRS 102 confirms that the depreciable amount of an asset should be allocated to profit and loss using a systematic basis over the useful life of the asset. In this instance, depreciation of an asset will begin when the asset becomes first available for use. An asset becomes first available for use when it is in the location and condition necessary for it to be capable of operating in the manner in which the members intended. Depreciation then ceases when the asset is derecognised from the LLP's balance sheet.

Example – an idle asset

An LLP uses an item of machinery in its production process. The LLP's policy in respect of this machine is to depreciate it under the 'usage method'. This is because the machine is only used at a certain point in the production schedule which occurs only at certain times during the year. The LLP has not depreciated the machine in the months when the machine was idle.

Paragraph 17.20 says that depreciation does not cease when the asset becomes idle or is retired from active use. The only exception to this would be where the asset has been written down to nil (ie fully depreciated). However, in circumstances when the usage method of depreciation is used, the depreciation charge can be zero at times when there is no production.

When considering the depreciation policy, the LLP must take into account a number of factors to ensure that the depreciation method employed is most appropriate in the LLP's circumstances. Such factors can include:

- The LLP's expected use of the asset.
- The expected physical wear and tear.
- Technical or commercial obsolescence.
- Legal or similar limits on the use of the asset.

The depreciation method employed by the entity must be the method that best reflects the pattern in which the LLP will use the asset and therefore consume the economic benefits associated with the asset. The two most common methods of depreciation used in practice are the straight-line method and the reducing balance method (also referred to as the 'diminishing balance' method). In addition, the LLP may consider the units of production method to be applicable in certain circumstances.

Impairment of assets

22 Impairment – introduction

9.22 An asset (tangible or intangible) is deemed to be impaired when the LLP is unable to recover the carrying value (all, or part thereof) on the balance sheet, either by continued use in its ongoing business or through sale. An impairment may arise either because of something that has happened to the asset or as a consequence of factors affecting the business or economic environment in which the asset is being used. In such circumstances, an adjustment is required to reduce the carrying value of the asset. One of the underlying principles in financial reporting is that assets should not be carried in the balance sheet at any more than their recoverable amount and therefore at each reporting date all assets should be reviewed for any indicators of impairment and consideration given as to whether any write-down to recoverable amount should take place by the LLP.

The principal section in FRS 102 covering impairment is Section 27 *Impairment of Assets*. Section 27 deals with the impairment of all assets (tangible and intangible) including inventories. However, Section 27 does not deal with the impairment of deferred acquisition costs and intangible assets which arise through contracts that fall under the scope of FRS 103 *Insurance Contracts*. In respect of tangible and intangible assets, the objectives of Section 27 are to ensure that:

- fixed assets and goodwill are recorded in the financial statements at no more than their recoverable amount;
- any resulting impairment loss is measured and recognised on a consistent basis; and
- sufficient information is disclosed in the financial statements to enable users to understand the impact of the impairment on the financial position and performance of the reporting LLP.

The term 'fixed assets' will also include investments made by the LLP in other undertakings. In respect of goodwill and fixed assets other than investments, an impairment charge could potentially impact both the LLP's own profit and loss account and the consolidated profit and loss account. In respect of investments, an impairment charge will only affect the LLP's own accounts.

23 Indicators of impairment

9.23 A review for impairment is required if events or changes in circumstances indicate that the carrying value of the fixed asset or goodwill may not be recoverable.

For assets other than inventories, Section 27 sets out examples of events and changes in circumstances that indicate that impairment may have occurred, and these include:

- the decline of an asset's market value during the accounting period in excess of what would otherwise be expected through normal passage of time or use;
- significant changes which have had an adverse effect on the LLP taking place during the accounting period (or which will take place in the near future) relating to the

technological, market, economic or legal environment in which the LLP operates, or in the market to which an asset is dedicated;

- increases in interest rates or other market rates of return on investments which are likely to materially affect the discount rate the LLP uses in calculating an asset's value in use and decrease the asset's fair value less costs to sell; and/or
- the net assets of the LLP being more than the estimated fair value of the LLP as a whole.

The above indicators relate to *external* sources of information which the LLP should consider when assessing assets for impairment. There are also some *internal* sources of information which should also be taken into consideration which include:

- evidence of obsolescence or physical damage to the fixed asset;
- a significant event(s) which has an adverse effect on the LLP having taken place (or about to take place in the near future) in the extent to which, or the manner in which, an asset is used or is expected to be used. For example, if the asset will become idle, the LLP plans to discontinue or restructure an operation to which an asset belongs, the LLP plans to dispose of an asset before the previously assessed expected date of disposal or the reassessment of the useful life of an asset to a much lower previously assessed useful life; and
- assessing available evidence from the LLP's internal records which indicate that the economic performance (ie operating results and cash flows) of an asset is, or may be, worse than previously expected.

When the LLP concludes that there is evidence that an asset is impaired, there should be a review undertaken of:

- the remaining useful life;
- the depreciation (or amortisation) method; or
- the residual value for the asset.

Once this review is undertaken, one of the above must be adjusted in accordance with either Section 17 *Property, Plant and Equipment* or Section 18 *Intangible Assets other than Goodwill*. This applies even if no impairment loss is recognised for the respective asset. Changes in the above estimates will be applied prospectively (ie in the period the change arises where the change affects that period only or in the period of change and in future periods) as such changes will relate to a change in accounting estimate under Section 10 *Accounting Policies, Estimates and Errors*.

24 Recognition and measurement of impairment losses

9.24 An impairment review comprises a comparison of the carrying amount of the fixed asset or goodwill with its recoverable amount. Recoverable amount is the *higher* of its fair value less costs to sell and its value in use.

Example – calculation of fair value but not value in use

An LLP is undertaking an impairment review of one of its assets. It has established the fair value of the asset less costs to sell but is unable to calculate value in use and is therefore unsure whether, or not, the asset has suffered any impairment. The fair value less costs to sell figure is higher than the asset's carrying amount stated in the LLP's balance sheet.

It is not always considered necessary to determine both fair value less costs to sell and value in use because if *either* of these amounts are higher than the asset's carrying amount, the asset is not impaired and therefore it will not be necessary to calculate the other figure.

To the extent that the carrying amount exceeds the recoverable amount, the fixed asset or goodwill is impaired and should be written down. The impairment loss should be recognised in the profit and loss account unless it arises on a previously revalued fixed asset. Where the impairment is caused by a clear consumption of economic benefits, it should be recognised in the profit and loss account. Other impairments of revalued fixed assets should be treated as a revaluation decrease in accordance with the relevant section of FRS 102 (for example Section 17 *Property, Plant and Equipment*).

Example – impairment of a revalued asset

An LLP has a building in its balance sheet that is accounted for in accordance with Section 17 *Property, Plant and Equipment* under the revaluation model. The amount of the impairment amounts to £70,000 and there is an associated revaluation surplus in the equity section of the LLP's balance sheet directly relating to the building amounting to £80,000.

Paragraph 27.6 says that an impairment loss of a revalued asset is to be treated as a revaluation decrease in accordance with the relevant section of FRS 102 (in this instance it will be Section 17). Section 17 says that a revaluation decrease is recognised in other comprehensive income to the extent of any previously recognised revaluation increase accumulated in equity. Therefore, the entries for the impairment loss will be:

Dr Revaluation surplus	£70,000
Cr Buildings (property, plant and equipment)	£70,000

This will result in the revaluation surplus in the LLP's balance sheet going from £80,000 to £10,000.

If, on the other hand the impairment loss amounted to £90,000 then the entries will be:

Dr Revaluation surplus	£80,000
Dr Profit and loss	£10,000

Cr Buildings (property, plant £90,000
and equipment)

This is because when a revaluation decrease exceeds the accumulated revaluation gains that have been accumulated in equity any excess is recognised in profit or loss.

Fair value less costs to sell

9.25 Fair value less costs to sell is the amount which could be received by the LLP from the sale of an asset in an arm's-length transaction that is entered into between knowledgeable and willing persons. Deducted from this value are the costs directly associated with the sale of the asset, such as any directly attributable legal fees. The best evidence of fair value less costs to sell might be found within a binding agreement (which outlines the sale proceeds and any associated costs inherent with the sale). Alternatively, a market value can be sourced from an 'active market'. An 'active market' for the purposes of impairment is a market in which:

- the items traded within the market are homogeneous;
- willing buyers and sellers can normally be found at any time; and
- prices are available to the public.

If a binding sales agreement does not exist, nor an active market for an asset, then fair value less costs to sell should be deciphered using the best information available to the LLP which might reflect the amount that the LLP could obtain at the reporting date from disposal of the asset in an arm's-length transaction (ie on normal commercial terms). The LLP should also consider any other recent transactions for similar assets in the same industry and the outcomes of those transactions.

Value in use

9.26 The value in use of an asset is the present value of the future cash flows obtainable as a result of the asset's continued use, including those that would arise from its ultimate disposal. Whilst value in use should be estimated for individual assets where reasonably possible, in practice, it is the utilisation of groups of assets and liabilities, together with their associated goodwill, that generates cash flows. Hence, value in use will usually have to be estimated for groups of assets and liabilities. These groups are referred to as cash-generating units ('CGU'). Because it is necessary to identify only material impairments, in some cases it may be acceptable to consider a group of CGUs together rather than on an individual basis.

CGUs are identified by dividing the total income of the LLP into as many largely independent income streams as is reasonably practicable in the light of the information available to management. In general terms, the income streams are likely to follow the way in which management monitors and makes decisions about how the different lines of business of the LLP are developed.

Central assets, such as group or regional head offices, and working capital may have to be apportioned across the units using a logical and systematic basis. The resulting CGUs will be complete and non-overlapping, so that the sum of the carrying amounts of the units equals the carrying amount of the net assets of the LLP as a whole.

Cash flows

9.27 Section 27 sets out the rules that need to be applied when determining the expected future cash flows of the CGUs. The calculations should include any allocation of central overheads, but must exclude cash flows relating to financing and tax, and they should be based on reasonable and supportable assumptions. The cash flows should be consistent with the most up-to-date budgets and plans that have been formally approved by management. Cash flows for the period beyond that covered by formal budgets and plans should assume a steady or declining growth rate for subsequent years (unless an increasing rate can be justified).

Future cash flows should be estimated for CGUs or individual fixed assets in their current condition. They should not include:

- future cash outflows or related costs savings or benefits that are expected to arise from a future restructuring for which the LLP is not yet committed; or
- future capital expenditure that will improve or enhance the CGU or assets in excess of their originally assessed standard of performance.

In the case of a newly acquired CGU such as a subsidiary, the purchase price will reflect the synergies and other opportunities for making more effective use of the assets as a result of the acquisition. In some of these cases, in order to obtain the benefits from its investment, it may be necessary for the purchaser to undertake related capital expenditure and reorganisations. In these situations, when performing impairment reviews up to the end of the first full year after acquisition (and subsequently, if still appropriate), such capital expenditure and reorganisation costs and benefits should be included in assessing the future cash flows of the investment, to the extent that the investments or reorganisations are still to be incurred. The costs and benefits applied in impairment reviews in subsequent periods should be consistent with those included within the budgets and plans produced and utilised for the initial impairment review.

Discount rate

9.28 The present value of the CGU under review should be calculated by discounting the expected future cash flows. The discount rate used should be an estimate of the rate that reflects current market assessments of the time value of money and the risks specific to the asset for which the future cash flow estimates have not been adjusted. Discount rates used in the present value calculation should be on a pre-tax basis.

Estimates of this market rate may be made by a variety of means, including reference to:

- the rate implicit in market transactions in similar assets;

- the current weighted average cost of capital (WACC) of a listed company whose cash flows have similar risk profiles to those of the CGU; or
- the WACC for the LLP, *but only if* adjusted for the particular risks associated with the CGU.

Using a discount rate equal to the rate of return that the market would expect on an equally risky investment is a method of reflecting the risk associated with the cash flows in the value in use measurement. It is likely that this method will be the easiest method of reflecting risk. However, an acceptable alternative is to adjust the cash flows for risk and to discount them using a risk-free rate (eg a government bond rate). Whichever method of reflecting risk is adopted, care must be taken that the effect of risk is not double-counted by inclusion in both cash flows and the discount rate.

If the LLP chooses to use the third option above, then the WACC for the LLP is based on the combined cost of equity and cost of debt. In terms of calculating the cost of equity, the LLP might consider ascertaining the expected return required by a private equity or venture capital investor for a business in the same industry. For the cost of debt, the post-tax rate of the cost of debt to the business should be used.

25 Allocation of impairment losses

9.29 To the extent that the carrying amount of the CGU exceeds its recoverable amount, the CGU is impaired. The impairment loss should be accounted for in accordance with paragraph 27.21 of FRS 102 and allocated to reduce the carrying amount of the assets of the CGU in the following order:

- first, to reduce any goodwill in the CGU; and then
- to the other assets in the CGU, on a pro rata basis of the carrying amount of each asset in the CGU.

Care must be taken in allocating impairment losses because an LLP cannot reduce the carrying amount of any asset in the CGU below the highest of:

- its fair value less costs to sell (where this can be established);
- its value in use (where this can be established); and
- zero.

If any excess amount remains because of this restriction, it must be allocated to the other assets of the unit pro-rata on the basis of the carrying amount of those other assets.

Example – allocation of an impairment loss

An LLP has undertaken an impairment test on one of its groups of assets that is considered to be a CGU. Financial statement extracts for the year-ended 30 September 2017 are as follows:

Goodwill	£130,000
Office equipment	£200,000

The CGU has suffered an impairment loss of £150,000 during the year as the LLP has received widely publicised criticism about the services of its subsidiary which has had a detrimental effect on its business.

The members have undertaken an exercise in calculating fair value less costs to sell and value in use of goodwill. They have determined that the fair value less costs to sell is £60,000 and the value in use is £50,000. The members consider it is not possible to arrive at a figure for fair value less costs to sell or value in use for office equipment.

The impairment loss of £150,000 will first be allocated to goodwill, with the remainder being applied to the office equipment. However, neither the goodwill nor any asset in a CGU can be reduced below the highest of:

- fair value less costs to sell (if determinable);
- value in use (if determinable); or
- zero.

As fair value less costs to sell is higher than value in use, goodwill is to be carried at £60,000, so of the £150,000 impairment £70,000 (£130,000 less £60,000) will be allocated to goodwill, with the remaining £80,000 being charged against office equipment. Following the allocation of the impairment charge, the financial statement extracts will be as follows:

Goodwill	£60,000
Office equipment	£120,000

---

26 Additional requirements for goodwill impairment

9.30 Paragraph 27.24 of FRS 102 recognises that goodwill, on its own, cannot be sold and it also does not generate cash flows for an LLP which are independent of the cash flows of other assets. This has the consequence that it is not possible to measure the fair value of goodwill directly and hence the fair value should be derived from the measurement of fair value of the CGU of which the goodwill forms part of.

Goodwill acquired in a business combination is impairment tested from the date of acquisition. It is then allocated to each of the acquirer's CGUs which are expected to benefit from the synergies of the combination, regardless of whether, or not, other assets or liabilities have been assigned to those units.

Part of the recoverable amount of the CGU may belong to the non-controlling interests (previously referred to as 'minority interests') and therefore for the purposes of impairment testing of a non-wholly-owned CGU that has goodwill, the carrying value of that unit is notionally adjusted before being compared with recoverable amount. This is achieved by grossing up the carrying amount of goodwill which has been allocated to the unit to include the goodwill attributable to the non-controlling interest. Once this has been completed, the notionally-adjusted carrying value is then compared with recoverable amount to determine whether the CGU is impaired.

Example – apportionment of an impairment loss

LLP A acquired 80% of the net assets of LLP B on 1 January 2017 (the date of acquisition). The finance manager is undertaking an impairment test on the goodwill acquired in LLP B but is unsure as to the starting point and how the apportionment of such an impairment loss would be split.

Goodwill which has been impaired in a business combination is impairment tested from the date of acquisition. Once this has been established and the impairment calculated, it is then allocated to each of the cash-generating units which are expected to benefit from the synergies of the combination, regardless of whether other associated assets or liabilities of the acquiree are assigned to those units.

20% of the impairment loss will belong to the non-controlling interests (minority interests) as LLP A only acquired 80% of the value of LLP B's net assets. As a result, 20% of the recoverable amount of the cash-generating unit with the goodwill in it will belong to the non-controlling interests. The finance manager should notionally adjust the carrying amount of the cash-generating unit before comparing the unit to its recoverable amount. The finance manager will do this by grossing up the carrying amount of goodwill so it includes the goodwill belonging to the non-controlling interests. It is this 'grossed up' goodwill which is compared to the recoverable amount to determine whether the cash-generating unit is impaired.

Leases

27 Leases – introduction

9.31 The accounting and disclosure requirements for leases is dealt with in Section 20 *Leases* of FRS 102, which identifies two distinct types of lease arrangement: finance leases and operating leases.

The correct classification of leases cannot be over-emphasised because the accounting treatment between a finance and an operating lease is significantly different. One of the main overarching principles in financial reporting is the concept of *substance over form* and the issue of lease transactions illustrates the need for the substance and not the legal form of a transaction to be considered. When the 'substance' of a transaction is referred to, it means the transaction's 'commercial reality' and it is the commercial reality which will often be markedly different than the transaction's legal form. The concept of 'off-balance sheet finance' has been in existence for several years and leases lend themselves to a host of scenarios which could give rise to leases being off-balance sheet and hence treated as an operating lease when, in reality, the lease should be treated as a finance lease and hence shown on the LLP's balance sheet. Standard-setters are aware of the concept of off-balance sheet finance and hence place emphasis on the substance of the arrangement in an attempt to lessen the scope for off-balance sheet finance to occur. However, the attempts by the standard-setters to close such 'loopholes' in leasing transactions does not stop some LLPs from deliberately engineering leasing arrangements to achieve a desired outcome and hence it is possible that in the future further changes to lease accounting might take place in further attempts to combat off-balance sheet finance.

Focus

- In September 2016, the Financial Reporting Council (FRC) issued a consultation document outlining their approach to changing FRS 102 as part of its triennial review to reflect changes in International Financial Reporting Standards (as FRS 102 is primarily based on *IFRS for SMEs*). The FRC have proposed to change the accounting for leases to bring Section 20 of FRS 102 in line with IFRS 16 *Leases*. IFRS 16 contains a single model for lessees and requires the majority of leases to be classified as finance leases, hence reported on the balance sheet. Exceptions to this treatment in IFRS 16 apply to short-term leases and low-value leases.
- This change will have a significant impact and therefore (at the time of writing) the FRC have proposed that any changes to lease accounting will not apply until accounting periods beginning on or after 1 January 2022 and it is likely that early-adoption will be permitted. At the time of writing, the FRC were planning on issuing exposure drafts relating to the triennial review in two phases. The Phase 1 exposure draft was scheduled for issuance towards the end of the first quarter of 2017 and the Phase 2 exposure draft (which will contain proposals for changes to lease accounting) is scheduled for issuance towards the end of the third quarter of 2017.

28 Finance leases

9.32 A finance lease is a lease that transfers substantially all the risks and rewards of ownership of an asset to the lessee. Whilst there are a number of factors to consider, paragraph 20.5 and 20.6 of FRS 102 outlines various indicators that a lease is a finance lease as follows:

- ownership of the asset is transferred to the lessee at the end of the lease term;
- an option exists in the lease for the lessee to purchase the asset at a lower price than fair value at the date on which the option becomes exercisable and that it is reasonably certain at the inception of the lease that the lessee will exercise this option;
- the term of the lease is for the major part of the useful economic life of the asset being subjected to the lease (regardless of whether title is not transferred);
- at the start of the lease, the present value of the minimum lease payments is equivalent to at least substantially all of the fair value of the leased asset; and

- the asset which is leased is of such a specialised nature that only the lessee can use it without major modifications to the asset being made.

The above indicators can, either individually or in combination, normally lead a lease being classified as a finance lease. There are a further three indicators which could also lead a lease being classified as a finance lease as follows:

- where the lessee can cancel the lease and the lessor's losses associated with the termination of the lease are met by the lessee;
- gains or losses in the residual value of the leased asset accrue to the lessee; and
- the lessee has the ability to continue to lease the asset at the end of the primary lease term at a rent which is substantially lower than market rent (often called a 'peppercorn' rent).

Whilst Section 20 outlines these indicators of a finance lease, the section does acknowledge that these examples are not always conclusive. A key theme in Section 20 is whether the risks and rewards of ownership of the asset passes from the lessor to the lessee. If risks and rewards do not pass from lessor to lessee then the lease is not classed as a finance lease, but is instead classed as an operating lease.

At the inception of a finance lease, both the leased asset and the related finance lease creditor should be recorded on the balance sheet at amounts equal to the fair value of the leased asset or, if lower, the present value of the minimum lease payments, determined at the start of the lease. Any incremental costs associated with the lease (eg fees incurred in negotiating the lease) are added to the cost of the asset. Depreciation should be charged in accordance with the provisions in Section 17 *Property, Plant and Equipment*. Depreciation should be charged over the shorter of the lease term and the estimated useful life of the asset when there is no reasonable certainty that the lessee will obtain ownership by the end of the lease term.

Each rental payment is split between the finance charge (the interest) and the capital element. This is done using the *effective interest method*. The effective interest method is a method of calculating the amortised cost of a financial asset or financial liability and then allocating the interest income or interest expense over the relevant period.

Example – lessee accounting calculations for a lease liability

An item of machinery with a useful life of ten years can be purchased outright by an LLP for £42,800. Alternatively, use of the asset may be obtained by means of a finance lease.

Under this arrangement, the LLP (the lessee) would be responsible for insurance and maintenance and would be required to make five annual payments of £11,600 all payable in advance. After the primary period of five years, the lessee would have the option to continue leasing the asset for an indefinite period for a nominal (a 'peppercorn') rental.

It is assumed that the fair value of £42,800 provides an acceptable approximation to the present value of the minimum lease payments determined at the inception of the lease, discounted at the interest rate implicit in the lease.

The interest rate implicit in the lease can be calculated using the internal rate of return function in Excel. To calculate this, use the amount capitalised (£42,800) as the opening liability and ensure this is a negative value in the spreadsheet. Then include the five annual payments of £11,600, hence the spreadsheet will show:

Cell A1: (£42,800)

Cell A2: £11,600

Cell A3: £11,600

Cell A4: £11,600

Cell A5: £11,600

Cell A6: £11,600

The formula will be =IRR(A1:A6) and this calculates the effective interest rate to be 11.07% and this is the rate used to allocate the interest over the life of the lease as follows:

Year	Liability b/f	Interest @ 11.07%	Cash flow	Liability c/f
	£	£	£	£
1	42,800	4,738	(11,600)	35,938
2	35,938	3,978	(11,600)	28,316
3	28,316	3,135	(11,600)	19,851
4	19,851	2,198	(11,600)	10,449
5	10,449	1,151	(11,600)	-
		15,200		

The net book value of assets held under finance leases is required to be disclosed in the accounts, along with the depreciation charged thereon. In year 1, the LLP will account for the finance lease as follows:

Dr Property, plant and equipment	£42,800
Cr Finance lease creditor	£42,800

Being fixed asset acquired under a finance lease

Dr Interest paid (profit and loss)	£4,738
Cr Finance lease creditor	£4,738

Being year 1 interest calculated using the effective interest method

Dr Finance lease creditor £11,600
Cr Cash at bank £11,600
Being payment to finance lease company

29 Operating leases

9.33 An operating lease is a lease which does not transfer substantially all of the risks and rewards incidental to ownership. Rentals payable under an operating lease should be charged on a straight-line basis over the lease term, unless:

- another systematic basis represents the time pattern of the LLP's benefit (this can apply even if the payments are not made on this basis); or
- payments to the lessor are structured in such a way so as to increase in line with expected general inflation (which is based on published indexes or statistics) to compensate for the lessor's expected inflationary cost increases. However, it should be kept in mind that if payments to the lessor vary because of factors other than general inflation, this condition will not be met.

Property leases give rise to two particular situations where the cash rental payments may be different from the amount that should be charged to the profit and loss account. These are: (1) where an LLP has been granted a rent-free period; and (2) where it is paying rent on vacant property.

In negotiating a new lease or renewing an existing lease, the lessor may provide incentives for the LLP to enter into the agreement. Examples of such incentives are an upfront cash payment to the lessee or an initial period of the lease term that may be rent-free or at a reduced rent. The nature of the incentives must be examined to establish if they are for the lessee's or the lessor's benefit. This is important because the financial statements must reflect the substance of the transaction.

Lease incentives are dealt with in paragraph 20.15A of FRS 102. Assuming the lease incentive is for the benefit of the lessee, the financial effect (regardless of the form the incentive takes) should be spread over the period of the lease (which is usually on a straight-line basis). This accounting treatment is somewhat different than under previous UK GAAP (UITF 28 *Operating lease incentives*) which required the incentive to be spread over the shorter of the lease term and a period ending on a date from which it is expected the prevailing market rental will be payable.

Example – lease incentive calculation

An LLP is negotiating a ten-year lease. The annual rental will be £20,000 but it is agreed that the lessee will be entitled to an incentive of a rent-free period for the first six months.

The lease incentive is £10,000 (six-months rent-free) and paragraph 20.15A says that this should be spread over the lease term (ten years) hence £1,000 per annum, so the rental expense in profit and loss will be £19,000 per annum net of the lease incentive.

The total payment to the lessor over the ten-year period will be £190,000 and the annual lease expense will be £190,000/10 years = £19,000. The LLP's balance sheet at the end of year 1 will show an accrual of £9,000 (the annual expense of £19,000 less the payment made in the first year of £10,000).

Provisions for vacant property are dealt with in **9.8** above.

Events after the end of the reporting period

30 Accounting for events after the reporting period

9.34 The Regulations require that all liabilities and losses which have arisen, or are likely to arise, relating to the period prior to the balance sheet date should be taken into account – either by way of recognition within the financial statements or by way of disclosure. This includes those which only become apparent between the balance sheet date and the date on which the accounts are approved by the members. Such items are referred to as 'events after the end of the reporting period' (often referred to as 'post balance sheet events') the accounting for which is dealt with in Section 32 *Events after the End of the Reporting Period.*

Section 32 distinguishes between two types of event:

- adjusting events; and
- non-adjusting events.

31 Adjusting events

9.35 Adjusting events are those occurring after the balance sheet date which provide additional evidence of conditions which were in existence at that date. The accounts should be changed to take account of this additional evidence. Examples of adjusting events include:

- The subsequent determination of the purchase price or of the proceeds of sale of assets purchased or sold before the year end.
- A valuation of a property that provides evidence of an impairment in value.
- The receipt of a copy of the financial statements or other information in respect of an unlisted company in which the LLP has an interest that provides evidence of an impairment in the value of a long-term investment.
- The receipt of proceeds of sales after the balance sheet date or other evidence concerning the estimated selling price (or fair/market value) of stocks.
- The receipt of evidence that the previous estimate of accrued profit on a long-term contract was materially inaccurate.

- The renegotiation of amounts owing by debtors or the insolvency of a debtor.
- The discovery of errors or frauds which show that the financial statements were incorrect.

Events after the balance sheet date which indicate a deterioration in operating results and in the financial position of the LLP may highlight issues as to whether the accounts should be prepared on a going concern basis (see Chapter 10).

Example – discovery of fraud

An LLP has an accounting reference date of 30 April. The LLP has prepared its financial statements for the year-ended 30 April 2018 and the auditors completed their detailed on-site fieldwork on 27 June 2018. During the audit work, the audit senior noticed large cash discrepancies throughout the year which had been written off to sundry expenses within the LLP's profit and loss account to agree the bank reconciliation statement. The audit manager and audit senior calculated that the value of the cash discrepancies amounted to £75,000 which is considered material to the financial statements. It was later found that a member of the accounts staff at the LLP had been stealing cash on a regular basis due to a distinct lack of segregation of duties and controls over the cash cycle within the accounts department.

The financial statements of the LLP should be adjusted to reflect the discovery of the fraud. This accords with the requirements in Section 32 of FRS 102 at paragraph 32.5(e) which says that the discovery of fraud or errors are adjusting events after the end of the reporting period and therefore should be adjusted within the financial statements.

Example – settlement of a court case

An LLP has a year-end date of 31 March 2018. At that date the company was in dispute with one of its clients who had brought a legal claim against the firm. The client alleged suffering financial loss due to advice received from the LLP. At the year-end date the legal advisers were not able to confirm whether the LLP would be successful in its defence and, as such, the accountant made disclosure of a contingent liability.

On 23 June 2018 (some three days before the financial statements were to be authorised for issue by the members), the court found in favour of the client and ordered the LLP to pay damages of £20,000 plus legal fees of £7,000. The accountant has suggested that the contingent liability disclosure remain within the financial statements and the damages and costs be accounted for within the 2019 financial statements.

Paragraph 32.5(a) is specific on such issues. The settlement of a court case after the end of a reporting period is an adjusting event. While the company was not able to recognise a provision in accordance with Section 21 *Provisions and Contingencies* due to the recognition criteria not being met, the LLP is now required to create a new provision in accordance with Section 32 at paragraph 32.5(a). This particular paragraph is also specific in that the entity must not merely disclose a contingent liability because the settlement provides additional evidence to be considered in determining whether the recognition criteria for a provision has been met in accordance with Section 21 to FRS 102.

---

32 Non-adjusting events

9.36 Non-adjusting events relate to conditions which did not exist at the balance sheet date. They do not result in the LLP's financial statements requiring amendment, but should be disclosed if they are material and hence non-disclosure would affect the ability of users of the accounts to have a proper understanding of the financial position of the LLP. Section 32 includes the following examples of non-adjusting events:

- A major business combination after the balance sheet date or disposal of a major subsidiary.
- Announcing a plan to discontinue an operation.
- Major purchases and disposals of assets, or expropriation of major assets by government.
- The destruction of a major production plant by a fire after the balance sheet date.
- Announcing or commencing the implementation of a major restructuring.
- Issues or repurchases of the LLP's debt instruments.
- Abnormally large changes after the balance sheet date in asset prices or foreign exchange rates.
- Entering into significant commitments or contingent liabilities, for example, by issuing significant guarantees.
- Commencing major litigation arising solely out of events that occurred after the balance sheet date.

Whilst these are listed as non-adjusting events, the circumstances surrounding them should always be considered. In some cases, it may be that they are the best indicator of circumstances at the balance sheet date where no other evidence is available.

Example – contingent asset

LLP A instigated legal proceedings against Company B Ltd on 20 April 2018 because Company B had failed to comply with the terms of a contract to supply goods. As a result of its failure to adhere to the terms of the contract, LLP A has suffered significant losses due to its customers sourcing alternative goods elsewhere. LLP A has a year-end of 31 July 2018.

Company B Ltd has filed a defence with the court and the case was heard on 2 August 2018. Prior to the court case, LLP A's legal advisers were not able to reliably estimate any potential costs which may become refundable if LLP A was successful in its case. However, the court ordered that Company B pay costs of £15,000. The accounts manager at LLP A is proposing to recognise this reimbursement of cost as a debtor in the financial statements to 31 July 2018.

Paragraph 32.7(b) states that an amount that becomes receivable as a result of a favourable judgement or settlement of a court case after the reporting date, but before the financial statements are issued, is a contingent asset at the reporting date. As a result, the LLP would be unable to recognise a receivable, but would instead make disclosure of a contingent asset.

Related parties

33 The source of disclosure requirements

9.37 The Companies Act 2006 contains specific legislation and disclosure requirements aimed at preventing directors from taking financial advantage from their position. The special relationship that exists between an LLP and its members means that none of this is reproduced in the Regulations. The only disclosure requirements contained within the Regulations are those which deal generally with members' interests (see Chapter 5).

LLPs do, however, have to comply with the full and more onerous requirements of Section 33 *Related Party Disclosures*.

34 The general requirements of Section 33

9.38 The objective of Section 33 is to ensure that the LLP's financial statements contain the disclosures necessary to draw attention to the possibility that the reported financial position and results may have been affected by the existence of related parties and by material transactions with them. Section 33 requires disclosure of a material transaction undertaken by the LLP with a related party, irrespective of whether a price is charged. Where the LLP is controlled by another party, disclosure is required of the name of that controlling party, irrespective of whether any transactions have taken place with it.

The SORP outlines issues concerning related parties in paragraphs 128 to 131. Small LLPs reporting under Section 1A *Small Entities* of FRS 102 are required to comply with the disclosure requirements of this section (related party disclosures are in Appendix C *Disclosure requirements for small entities*) in Section 1A.

35 Identifying related parties

9.39 Under Section 33 of FRS 102, a related party is a person (or entity) which is related to the LLP preparing financial statements (a reporting LLP). In addition:

- A person or a close family member of that person is related to the reporting LLP if that person:
  - — has control, or joint control, over the reporting LLP;
  - — has significant influence over the reporting LLP; or

  - — is a member of the key management personnel of the reporting LLP or of a parent of the reporting LLP.

Section 33 then goes on to explain about how businesses may be related to a reporting LLP. This occurs when any of the following conditions apply:

- the entity and the reporting LLP are members of the same group (meaning each parent, subsidiary and fellow subsidiary is related to the others);
- the entity is an associate or joint venture of the LLP;
- both parties are joint ventures of the same party;
- one party is a joint venture of a third party and the other party is an associate of the third party;
- the entity is a post-employment benefit plan for the benefit of employees of either the reporting LLP or an entity related to the reporting LLP. If the reporting LLP is itself such a post-employment benefit plan, the sponsoring employees are also related to the reporting LLP;
- the entity is controlled or jointly controlled by a person or a close family member of that person related to the reporting LLP; and
- the party is an entity that is controlled, jointly controlled or significantly influenced by, or for which significant voting power in such entity resides with directly or indirectly, any individual referred to above or is a member of the key management personnel.

The Glossary to FRS 102 defines control as *'the power to govern the financial and operating policies of an entity so as to obtain benefits from its activities.'* Common control is deemed to exist when both parties are subject to control from boards having a controlling nucleus of directors or members in common.

The difference between control and influence is that control brings with it the ability to cause the controlled party to subordinate its separate interests, whereas the outcome of the exercise of influence is less certain.

Where one party has influence over the financial and operating policies of the other party to an extent that the other party might be inhibited from pursuing, at all times, its own separate interests; or where the parties, in entering into a transaction, were subject to influence from the same source to such an extent that one of the parties to the transaction subordinated its own separate interests, then in both of these situations, control is said to exist and the two parties are deemed related.

The term 'key management personnel' should not be interpreted to mean that all members of an LLP are to be automatically regarded as related parties. Whether the members are related will depend upon the degree of control they have over the day-to-day activities of the LLP. In a small LLP, it may be the case that all the members are directly involved in its management and, as such, should be regarded as related. However, in a large LLP, management may be devolved to a small number of members who should be presumed to be related. The reference to key management in Section 33 means that designated members will usually be related parties. In certain circumstances, key management personnel may also include individuals who are not members of the LLP, for example the Head of Finance or the Head of Human Resources.

The fact that some members of an LLP are also members of another LLP is not of itself sufficient to make the two entities related. The extent to which they have control of both LLPs, and are in a position to influence transactions between the two entities, will have to be considered.

The issue surrounding close family members of a related party has been clarified in Section 33 to FRS 102. Section 33 regards a related party's children, spouse and domestic partner and the dependants of a person or his/her spouse or domestic partner to be related parties (this is also clarified it the definition of 'close members of the family a person' in the Glossary to FRS 102).

36 Identifying related party transactions

9.40 A transaction is entered into with a related party when the LLP provides goods, services or incurs obligations with a related party. A key point to emphasise where this concept is concerned is that a price does *not* have to be charged for the related good, service or obligation. The idea behind related party disclosures is to ensure that the user can understand that the reported financial results may have been affected by the existence of related parties and transactions with those related parties. Regardless of whether a price is charged or not, if the transaction is a material related party transaction ('material' being in the context of both monetary amount and nature) then it should be disclosed in the financial statements.

The following are some examples of transactions that would need disclosure if they are with a related party:

- purchases or sales of goods which covers both finished and unfinished goods;
- the purchase or sale of property or other assets;
- rendering or receipt of services;
- transactions involving lease arrangements;
- the transfer of research or development;
- transfers under licence agreements;
- transfers that arise through financing arrangements (for example a loan);
- guarantees and collateral;
- the settlement of liabilities on behalf of the LLP or by the LLP on behalf of another related party; and
- the participation by a parent or a subsidiary in a defined benefit pension plan that shares risks between the members of the group.

37 Exemptions from disclosure

9.41 There are some exemptions from disclosure, and these are set out below:

- in a parent LLP's accounts, transactions with wholly-owned subsidiaries;
- in wholly-owned subsidiary entities accounts, transactions with their parent and with other subsidiaries that are wholly-owned within the group;
- remuneration in respect of services as an employee;
- a state (whether it is a national, regional or local government) that has control, joint control or significant influence over the LLP; and
- another entity which is a related party because the same state has control, joint control or significant influence over both the reporting LLP and the other entity.

38 Information that should be disclosed

9.42 For each related party transaction, the following should be disclosed:

- Details of parent-subsidiary relationships regardless of whether there have been any transactions between the related parties. The reporting LLP must disclose the name of its parent and, if different, the ultimate controlling party.
- Compensation paid to key management personnel in total.
- A description of the relationship between the LLP and the other party.
- Information relating to the related party transactions which should also include:
  - the amounts involved;
  - outstanding balances at the reporting date including terms and conditions, whether the outstanding balances are secured and the nature of the consideration to be provided in discharging the obligation as well as any guarantees given or received by the LLP;
  - any provision for doubtful debts due from related parties; and
  - amounts written off in the period in respect of debts due to or from related parties.

Comparative information should also be presented.

The above disclosures are required to be separately presented for each of the following categories:

- entities with control, joint control or significant influence over the entity;
- entities over which the LLP has control, joint control or significant influence;
- key management personnel of the LLP or its parent (in totality); and
- other related parties.

39 Small LLPs

9.43 Paragraph 27A to the SORP requires small LLPs qualifying for, and choosing to, apply the small entities' regime to comply with the disclosure requirements of Section 1A of FRS 102 rather than the disclosure requirements of the SORP.

Related party issues for small LLPs are less onerous than the requirements of Section 33 of FRS 102. Paragraph 1AC.34 requires the following information in respect of the parent of the smallest group for which consolidated financial statements are drawn up of which the small LLP is a member:

(a) the name of the parent which draws up the consolidated financial statements;

(b) the address of the parent's registered office (whether in or outside the UK); or

(c) if it is unincorporated, the address of its principal place of business.

Section 1A does not require disclosure of all related party transactions. Indeed, the disclosure requirements of Section 1A in FRS 102 are less onerous than in Section 33 and a small LLP need only disclose those material transactions which it has entered into with:

- owners holding a participating interest in the small LLP;
- entities in which the small LLP has a participating interest; and
- the small LLP's members,

which have not been carried out under normal market conditions. FRS 102 does not define what 'normal market conditions' are and hence the advice is to carefully consider the arrangement and then arrive at a conclusion as to whether the transaction has, or has not, been concluded under normal market conditions. If the conclusion is that the transaction has been concluded under normal market conditions, no disclosure is required. However, if the conclusion is that the transaction has not been concluded under normal market conditions, disclosure must include:

(a) the amount of such transactions;

(b) the nature of the related party relationship; and

(c) other information about the transactions which are necessary for an understanding to be obtained about the financial position of the small LLP.

In practice, it may be challenging to decipher whether a transaction has, or has not, been concluded under normal market conditions. Paragraph 1AC.35 of FRS 102 only requires disclosure of material transactions with specified related parties that have not been concluded under normal market conditions. However, a small LLP may choose to disclose all transactions with such related parties and if this is the case, the small LLP would still be complying with legislation.

Focus

- The SORP acknowledges that the accounts of small LLPs must give a true and fair view. As a result, judgement will be needed when considering whether disclosures over and above the requirements of Section 1A are needed to achieve a true and fair view. This is particularly relevant to related parties. In addition, the SORP requires small LLPs to make the disclosures about how loans and other debts due to members rank in relation to other unsecured creditors. Such a disclosure is not required under FRS 102, Section 1A, but is a requirement of the SORP to enable the LLP's financial statements to give a true and fair view. This is because LLPs do not have any of the capital maintenance provisions that apply to companies.

Chapter summary

- There are certain sections of FRS 102 which will be particularly relevant to LLPs and these must be carefully considered during the preparation of the LLP's financial statements.
- Provisions for liabilities can only be recognised when the criteria in Section 21 *Provisions and Contingencies* has been met. Contingent assets and contingent liabilities are not recognised in the financial statements, but are instead disclosed.
- An obligation can either be a legal obligation or a constructive obligation.
- Retirement benefits to members of the LLPs can pose particularly complex challenges for preparers of LLP financial statements.
- Retirement benefits can arise via a defined contribution or a defined benefit pension plan and the accounting treatment for both types of plans are significantly different.
- Tangible fixed assets can only be recognised on a balance sheet when it is probable (ie more likely than not) that future economic benefits associated with the asset will flow to the LLP and the cost of the asset can be reliably measured.
- After initial recognition, an item of property, plant and equipment can be measured at historic cost or revaluation; although the revaluation model is unavailable to micro-entity LLPs reporting under FRS 105.
- FRS 102 places more emphasis on the use of 'component accounting'.
- Assets must be reviewed for indicators of impairment at each balance sheet date and impairments are to be accounted for under the provisions of Section 27 *Impairment of Assets* in FRS 102.
- Leases are dealt with in Section 20 *Leases* and the concept of 'finance' and 'operating' leases is recognised.
- The Financial Reporting Council have intimated that they intend to overhaul lease accounting to bring FRS 102 in line with IFRS 16 *Leases* in the future.

- The interest in a finance lease is accounted for using the effective interest method.
- Financial statements of LLPs must consider events after the end of the reporting period and such events can be adjusting events or non-adjusting events.
- Related party transactions are dealt with in Section 33 *Related Parties* in FRS 102 and there are specific disclosure requirements for transactions with related parties. Small LLPs have less onerous disclosure requirements where they comply with Section 1A *Small Entities* of FRS 102.

Chapter 10

Going concern

Signposts

- LLPs will prepare financial statements on a going concern basis when it is expected the LLP will continue in business for the foreseeable future (see **10.1**).
- If the LLP is going to be liquidated, cease trading or the members have no realistic alternative but to liquidate the LLP or cease trading, an alternative basis is used for preparing the financial statements (see **10.1**).
- Going concern is considered to be a material concept in all entities – regardless of whether they are cash-rich and profit-making or not (see **10.1**).
- Auditors may qualify their auditor's report if there are uncertainties surrounding the going concern presumption and adequate disclosures have not been made in the financial statements (see **10.1**).
- The members are responsible for assessing the going concern of the LLP when preparing the financial statements (see **10.2**).
- Auditors should consider whether the members have undertaken an assessment of going concern for a period of at least 12 months from the date of approval of the financial statements (not 12 months from the balance sheet date) (see **10.2**).
- There are a number of risk factors which can be regarded as being indicative of a potential going concern problem (see **10.3**).
- If an LLP is part of a group and is relying on its parent or another member of the group for financial support, confirmation should be obtained in writing (see **10.4**).
- There are three possible conclusions relating to an assessment of going concern (see **10.5**).
- Members should ensure disclosure notes are adequate where there is significant doubt about the going concern of an LLP (see **10.6**).
- Auditors will usually consider the going concern presumption up to the point at which the auditor's report is to be signed (see **10.7**).
- Any concerns the auditor has relating to going concern will be discussed with the LLPs members and management and there are certain issues relating to the going concern assessment which the auditor will pay close attention to (see **10.8**).
- The auditor can express various opinions depending on the effect of going concern assessments (see **10.9**).

1 The going concern concept

10.1 Going concern is a fundamental principle underlying the preparation of the accounts of all entities. Accordingly, the majority of LLP accounts will be prepared on the basis that the LLP will continue in operational existence for the foreseeable future, known as the 'going concern basis'. The term 'foreseeable future' is taken to mean for a period of at least 12 months from the date of approval of the LLP's financial statements. The Limited Liability Partnership Act (LLPA) states that an LLP is presumed to be carrying on business as a going concern unless the accounts say otherwise. Application of Section 3 *Financial Statement Presentation* to FRS 102 *The Financial Reporting Standard applicable in the UK and Republic of Ireland* also requires that an LLP should prepare its accounts on the going concern basis, unless the LLP is being liquidated or has ceased trading, or the members have no realistic alternative but to liquidate the LLP or to cease trading. In these circumstances, it may be appropriate to prepare the accounts on an alternative basis (normally the 'break-up' basis). Paragraph 3.9 to FRS 102 does not make specific reference to the 'break-up' basis, but says that where there are material uncertainties which cast doubt on the LLP's ability to continue as a going concern, and hence the LLP does not prepare accounts under the going concern basis, the basis on which the financial statements are prepared is disclosed.

Going concern is a central issue to all LLP's regardless of whether they are profitable and cash-rich. Indeed, unforeseen events may take place even in the most profitable of LLP's which may call the ability for the LLP to continue as a going concern into question. In times of economic difficulties (eg recession) going concern needs to be very carefully considered and the auditors need to ensure that sufficient and appropriate audit evidence is obtained where the LLP's going concern status is concerned. In some cases, the auditors may deem the going concern basis to be inappropriate in the LLP's circumstances which could have implications for the auditor's overall conclusion on the financial statements.

In preparing the accounts, the members will need to carry out such procedures as they consider necessary to satisfy themselves as to whether the going concern basis is appropriate. There may be factors about the business which cast doubt as to the going concern status of the LLP, for example a downturn in profitability or the renegotiation of necessary bank facilities, the outcome of which negotiations may be unknown at the time of approving the financial statements. In these circumstances, the members will need to consider the actions that can be taken to mitigate those concerns. Disclosure of both the concerns and the mitigating action, together with why the members consider the accounts give a true and fair view of the position of the LLP, is required in the accounts.

Focus

- The SORP requires LLPs which are classed as small to comply with the disclosure requirements of Section 1A *Small Entities* in FRS 102. Going concern disclosures for small LLPs are not mandatory under Section 1A but are, instead, an encouraged disclosure under paragraph 1AD.1(c). Members are advised to make adequate going concern disclosures when there are material uncertainties relating to going concern so that the financial statements give a true and fair view.

Where there are uncertainties associated with the ability of the LLP to continue as a going concern, and the accounts do not include sufficient disclosure, the accounts may not give a true and fair view (this is particularly the case for small LLPs where disclosure of going concern is encouraged rather than mandated), and this will be considered by the auditors who, as a consequence, may qualify their audit opinion. The effect on an auditor's report relating to the going concern presumption is considered later in the chapter.

Section 3 to FRS 102 considers the presentation of financial statements under the going concern presumption and also specifies the actions to be taken by the members when they consider the going concern presumption to be inappropriate in the LLP's circumstances.

Example – cessation of trade after the reporting period

An LLP is preparing financial statements to 31 December 2017. Over the last couple of years, the LLP has seen a decline in profitability and on 3 March 2018 one of its major customers ceased trading with immediate effect. The liquidators of the customer have confirmed that once the liquidation is complete there will be no funds available to pay unsecured creditors (of which the LLP is one of those unsecured creditors). The LLP's bank has also refused to renew borrowing facilities which are due for renewal on 1 April 2018 and the bank have also 'called in' the overdraft. The members have all agreed unanimously that they have no alternative but to also cease to trade with immediate effect. The question arises as to whether the financial statements as at 31 December 2017 should be prepared on a going concern basis in view of the fact that the customer ceased trading and the bank have refused to renew borrowing facilities after the year-end date has passed.

The concept of going concern is also considered in FRS 102 at Section 32 *Events after the End of the Reporting Period*. In this context, FRS 102 prohibits an LLP from preparing its financial statements under the going concern concept if, after the end of the reporting period, the members determine it necessary to either liquidate the LLP or to cease trading, or have no realistic alternative but to cease trading. As a result, the LLP must not prepare the financial statements under the going concern basis but on an alternative basis (eg the break-up basis).

The above example is an illustration of an issue which might arise after the LLP's year-end has passed. When the members of an LLP conclude that the going concern basis cannot be used to prepare the financial statements, the effect is so pervasive that Section 32 requires a fundamental change in the basis of accounting as opposed to merely adjusting the amounts recognised within the original basis of accounting. In the example above, the requirements in paragraph 3.9 would apply and the LLP should disclose:

- any material uncertainties the LLP may have in making its assessment of the LLP's ability to continue as a going concern; and
- when the LLP does not prepare its financial statements under the going concern basis, it should disclose that fact and the basis on which the LLP has prepared its financial statements (eg a break-up basis).

2 Evidence supporting going concern assessments

10.2 Paragraph 3.8 to FRS 102 requires that, when preparing accounts, the members should assess whether there are significant doubts about the LLP's ability to continue as a going concern. This assessment is required to be made for what is termed the 'foreseeable future'. The term 'foreseeable future' is not defined in accounting standards; however, disclosure is required where the review period considered by members is less than one year from the date of approval of the accounts (not the accounting period end). UK auditing standards (specifically ISA (UK) 570 *Going Concern*) requires that, where the period considered is less than one year from the date the accounts are approved and this fact is not disclosed, it should be referred to in the auditor's report. As a consequence of these requirements, most LLPs will consider a period of at least 12 months from the date of approval of the accounts.

Care needs to be taken with the application of ISA (UK) 570 to ensure that the review period is correct (ie 12 months from the date of approval of the financial statements) because this differs from the mainstream ISA 570 *Going* Concern issued by the International Auditing and Assurance Standards Board which says the review period should be 12 months from the date of the financial statements. The UK version of this standard is more stringent in its approach.

The extent of evidence required to support the members' assessment of going concern will depend on a number of factors. These include:

- The extent to which the LLP's financial resources exceed its requirements.
- The size and complexity of the LLP's operations.
- The extent to which the LLP is operating in a high-risk industry.

For some LLPs, where they are trading profitably and have adequate working capital available, the extent of documented evidence could be fairly limited.

In other cases, where the position is less certain, it may be necessary to prepare cash flow projections for subsequent periods comparing these with available, or likely to be available, facilities. Where such projections are considered necessary, they should be completed in sufficient detail to take full account of both future trading and the impact of any major transactions, such as proposed acquisitions or major capital investment programmes.

It is the members' responsibility to consider whether (or not) the going concern basis is appropriate in the LLP's circumstances and the assessment needs to be carefully considered in light of all facts pertinent to the LLP. If the LLP is subjected to external audit, the auditors will not be responsible for considering whether the going concern basis is appropriate, but instead they will be responsible for obtaining sufficient and appropriate audit evidence concerning the members' adoption of the going concern basis and whether the auditors are in agreement that this basis is appropriate. If the auditors disagree and adequate disclosure is not made, there will be implications for the auditor's opinion.

3 Risk factors indicating a significant level of concern

10.3 Whether something is significant or not will depend on the circumstances of the individual LLP. There are, however, a number of risk factors that can be regarded as being indicative of a potential going concern problem. These include:

General business considerations

- Fundamental changes in the market or technology to which the LLP cannot adapt adequately.
- Regulatory changes to which the LLP cannot adapt.
- Political or 'global' factors which may cause a significant effect on the LLP's operations.
- Loss of particular skills or technical expertise which might give it an advantage over competitors.
- The existence of major litigation, where an adverse judgment would imperil the LLP's continued existence or seriously damage its reputation.

General financial considerations

- The LLP's accounts indicate an excess of liabilities over assets.
- The LLP's accounts indicate net current liabilities.
- Significant liquidity or cash flow problems.
- Inability to pay creditors by the due dates.
- Deteriorating relationship with bankers or financiers.
- Denial of trade credit.
- Major losses or cash flow problems since the balance sheet date.
- The LLP has provided significant loans or guarantees, and there is a threat that these might be called in or that the borrower may not be able to make repayments.
- The LLP is dependent on financial support provided by another party (for example, a parent entity or fellow group member), and there is concern that the other party may be unable to provide the level of support needed to enable the LLP to stay in business.
- Cash flow forecasts suggesting net cash outflows.

Difficulties with external financing

- The LLP has experienced difficulties in the past in obtaining external finance facilities and/or complying with the related terms and covenants.
- The LLP has recently undertaken, or is planning to undertake, a major restructuring of debt.
- Borrowing facilities are under negotiation or are due for renewal in the next year.

- There are no planned alternative arrangements should current facilities not be extended.
- Borrowing agreements or executory contracts include clauses relating to debt covenants or subjective clauses (for example, a 'material adverse change' clause) that may trigger a request for repayment.
- The LLP has breached some of the terms or covenants, giving rise to the risk that the facilities may be withdrawn or not renewed.
- Terms or covenants of renewed financing are changed and become more difficult to comply with (for example, increased interest rates or charges).
- The finance facility is secured on assets (for example, properties) that have decreased in value below the amount of the facility.

Dependence on counterparties

- Loss of key members or staff.
- Loss of key customers.
- Evidence that suppliers providing essential goods or services are facing financial difficulties.
- Denial of (or reduction in) normal terms of trade by suppliers.
- The LLP is unable to find alternative suppliers.

The indicators above are not designed to be an 'exhaustive' list and there may be other indicators that the LLP's ability to continue as a going concern is called into question. Essentially, where there is material uncertainty relating to the LLP's ability to continue as a going concern then adequate disclosure should be made in the financial statements.

Example – material uncertainty relating to going concern

An LLP is preparing its financial statements for the year-ended 31 December 2017. 90% of the LLP's income is derived from a government contract which was awarded to the LLP in 2014 for a period of three years.

The contract ends on 31 March 2018 and the LLP is currently putting together a proposal to re-tender for the contract. If the contract is not awarded to the LLP this will cast significant doubt on its ability to continue in existence for the foreseeable future. The government's deadline for the tenders is 30 April 2018 and a decision is expected to be made by 30 June 2018. The LLP is confident that they will be awarded the contract for a further three-years and the financial statements are due to be approved by the members on 30 April 2018.

Clearly there is a material uncertainty regarding the LLP's ability to continue as a going concern because they will not know the outcome of their tender until the end of June 2018, by which time the financial statements will have been approved. The LLP should make adequate disclosure in their financial statements about this material uncertainty and, assuming the disclosures made by the LLP are judged to be adequate, the auditors should include a paragraph headed 'Material Uncertainty Related to Going Concern' paragraph within their report which cross-references the user to the relevant note in the LLP's financial statements.

Focus

- Under the previous ISA (UK and Ireland) 570, any going concern uncertainties would have been included in an Emphasis of Matter paragraph. This requirement changed in the revisions to ISA (UK) 570 and hence where adequate disclosure of a material uncertainty is made in the LLP's financial statements, paragraph 22 of ISA (UK) 570 now requires a separate section under the heading 'Material Uncertainty Related to Going Concern' as opposed to the use of an Emphasis of Matter paragraph.

4 Reliance on the support of other entities within a group

10.4 Where an LLP which is part of a group relies upon its parent or another member of that group for financial support, confirmation should be obtained in writing. This is usually done by way of a 'letter of support' (or 'comfort letter') issued by the parent to the LLP. The members of the LLP will need to satisfy themselves that the parent is in a strong enough financial position to provide the necessary support. The auditors will require sight of the letter of support, and will also carry out their own procedures in relation to the financial position of the parent and its ability to provide additional support were the LLP to need it. This is because the auditors cannot simply rely on the letter of support from the parent as it is internally-generated – audit evidence must be sufficient and appropriate.

In some cases, a letter of support may be required from the LLP to a subsidiary where that entity's ability to continue as a going concern is dependent upon financial support from the LLP. The LLP should consider the effect such support will have on its own ability to continue in operational existence.

5 Conclusions in relation to going concern

10.5 Once the members have carried out their assessment, there are three possible conclusions:

- there are no material uncertainties that lead to significant doubt about the LLP's ability to continue as a going concern;
- there are material uncertainties that lead to significant doubt about the LLP's ability to continue as a going concern, but the going concern basis remains appropriate; or
- the use of the going concern basis is not appropriate.

Generally, an LLP will not make any disclosures within the financial statements when there are no material uncertainties which lead to significant doubt about the ability of the LLP to continue as a going concern. However, where there are significant doubts about the LLP's ability to continue as a going concern, adequate disclosures should be made in the LLP's financial statements.

6 Disclosure where there is significant doubt

10.6 The adequacy of disclosure made by the members will be assessed by the auditors, but the disclosure will not normally be regarded as adequate, unless it contains the following:

- A statement of the specific nature of the material uncertainties that give rise to significant doubt.
- A statement of the assumptions made by the members, which should be clearly distinguishable from the relevant facts.
- Where appropriate and practicable, a statement regarding the members' plans for resolving the matters giving rise to the uncertainty.
- Details of any relevant actions taken by the members.
- An explanation of why the going concern basis has been adopted.

These statements should be given reasonable prominence within the accounts, and are usually best positioned in the accounting policies note under the 'Basis of preparation' heading although it is not uncommon for some LLP's to make these disclosures under a separate 'Going concern' heading.

Due to the pervasive nature of going concern, if the disclosures are considered to be inadequate by the auditors it will have an impact on the auditor's opinion. In all cases the auditors will try to resolve any issues as the auditors would ordinarily only issue a qualified opinion as a 'last resort'

All LLPs, whether audited or not, must ensure that any uncertainties relating to going concern are adequately disclosed as the members have a duty to prepare financial statements which give a true and fair view. This requirement also applies to small LLPs.

7 Reassessment prior to approving the accounts

10.7 The members' assessment of going concern, and the information supporting that assessment, will usually be prepared at a date in advance of the accounts being approved. In addition, the auditors may perform some of their work on the appropriateness of the going concern basis whilst carrying out other fieldwork. This may be completed some time before the accounts are approved. At the time that the accounts are approved, the members will need to revisit their assessment and consider any further factors that have come to light up until the date the accounts are approved. The auditors will similarly need to update their procedures, both by discussion with the members and by review of any further evidence which has become available.

Care needs to be taken by all parties where the reassessment is concerned. This is because the date of approval of the financial statements and the date of the auditor's report will normally take place on the same day. All events and transactions which may give rise to going concern issues need to be considered and therefore users' of the LLP's financial statements will expect that all such issues have been taken into consideration up to and including the date of approval of the financial statements and the date of the auditor's report. Auditors must therefore ensure that the work they carry out on the LLP's going concern presumption is as near to the date of the auditor's report as possible. Failing to do this may result in a failing to detect a material transaction or event that could call into question the LLP's ability to continue as a going concern and hence increase audit risk (the risk that the auditor forms an incorrect opinion on the financial statements).

8 Assessments made by auditors

10.8 In carrying out their work, the auditors will need to assess whether the going concern concept is appropriate and also consider the adequacy of any disclosures about the LLP's ability to continue as a going concern that are made in the accounts. It is *not* the auditor's responsibility to conclude whether the LLP is a going concern – this is the responsibility of the members. The auditor's responsibility is to obtain sufficient and appropriate audit evidence to corroborate the members' assertion about the going concern status of the LLP.

The auditors will discuss factors affecting the ability of the LLP to continue in business with the members and the LLP's management, and also examine the financial information available to support the members' opinion, such as the latest management accounts or budgets and projections. They may also request copies of other supporting details, such as correspondence with bankers and other providers of finance.

The auditors will pay particular attention to the following:

- the period covered by the projections;
- how recently those projections have been updated;
- past history as to the reliability of projections prepared by the LLP;
- whether the projected income is reasonable in the context of existing clients and customers and known marketing activity for the future;
- whether assumptions as to profit and levels of work in progress, debtors and creditors are consistent with the history of the business;
- whether projected and necessary capital expenditure has been included;
- whether all payments during the period are taken into account, including members' remuneration and drawings, and annuities to former members;
- whether the assumptions made are consistent with each other;
- whether the assumptions used in respect of financing match what is available to the LLP and whether interest rates utilised are realistic;
- whether consideration has been given to the sensitivity of the projections to changes in the underlying assumptions; and

- that periods where cash is most critical have been identified and that an assessment of headroom above available facilities has been made.

Where critical points within the cash flow are identified, the actions which can be taken by the members to mitigate the impact will also be considered. The above list is **not** an exhaustive list of procedures which the auditor may adopt and further specific procedures may be needed and implemented by the auditor to confirm the appropriateness of the LLP's going concern ability.

9 Effect on the auditor's report

10.9 There are a number of effects that going concern can have on the auditor's report, dependent on the circumstances of the individual LLP. ISA (UK) 570 considers all the permutations of circumstances that can arise, the further procedures the auditor may have to undertake, and the effect on the auditor's report. The effects on the auditor's report are summarised in Table 10.1:

Table 10.1 Effects of going concern assessments on the auditor's report

Situation	Impact on auditor's report
No material uncertainty about ability to continue as a going concern	Unqualified
Material uncertainty about ability to continue as a going concern, but the circumstances are explained fully and adequately in the notes to the accounts	Unqualified report, but with a separate section under the heading 'Material Uncertainty Related to Going concern'
Material uncertainty about the LLP's ability to continue as a going concern, but the circumstances are not explained fully or adequately in the notes to the accounts	Qualified on grounds of disagreement regarding disclosure ('except for') or adverse opinion (accounts do not give a true and fair view)
The auditors are unable to obtain such information and explanations as they consider necessary from the LLP's members' or management	Qualified on grounds of limitation of scope (insufficient evidence) (disclaimer – auditor is unable to say whether the accounts give a true and fair view)
The period to which the members have paid particular attention in assessing the going concern basis is less than one year from the date of approval of the financial statements, and the auditors believe this to be unreasonably short	Disclaimer as a result of limitation of scope (insufficient evidence), possibly with disagreement regarding disclosure if the members have also failed to disclose the period
The period to which the members have paid particular attention in assessing the going concern basis is less than one year from the date of approval of the accounts, but this has been disclosed	Unqualified (including an 'Emphasis of Matter' paragraph where appropriate)

The period to which the members have paid particular attention in assessing the going concern basis is less than one year from the date of approval of the accounts, and the members have not disclosed that fact	Qualified on grounds of disagreement regarding disclosure ('except for')
The auditors disagree with the preparation of the accounts on the going concern basis	Adverse opinion (accounts do not give a true and fair view)
The accounts, in order to give a true and fair view, are prepared on a basis other than the going concern basis	Unqualified. The auditor may include an 'Emphasis of Matter' paragraph, drawing attention to the basis of preparation

---

Example auditor's report extract – use of going concern assumption is appropriate but a material uncertainty exists (based on ISA (UK) 700 (Revised June 2016) *Forming an Opinion and Reporting on Financial Statements*)

Opinion

Express audit opinion.

Basis for Opinion

Include a paragraph describing the basis for the auditor's opinion.

Material Uncertainty Related to Going Concern

Without qualifying our opinion, we draw attention to Note 20 in the financial statements which indicates that the LLP has incurred a net loss of £65,000 during the year ended 31 December 2017 and, as at that date, the LLP's current liabilities exceeded its total assets by £32,000. These conditions, along with other matters as set forth in Note 20, indicate the existence of a material uncertainty that may cast significant doubt about the LLP's ability to continue as a going concern.

Example auditor's report extract – material uncertainty exists but has not been adequately disclosed and a qualified 'except for' opinion is considered appropriate (based on ISA (UK) 700 (Revised June 2016))

Qualified Opinion

In our opinion, except for the incomplete disclosure of the information referred to in the Basis for Qualified Opinion paragraph, the financial statements give a true and fair view of the financial position of the LLP as at 31 December 2017 and of its financial performance and its cash flows for the year then ended in accordance with United Kingdom Generally Accepted Accounting Practice and the Statement of Recommended

Practice – Accounting by Limited Liability Partnerships and have been prepared in accordance with the requirements of the Companies Act 2006 as applied to Limited Liability Partnerships.

Basis for Qualified Opinion

The LLP's overdraft expired and is due to be repaid on 31 March 2018. The LLP has been unsuccessful in negotiating or re-financing this overdraft. This situation indicates the existence of a material uncertainty that may cast significant doubt about the LLP's ability to continue as a going concern and therefore the LLP may be unable to realise its assets and discharge its liabilities in the ordinary course of business. The financial statements (and notes thereto) do not fully disclose this fact.

Example auditor's report extract – material uncertainty exists but has not been adequately disclosed and an adverse opinion is considered appropriate (based on ISA (UK) 700 (Revised June 2016))

Adverse Opinion

In our opinion, because of the omission of the information mentioned in the Basis for Adverse Opinion paragraph, the financial statements do not give a true and fair view of the financial position of the LLP as at 31 December 2017 and of its financial performance and its cash flows for the year then ended in accordance with United Kingdom Generally Accepted Accounting Practice and the Statement of Recommended Practice – Accounting by Limited Liability Partnerships.

Basis for Adverse Opinion

The LLP's overdraft expired on 29 December 2017 and the overdraft was repayable on 31 December 2017. The LLP has been unsuccessful in negotiating or re-financing this overdraft and is considering filing for bankruptcy. These events indicate a material uncertainty that may cast significant doubt on the LLP's ability to continue as a going concern and therefore it may be unable to realise its assets and discharge its liabilities in the normal course of business. The financial statements (and notes thereto) do not disclose this fact.

Chapter summary

- Going concern is considered to be a fundamental concept in the preparation of financial statements and the responsibility for assessing whether, or not, an LLP is a going concern rests with the members.
- Auditors are responsible for assessing the members' assessment as to the going concern ability of the LLP; it is not the auditor's responsibility to conclude whether the LLP is a going concern.

- Going concern should be considered for a period of at least 12 months from the date of approval of the financial statements, not 12 months from the balance sheet date.
- The extent of the auditor's evidence required to support the members' assessment of going concern will depend on a number of factors including the size and complexity of the LLP.
- Risk factors indicating a material uncertainty relating to going concern can include general business considerations, financial considerations, availability of external financing and dependence on third parties.
- A letter of comfort in addition to other audit procedures will be needed when the LLP is a member of a group and there are uncertainties related to going concern.
- When there is significant doubt about the LLP's ability to continue as a going concern, and the members have made adequate disclosure, the auditor's report must contain a separate section headed 'Material Uncertainty Related to Going Concern' which cross-references the user to the relevant disclosure note in the accounts.
- Going concern procedures must be undertaken up to the point at which the members approve the financial statements and the auditor's report is signed.
- If the auditors do not agree that the going concern basis is appropriate and the members have not made any disclosures in respect of going concern, the auditor's report must express an adverse opinion.

Chapter 11

Consolidated financial statements

Signposts

- An LLP may acquire a controlling investment in another undertaking (see **11.1**).
- When a parent-subsidiary relationship exists, the parent LLP must prepare consolidated financial statements which show the results of the group as a single economic entity (see **11.1**).
- The process of preparing consolidated financial statements can be complicated and therefore a logical approach is needed (see **11.2**).
- The parent LLP must have 'control' over the financial and operating policies of the subsidiary in order for a parent-subsidiary relationship to exist and control can be obtained in a variety of ways (see **11.3**).
- Uniform accounting policies and year-ends should be used for all members of the group in preparing consolidated financial statements (see **11.4**).
- If a parent LLP owns less than 100% of the net assets of a subsidiary, the remaining balance will be owned by the non-controlling interests (previously referred to as 'minority interests') (see **11.5**).
- There are additional considerations which should be taken into account when there has been a change in group structure during the year (see **11.6–11.8**).
- In addition to obtaining a subsidiary (when control is achieved), there are other forms of investment which do not result in control that an LLP can invest in (see **11.10** and **11.11**).

1 Introduction

11.1 It is not unusual for an LLP to either set up other entities through which to carry out certain parts of its trade or, as discussed in Chapter 12, acquire a controlling investment in another undertaking (ie a subsidiary). Legislation and UK GAAP may, in such circumstances, require the LLP to prepare consolidated accounts, which aggregate the accounts of the LLP and the other undertakings, as well as its own entity accounts.

The main section of FRS 102 *The Financial Reporting Standard applicable in the UK and Republic of Ireland* which governs the accounting for groups is Section 9 *Consolidated and Separate Financial Statements* although Section 19 *Business Combinations and Goodwill* is also closely related. The objective of a consolidated set of LLP financial statements is to show the results of the group in line with its economic substance – which is that of a single reporting entity. Generally accepted accounting practice (GAAP) recognises that the financial statements of a parent LLP would not, in themselves, present a full picture of the group's economic activities or financial position. The consolidated financial statements will, therefore, reflect the extended business unit which conducts activities under the control of the parent. The cost of the investment in the subsidiary in the parent LLP's individual financial statements is replaced by goodwill and then on a line-by-line basis the subsidiary's assets, liabilities, income and equity is added in 100% to represent the control obtained by the parent LLP.

All intra-group trading (and the effects thereof) are eliminated during the consolidation process. This is because if intra-group trading (and the effects) were not eliminated on consolidation then the consolidated profit and loss account and consolidated balance sheet would be seriously distorted. For example, intra-group 'sales' are only true sales when the sale occurs with a third party outside of the group structure. If intra-group sales are not removed, the consolidated sales figure will be overstated; similarly, if intra-group debtors and intra-group creditors are not eliminated on consolidation, they, too, will be overstated in the consolidated financial statements.

Focus

- The upshot of eliminating intra-group activity results in the consolidated financial statements presenting the financial results of the group as if the group structure did not exist; in other words, the consolidated financial statements show the results of the group as a single trading entity with parties external to the group.

2 Preparing consolidated financial statements

11.2 The requirements as to when consolidated financial statements (group accounts) must be prepared, and the available exemptions, are considered in Chapter 2. An overview of how group accounts are prepared is as follows:

- Understand the group structure and establish those entities where the LLP has control (keep in mind that control does not necessarily have to be established through a percentage of ownership interest – control can exist even when the LLP owns less than 51% of the net assets of the subsidiary – see the next section).
- Ensure uniform accounting year-ends and accounting policies are used for all members of the group. Where uniform accounting policies are impracticable, adjustments will need to be made to the subsidiary's financial statements for consolidation purposes.
- Eliminate intra-group trading and the results of intra-group trading (eg intra-group debtors and intra-group creditors).
- Consolidate the results of the parent and all its subsidiaries, paying careful attention to goodwill calculations for any subsidiaries acquired during the reporting period.

For subsidiaries which have been acquired during the accounting period, the fair value of the purchase consideration used in the calculation of goodwill should be carefully assessed.

This is because the SORP requires the profit share promised to the new members in the enlarged LLP to be assessed in order to establish if a portion of that remuneration represents consideration for the acquired business rather than future members' remuneration. The substance of the arrangement needs to be carefully scrutinised and legal advice should be obtained where considered necessary.

The SORP cites an example whereby the members of an acquired entity were awarded an increased profit share for a certain amount of time after the acquisition which then falls back to normal levels. It could be suggested that the short-term excess amounts formed part of the purchase consideration and hence the substance of the arrangement should be carefully assessed to ensure appropriate treatment.

Where non-controlling interests (referred to as 'minority interests' in previous UK GAAP) are concerned, these are usually shown within the consolidated balance sheet as a deduction from net assets (see section 5).

3 Understanding control

11.3 In accounting terms, an LLP will be the parent LLP of another undertaking if it exercises control over that undertaking. Both legislation and Section 9 refer to 'undertakings', which means that the LLP needs to consider not just companies and LLPs in which it has an interest, but also other vehicles, such as partnerships and unincorporated businesses.

The Glossary to FRS 102 defines control as 'the power to govern the financial and operating policies of an entity so as to obtain benefits from its activities'. Control is deemed to exist, and hence the LLP is the parent LLP of another undertaking, if any of the following apply:

- The LLP owns (directly or indirectly through subsidiaries) a majority of the voting rights in the undertaking (only in exceptional circumstances could such ownership not constitute the achievement of control).
- The LLP is a member of the undertaking and has the right to appoint or remove directors holding a majority of the voting rights at meetings of the board on all, or substantially all, matters.
- The LLP has the power to govern the financial and operating policies of the undertaking under either a statute or by way of an agreement.
- The LLP has the power to cast the majority of votes at meetings of the undertaking and control of the undertaking is by that board or body.
- The LLP has options or convertible financial instruments that are currently exercisable, or by having an agent with the ability to direct the activities for the benefit of the controlling undertaking.
- The LLP has the power to exercise, or actually exercises, dominant influence or control over the undertaking and the LLP and the undertaking are managed on a unified basis (two or more undertakings are managed on a unified basis if the whole of the operations of the undertakings are integrated and they are managed as a single

unit. Unified management does not arise solely because one undertaking manages another).

The term 'dominant influence' refers to the situation where an LLP can use its position to achieve the operating and financial policies which it desires, notwithstanding the rights or influence of any other party. Such influence may, or may not, be explicit in nature. Determining whether there is dominant influence requires consideration of how this is effected in practice, by reference to the way in which the LLP interacts with the potential subsidiary. The fact that the LLP has the ability to exercise dominant influence, but chooses not to, will not of itself be sufficient to establish a parent-subsidiary relationship.

4 The preparation of consolidated financial statements

11.4 Consolidation is the process of adjusting and combining financial information from the individual accounts of a parent LLP and its subsidiaries, to prepare consolidated financial statements that present financial information for the group in line with that of its economic substance; ie as a single economic entity. Paragraph 9.17 of FRS 102 says that uniform group accounting policies should be used in preparing the consolidated financial statements for like transactions and other events and conditions in similar circumstances. It may, therefore, be necessary to make adjustments to amounts shown in a subsidiary's accounts at the time of consolidation where the subsidiary uses accounting policies which are different from those adopted in the consolidated financial statements. Particular attention is likely to be required to any overseas subsidiaries, as local accounting practice or legislation may differ from that in the UK.

Paragraph 9.16 of FRS 102 requires that the accounts of the subsidiaries to be used in preparing the consolidated financial statements should, where practicable, be for the same financial year end, and for the same accounting period, as those of the parent LLP. However, this may not be practicable, particularly in the case of overseas subsidiaries, where legislation in a particular country may dictate the year-end. Where possible, interim accounts for that subsidiary should be used; however, if this is impracticable, earlier accounts of the subsidiary may be used, provided they are prepared for a financial year that ended not more than three months earlier. Outside this period, legislation requires that interim accounts be prepared.

All intra-group trading and the effects of intra-group trading should be eliminated on consolidation. The objective of this elimination process is so that the consolidated financial statements show the trading results of the group as if it were a single reporting entity (ie the consolidated accounts show the results of the group's trading with the outside world which does not include any intra-group trading).

Example – intra-group trading

LLP A has a wholly-owned subsidiary (Sub B) and the group's year-end is 31 December 2017. During the year LLP A has provided services to Sub B amounting to £15,000 which have been reflected as cost of sales in Sub B's individual financial statements. At the year-end Sub B owed LLP A an amount of £3,000.

All intra-group trading (and the effects thereof) have to be eliminated on consolidation to show the results of the group as if it were a single reporting entity. Therefore, in the consolidated financial statements of the group the eliminations will be:

Dr Sales	£15,000 (this reduces LLP A's sales)
Cr Cost of sales	£15,000 (this reduces Sub B's cost of sales)
Being elimination of intra-group sales during the year	
Dr Creditors	£3,000 (this reduces Sub B's creditors)
Cr Debtors	£3,000 (this reduces LLP A's debtors)
Being elimination of intra-group debt at the year-end	

This will have the effect of enabling the consolidated financial statements to reflect the trading with entities which are outside of the group (ie with the outside world) as well as reducing debtors and creditors for the effects of intra-group trading at the year-end.

Intra-group transactions may result in profits or losses being reflected in the book value of assets to be included in the consolidation. Such profits or losses should be eliminated in full, because, for the group as a whole, no profits or losses have arisen.

Example – unrealised profit in in stock at year-end

LLP A has a wholly-owned subsidiary (Sub B) and the group's year-end is 31 December 2017. On 29 December 2017, Sub B sold goods to LLP A for £6,000 which resulted in a profit on sale for Sub B of £3,000. All of these goods were in LLP A's stock at the year-end.

The unrealised profit in stock remains in LLP A's stock figure at the year-end (because this would have been valued at cost of £6,000). However, the £3,000 profit is merely an intra-group profit in stock and in order to reduce stock back down to cost to the group (to accord with the principles in Section 13 *Inventories* which says that stock should be valued at the lower of cost and estimated selling price less costs to complete and sell), LLP A will have to eliminate the profit by:

Dr Closing stock (consolidated profit and loss account)	£3,000
Cr Closing stock (consolidated balance sheet)	£3,000

This will then bring the stock value down to cost to the group.

---

5 Non-controlling interests

11.5 Where the LLP controls less than 100% of a subsidiary, the interest it does not control is referred to as a non-controlling interest. The term 'minority interest' may be more familiar with preparers of LLP financial statements but FRS 102 refers to them as 'non-controlling interest'.

Within the consolidated balance sheet, non-controlling interests are most usually shown as a deduction from net assets. The consolidated profit and loss account should show separately the aggregate of profit or loss on ordinary activities for the period attributable to the non-controlling interests. Profits or losses arising in a subsidiary should be apportioned between the controlling and non-controlling interests, in proportion to their respective interests held over the period in which the profit or loss arose. Where the losses in a subsidiary attributable to the non-controlling interest result in its interest being one of net liabilities rather than net assets, the group should make provision to the extent that it has any commercial or legal obligation to provide finance that may not be recoverable in respect of the accumulated losses attributable to the non-controlling interest.

Example – consolidated profit and loss account showing non-controlling interests

	2017	**2016**
	£'000	£'000
Turnover	10,000	9,000
Cost of sales	(6,000)	(4,000)
Gross profit	4,000	5,000
Other operating costs	(2,000)	(1,000)
Other operating income	700	500
Operating profit	**2,700**	**4,500**
Interest payable and similar expenses	(800)	(900)
Profit on ordinary activities before tax	**1,900**	**3,600**
Tax on profit on ordinary activities of subsidiaries	–	–
Profit on ordinary activities after tax	**1,900**	**3,600**
Equity non-controlling interests	102	–
Profit for the financial year before members' remuneration and profit shares	**2,002**	**3,600**
Members' remuneration charged as an expense	(1,200)	(1,200)
Profit for the financial year available for discretionary division among members	**802**	**2,400**

6 Changes to the group structure during a financial period

11.6 Chapter 12 considers in more detail the accounting implications of business combinations during a financial period. However, when preparing consolidated financial statements where there has been a change in the group structure during the period, the following specific considerations should be taken into account.

Acquisitions

11.7 In a business combination, Section 19 *Business Combinations and Goodwill* requires that the identifiable assets and liabilities of the acquired subsidiary are brought into the consolidation at their fair values at the date that the undertaking becomes a subsidiary.

There may be occasions when a parent owns, say, 70% of a subsidiary and then increases this ownership interest by acquiring further ownership interest from the non-controlling interests to, say, 90%. When the parent increases its controlling interest in a subsidiary Section 9 does not allow the parent to revalue the identifiable assets and liabilities including any provisions for contingent liabilities to fair value; nor does it permit any additional goodwill being recognised. Instead, any increases in the parent's ownership interest is accounted for as a transaction between the equity holders.

Example – increases in ownership interest

LLP A has owned 60% of the net assets of Undertaking B for several years and has a year-end of 31 December. During the year to 31 December 2017, LLP A acquired a further 30% of the net assets of Undertaking B thus taking its ownership interest to 90% at a cost of £4,000.

Paragraph 22.19 to FRS 102 says that changes in a parent's controlling interest in a subsidiary which do not result in a loss of control are to be accounted for as transactions with equity holders in their capacity as equity holders. Any difference (if any) between the amount by which the non-controlling interest is changed and the fair value of the consideration paid or received is recognised directly in equity and attributed to equity holders of the parent. The parent will not recognise any change in the carrying value of assets (which includes goodwill) or liabilities as a result of the transaction. Therefore, LLP A will record the transaction as:

Dr Non-controlling interests	£4,000
Cr Cash at bank	£4,000

The above example highlights an example of where the parent increases its ownership interest in stages. It might be the case that the LLP achieves control in stages and in such situations the transaction is accounted for in accordance with paragraphs 19.11A and 19.14 of FRS 102. Paragraph 19.11A says that when control is achieved following a series of transactions, the cost of the business combination is the total of the fair values of the assets given, liabilities assumed and equity instruments issued by the acquirer at the date of each transaction in the series. The cost is then allocated by recognising the acquiree's identifiable assets and liabilities and a provision for contingent liabilities at fair value and any difference will be goodwill and therefore accounted for in accordance with paragraphs 19.22–19.24 of FRS 102.

Example – control achieved in stages

LLP A acquired a controlling interest in Undertaking B in two transactions as follows:

30 June 2017: 15% holding at a cost of £33,000 when the fair value of the net assets of Undertaking B amounted to £180,000.

31 March 2018: 45% holding at a cost of £162,000 when the fair value of the net assets of Undertaking B amounted to £290,000.

The cost of the business combination is £195,000. The group share of the fair value of the assets at the date that control is achieved is £174,000 (60% x £290,000). Goodwill is therefore £21,000 (£195,000 less £174,000).

Disposals

11.8 When an undertaking ceases to be a subsidiary during a period, the consolidated financial statements for that period should include its results up to the date that it ceases to be a subsidiary, together with any gain or loss arising on that cessation. If control is lost (hence the subsidiary falls to be classed as either an associate or a simple investment), the gain or loss on the disposal is calculated as the difference between:

- the proceeds from the disposal; and
- the proportion of the carrying value of the amount of the subsidiary's net assets, including any related goodwill, disposed of (or lost) as at the date of disposal (or as at the date that control is lost).

If a disposal occurs but the parent still retains control (ie the disposed element does not result in the LLP owning less than 51% of the net assets of the undertaking) then no gain or loss is recognised on the disposal. Instead the disposal is accounted for as a transaction between equity holders and the non-controlling interests is changed to reflect the parent's partial disposal.

Example – outright disposal of a subsidiary

LLP A has undertaken a strategic review of its business and has decided to dispose of its entire ownership interest in Undertaking B. The group has a year-end of 31 October and the sale completed on 31 August 2017 for a sum of £100,000. The net assets of the subsidiary were valued at £98,700.

The resulting profit on disposal amounts to £1,300 (£100,000 proceeds less disposal of the subsidiary at fair value of £98,700) and this gain will be recognised in the LLP's profit and loss account (income statement).

Accounting for interests in undertakings that do not give rise to control

11.9 Whilst an outright controlling interest via a subsidiary is probably the most common form of interest that an LLP will have in another entity, other lesser interests, where the LLP does not control the activities of the other entity, are also possible.

Associate

11.10 In this situation, the LLP holds a participating interest, and exercises *significant influence* over the other entity. The term 'significant influence' means that the LLP has the ability to participate in the financial and operating polices of the associate but it does not control (or have joint control over) the associate. In practical terms, the LLP has a long-term interest and is actively involved, and influential, in the direction of its investee, through its participation in policy decisions covering the aspects of policy relevant to the LLP, including decisions on strategic issues such as:

- the expansion or contraction of the business, participation in other entities or changes in products, markets and activities of its investee; and
- determining the balance between dividend and reinvestment.

Section 14 *Investments in Associates* in FRS 102 contains an assumption that a holding of 20% or more of the shares of an entity is presumed to be a participating interest, unless the contrary can be clearly demonstrated. The presumption is rebutted if the interest is either not for the long term or is not beneficial.

Section 14 requires that the equity method of accounting be used when including the associate in its own consolidated accounts. The LLP Regulations were amended by SI 2016/575 which allows the equity method of accounting to be applied to participating interests in the LLP's own individual financial statements.

The equity method of accounting is a method whereby the equity investment is initially recognised at the transaction price (which should also include all transaction costs) and it is then subsequently adjusted to reflect the investor's share of the profit or loss, other comprehensive income and equity of the associate.

Example – equity accounting for an associate

On 31 December 2017, Indigo LLP invested a sum of £10,000 in Purple in return for a 25% holding in the net assets of Purple. On 31 December 2018 the resulting profit in Purple was £7,000.

On 31 December 2017, Indigo will account for its investment in its associate as follows:

Dr Investment in associate	£10,000
Cr Cash at bank	£10,000

This represents the initial investment in Purple.

On 31 December 2018, Indigo will reflect its share of Purple's profit in its consolidated profit and loss account so under equity accounting the entries will be:

Dr Investment in associate (25% × £7,000)	£1,750
Cr Profit and loss account	£1,750

In the consolidated profit and loss account, the LLP's share of its associate's operating result should be included immediately before the group operating result. From the level of profit before tax, the LLP's share of the relevant amounts for associates should be included within the amounts for the group. In the balance sheet, the LLP's share of the net assets of the associate should be included and separately disclosed as part of investments. Goodwill arising on the LLP's acquisition of its associate, less amortisation and, where necessary, impairment, should be included in the carrying amount for the associate but should be disclosed separately. In the profit and loss account, the amortisation or other write down of such goodwill should be separately disclosed as part of the LLP's share of the associate's results.

Joint ventures

11.11 The accounting for joint ventures is dealt with in FRS 102 at Section 15 *Investments in Joint Ventures*, and this section applies to:

- accounting for joint ventures in the LLP's consolidated financial statements;
- investments in joint ventures in the individual financial statements of a venturer which is not a parent; and
- investments in jointly controlled operations and jointly controlled assets in the separate financial statements of a venturer which is a parent.

A joint venture will exist where the LLP holds a long-term interest in another venture, and shares control under a contractual arrangement. The joint venture agreement can override the rights normally conferred by ownership interests, with the effect that:

- acting together, the venturers can control the venture and there are procedures for such joint action; and
- each venturer has (implicitly or explicitly) a veto over strategic policy decisions.

There is usually a procedure for settling disputes between investors and, possibly, for terminating the joint venture.

Joint ventures can take the form of jointly controlled operations, jointly controlled assets or jointly controlled entities. The key aspect of the joint venture is that there must be a contractual arrangement in place in which two (or more) parties undertake an economic activity which is subjected to joint control.

Focus

- It is important that there is a contractual agreement in place which establishes joint control and that this agreement is in writing. Indeed, the definition of 'joint control 'in the Glossary to FRS 102 defines the term as:

  'The contractually agreed sharing of **control** over an economic activity. It exists only when the strategic financial and operating decisions relating to the activity require the unanimous consent of the parties sharing control (the **venturers**).'

- Note the start of the definition 'The contractually agreed sharing of control …'.

When including the joint venture in its consolidated accounts, the LLP should use the equity method showing, in addition to the amounts included under the equity method (as outlined for associates above), on the face of the balance sheet, the LLP's share of the gross assets and liabilities of the joint venture, and, in the profit and loss account, the LLP's share of its turnover (which should be distinguished from that of the group).

7 Appendix – illustrative consolidated balance sheet

11.12 The following illustrative consolidated balance sheet is an example only and some LLP consolidated balance sheets may contain additional information from that shown in the following illustration.

	Note	2017	2016
		£'000	*£'000*
Fixed assets			
Intangible assets	8	X	X
Tangible assets	9	X	X
Investments	10	X	X
		X	X
Current assets			
Debtors	11	X	X
Cash at bank and in hand	12	X	X
Creditors: amounts falling due within one year		(X)	(X)
Net current assets		X	X
Total assets less current liabilities		**X**	**X**

Creditors: amounts falling due after more than one year	14	**(X)**	**(X)**
Provisions for liabilities	15	**(X)**	**(X)**
Pension scheme liability	26	**(X)**	**(X)**
Equity non-controlling interests		X	X
Net assets attributable to members	1	**Y**	**Y**
Represented by:			
Loans and other debts due to members within one year			
Members' capital classified as a liability	16	X	X
Other amounts	16	X	X
		X	X
Loans and other debts due to members after more than one year			
Other amounts	16	X	X
		X	X
Equity			
Members' other interests - other reserves classified as equity	16	(X)	(X)
Revaluation reserve	16	(X)	(X)
		Y	**Y**
Total members' interests			
Loans and other debts due to members	16	X	X
Members' other interests	16	(X)	(X)
Amounts due from members	16	(X)	(X)
Total including pension scheme liability		(X)	(X)
Pension scheme liability		X	X
Total excluding pension scheme liability		X	X

Chapter summary

- Consolidated financial statements are dealt with in FRS 102 in Section 9 *Consolidated and Separate Financial Statements* with close interaction with Section 19 *Business Combinations and Goodwill.*
- Intra-group trading and the effects thereof must be eliminated when preparing the consolidated financial statements so that the consolidated financial statements show the results of the group in line with its economic substance; which is that of a single reporting entity.
- In addition to intra-group trading, any intra-group profit should also be eliminated (such as intra-group profit in stock).
- For subsidiaries that have been acquired during the accounting period, the fair value of the purchase consideration used in the calculation of goodwill should be carefully assessed, especially in light of profit-sharing arrangements for members in the enlarged LLP.
- Control usually arise when a parent LLP acquires a subsidiary and the parent has an ownership interest of more than 50% (although other characteristics of control can also be present which will need consideration on a case-by-case basis).
- Uniform accounting policies and accounting reference dates should be used when preparing consolidated financial statements.
- Non-controlling interests will arise when the parent owns less than 100% of the net assets of the subsidiary. Non-controlling interests are usually shown as a deduction from net assets in the consolidated balance sheet.
- Where a parent increases its controlling interest in a subsidiary, the transaction is treated as one between equity holders in their capacity as equity holders.
- When an undertaking ceases to be a subsidiary, the consolidated financial statements should include that undertaking's results up to the date that it ceases to be a subsidiary, together with any gain or loss arising on disposal.
- Where a disposal occurs, but the parent still retains control, no gain or loss on disposal is recognised. Instead the disposal is accounted for as a transaction between equity holders and non-controlling interests are changed to reflect the parent's partial disposal.
- Joint ventures should have a contractual agreement in place and can take the form of jointly controlled operations, jointly controlled assets or jointly controlled entities.
- When including a joint venture in the consolidated financial statements, the equity method of accounting should be used.

Chapter 12

Business combinations

Signposts

- An LLP can acquire another business either by taking a direct investment or by acquiring the assets (see **12.1**).
- Under UK GAAP there are two methods of accounting for a business combination: the 'purchase method' or 'merger accounting' (see **12.2**).
- Strict rules govern the use of merger accounting but are particularly relevant to partnerships which are transferring to LLP status (see **12.2**).
- There are three steps involved in applying the purchase method (see **12.3**).
- The date of acquisition may not necessarily be the date on which control is obtained (see **12.7**).
- The consideration paid by a parent LLP for an ownership interest in another undertaking may take several different forms and may not necessarily just be simply in cash (see **12.8**).
- Care needs to be taken to ensure the accounting for 'contingent consideration' is applied correctly (see **12.8**).
- In dealing with a business combination, an LLP should also have regard to not only those parts of the agreement which deal with the consideration, but also to those parts of the agreement which deal with the arrangements entered into for profit-sharing with any new members joining the LLP from the acquired entity (see **12.8**).
- At the date of acquisition, assets and liabilities of the acquired entity are to be valued at fair value and various factors should be taken into account when arriving at fair values (see **12.9**).
- When an LLP acquires the business assets and liabilities of an entity rather than making an investment, the primary difference is that goodwill arising on acquisition will be recorded on the LLP's own balance sheet (see **12.10**).
- Goodwill under FRS 102 cannot have an indefinite useful life and must be amortised on a systematic basis over its expected useful economic life (see **12.11**).
- Internally-generated goodwill cannot be recognised on the LLP's balance sheet (see **12.11**).

- A reassessment exercise should be carried out if the goodwill arising on a business combination is negative (ie a 'bargain purchase' has taken place) to ensure the completeness of assets and liabilities and the accuracy of the cost of the combination (see **12.11**).
- There are additional requirements in respect of goodwill impairment under FRS 102 (see **12.12**).
- There are three criteria which must be met before merger accounting can be applied (see **12.13**).
- The SORP recommends merger accounting be used (where permitted) so as to reflect the initial 'conversion' to LLP (see **12.13** and **12.14**).
- There are accounting consequences in respect of a merger which differ from the investment by a parent in a subsidiary (see **12.15**).

1 Introduction

12.1 This chapter considers the accounting consequences of an LLP acquiring another business, either by taking a direct investment (equity, partnership share, etc) or by acquiring the assets, liabilities and trade without making a direct investment in the disposing entity.

In each of these circumstances, there are accounting implications both for the LLP's accounts and for the consolidated financial statements where the LLP is required to prepare them (see Chapter 2 for the exemptions from the requirement to prepare consolidated financial statements, and Chapter 11 for more detailed considerations regarding the preparation and presentation of consolidated financial statements).

2 General accounting principles for business combinations

12.2 There are currently two possible methods of accounting for a business combination within a set of consolidated financial statements: the purchase method or merger accounting. The purchase method was previously referred to as the 'acquisition' method of accounting in previous UK GAAP. With regards to merger accounting, the conditions which must be met before merger accounting can be applied are discussed below. The rules contained within accounting standards are extremely strict and, as a result, mergers in the corporate environment are relatively rare. The strict criteria for merger accounting are particularly relevant to partnerships transferring to LLP status as, historically, most partnerships have regarded any business combination with another partnership as a merger. However, a large number of these combinations would not meet the accounting requirements for merger accounting and, therefore, fall to be treated as acquisitions and hence the purchase method would be applied.

In addition to the requirements set out in legislation, accounting for business combinations is governed by the provisions in FRS 102 (September 2015) *The Financial Reporting Standard applicable in the UK and Republic of Ireland* at Section 19 *Business Combinations and Goodwill.*

> **Focus**
>
> - Micro-entity LLPs whose individual financial statements are consolidated in with those of a parent are unable to apply FRS 105 *The Financial Reporting Standard applicable to the Micro-entities Regime* (see Chapter 14).

Section 19 provides guidance on the identification of the acquirer, measuring the cost of the business combination and the allocation of this cost to the assets acquired and the liabilities and provisions (including contingent liabilities) assumed in the business combination. The accounting treatment for goodwill is also addressed in Section 19.

The scope of Section 19 does not, however, apply to:

- the formation of a joint venture; or
- the acquisition of a group of assets which would not constitute a business.

In financial reporting terms, a business combination is the bringing together of separate businesses into one reporting business. In almost all cases, a business combination will result in one party obtaining control of one or more other businesses within the combination from the date of acquisition (the date of acquisition being the date on which control is obtained by the parent).

Some business combinations can be very complex in terms of how they are structured depending on the reasons for the combination and occur by the issue of equity instruments (shares), the transfer of cash (or cash equivalents) or other assets. In some combinations there may well be a mixture of equity instruments, cash/cash equivalents or other assets, and in some combinations, there may well be a new entity set up that will control the combined entities or net assets transferred or it could involve the restructuring of existing combined entities.

3 Principles of the purchase method

12.3 The overarching principle of consolidated financial statements is that they should present the financial position and results of the parent and its subsidiary undertakings in line with the group's economic substance, which is that of a single LLP. All business combinations which fall under the scope of Section 19 are accounted for by applying the purchase method with the exceptions of group reconstructions which may be accounted for by applying the merger accounting method and public benefit entity combinations which are in substance a gift or a merger and hence would be accounted for under Section 34 *Specialised Activities* of FRS 102.

There are three steps in applying the purchase method:

- identify the acquirer;
- measure the cost of the business combination; and

- at the date of acquisition, allocate the cost of the business combination to the assets acquired and liabilities (including provisions and contingent liabilities) assumed.

Identify the acquirer

12.4 The acquirer is the parent LLP which obtains control of the other combining business(es). Control has to be obtained and for the purposes of Section 19 'control' is the power to govern the financial and operating policies of an entity or business in order that the parent LLP can benefit from its activities.

Measure the cost of the business combination

12.5 The cost of a business combination is the total of:

- the fair values at the date of acquisition of assets given, liabilities incurred (or assumed) and equity instruments which are issued by the acquirer in exchange for control of the acquiree; and
- costs which are directly attributable to the business combination.

Focus

- If control of a business is achieved in a series of transactions (often referred to as 'step' or 'piecemeal' acquisitions), the cost of the business combination is the aggregate of the fair values of the assets given, liabilities assumed and equity instruments issued by the acquirer at the date of each transaction in the series.

Allocate the cost of the business combination

12.6 The cost of the business combination is allocated at the date of acquisition. This occurs by the parent LLP recognising the acquiree's identifiable assets and liabilities and a provision for contingent liabilities (which satisfy the recognition criteria) at their fair values.

When the group acquires a new subsidiary, the parent LLP is treated as having acquired the assets and liabilities at their 'fair value' at the date of acquisition, and the income and expenditure of the subsidiary is only included in the consolidated profit and loss account from the date of acquisition. For the purposes of business combinations, the date of acquisition is the date on which control is passed to the parent LLP and may not necessarily be the same date on which completion of the transaction occurs and purchase consideration is transferred.

In preparing the consolidation, the cost of the investment in the subsidiary shown on the balance sheet of the parent LLP will nearly always differ from the fair value of the assets and liabilities of the subsidiary at the date of acquisition. The difference between the aggregate fair values of the assets and liabilities and the purchase consideration (cost of investment) represents either positive or negative goodwill, the accounting treatment of which is discussed at **12.11**.

4 Determining the date of acquisition

12.7 When a parent LLP acquires a subsidiary, the date of acquisition is the date on which control passes to the parent LLP. The date that control passes is a matter of fact and it cannot be artificially altered, for example by including within the purchase and sale agreement some other 'effective' date. It can usually be assumed that control passes on the date on which an offer to purchase becomes unconditional.

Care must be taken in determining the date of acquisition because control may not necessarily pass on the date that the purchase consideration is transferred. Indeed, as is often the case in such matters, consideration may well be paid in instalments or certain portions of the consideration may be contingent on future occurrences (or non-occurrences).

Where there is an earn-out arrangement, or consideration is payable in instalments, the date of acquisition is not usually deferred, and all the circumstances should be considered in order to determine when control passes. Once control passes to the parent LLP, there becomes a parent-subsidiary relationship, and unless the group is small, consolidated financial statements will be needed.

5 Purchase consideration

12.8 The cost of a business combination is generally the aggregate of:

- the amount of cash paid;
- the fair value of any other purchase consideration given by the acquirer; and
- the directly attributable expenses of the acquisition (ie those costs which would have been avoided had the combination not taken place).

The cost of the combination will determine the initial carrying value of the investment on the parent LLP's own balance sheet.

The fair value of purchase consideration is determined by reference to the following:

- *Cash and other monetary items* (for example, monetary assets given or liabilities assumed) – the amount paid or payable.
- *Interest in the LLP.* Where there has been a valuation of the LLP at, or shortly prior to, the acquisition of the newly acquired entity, it may be possible to value the consideration by reference to such a valuation (for example, where the members or shareholders of the acquired entity become members of the LLP). However, the SORP acknowledges that, for any type of entity in which there is no ready market for its securities or other interests, the best estimate of value may be obtained by valuing the acquired entity.

- *Non-monetary consideration.* Estimated by reference to market prices, estimated realisable values, independent valuations or other available evidence.

It is not unusual for an acquisition agreement to provide for part of the purchase consideration to be deferred to a future date (deferred consideration) or to be contingent upon the occurrence of some future event (contingent consideration).

Paragraph 19.12 of FRS 102 (September 2015) says that when a business combination agreement makes provision for an adjustment to the cost of the combination which is contingent on future events, the parent LLP should include the estimated amount of that adjustment in the cost of the combination at the date of acquisition when the adjustment is probable (ie more likely than not) and can be measured reliably.

If, at the date of acquisition, such an adjustment was not recognised because it was not probable or could not be reliably measured (or both), but then subsequently becomes probable and can be reliably estimated, the additional consideration is to be treated as an adjustment to the cost of the business combination. Although it is not explicitly stated in the standard itself, any adjustment made to the cost of the business combination should be made to goodwill until the consideration is finally established and payable in accordance with the sale/purchase agreement. Conversely, the adjustments to provisional fair values of assets and liabilities acquired to reflect new information obtained are finalised within 12 months from the date of acquisition and hence such adjustments are applied retrospectively as if they had occurred at the date of acquisition. Beyond 12 months from the date of acquisition, any adjustments to the initial accounting for a business combination must be recognised only to correct a material error and in such cases the provisions in Section 10 *Accounting Policies, Estimates and Errors* will apply.

The rules for finalising provisional fair values is a concession which allows the parent LLP to finalise fair values that it was not initially possible to finalise due to time constraints. This is notably different than the situation with contingent consideration whereby an initial estimate is made and is then later adjusted, based on future events.

Example – contingent consideration adjustments

LLP A acquires a wholly-owned subsidiary, Undertaking B, for £15 million. The terms of the sale agreement require the parent LLP to seek protection from false representation made by Undertaking B's sellers. At the completion date, LLP A will pay the sellers of Undertaking B £14 million in cash and the remaining £1 million will be placed in an escrow account and will be payable to the sellers of Undertaking B one year after the date of completion if no false representations claims have been made.

At the date of acquisition, it would be impossible for LLP A to establish whether any false representation claims will be made and hence no adjustment should be made to the combination's cost by the parent LLP at the date of acquisition.

However, if at the first anniversary of the sale, new facts emerge which indicate that there would be an adjustment to the amount held in the escrow account, the provisions in paragraphs 19.12 and 19.13 would be triggered. If it is assumed that the amount to be released to the previous owners of Undertaking B is to be £300,000, the refund of £700,000 to LLP A would be recognised as an adjustment to the purchase consideration and a consequential reduction in goodwill by that amount.

When considering accounting for a business combination by an LLP, reference should be made not only to those parts of the agreement that deal with the consideration, but also those parts dealing with the arrangements entered into for profit-sharing with any new members joining the LLP from the acquired entity. These arrangements may also include an element of contingent consideration. For example, the members from the acquired entity might be awarded an increased profit share for a limited period after the acquisition, which subsequently reduces back to a 'normal' level. In these circumstances, it will be necessary for the LLP to make an estimate of the future profits which will be earned by the LLP over this period and to include an estimate of the enhanced profit share element payable to such members as part of the cost of the business combination.

Focus

- Where members of the acquired entity have been awarded an increased profit share for a limited period of time post-acquisition, which subsequently reverts back to normal remuneration levels after this period of time has elapsed, this could suggest that the short-term excess amounts were part of the purchase consideration. In all cases, the sale and purchase agreement must be closely examined in order to determine the substance of the arrangement.

Deferred or contingent consideration should generally be included in the balance sheet as a liability at the time of acquisition. FRS 102 does not specify where the liability should be disclosed on the balance sheet; therefore, it could be within creditors or within provisions for liabilities. Where there is any estimation involved, the most appropriate position would usually be within 'Provisions for liabilities'.

Where the deferred or contingent consideration is to be satisfied by an enhanced profit share, rather than include the amount within provisions, it should be shown as part of members' other interests, preferably under a separate heading such as 'Members' interests in respect of deferred consideration'. As the conditions for triggering the entitlement to deferred or contingent consideration are reached, transfers should then be made to members' capital accounts or debt due to members, dependent on the terms agreed with the new members.

The cost of the combination should also include any expenses which are directly attributable to the combination (such as legal fees). These costs should not include any allocation of costs that would have been incurred irrespective of whether or not the acquisition had been entered into, such as management remuneration.

6 Determining the fair value of assets and liabilities

12.9 The assets and liabilities to be included in the assessment of fair value are all those which existed at the date of acquisition. In determining fair value, the following should be taken into account:

- the conditions in existence at the date of acquisition;
- fair value should not reflect any changes resulting from the LLP's intentions or actions taken subsequent to the date of acquisition;
- fair value should not reflect any impairment, or other changes, resulting from events subsequent to the acquisition;
- provisions or accruals for future operating losses or other costs expected to be incurred as a result of the business combination should not be included; and
- only those liabilities for terminating or reducing the activities of the acquiree should be recognised to the extent that the parent LLP has, at the date of acquisition, an existing liability for restructuring which meets the recognition criteria in Section 21 *Provisions and Contingencies.*

Fair value should be assessed by reference to the LLP's accounting policies. Therefore, where accounting policies differ between the LLP and the entity acquired, the values of the assets and liabilities should be adjusted to bring them into line with the acquiring LLP's accounting policies.

The general requirement within Section 19 is that the fair value exercise should be completed, if possible, by the date on which the first accounts including the acquired business are approved by the members. This may not always be possible, particularly where the date of acquisition is close to the year-end. In these circumstances provisional valuations should be made, which should be amended, if necessary, in the next accounts. Although not specifically stated in Section 19, the corresponding adjustment to the combination's cost will be to goodwill. The accounts for the first year post acquisition should make it clear that the fair values are provisional. Any adjustments to the initial accounting for a business combination beyond 12 months from the date of acquisition should only be recognised to correct a material error in accordance with Section 10 *Accounting Policies, Estimates and Errors.*

It is not unusual for sale and purchase agreements to include values for the assets and liabilities of the acquired business. These may, however, differ from the fair values of such assets and liabilities. Fair value guidance is provided in FRS 102 at paragraphs 11.27 to 11.32 and paragraph 11.28 outlines various valuation techniques which can be employed to arrive at a fair value assessment. Such techniques can include:

- using recent arm's-length market values for identical assets;
- current fair values of other similar assets;
- discounted cash flow analysis; and
- option pricing models.

The general principles for determining the fair values of different classes of assets and liabilities are set out below:

- *Tangible fixed assets.* The lower of the recoverable amount and depreciated replacement cost. Where similar assets are bought and sold on the open market (for example, property), the value should be determined by reference to market value.
- *Intangible fixed assets.* These must be capable of being valued separately to the underlying business before they can be recognised. The fair value should be determined by reference to replacement cost, which will usually be market value.
- *Stocks and work in progress.* The lower of replacement cost or estimated selling price less costs to complete and sell. Replacement cost is the cost at which the stocks would have been replaced by the acquired entity, reflecting its normal buying process and the sources of supply and prices available to it. Current cost would include members' time as discussed in **Chapter 5**.
- *Quoted investments.* Market price (adjusted if necessary for unusual price fluctuations or for the size of holding).
- *Monetary assets and liabilities.* The fair value should take into account the amounts expected to be received or paid.
- *Contingent assets and liabilities.* Contingent assets and liabilities should only be included if the contingency exists at the date of acquisition. The value should be based on a reasonable estimate of expected outcome.
- *Businesses sold or acquired exclusively with a view to subsequent resale.* Where a purchaser has been identified or is being sought and the disposal is reasonably expected to occur within approximately one year of the date of the acquisition, the operation should be valued at an estimate of the sales proceeds. Such items should be included as a single asset within current assets.
- *Pensions and other post-retirement benefits.* For a funded scheme, the amount of the surplus or deficiency should be recognised as an asset or liability respectively. An asset should, however, only be recognised to the extent that it can be recovered through reduced contributions or through refunds from the scheme. For unfunded schemes the valuation of accrued obligations should be recognised as a liability.

7 Acquisition of business assets and liabilities

12.10 Similar accounting provisions will apply where an LLP acquires the assets and liabilities of a business rather than making an investment therein.

The principal difference is that any goodwill arising will be recorded on the LLP's own balance sheet instead of only on the consolidated balance sheet. In these circumstances, amortisation of goodwill will be charged against, and directly affect, the profits of the LLP available for distribution to the members.

8 Goodwill

12.11 A successful business will be worth more than the sum of its net assets, and therefore has 'goodwill'. FRS 102 (September 2015) at Section 18 *Intangible Assets other than Goodwill* prohibits the recognition of internally-generated goodwill at paragraph 18.8C(f). FRS 102 deals with goodwill and other intangible assets in a separate section (Section 19 *Business Combinations and Goodwill*) and is defined as *'future economic benefits arising from assets that are not capable of being individually identified and separately recognised.'* Goodwill under the provisions in FRS 102 will only generally appear in the LLP's balance sheet as a result of a business combination. A number of partnerships include goodwill on their balance sheet. In some circumstances, this arises not as a result of the acquisition of another business, but instead as part of a revaluation exercise to calculate the cost of capital for new partners. Such goodwill does not represent goodwill arising as a result of a business combination which brings together separate entities into one reporting entity and, as a result, cannot be recognised on transition to an LLP.

Unlike previous UK GAAP, goodwill is always considered to have a limited useful economic life, and paragraph 19.23(a) requires goodwill that satisfies the recognition and measurement criteria in paragraph 19.22 to be amortised on a systematic basis over that useful economic life. If the LLP is unable to make a reliable estimate of the useful economic life of goodwill, then paragraph 19.23(a) of FRS 102 (September 2015) says that the life shall not exceed ten years.

Focus

- The useful economic life of ten years was increased from five years in the September 2015 edition of FRS 102. This was as a result of the EU Accounting Directive increasing the life from five years to ten.

The useful economic life of goodwill which cannot be attributed a reliably measurable useful life has been subject to a considerable reduction when compared to previous UK GAAP. FRS 10 *Goodwill and intangible assets* contained a rebuttable presumption that the useful economic life of goodwill is 20 years or less. An important point to emphasise is that the ten-year rule only applies to goodwill (or other intangible assets) where the members are unable to assign a useful economic life and in many cases an amortisation period in excess of ten years may well be appropriate and the LLP may have justifiable reasons for choosing such a period. The use of professional judgement in this area is a critical aspect and paragraph 19.25(g) requires the LLP to disclose supporting reasons for the useful life of goodwill where the useful life exceeds ten years.

A further point to consider is an LLP which previously considered its goodwill to have an indefinite useful economic life. Under FRS 102, Section 19, all goodwill and intangible assets will have a finite useful life and therefore on transition to FRS 102, LLP's that have not been previously amortising goodwill on the grounds that they consider it to have an indefinite useful life will need to change the accounting policy and arrive at a reliable estimate of the useful economic life of the goodwill and amortise it systematically over that useful life. If the members cannot ascertain a reliable useful economic life, then the ten-year rule in FRS 102 will apply.

Focus

- The ten-year rule in respect of goodwill only applies where the members are unable to reliably estimate the useful economic life. Under previous UK GAAP, goodwill may have been amortised over, say, 20 years and at the date of transition it could have a remaining life of 15 years left. In the vast majority of cases, it is likely that this will still be appropriate and hence on transition, the LLP will continue amortising the goodwill over the remaining 15 years. There would have to be a change in circumstance to justify why the useful life should be changed on transition and, even then, ten years may not be the answer. LLPs will need to consider whether there has been a change in circumstances that may have occurred and use the previous useful economic life (such as 20 years as above) as a starting point and then apply a prospective adjustment to the useful life when the change occurred.

The key to developing an amortisation policy is for the members to assess the LLP's accounting policy in respect of amortisation and to consider whether this policy genuinely reflects the position of the acquired business. Different LLP's operating in different industries will have varied accounting policies in respect of amortisation of goodwill and consideration needs to be given of the nature and stability of the acquired business and its product lifecycles.

In rare circumstances, the cost of a business combination may be less than the fair value of the assets and liabilities acquired (often referred to as a 'bargain purchase'). Such situations are quite rare and usually only arise in distressed business sales because the exiting members want a quick exit route out of the business due to difficult trading conditions or the members may want to retire quickly and are therefore willing to accept a reduced selling price for a quick sale. In such cases, 'negative goodwill' arises and the provisions in paragraph 19.24 will be triggered. There are three steps that an LLP should take where negative goodwill is concerned:

- Go back to the identification and measurement of the acquiree's assets, liabilities and provisions for contingent liabilities and assess them for completeness as well as reassessing the accuracy of the cost of the combination. The objective of this reassessment is to ensure that assets are not overstated and liabilities have not been omitted.
- Should negative goodwill still exist following this reassessment, then it should be recognised separately on the face of the balance sheet immediately below goodwill, followed by a subtotal of the net amount of goodwill and the excess.
- In subsequent accounting periods, recognise the excess up to the fair value of non-monetary assets acquired in profit or loss in the periods in which the non-monetary

assets are recovered. Any excess which exceeds the fair value of non-monetary assets acquired are recognised in the LLP's profit and loss account in the periods which are expected to benefit.

9 Impairment of goodwill

12.12 The overarching principle in financial reporting is that assets should not be carried in the balance sheet at any more than their recoverable amount. For this reason, the LLP should undertake a review of their assets at each reporting date and consider whether such assets are capable of being recovered at their carrying value. If, as a result of the assessment, the LLP considers that assets will not be recovered at their carrying value then a write-down to recoverable amount will be needed (this is known as an 'impairment').

Section 27 *Impairment of Assets* of FRS 102 gives guidance to LLPs on conducting a review for impairment. Paragraph 19.23(b) also specifically requires an LLP to follow Section 27 for the recognition and measurement of goodwill impairment and there are additional specific requirements in respect of goodwill impairment contained in paragraphs 27.24–27.27.

Goodwill acquired in a business combination is allocated to each cash-generating unit which is expected to benefit from the synergies of the business combination regardless of whether other assets or liabilities of the acquiree have been assigned to those units.

For subsidiaries which are not wholly-owned by the parent LLP, part of the recoverable amount of a cash-generating unit (CGU) is attributable to the non-controlling interests in goodwill. In recognition of this, paragraph 27.26 requires the carrying value of that unit to be notionally adjusted before being compared with its recoverable amount. This is done by grossing up the carrying value to include the goodwill attributable to the non-controlling interest. This grossed up value is then compared to recoverable amount to ascertain whether the CGU is impaired.

Example – notionally adjusted goodwill

Parent LLP acquired an 80% ownership interest in Sub LLP on 1 January 2017 (the date of acquisition) for £340 million. At the date of acquisition, the fair value of Sub LLP's net assets and contingent liabilities is £300 million. Group policy is to recognise goodwill to the extent of the parent's own as follows:

1. Fair value of net assets and contingent liabilities	£300m
2. Goodwill (*)	£100m
3. Non-controlling interests (£300m x 20%)	£60m

*Goodwill

Cost of investment	£340m
Less net assets acquired in the combination	(£240m)
Goodwill	£100m

On 31 December 2017, the Group carries out an impairment test and assesses the recoverable amount to be £200 million. Sub LLP's net assets of £300 million are being depreciated over their useful economic lives of ten years and there is no residual value expected at the end of this useful life. The members have also decided to write off the goodwill over a five-year period.

Part of the £200 million recoverable amount will belong to the non-controlling interests' share of goodwill that has not been recognised. Paragraph 27.26 of FRS 102 requires the carrying value of Sub LLP to be notionally increased by the goodwill attributable to the non-controlling interests. Once this has been done, this grossed up value is then compared to the recoverable amount of £200 million to assess if it is impaired. This can be illustrated as follows:

	£m	£m
Goodwill (£100m × 4/5)		80
Unrecognised non-controlling interest (W1)		20
Gross carrying value of identifiable net assets	300	
Accumulated depreciation	(30)	
		270
Notionally adjusted carrying value		370
Recoverable amount		(200)
Impairment loss		170

W1

Goodwill attributable to Parent LLP's interest of 80% was £100 million, therefore goodwill for the non-controlling interests is ¼ of the 80%, thus £25 million and so at the end of 2017 it is £20 million (£25m × 4/5).

The impairment loss then needs to be allocated. It is first allocated to goodwill of £80 million (see above) as the remaining £20 million belongs to the non-controlling interest.

	Carrying value of CGU		**Impairment**	**Post-impairment**
	£m	£m	£m	£m
Goodwill attributable to the parent		80	(80)	
Gross carrying amount of identifiable assets	300			
Accumulated depreciation	(30)			
		270	(70)	200
Carrying value		350		
Recoverable amount		200		
Impairment loss in the parent		150	(150)	

The impairment loss in the parent can be proved as follows:

Total impairment loss for notional purposes	£170m
Less goodwill belonging to non-controlling interests	(£20m)
Impairment loss recognised	£150m

In situations where the parent LLP cannot allocate goodwill to individual CGUs (or groups thereof) on a non-arbitrary basis, then it should test goodwill for impairment by determining the recoverable amount of either:

- the acquired undertaking in its entirety if the goodwill relates to an acquired entity which has not been integrated into the reporting entity; or
- the entire group but excluding those entities which have not been integrated where the goodwill relates to an undertaking which has been integrated.

In order to carry out this correctly, the LLP must separate goodwill into that portion which relates to entities that have been integrated and the portion which relates to goodwill which have not been integrated.

Focus

- LLPs following the provisions of FRS 102 (September 2015) should keep in mind that an impairment loss recognised for goodwill in an accounting period cannot be reversed in a subsequent period.

10 Application of merger accounting

12.13 The SORP only allows merger accounting for group reconstructions so as to be consistent with the requirements in FRS 102. Merger accounting is not the acquisition of a subsidiary by a parent LLP – it is the combining of entities to create a new reporting entity. There is no controlling party in merger accounting and strict criteria exists to ensure that this is the case. All of the following criteria must be met for an entity combination to meet the definition of a merger:

- no party to the combination is purported to be an acquirer or an acquiree;
- there will be no significant change to the classes of beneficiaries of the combining entities or the purpose of the benefits provided as a result of the combination; and
- all parties in the combination (as represented by the members of the board) participate in establishing the management structure of the combined entity and also participate in the selection of management personnel with such decisions being made on the basis of a consensus between the parties to the combination rather than purely by exercise of voting rights.

> **Focus**
>
> - The LLP Regulations (SI 2008/1912 schedule 3, 10 and SI 2008/1911 schedule 4, part 1, 7) permits an acquisition to be accounted for as a merger if adoption of the merger method of accounting complies with UK GAAP. The Glossary to FRS 102 outlines the arrangements that meet the definition of a group reconstruction and paragraph 19.27 of FRS 102 also sets out the conditions which must be met in order for a group reconstruction to be accounted for using the merger method. Paragraph 19.27(a) says that the use of the merger method must not be prohibited by other relevant legislation. The LLP Regulations do not prohibit the use of the merger method.

Merger accounting is also dealt with in Section 19 of FRS 102. In respect of initial conversions, where the requirements in paragraph 19.27 are met in respect of group reconstructions, the SORP recommends that the merger accounting method be used (where permitted) so as to reflect the initial 'conversion' to LLP. The initial 'opening' balance sheet should follow the accounting policies of the LLP. Ordinarily, such transactions will be undertaken using book values rather than fair values and therefore the merger accounting method reflects the substance of the transactions.

When there is a 'true' merger, Section 19 of FRS 102 requires merger accounting to be used. Merger accounting may also be used when there is a business combination which meets the definition of a group reconstruction. Whilst Section 19 does not make merger accounting mandatory in the latter case, it is generally considered that merger accounting as opposed to the purchase method should be applied to group reconstructions in order for the accounts to give a true and fair view as merger accounting will reflect the substance of the transaction.

Considerations relating to transition from a partnership to an LLP are dealt with in more detail in Chapter 13. However, in general, these should be accounted for as group reconstructions using merger accounting.

11 Conditions permitting merger accounting

12.14 FRS 102 (September 2015) allows a group reconstruction to be accounted for using merger accounting provided that three conditions are met:

- the use of the merger accounting method is not prohibited by law;
- the ultimate equity holders remain the same, and the rights of each equity holder, relative to the others, are unchanged; and
- no non-controlling interest in the group's net assets is altered by the transfer.

The SORP acknowledges that new start-ups and existing businesses (which include both partnerships and limited companies) might choose to become an LLP. When this happens, the SORP requires merger accounting to be used provided that the transfer complies with the three criteria above.

12 The accounting consequences of a merger

12.15 Where all of the criteria for merger accounting are met, the accounting in the consolidated financial statements is as follows:

- the net assets of the two entities are combined using their existing book values – no fair value adjustments are required because existing book values reflects the substance of the transaction;
- adjustments will, however, need to be made as necessary to ensure that the same accounting policies are applied;
- no positive goodwill or negative goodwill will be recognised;
- the results of all the combining entities are brought into the financial statements of the combined entity from the start of the financial year in which the combination took place and are adjusted in order to achieve uniformity of accounting policies; and
- the comparative amounts should be restated to the aggregate of the amounts recorded by the two entities in the previous period, adjusted as necessary to achieve uniformity of accounting policies.

When comparatives are restated so as to achieve uniformity of accounting policies, there will often be a difference between the amounts reported as attributable to owners by the predecessor undertaking and the members' interests in the opening balance sheet of the LLP. In such cases the SORP requires that such differences are not dealt with in the financial statements of the LLP.

The SORP also identifies additional factors which LLPs should consider when adjusting comparative information:

- whether the predecessor undertaking's accounting policies require amendment as they are not compliant with the requirements of FRS 102;
- whether the predecessor undertaking's accounting policies are to be amended voluntarily; and
- whether any of the members' rights change on transition together with the effects of those changes.

Chapter summary

- There are two possible methods of accounting for a business combination: the purchase method and the merger method.
- Strict conditions exist in UK GAAP and legislation where the merger method is concerned.
- There are three steps involved in the purchase method: identify the acquirer; measure the cost of the business combination; and allocate the cost of the combination.

- The date of acquisition is the date on which control passes to the parent LLP which might be different than the date on which legal completion takes place.
- Assets and liabilities of the acquired business should be fair valued when the purchase method of accounting is being used.
- Goodwill arises when the value of the consideration is higher or lower than the fair value of the net assets acquired.
- Positive goodwill is capitalised and amortised over its useful economic life. Negative goodwill is recognised in profit or loss in the periods in which the non-monetary assets are recovered.
- Goodwill must be tested for impairment.
- The SORP recommends that the merger accounting method be used (where permitted) so as to reflect the initial conversion of a partnership to an LLP.
- Book values, as opposed to fair values, are used in a merger to reflect the substance of the arrangement.

Chapter 13

The transition from partnership to LLP

Signposts

- Whilst the conversion to LLP may seem attractive, it is not without its costs in terms of internal time and professional fees (see **13.1**).
- In the event of the LLP becoming insolvent, the capital may not be returned to the members (see **13.2**).
- Whilst all, or the vast majority of, assets and liabilities would be transferred from the partnership into the LLP, the former partners may decide that some assets and liabilities remain in the former partnership (see **13.3**).
- Retirement benefits to former partners need careful consideration (see **13.3**).
- When the transfer of assets and liabilities into the LLP is to take place, they should be brought in at amounts which have been calculated in accordance with the LLPs accounting policies which should be compliant with FRS 102 (see **13.4**).
- For new LLPs which are groups, there are a number of steps they must take to establish the basis on which any consolidated financial statements are to be constructed (see **13.5** and **13.6**).
- In order for an LLP to qualify as a group reconstruction and adopt merger accounting, the interests of the members in the LLP should be in the same proportions as their 'share' in the partnership immediately prior to the transfer to the LLP (see **13.7**).
- Pro-forma comparative information should be presented in the financial statements of the first period after incorporation for a single-entity LLP formed from the transfer or incorporation of an existing entity (see **13.8**).
- The SORP contains some additional guidance where there is a delay in forming the LLP and the transfer of the existing partnership into the LLP (see **13.8**).
- There are specific issues which auditors need to consider in the first year of transition (see **13.9**).

1 Introduction

13.1 The combination of the advantages of limited liability and the concept of partnership makes conversion of existing partnerships to LLP status attractive and is the main reason why LLPs have increased in popularity over recent years. It is not, however, without its costs, not only in respect of the internal time and professional fees involved in effecting the transfer, but also with regard to the accounting and auditing requirements, a number of which will be unfamiliar to some partnerships that choose to 'convert' (see below). In addition, the financial affairs of the LLP will be in the public domain through the filing of annual accounts with the Registrar of Companies (Companies House).

In this chapter, we look specifically at some of the accounting issues surrounding the transition of a partnership to an LLP.

2 How much capital?

13.2 Whereas the liability of individual members is significantly reduced from that within a partnership (hence 'limited liability'), in the event of the insolvency of the LLP the capital may not be returned to the members. It is important, therefore, to take this into consideration when determining the level of existing partnership capital which should be introduced into the new LLP. Although there are obvious attractions to keeping the level of capital as low as possible, it should be noted that third parties such as banks and regulators may require the subordination of amounts due to members and/or require minimum amounts to be retained within the LLP.

3 The assets and liabilities to be transferred

13.3 In most circumstances, it would be anticipated that all, or the vast majority of, assets and liabilities would be transferred from the partnership to the new LLP. The former partners may, however, decide that some assets and liabilities should remain in the former partnership.

One particular area for consideration is the treatment of liabilities to former partners. Some partnerships have sought to leave the retirement benefits due to former partners as a liability of the partnership rather than transfer that liability to the LLP. Such a course of action will normally require the consent of those former partners, and they may also require the liabilities to be underwritten by the LLP. The accounting treatment of post-retirement liabilities is dealt with in **9.11** to **9.16**. Similar accounting treatments will also apply to any other liabilities of the former partnership—and careful consideration has to be given as to whether or not the LLP will be required to recognise the liability, as this will depend upon the probability that it may be required to make any payment. Even if no provision is required to be recognised in the accounts, the possibility of a future liability should be disclosed as a contingent liability of the LLP and the requirements in Section 21 *Provisions and Contingencies* of FRS 102 should be considered.

4 Alignment of accounting policies

13.4 On transferring assets and liabilities to the LLP, the amounts at which they are initially recorded in the accounts should be calculated by reference to the accounting policies to be adopted by the LLP. The accounting policies selected must be compliant with the requirements of FRS 102. Where the LLP is a micro-entity and is reporting under FRS 105 *The Financial Reporting Standard applicable to the Micro-entities Regime*, it should be borne in mind that micro-entity LLPs will not have any accounting policy options available to them under the micro-entities framework (other than some transitional options on transition to the standard). Dependent on the policies adopted by the partnership, these could vary significantly from those shown in the accounts of the predecessor partnership. This will be particularly relevant where the partnership had prepared accounts for its own purposes other than on the 'true and fair' basis, making adjustments to that basis only for the purposes of its tax return. Areas where differences may arise include:

- Provisions for retirement benefits to former partners to the extent that the liability to meet the cost is transferred to the LLP (see **9.11–9.16**).
- Derecognition of provisions which do not meet the definition within Section 21 of FRS 102 or Section 16 *Provisions and Contingencies* in FRS 105 (for example, provisions for possible future PI claims) (see **9.2–9.10**).

The particular issues facing partnerships with subsidiary undertakings are discussed below.

5 Groups

13.5 The majority of partnerships with subsidiary undertakings, irrespective of whether those subsidiaries are companies or other partnerships, will not historically have prepared consolidated (group) accounts in the form required by UK GAAP. The partnership may well have prepared some form of group accounts, probably an aggregation of the results and balance sheets, but these are unlikely to be sufficient going forward as they will more than likely not accord to the principles in UK GAAP, notably Section 9 of FRS 102, *Consolidated and Separate Financial Statements* (note: groups are not within the scope of FRS 105).

There are a number of steps that the LLP must take in order to establish the basis on which any group accounts should be constructed. It will need to:

- Ascertain those investments of the partnership which fall to be treated as subsidiaries. In simple terms, this will be those other entities in which the LLP has a controlling interest (see **Chapter 11**).
- Determine whether or not group accounts are required by reference to the combined size of the LLP and its subsidiaries. (The circumstances where group accounts are not required are considered in **Chapter 2**).
- Determine the cost of investment in those subsidiaries. For companies, this will be the amount paid to acquire the shares, which should already be recorded as an investment in the accounts of the partnership. For an investment in a partnership, the cost of investment will be the amount of capital held in that partnership.

- Where a subsidiary has been previously acquired, ascertain whether or not it is practical to determine the fair values of assets and liabilities at the date of acquisition (the date of acquisition being the date on which control is passed to the parent LLP). Where a subsidiary is a company or partnership formed by the previous partnership to undertake certain parts of the partnership's business no further analysis should be necessary.
- If intra-group trading has taken place, identify the amounts as these will need to be eliminated from consolidated accounts (both the intra-group trading and the effects of such trading eg intra-group debtors/creditors will need to be eliminated) so that the consolidated financial statements present the results of the group in line with its economic substance, ie as if it were a single reporting entity.
- Where assets are sold between group members at a profit (for example, fixed assets or stock); identify the profit element in order that it can be eliminated from the consolidated accounts.

Example – intra-group profit in stock at the year-end

LLP A sold goods for resale to Subsidiary B (B) for £2,000 which represents cost plus 25%. At the year-end goods of £1,200 were still in stock and included in B's stock count. The selling price is therefore made up as follows:

Cost	£1,600
Profit	£400 (ie 25% of cost)
Sales price	£2,000

The unrealised profit in stock is £240 (£1,200/£2,000 x £400) and is removed by crediting closing stock in the consolidated balance sheet and debiting closing stock in the consolidated profit and loss account. The objective of this is to reduce the closing stock valuation to cost to the group. If this profit were not eliminated, the closing stock value in the consolidated financial statements would be overstated as the stock valuation would not be at cost to the group.

In reality, the step which is most likely to cause difficulties is the identification of assets and liabilities associated with past acquisitions. Whether or not it is possible to determine the fair value of assets and liabilities at the date of acquisition will depend on the extent of the records maintained by the partnership and the period of time that has elapsed since the acquisition. The method suggested below may give an adequate approximation, particularly for subsidiaries acquired some time previously.

13.6 As a matter of accounting principle, the consolidated financial statements should not include any profits earned by a subsidiary prior to acquisition. An adjustment should therefore be made in the consolidated accounts to remove any such profits from the cumulative reserves of the group. The corresponding entry to this adjustment should be made against the cost of investment, along with the elimination of the share capital of the subsidiary. Any difference between the cost of investment and pre-acquisition reserves and share capital, together with any adjustments to reflect fair value, should be treated as goodwill and be amortised in the consolidated profit and loss account on a systematic basis over the estimated useful economic life of the goodwill (note under FRS 102, all goodwill will have a finite useful life). Where the partners are unable to arrive at a reliably measurable useful economic life, the maximum timescale that this goodwill can be written off over is ten years.

The following example illustrates the position where it has not been possible to determine the fair values of the assets and liabilities in a previously acquired subsidiary.

Example – previously acquired subsidiary

X & Co (a partnership) acquired Y Ltd a number of years ago for £200. At that date, share capital was £30 and profit and loss reserves were £70. Net assets, therefore, were £100. At the current year end, the balance sheet of Y Ltd is as follows:

	£
Assets	400
Share capital	30
Profit and loss account	370
	400

In preparing the consolidated accounts, the newly formed LLP first needs to aggregate its balance sheet and profit and loss account with that of Y Ltd. It will then raise a journal which will debit share capital by £30, debit profit and loss by £70, debit goodwill by £100 (£200 – £100), and credit cost of investment by £200. The goodwill will then require amortisation in accordance with the accounting policy determined by the LLP.

---

6 Presenting the transition in the accounts

13.7 As discussed in Chapter 12, the transition from partnership to LLP should be accounted for using the merger accounting method instead of the purchase method of accounting (see below). The LLP Regulations (SI 2008/1912 schedule 3, 10 and SI 2008/1911 schedule 4, part 1, 7) allows an acquisition to be accounted for as a merger if the adoption of merger accounting complies with UK GAAP. The Glossary to FRS 102 defines a 'group reconstruction' as:

> 'Any one of the following arrangements:
>
> (a) the transfer of an equity holding in a **subsidiary** from one group entity to another;
>
> (b) the addition of a new **parent** entity to a **group**;
>
> (c) the transfer of equity holdings in one or more subsidiaries of a group to a new entity that is not a group entity but whose equity holders are the same as those of the group's parent; or

(d) the combination into a group of two or more entities that before the combination had the same equity holders.'[1]

In addition, paragraph 19.27 of FRS 102 sets out the conditions which must be met in order that a group reconstruction can be accounted for using the merger accounting method. One of the conditions in paragraph 19.27(a) says that the use of the merger accounting method must not be prohibited by company law or other relevant legislation. The LLP Regulations do not prohibit the use of the merger method.

Paragraph 19.27(b) also says that the ultimate equity holders must remain the same, and the rights of each equity holder, relative to the others, are unchanged.

Paragraph 19.27(b) is written in the context of corporate entities. Putting this definition into the context of a partnership, in order for the transfer to an LLP to qualify as a group reconstruction, and hence being eligible to apply merger accounting, the interests of members in the LLP should be in the same proportions as their 'share' in the partnership immediately prior to the transfer. Both the amount of capital introduced and profit-sharing arrangements will need to be taken into account when determining if the criteria have been met.

The application of this requirement means that it may be preferable not to combine the retirement or appointment of partners or members with transition to an LLP, nor should the relative benefits of partners/members be altered at this stage. Where the requirements of paragraph 19.27 are not met, the transfer should be accounted for as an acquisition (and hence the use of the purchase method) and the assets and liabilities transferred would need to be restated to their fair values at the date of acquisition and the 'consideration' for the acquisition determined by reference to the value of the business of the partnership transferred. Goodwill will arise as a consequence of the difference between the two values, and this will have to be recognised on the balance sheet and amortised through the profit and loss account of the LLP over its useful economic life. For a partnership in the services sector, the value of the business taken as a whole, compared to the value of its underlying assets and liabilities, could well be significantly different. The amount of goodwill, and the impact on the profit and loss account, could therefore be substantial.

13.8 The SORP requires that single entity LLPs formed from the transfer or incorporation of an existing entity should present comparative pro-forma information in the financial statements of the first period after incorporation. The corresponding amounts should be stated using the same accounting policies as those adopted by the LLP. For the reasons discussed above, the amounts shown by the comparative figures may differ from those in the equivalent partnership accounts, resulting in a consequential difference between partners' interests and members' interests. This difference should not be reflected in the accounts of the LLP, which should be prepared on the basis that the LLP has always existed and has always prepared accounts in accordance with its selected accounting policies.

It is frequently the case that there is a delay between forming the LLP and the transfer of the existing partnership undertaking. In these cases, there is a conflict between the

1 FRS 102 Glossary 'group reconstructions'.

requirements to present a profit and loss account that complies with statutory requirements (ie covering only the period from the transfer of the previous undertaking) and information that provides a meaningful comparative of what is effectively the same business. The SORP considers this issue in some detail in Appendix 4. Appendix 4 considers two potential alternative ways of presenting the LLP's results based on a scenario where Entity A establishes an LLP on 1 April, transfers its trade and assets to the LLP on 1 July and has a year-end of 31 December and prepares entity-only accounts. The two potential alternative options are as follows:

- bring in the net asset book values at the date of transfer of trade and assets. Profits are recognised which arise in the LLP from the incorporation date (1 April) but will only include transactions from the date of transfer which is from 1 July to 31 December (as the LLP did not undertake any trading transactions before the date of transfer); or
- bring in the net book values at 1 January and include the results for the 12-month accounting period from 1 January to 31 December so as to be consistent and comparable with Entity A's reporting period.

The SORP recommends the following presentation:

- A statutory profit and loss account for the period from transfer of business to the reporting date.
- Disclosure of the 12-month period to the reporting date.
- Pro-forma comparatives for the previous reporting period.

This can be contrasted with the position where a group transfers to LLP status. In these circumstances, the group reconstruction provisions of Section 19 of FRS 102 require that comparative figures be presented for the previous year. These will not be pro-forma and will, therefore, fall within the scope of the auditor's report. Whilst an LLP presenting consolidated financial statements does not have to present the individual LLP's profit and loss account within the financial statements, the Companies Act 2006 requires that it still be prepared for the information of members. Similar principles to those discussed above will therefore apply.

It is recommended that those partnerships considering transfer to LLP status carry out some initial calculations of the impact that changes in accounting policies could have and how this affects existing partners' interests. Such changes can then be explained and discussed with the partners.

7 Audit issues arising in the first year of transition

13.9 There are a number of potential issues which will affect the audit of an LLP formed from a partnership in its first year.

The majority of partnerships do not have their accounts audited and, therefore, it will be for the auditors to determine whether they are able to obtain sufficient and appropriate audit evidence as to the accuracy of the opening balance sheet of the LLP to enable them to state that the accounts for the current reporting period give a true and fair view. Whilst it should usually be possible to form an opinion on the closing balance sheet, the opening figures will impact the amounts included in the profit and loss account, and qualification with respect to limitation in audit scope may be required.

It may be possible to restrict the qualification to a specific account area, for example work in progress, if the auditors are able to perform audit procedures that allow them to meet the requirements of ISA (UK) 510 (Revised June 2016) *Initial Audit Engagements – Opening Balances.*

Further complications may arise in considering the status of any comparative figures and their impact on the auditor's report.

For a single entity LLP formed from an existing partnership, the comparative information is only included as a pro-forma and can therefore be excluded from the scope of the auditor's report. Where this is the case, the presentation of the comparatives in the accounts should make it clear that they are unaudited pro-forma information, and this fact should also be made clear in the scope paragraph of the auditor's report.

The position for a group headed by a new LLP which is required to present comparative information in accordance with paragraph 19.30 of FRS 102 may be more complex. In particular, where the comparative information has not been subject to audit, reference to this fact will be required in the auditor's report in a similar way to that referred to above.

Chapter summary

- Careful thought must be given when considering transferring to LLP status because the transfer will incur additional costs and impose more burdens on the partners in terms of accounting and audit-related issues.
- LLPs have limited liability and in the invent of insolvency of the LLP, capital may not be returned to the members.
- Some assets and liabilities may be kept in the old partnership rather than transferred into the LLP.
- On conversion to LLP status, the partners must consider whether the accounting policies are appropriate to the LLP as well as being compliant with accounting standards (such as FRS 102/FRS 105).
- LLPs may have to prepare group accounts (consolidated financial statements) in some situations which follow the principles laid down in FRS 102.
- Transitioning from partnership to LLP will often be effected using the merger method of accounting provided that it meets the criteria in law and complies with paragraph 19.27 of FRS 102.
- If the LLP becomes subject to audit (either voluntarily or mandatorily), then there are a number of potential issues which will affect the audit of an LLP formed from a partnership in its first year (such as opening balances on conversion).

Chapter 14

Micro-entities

Signposts

- SI 2016/575 amended the Regulations applicable to LLPs and these amendments apply for accounting periods starting on or after 1 January 2016 (with early-adoption permissible) (see **14.1** and **14.3**).
- A Micro LLP can use FRS 105 *The Financial Reporting Standard applicable to the Micro-entities Regime* if it so chooses. If the micro LLP prepares its financial statements under FRS 105, it must not apply any provisions in the LLP SORP (see **14.5**).
- There are some notable key features of FRS 105 which should be understood at the outset (see **14.7**).
- Whilst FRS 105 is considered to be the least complex accounting standard in UK GAAP, it may not be appropriate to some micro LLPs and various factors should be considered prior to applying the standard (see **14.8**).
- There are some significant differences in accounting in FRS 105 when compared to the previous FRSSE (see **14.9**).
- The provisions in FRS 105 are examined in this chapter at paragraphs **14.10** to **14.134**.

1 Introduction

14.1 In 2015, the Companies Act 2006 was amended to reflect the provisions in the EU Accounting Directive (the Accounting Directive) and these changes primarily affected small companies and micro-entities in terms of the levels of disclosures that such entities are mandated to make in their financial statements.

LLPs are not subject to the Accounting Directive, but are subject to a very similar accounting regime to limited companies; for example, the requirement to file financial statements at Companies House for placing on the public record.

In May 2016, the Department for Business Innovation and Skills (BIS) (which was replaced by the Department for Business, Energy and Industrial Strategy in July 2016) issued SI 2016/575 which amended legislation relating to the accounting and audit regulatory framework for LLPs. In addition, the Regulations introduced an exemption from certain financial reporting requirements for very small (micro) LLPs as well as very small (micro) partnerships, including limited partnerships that are 'qualifying partnerships' under the Partnerships (Accounts) Regulations 2008 (SI 2008/569). The Regulations themselves are deregulatory in nature and reduce the burdens in respect of financial reporting and audit for small and micro LLPs. In addition, the Regulations achieve consistency with the financial reporting regime for companies.

From a legislative perspective, the Regulations amend the following legislation:

- the Limited Liability Partnerships (Accounts and Audit) (Application of Companies Act 2006) Regulations 2008 (SI 2008/1911) (which applies to LLPs, with modifications, provisions of the Companies Act 2006 regarding accounts and audit);
- the Small Limited Liability Partnerships (Accounts) Regulations 2008 (SI 2008/1912) (which applies to LLPs, with modifications, provisions of the Small Companies and Groups (Accounts and Directors' Report) Regulations 2008 (SI 2008/409));
- the Large and Medium-sized Limited Liability Partnerships (Accounts) Regulations 2008 (SI 2008/1913) (which applies to LLPs, with modifications, provisions of the Large and Medium-sized Companies and Groups (Accounts and Reports) Regulations 2008 (SI 2008/410));
- the Small Companies (Micro-Entities' Accounts) Regulations 2013 (SI 2013/3008) (which introduced a micro-entities regime for companies that was not applied to qualifying partnerships);
- the Partnerships (Accounts) Regulations 2008 (SI 2008/569); and
- the Large and Medium-sized Companies and Groups (Accounts and Reports) Regulations 2008 (SI 2008/410) (which contains provisions regarding the preparation of accounts for large and medium-sized companies).

14.2 In May 2016, BIS estimated that there were some 58,000 LLPs in the UK and around 98% of LLPs are small and hence will benefit significantly from the deregulatory changes. BIS also expect that the deregulatory changes will be of benefit to some medium-sized and large LLPs as well as groups that include both companies and LLPs within their structures.

One of the notable features of SI 2016/575 was to introduce a micro-entities regime for LLPs and qualifying partnerships (previously LLPs were unable to apply the micro-entities' regime in the preparation of financial statements). However, following a consultation, the majority of respondents agreed with the proposal to introduce a micro-entities regime for LLPs and qualifying partnerships and the respondents encouraged BIS to make the legislative changes as soon as possible, which they did when they issued SI 2016/575.

Effective date

14.3 The Regulations are effective for accounting periods starting on or after 1 January 2016 and the LLP SORP (issued on 26 January 2017) has been revised to reflect the provisions of SI 2016/575. The LLP SORP is also effective for accounting periods starting on or after 1 January 2016. However, early-adoption of the revised LLP SORP is also permitted for accounting periods starting on or after 1 January 2015, provided that The Limited Liability Partnerships (Accounts and Audit) Regulations 2016 (SI 2016/575) are applied from the same date.

> **Focus**
>
> - The thresholds which determine whether an LLP is micro, small, medium-sized or large have been increased in line with those for companies (see **Chapter 2**).

2 Micro-entities regime

14.4 Until May 2016, the micro-entities' framework could only be used by companies. However, following the issuance of SI 2016/575 the smallest of LLPs (micro LLPs) may be eligible to use FRS 105 *The Financial Reporting Standard applicable to the Micro-entities Regime*.

In order to be eligible to apply FRS 105 a micro LLP must meet two out of the following three criteria:

- turnover of not more than £632,000;
- a balance sheet total (fixed assets plus current assets) of not more than £316,000; and
- not more than ten employees.

> **Focus**
>
> - It is also worth emphasising that the micro-entities' framework is not available to financial, insurance or credit institutions. In addition, charities are unable to apply FRS 105 and LLPs whose financial statements are consolidated in with those of a parent are unable to use the standard. Therefore, the first concern when deciding whether to apply FRS 105, or not, would be to consider whether the LLP is undertaking a business activity which is permitted to apply the standard, or whether the LLP has its financial statements consolidated in with those of a parent.

14.5 FRS 105 was first issued in July 2015 and was subsequently amended by the Financial Reporting Council in May 2016 to reflect the fact that LLPs can now use the standard.

> **Focus**
>
> - Micro LLPs applying FRS 105 are scoped out of the requirements of the LLP SORP. Paragraph 3 of the LLP SORP confirms that LLPs applying FRS 105 should only have regard to the provisions of FRS 105. This is because the LLP SORP complements the requirements of FRS 102 *The Financial Reporting Standard*

applicable in the UK and Republic of Ireland and not FRS 105 (there are some quite significant differences between the provisions in FRS 102 and FRS 105). Where FRS 105 does not deal with a specific transaction, the micro LLP must refer to the *Concepts and Pervasive Principles* contained in Section 2 of FRS 105. It must not refer to the LLP SORP.

The Financial Reporting Council decided to 'carve out' the micro-entities regime into its own FRS because of the significantly reduced disclosures the micro-entities regime imposes on reporting entities under its scope and the simplifications that have been made in FRS 105. In addition, there are no accounting policy options available to micro-entities, other than some transitional options on first-time adoption of FRS 105, hence it was sensible to have a standalone standard for micro-entities.

While FRS 105 is considered to be the least complicated standard in the suite of UK GAAP, each entity that is eligible to apply it should consider whether the regime meets their individual needs. This is because while FRS 105 will be appropriate for some LLPs, it will not necessarily be appropriate for them all. For example, some of the accounting policy options that are found in FRS 102 are not available in FRS 105 (such as the option to revalue fixed assets). Such issues are discussed in **14.8**.

3 FRS 105 *The Financial Reporting Standard applicable to the Micro-entities Regime*

14.6 Micro LLPs are eligible to use FRS 105 if they meet the size criteria (see **14.4** above) and are also not in a business that is precluded from using the standard, for example the LLP is not a financial institution. FRS 105 was first issued in July 2015 but the Financial Reporting Council issued amendments to FRS 105 which apply specifically for LLPs as the scope of the standard was widened to cater for LLPs when SI 2016/575 was issued.

The structure of FRS 105 is different than FRS 102 because some sections of FRS 102 are not applicable to micro-entities. The following table reconciles the structural differences:

Section	FRS 102 (September 2015)	FRS 105 (July 2015)
1	Scope	Scope
1A	Small Entities Appendix A: Guidance on adapting the balance sheet formats Appendix B: Guidance on adapting the profit and loss account formats Appendix C: Disclosure requirements for small entities Appendix D: Additional disclosures encouraged for small entities	N/A

Section	FRS 102 (September 2015)	FRS 105 (July 2015)
2	Concepts and Pervasive Principles	Concepts and Pervasive Principles
3	Financial Statement Presentation	Financial Statement Presentation
4	Statement of Financial Position	Statement of Financial Position
5	Statement of Comprehensive Income and Income Statement Appendix: Example showing presentation of discontinued operations	Income Statement
6	Statement of Changes in Equity and Statement of Income and Retained Earnings	Notes to the Financial Statements Appendix: Company law disclosure requirements
7	Statement of Cash Flows	Subsidiaries, Associates, Jointly Controlled Entities and Intermediate Payment Arrangements
8	Notes to the Financial Statements	Accounting Policies, Estimates and Errors
9	Consolidated and Separate Financial Statements	Financial Instruments
10	Accounting Policies, Estimates and Errors	Inventories
11	Basic Financial Instruments	Investments in Joint Ventures
12	Other Financial Instruments Issues Appendix: Examples of hedge accounting	Property, Plant and Equipment and Investment Property
13	Inventories	Intangible Assets other than Goodwill
14	Investments in Associates	Business Combinations and Goodwill
15	Investments in Joint Ventures	Leases
16	Investment Property	Provisions and Contingencies Appendix: Examples of recognising and measuring provisions

Section	FRS 102 (September 2015)	FRS 105 (July 2015)
17	Property, Plant and Equipment	Liabilities and Equity
18	Intangible Assets other than Goodwill	Revenue Appendix: Examples of revenue recognition under the principles in Section 18
19	Business Combinations and Goodwill	Government Grants
20	Leases	Borrowing Costs
21	Provisions and Contingencies Appendix: Examples of recognising and measuring provisions	Share-based Payment
22	Liabilities and Equity Appendix: Example of the issuer's accounting for convertible debt	Impairment of Assets
23	Revenue Appendix: Examples of revenue recognition	Employee Benefits
24	Government Grants	Income Tax
25	Borrowing Costs	Foreign Currency Translation
26	Share-based Payment	Events after the End of the Reporting Period
27	Impairment of Assets	Specialised Activities
28	Employee Benefits	Transition to this FRS
29	Income Tax	N/A
30	Foreign Currency Translation	N/A
31	Hyperinflation	N/A
32	Events after the End of the Reporting Period	N/A
33	Related Party Disclosures	N/A

Section	FRS 102 (September 2015)	FRS 105 (July 2015)
34	Specialised Activities Agriculture Extractive Activities Service Concession Arrangements Financial Institutions Retirement Benefit Plans: Financial Statements Heritage Assets Funding Commitments Incoming Resources from Non-exchange Transactions Public Benefit Entity Combinations Public Benefit Entity Concessionary Loans Appendix A: Guidance on funding commitments Appendix B: Guidance on incoming resources from non-exchange transactions	N/A
35	Transition to this FRS	N/A

Key features of FRS 105

14.7 Some of the notable key features of FRS 105 are shown in the following table:

Issue	FRS 105
Primary statements	There are only two primary statements required under FRS 105: a balance sheet and a profit and loss account. There is no requirement for a micro LLP to prepare a cash flow statement or a statement of changes in equity.
Condensed financial information	The information presented in the balance sheet and profit and loss account is condensed; for example, fixed assets are not split between intangible fixed assets, tangible fixed assets and investments. This is because the statutory formats are only preceded by letters. The statutory formats do not contain any items preceded by Roman or Arabic numerals.
Fair values and revaluation amounts	No asset or liabilities are allowed to be measured at fair value or at revaluation amounts. The consequence of this is that any previous revaluations will have to be removed on transition because the legislation does not recognise fair value or revaluation accounting. This rule also applies to an LLP that may have an investment property on the balance sheet; hence careful consideration should be given to the appropriateness of FRS 105 where an LLP has previously revalued an asset or has an investment property which it has previously carried at open market value at each balance sheet date.

Issue	FRS 105
Disclosure requirements	The disclosure requirements for a micro LLP are significantly fewer than what was the case under, say, the FRSSE. The disclosure requirements are outlined in Section 6 *Notes to the Financial Statements* in FRS 105, but Section 6 contains an Appendix which is an integral part of the standard which 'drills down' on the disclosure requirements in more detail.
True and fair view	Micro LLPs preparing financial statements in compliance with the minimum legal requirements will result in financial statements that are *presumed* to give a true and fair view. There is no requirement, therefore, for the members to consider any additional disclosure information that may be needed.
Simplified accounting treatments	FRS 105 simplifies the accounting treatment for some transactions; for example there is no requirement to impute market rates of interest for loans that are not entered into at market rates as the effective interest method is not used in FRS 105.
No accounting policy choices	All accounting policy options have been removed in FRS 105 (with the exception of some transitional options). The mandatory treatments result in earlier recognition of income/expenses in the profit and loss account rather than deferred in the balance sheet. Therefore, costs such as development and borrowing costs are recognised immediately in profit or loss; there is no option to capitalise such expenses.
More helpful guidance included	In many instances, the requirements of FRS 105 do not differ from those of the FRSSE. However, more guidance is provided in FRS 105 to help preparers apply and interpret the treatment required.
Terminology	Terminology used in FRS 105 is consistent with that of FRS 102; hence the standard refers to the balance sheet as a 'statement of financial position'. A Table of Equivalence is included in Appendix II to FRS 105 for convenience.

Considerations when assessing the appropriateness of FRS 105 for an LLP

14.8 LLPs and professional advisers should carefully consider the appropriateness of FRS 105 on a case-by-case basis. The standard itself will be suitable for the majority of micro LLPs; however, it may not necessarily be suitable for them all. Some factors to take into consideration include:

- **Information placed in the public domain**. The micro-reporting regime offers the opportunity to file considerably less detail at Companies House in the way of disclosures than, say, a small LLP reporting under FRS 102, Section 1A. This may be an attractive option to most micro LLPs given the fact that abbreviated financial statements are abolished for accounting periods starting on or after 1 January 2016.
- **Pace of growth**. If the micro LLP is new and is expected to grow at a rapid rate, it may be worthwhile considering bypassing FRS 105 in favour of FRS 102, Section 1A. This could avoid the need to do a transition from FRS 105 to FRS 102 if the LLP outgrows FRS 105 in a relatively short period of time.

- **Access to finance and credit**. Some micro LLPs preparing their financial statements under the micro-entities' regime may have to produce certain non-statutory information in order to be able to secure finance and credit. This, of course, may incur extra costs and as the micro-entities' regime is (at the time of writing) still in its infancy, and there are concerns about the impact of the limited disclosure requirements.
- **Balance sheet position**. FRS 105 does not allow micro LLPs to revalue assets or carry assets at fair value. On transition, a micro LLP must remove all previous revaluations and fair value amounts and restate any assets previously carried at revaluation or at fair value to historic cost values. This, of course, could have a detrimental impact on the balance sheet position and careful consideration needs to be given to the impact that transitioning to FRS 105 might have where the LLP has previously measured asset at fair value or under the revaluation model.
- **Profitability**. As FRS 105 does not allow any accounting policy options, issues such as borrowing costs and development costs may need to be considered if the LLP enters into such transactions and the impact that such costs will have on the LLP's profitability. This is because under FRS 105, an LLP has no option but to write such costs off to profit or loss.
- **Client deliverables**. The micro-entities' regime is intended to be deregulatory and the information disclosed is very limited. Some practitioners may advise against using FRS 105 on the grounds that the information is potentially insufficient as a basis for discussion with the client in order to make informed management decisions.
- **Ease of use of FRS 105**. The accounting treatments in FRS 105 have been simplified in many areas; most notably in respect of financial instruments and this may prove to be of significant benefit to the LLP. For most LLPs, the lack of detail in the financial statements may be of benefit to members who may only want to have simplified financial statements.

FRS 105 versus the FRSSE/SORP

14.9 As mentioned earlier in the chapter, there are some notable differences between FRS 105 and the FRSSE which preparers of LLP financial statements need to understand. In many instances, the requirements of FRS 105 do not differ from the FRSSE; however, as there is a lack of accounting policy options available under FRS 105, this could impact on previous accounting treatments.

The table below outlines some of the most notable differences between FRS 105 and the FRSSE:

Subject	FRSSE/SORP	FRS 105
True and fair view	The FRSSE requires more disclosures in order that the financial statements give a true and fair view.	Financial statements prepared under the minimum legal requirements are presumed to give a true and fair view. This means that the members of the LLP need not consider any other disclosures to give a true and fair view.

Subject	FRSSE/SORP	FRS 105
Profit and loss account format	The profit and loss account was much more detailed under the FRSSE/SORP.	The LLP's profit and loss account under FRS 105 follows the structure of a Format 2 profit and loss account (expenses by nature) as follows: Turnover Other income Cost of raw materials and consumables Staff costs Depreciation and other amounts written off assets Other charges Tax Profit or loss for the financial year before members' remuneration and profit shares
Fair values and revaluation amounts	Under the FRSSE, an LLP could revalue assets or carry assets at fair value. This was particularly the case for investment property.	The micro-entities' legislation does not recognise fair value or revaluation accounting. As a consequence, all previous revaluation and fair value amounts must be removed on transition.
Borrowing and development costs	Borrowing and development costs could have been capitalised if this was the accounting policy applied.	Borrowing and development costs must be written off to profit or loss as they are incurred.
Disaggregation of the balance sheet	There was more disaggregation of amounts shown in the balance sheet.	There is no disaggregation of the balance sheet in the notes as the statutory formats are only preceded by letters. They are not preceded by Roman or Arabic numerals.
Defined benefit pension plans	The accounting treatment was far more complex and required actuarial valuations in order to complete the accounting input and associated disclosure requirements.	Defined benefit pension plans are accounted for as a defined contribution plan. A micro LLP must, however, recognise a liability in respect of a schedule of contributions which relates to a deficit in a defined benefit pension plan.
Intangible assets	Intangible assets that were separately identifiable were recognised separately.	No separate recognition of identifiable intangible assets in a trade and asset acquisition.

4 Financial statement presentation

14.10 Section 3 *Financial Statement Presentation* in FRS 105 explains how the micro LLP should present its financial statements and what a complete set of financial statements should comprise.

Going concern

14.11 As with companies, members of an LLP are required to assess whether the going concern basis of accounting is appropriate. Paragraph 3.3 of FRS 105 says that the going concern basis of accounting is appropriate unless the members either intend to liquidate the micro LLP or to cease trading, or the members have no realistic alternative but to do so.

Focus

- The members are required to consider all the information they have available concerning the future which is at least, but not limited to, 12 months from the date on which the financial statements are authorised for issue. The going concern assessment is not for a period of 12 months from the balance sheet date.

If the members do not regard the LLP as being a going concern, they must not adopt the going concern basis of preparing the financial statements. Ordinarily, in such situations, the members will prepare the financial statements on a 'break-up' basis.

FRS 105 says that the members of the LLP must take into account all available information about the future, which is at least, **but is not limited to**, 12 months from the date when the financial statements are authorised for issue. Therefore, if an LLP is expected to cease trading in, say, 18 months' time, it must not prepare the financial statements on the going concern basis because there is the intention to cease trading. The standard is clear; the members must consider the information at their disposal for a period of at least 12 months, not up to 12 months.

Consistency of presentation

14.12 The micro LLP must retain consistency with the way in which it presents and classifies items in the financial statements from one period to the next. This does not, however, preclude the micro LLP from changing the way it presents or classifies items if there is a significant change in the nature of the micro LLP's operations; or a review of the financial statements suggests that another presentation or classification would be more appropriate. In such situations, the micro LLP will apply the change in accordance with Section 8 *Accounting Policies, Estimates and Errors* which would require the micro LLP to reclassify comparative amounts (ie apply the change retrospectively) unless the reclassification is impracticable.

Focus

- The term 'impracticable' is defined in the Glossary as 'Applying a requirement is impracticable when the entity cannot apply it after making every reasonable effort to do so'.[1]

There may also be amendments made to FRS 105 by the Financial Reporting Council which requires a change in presentation in the micro LLP's financial statements. Again, such changes would also be accounted for under the provisions in Section 8 and hence applied retrospectively.

Comparative information

14.13 The micro LLP must present comparative information in respect of the preceding period for all amounts that are presented in the current period's financial statements. The exception to this rule would be where FRS 105 permits or requires otherwise.

Materiality

14.14 A micro LLP does not have to provide a specific disclosure if the information is considered to be immaterial. The Glossary to FRS 105 defines 'material' as:

> 'Omissions or misstatements of items are material if they could, individually or collectively, influence the economic decisions of users taken on the basis of the **financial statements**. Materiality depends on the size and nature of the omission or misstatement judged in the surrounding circumstances. The size or nature of the item, or a combination of both, could be the determining factor.'[2]

Complete set of financial statements

14.15 A complete set of financial statements for a micro LLP comprises:

- a balance sheet at the reporting date;
- notes included at the foot of the balance sheet; and
- a profit and loss account for the reporting period.

FRS 105 uses the term 'statement of financial position' for the balance sheet and 'income statement' for the profit and loss account, which are equally viable terms to use for the micro LLP's primary statements. It is expected that the majority of micro LLPs will continue to

1 FRS 105 Glossary **impracticable**.
2 FRS 105 Glossary **material**.

produce 'balance sheets' and 'profit and loss accounts' and hence this book uses traditional terminology for ease of reference. In addition, paragraph 3.12 of FRS 105 allows alternative titles to be used for the financial statements provided they are not misleading.

The micro LLP must produce comparative amounts in respect of the previous period for all amounts presented in the accounts. This means that in a set of complete financial statements for the micro LLP, it will present, as a minimum, two of each of the required financial statements and related notes.

5 Balance sheet (statement of financial position)

14.16 The balance sheet (referred to as the 'statement of financial position' in FRS 105) is dealt with in Section 4 *Statement of Financial Position*. There are two possible formats for the balance sheet: Format 1 and Format 2. It is important that the micro LLP is consistent, however, from one reporting period to the next.

Focus

- The balance sheet formats in Section 4 of FRS 105 refer to 'Called up share capital not paid' and 'Capital and reserves'. As LLPs will never have called up share capital, this line item cannot be used. References to 'Capital and reserves' should be substituted with 'Loans and other debts due to members' and 'Members' other interests'. The formats below reflect this requirement.

Format 1 balance sheet	2017	2016
	£	£
Fixed assets		X
Current assets	X	
Prepayments and accrued income	X	
Creditors: amounts falling due within one year	(X)	
Net current assets / (liabilities)		X/(X)
Total assets less current liabilities		X
Creditors: amounts falling due after more than one year		(X)
Provisions for liabilities		(X)
Accruals and deferred income		(X)
		X
Loans and other debts due to members		X
Members' other interests		X
		X

Format 2 balance sheet	2017	2016
	£	£
Assets		
Fixed assets		X
Current assets		X
Prepayments and accrued income		X
Loans and Other Debts due to Members/Members		X
Other Interests and Liabilities		
Loans and other debts due to members		X
Members other interests		X
Provisions for liabilities		X
Creditors		
Amounts falling due within one year	X	
Amounts falling due after one year	X	
		X
Accruals and deferred income		X
		X

> **Focus**
>
> - A micro LLP must classify a creditor as due within one year when it does not have an unconditional right, at the end of the reporting period, to defer settlement of the liability for at least 12 months after the reporting date.

6 Profit and loss account

14.17 The format of the profit and loss account is dealt with in Section 5 *Income Statement*. Under FRS 105, the micro LLP only has the option of preparing a Format 2 profit and loss account (expenses by nature). The line item 'Profit or loss' is substituted for 'Profit or loss for the financial year before members' remuneration and profit shares' and the illustration below reflects this requirement. Note: The line item for 'Tax' has been deliberately omitted as the LLP itself is not subject to taxation.

Profit and loss account	2017	2016
	£	£
Turnover	X	X
Other income	X	X
Cost of raw materials and consumables	(X)	(X)
Staff costs	(X)	(X)
Depreciation and other amounts written off assets	(X)	(X)

Profit and loss account	2017	2016
	£	£
Other charges	(X)	(X)
Profit or loss for the financial year before members' remuneration and profit shares	X/(X)	X/(X)

> **Focus**
>
> - Corrections of material errors and changes in accounting policies must be presented as retrospective adjustments of prior periods as opposed to adjustments of profit or loss in the period in which they arise.

7 Notes to the financial statements

14.18 Regulation 30 of the Limited Liability Partnerships (Accounts and Audit) (Application of Companies Act 2006) Regulations 2008 (SI 2008/1911) requires the notes of the micro LLP to be presented at the foot of the balance sheet. The notes must include details of any financial commitments, guarantees and contingencies as required by paragraph 55 of Part 3 of Schedule 1 to the Small LLPs Regulations.

The notes to the financial statements are dealt with in Section 6 *Notes to the Financial Statements*. However, there is an Appendix to Section 6 which is considered to be an integral part of FRS 105 and essentially 'drills down' on the disclosure requirements that a micro LLP must make.

> **Focus**
>
> - It is important that the disclosure requirements are checked for accuracy. This is because if they do not comply with requirements of Section 6, the micro LLP's financial statements will not be presumed to give a true and fair view. The presumption of true and fair only applies if the micro LLP has complied with the minimum legal requirements.

The Appendix to Section 6 spells out the exact disclosure requirements to comply with the law as follows:

1. The total value of financial commitments, guarantees and contingencies that are not included in the balance sheet to comply with paragraph 55(1) of Schedule 1 to the Small LLPs Regulations.
2. The total amount of any commitments concerning pensions must be separately disclosed to comply with paragraph 55(3) of Schedule 1 to the Small LLP Regulations.
3. The total amount of any commitments which are undertaken on behalf of, or for the benefit of:

    a) any parent, fellow subsidiary or any subsidiary of a micro-entity; or

b) any undertaking in which a micro-entity has a participating interest,

must be shown separately and those within a) must also be stated separately from those within b) (paragraph 55(4) of Schedule 1 to the Small LLPs Regulations).

In addition, the micro LLP must also provide an indication of the nature and form of any valuable security given by the micro LLP in respect of commitments, guarantees and contingencies within the above (paragraph 55(2) of Schedule 1 to the Small LLPs Regulations).

14.19 The disclosure requirements above are the minimum required by law and due to the presumption that the financial statements of a micro LLP prepared under the minimum legal provisions will give a true and fair view, the members need not consider any additional disclosures that may be necessary. However, this does not preclude the LLP from making voluntary disclosures which are beyond the scope of FRS 105. FRS 105 permits, but does not require, a micro LLP to include information which is additional to the micro LLP minimum accounting requirements. Where the micro LLP wishes to make additional voluntary disclosures, it must have regard to any requirement of Section 1A *Small Entities* in FRS 102 which relates to that information. It is expected that additional disclosures in respect of average number of employees and off-balance sheet arrangements will be required in the next edition of FRS 105 as these are required by law under the Companies Act 2006 (although at the time of writing this had not been issued in an Exposure Draft).

8 Subsidiaries, associates and jointly controlled entities

14.20 The first point worthy of note is that any entity which is required, or chooses, to present consolidated financial statements is excluded from the micro-entities regime and hence is not able to use FRS 105.

Where the micro LLP has investments in subsidiaries, associates, or jointly controlled entities they account for such investments under Section 9 *Financial Instruments* (see **14.26** to **14.39**).

9 Accounting policies, estimates and errors

14.21 FRS 105 says that accounting policies are the specific principles, bases, conventions, rules and practices which are applied by a micro LLP in preparing and presenting its financial statements.

Ordinarily, an LLP will follow the provisions in FRS 105 in respect of transactions, events, conditions and disclosures that are dealt with in the standard; although FRS 105 does acknowledge that the standard does not have to be followed if the effect would not be material.

Absence of specific guidance

14.22 In situations that FRS 105 does not deal with a transaction, event or condition, the members of the LLP must use judgement in developing and applying an accounting policy. The members must ensure that the policy they develop results in information that:

(a) represents faithfully the transactions, other events or conditions;

(b) reflects the economic substance of the transactions, other events and conditions, rather than legal form;

(c) is neutral, ie free from bias; and

(d) is prudent.

The members must have regard to the provisions in Section 2 *Concepts and Pervasive Principles* and a micro LLP is not required to provide any disclosures other than those required by Section 6 of the standard.

Focus

- It is important that the LLP selects and applies its accounting policies consistently for similar transactions, other events and conditions.

Changing accounting policies

14.23 There are two means by which a micro LLP will change an accounting policy:

(1) the change is required by FRS 105 (for example due to a change implemented by the Financial Reporting Council); or

(2) the members voluntarily make the change so that the financial statements provide reliable and more relevant information about the effects of transactions, other events or conditions on the micro LLP's financial position and financial performance.

When a micro LLP changes an accounting policy, it must apply the revised change retrospectively to comparative information for prior periods to the earliest date on which it is practicable to do so. This results in the financial statements reflecting the revised accounting policy as if that policy had always been in place. If it is impracticable to determine the individual-period effects of a change in accounting policy on comparative information for one, or more, periods presented, the micro LLP must apply the new accounting policy to the carrying amounts of assets and liabilities at the beginning of the earliest period for which retrospective application is practicable (which might be the current period).

Changing accounting estimates

14.24 Changes in accounting estimates are not changes in accounting policy and hence are not applied retrospectively. Instead, a change in accounting estimate (such as changing a fixed asset depreciation policy from 25% reducing balance to three-years straight line) is accounted for in the current year and going forwards (ie prospectively) if the change affects both the current period and future periods.

Prior period errors

14.25 FRS 105 says that 'prior period errors' are omissions from, and misstatements in, a micro LLP's financial statements for one, or more, periods and arises from a failure to use, or misuse of, reliable information which was available at the time the financial statements were authorised for issue and could have been expected to have been obtained and taken into account in the preparation and presentation of those accounts.

Prior period errors include:

- mathematical errors;
- mistakes in the application of the micro LLP's accounting policies;
- oversights;
- misinterpretation of facts; and
- fraud.

Prior period errors are corrected by restating the comparative amounts for the prior periods presented in the micro LLP's accounts. If the error arose before the earliest prior period presented, then it is corrected by restating the opening balances of assets, liabilities and loans and other debts due to members or members' other interests for the earliest prior period presented.

10 Financial instruments

14.26 Section 9 *Financial Instruments* of FRS 105 provides examples of financial instruments within its scope as follows:

(a) cash;

(b) accounts receivable and payable (trade debtors and creditors);

(c) commercial paper and commercial bills held;

(d) demand and fixed-term deposits with banks and similar institutions;

(e) bonds, loans and similar instruments;

(f) investments; and

(g) options, warrants, futures contracts, forward contracts and interest rate swaps.

For a micro LLP Section 9 does not deal with:

- financial instruments that are the micro LLP's own equity (see **14.101** to **14.103**);
- leases (see **14.79** to **14.89**);
- employers' rights and obligations under employee benefit plans (see **14.118**);
- reimbursement assets and financial guarantee contracts accounted for under Section 16 *Provisions and Contingencies* (see **14.90** to **14.100**); and
- contracts for contingent consideration in a business combination (see **14.76** to **14.78**).

Initial recognition of financial assets and financial liabilities

14.27 A financial asset or financial liability is only recognised when the micro LLP becomes a party to the contractual provisions of the instrument. When a micro LLP becomes a party to the contractual provisions of the instrument, it is always recognised initially at its cost. The cost is measured at the transaction price.

Some of the more common examples of financial assets and financial liabilities are shown in the table below:

Financial asset or financial liability	Initial recognition
Loan	The amount borrowed or loaned
Trade debtors or trade creditors	Invoice price (unless payment is deferred beyond normal credit terms (see **14.28**))
Investment	Cash paid to acquire the investment
Option	The premium paid to acquire the option

Deferred payment

14.28 If a micro LLP purchases stock, fixed assets or investment property or sells goods or services under terms which are beyond normal credit terms, the transaction price is the cash price available on the date of the transaction.

Example – deferred payment

An LLP provides services to one of its major clients and would normally expect payment from clients within 30 days. However, in this case, the members agree to defer payment for 14 months. The value of the services is £1,500 but would normally be £1,100 if payment is received within the usual credit terms.

The cash price for the services and therefore the transaction price is £1,100. The difference of £400 will be recognised as interest income and is allocated on a straight-line basis over the credit term (see **14.32** below).

Transaction costs

14.29 The treatment of transaction costs associated with a financial instrument will all depend on whether or not they are material. Transaction costs are added to the cost of a financial asset or deducted from the cost of a financial liability if they are material. If they are not material, they are recognised as an expense in profit or loss in the micro LLPs financial statements.

Example – bank loan

A micro LLP receives a bank loan of £2,000. The bank charges £175 in arrangement fees and the members conclude that the transaction costs are not material.

The transaction costs are recognised immediately as an expense.

Example – investment

A micro LLP purchases an investment in another LLP for £3,000 and incurs legal fees of £750. The members conclude that the legal fees are material.

The legal fees are included in the cost of the investment and hence the cost of the investment will be £3,750.

Subsequent measurement

14.30 Investments in preference shares, ordinary shares, subsidiaries, associates and jointly controlled entities are all to be measured at cost less impairment. There is no account taken of any transaction costs which the micro LLP may incur on sale or other disposal.

Focus

- All financial assets must be tested annually for impairment. See paragraphs **14.111** to **14.115**.

Any financial instrument which is not:

- preference or ordinary shares;
- an investment in a subsidiary, associate or joint venture; or
- a derivative,

is measured as follows:

- the transaction price;
- *plus*, in the case of a financial asset or *minus* in the case of a financial liability, transaction costs not yet recognised in profit or loss; plus
- the cumulative interest income or expense recognised in profit or loss to date; minus
- all repayments of capital and all interest payments or receipts to date; and
- *minus*, in the case of a financial asset, any reduction for impairment or uncollectibility.

Derivatives

14.31 The most common type of derivative financial instrument which a micro LLP may enter into is a forward foreign currency contract or an interest rate swap. Micro LLPs are not allowed to use fair value accounting and therefore when a micro LLP enters into a derivative instrument it accounts for it as follows:

- initially recognise the instrument at its transaction price; plus

- transaction costs not immediately recognised as an expense; minus
- impairment losses to date.

The derivative instrument is then allocated to the micro LLPs profit and loss account over the term of the contract on a straight-line basis. Another systematic basis can be used if the micro LLP so wishes if this alternative basis is deemed more appropriate.

Focus

- In some situations, a micro LLP may be contractually required to make payments under the contract or receive payments as the case may be. Any amounts payable or receivable are recognised in the micro LLP's financial statements as they accrue.

Allocating interest income or expense

14.32 Interest income or expense is to be allocated as follows:

(a) in respect of deferred payment arrangements, total interest income or expense is allocated on a straight-line basis over the term of the contract; and

(b) in all other cases, interest income or expense is allocated at a constant rate on the financial asset's or financial liability's carrying amount, excluding transaction costs not yet recognised in profit or loss.

Focus

- The rate of interest in (b) will usually be the contractual rate which may be variable or fixed rate.

Example – LLP receives a loan

On 1 July 2016, a micro LLP receives a loan of £10,000 and pays a loan arrangement fee of £500. The contractual rate of interest is 5% which is payable annually in arrears on 30 June. The loan is repayable in two years' time.

The members have concluded that the loan arrangement fee is material and therefore recognises the loan at its transaction price of £9,500 (£10,000 less £500). The transaction costs are recognised in profit or loss on a straight-line basis over two years and the loan is profiled as follows:

	Carrying value at 1 July	Interest at 5%	Transaction costs in P&L	Cash flow	Carrying value at 30 June
Year	£	£	£	£	£
2016	(9,500)	(500)	(250)	500	(9,750)
2017	(9,750)	(500)	(250)	10,500	–

Impairment of financial assets

14.33 There is a specific requirement in FRS 105 that a micro LLP must assess whether there is evidence of impairment of any financial asset. Usual indicators that a financial asset is impaired are:

- the micro LLP's customer is suffering from financial difficulty;
- there has been a breach of contract or default in payment;
- it is likely that the micro LLP's debtor will enter bankruptcy or similar financial reorganisation; or
- the micro LLP grants the debtor a concession which would not normally occur.

The list above is not exhaustive, but are the most likely indicators of impairment pertinent to a micro LLP. Financial assets should be tested for impairment on a case-by-case basis.

When the members determine that a financial asset is impaired, the impairment loss is recognised immediately in profit or loss.

In broad terms, an asset is impaired when the carrying amount in the micro LLP's financial statements is higher than recoverable amount. To put this concept into specifics it can be applied as follows:

Type of financial asset	When it may be impaired
Investments in shares, subsidiaries, associates and jointly controlled entities	When the asset's carrying amount exceeds the best estimate of the asset's selling price at the reporting date.
Derivative	When the derivative's carrying value exceeds the derivative's fair value less costs to sell.
Any other type of financial asset	When the asset's carrying amount exceeds the total of estimated net cash flows which can be generated from the asset. Net cash flows are discounted to present value when the time value of money is material and the discount rate will be the asset's current contractual interest rate.

Impairment tests on assets must be done each year. This is to ensure that assets are not stated in the micro LLP's balance sheet at any more than recoverable amount, as overstating assets would, of course, result in misleading information being presented in the balance sheet.

Example – Impairment loss

On 1 September 2017, the designated members of a micro LLP agree to make an interest-free loan to an unconnected party of £5,000. The loan is due to be paid on 31 August 2019. However, on 30 June 2019, the debtor lost a major customer and ran into financial difficulty and informed the designated members that he could only pay £3,000 to which the designated members agreed to.

The loan would be initially recognised at transaction price of £5,000 on 1 September 2017. In 2018/19 an impairment loss of £2,000 is recognised and the carrying amount of the loan is shown as follows:

	Carrying value at 1 September	Impairment	Cash flow	Carrying value at 31 August
Year	£	£	£	£
2017/18	5,000	–	–	5,000
2018/19	5,000	(2,000)	(3,000)	–

Reversals of an impairment loss

14.34 A micro LLP can reverse a previously recognised impairment loss when the conditions that gave rise to the original impairment loss have either reduced or cease to exist. This might apply when a micro LLP makes a provision for a bad debt against a trade debtor in one year, but then the trade debtor's credit-rating subsequently improves and hence the conditions giving rise to the impairment loss no longer apply. Any reversals of previously recognised impairment losses are recognised immediately in profit or loss.

Onerous contracts

14.35 An onerous contract is a contract in which the unavoidable payments that have to be made under the contract exceed the benefits expected to be received from the contract. FRS 105 requires a micro LLP to assess whether a derivative financial instrument (eg an interest rate swap) constitutes an onerous contract. A derivative instrument will become an onerous contract when the expected payments exceed the expected cash receipts under the contract.

Example – Interest rate swap

A micro LLP takes out a working capital loan with its bank for five years. The loan is at variable rates and in order to protect against fluctuating interest payments, the LLP takes out an interest rate swap. The terms of the swap mean that the LLP pays a fixed of interest and receives a variable rate of interest equivalent to the interest on the loan.

During the second year of the loan, the LLP was awarded a lucrative contract which it successfully completed and the members decided to repay the loan at the end of year two as there was surplus cash available. The interest rate swap cannot be terminated early and the members expect that the payments due under the interest rate swap will exceed the receipts. In this scenario, the interest rate swap has become onerous because the micro LLP will not derive a benefit from it. The micro LLP must therefore measure the present obligation under the provisions of Section 16 *Provisions and Contingencies* (see **14.90** to **14.100**).

Derecognition of a financial asset

14.36 There are three instances when a micro LLP can derecognise a financial asset:

(a) the contractual rights to the cash flows expire or are settled;

(b) the micro LLP transfers substantially all the risks and rewards of ownership; or

(c) no future economic benefits are expected from holding or disposing of the financial asset.

Example – customer goes into liquidation

A micro LLP has a year-end of 31 March 2017 and on that date a customer owed the LLP £72,000. The accountant is preparing the LLP's accounts and notices that this debt has been owed for some considerable time and has asked if a provision is needed against this debt. One of the designated members has received a letter from an insolvency practitioner notifying creditors that the customer has gone into liquidation and that it is expected there will be insufficient assets realised after the liquidation to pay any unsecured creditors. The micro LLP is one of those unsecured creditors.

The micro LLP should derecognise the trade debtor because no future economic benefits are expected to be received by holding the financial asset in the balance sheet.

Derecognition of a financial liability

14.37 A micro LLP should only derecognise a financial liability when it is discharged, cancelled or expires. Any gain or loss on the derecognition of a financial liability is recognised in profit or loss at the time of derecognition.

Offsetting financial assets and financial liabilities

14.38 Financial instruments should be presented gross in the balance sheet. A financial asset and a financial liability can only be offset (and hence the net amount shown in the balance sheet) when a micro LLP:

(a) has a legally enforceable right to set off the recognised amounts; and

(b) intends either to settle on a net basis, or to realise the asset and settle the liability simultaneously.

Disclosures relating to financial instruments

14.39 A micro LLP must determine the amount of any financial commitments, guarantees and contingencies that have not been recognised on the balance sheet that have arisen through financial instruments and disclose that amount within the total amount of financial commitments, guarantees and contingencies.

Disclosure must also be made of the nature and form of any financial asset given as security in respect of the micro LLP's commitments, guarantees and contingencies.

11 Stock and work in progress

14.40 The majority of LLPs are confined to professional practices and hence will more than likely have work in progress ongoing at the year-end. Issues concerning work in progress are discussed in **Chapter 7** but these generally relate to LLPs applying FRS 102; although similar principles for micro LLPs will be followed.

When a micro LLP has carried out work which has not met the revenue recognition criteria in Section 18 *Revenue* (see **14.104** to **14.109**), work in progress should be recognised. Work in progress should be recognised at the lower of cost and estimated selling price less costs to complete and sell. Applying this concept will mean that costs are only deferred to the extent that they are expected to be recovered against future revenue.

The 'cost' of work in progress will include any direct labour and direct overheads and hence the components of cost can comprise of more elements than simply the cost of raw materials. Other costs should only be included in work in progress to the extent that they are incurred in providing the related service. This means that costs such as administrative and selling costs would not be recognised when valuing a micro LLP's work in progress.

Overheads would normally be allocated to work in progress on the basis of the micro LLP's normal level of activity. Any abnormal overhead costs, such as costs of inefficiencies or the effect of abnormal procedural changes are not included in the valuation.

Micro LLPs that undertake professional services often use the value of unbilled fee-earner time at charge-out rates as a basis of calculating work in progress, and then reduce this value by the gross profit element included within the charge-out rates. Other micro LLPs have different methods, such as building up an hourly cost for each fee-earner from their salary and related costs plus an allocation of overheads.

It would be unusual for a micro LLP to have a complex system for calculating work in progress amounts and there are no weaknesses in having a simple method, provided it results in a calculation of work in progress which is reasonable and is consistently applied from one reporting period to the next.

Stock

14.41 Stock (referred to as 'inventory' in FRS 105) should always be valued at the lower of cost and estimated selling price less costs to complete and sell (referred to in previous UK GAAP as the 'lower of cost and net realisable value').

As with work in progress, 'cost' can include several elements and FRS 105 recognises the following costs which make up the components of the cost of stock:

- purchase price;

- import duties;
- irrecoverable taxes (such as input VAT if the micro LLP is not VAT-registered);
- transport costs;
- handling costs; and
- other costs which are directly attributable to the acquisition of finished goods, materials and services.

If the micro LLP receives any trade discounts, rebates or other similar discounts, these are deducted from the cost price.

If a supplier agrees to defer payment beyond normal credit terms, the purchase price is the cash price which is available on the date that the goods/services are acquired. Any excess of the deferred payment over the cash price is recognised as interest in the micro LLP's profit and loss account over the credit period.

Costs which are not included in the cost of stock

14.42 FRS 105 says that the cost of stock should not include the following expenses:

- abnormal amounts of wasted materials, labour or other production overheads;
- storage costs, unless those costs are necessary during the production process before a further production stage;
- administrative overheads that do not contribute to bringing inventories to their present location and condition; and
- selling costs.

Costs of conversion

14.43 It is fairly uncommon for a manufacturing entity to be a micro LLP, but just because this is uncommon, does not mean that it is impossible for a manufacturing entity to have LLP status. Manufacturing entities tend to convert raw materials into finished goods and therefore any costs of conversion incurred by a micro LLP will include costs directly related to the units of production, such as direct labour. In addition, a systematic allocation of fixed and variable production overheads will be included in the cost.

Focus

- Fixed production overheads are those indirect costs which remain relatively constant from one period to the next regardless of the levels of production (for example depreciation of machinery). Fixed production overheads are allocated to the costs of conversion on the basis of the **normal** capacity of production facilities. In periods of abnormally high production (for example, if the micro LLP receives a one-off large order), the amount of fixed overhead allocated to each unit of production is decreased so that stock is not measured above cost.

Agricultural produce harvested from biological assets

14.44 Micro LLPs involved in agriculture and have agricultural produce in stock at the year-end must value this agricultural produce on initial recognition (at the point of harvest) at the lower of cost and estimated selling price less costs to complete and sell. Section 27 *Specialised Activities* also applies to agriculture (see **14.126** to **14.129**).

Cost formulas and other techniques for measuring cost

14.45 FRS 105 permits the use of the first-in first-out method or weighted average cost formulas. Under no circumstances should a micro LLP use last-in first-out as this technique is not permitted in FRS 105.

Other techniques available include standard cost methods, the retail method or the most recent purchase price for measuring the cost of stock. Whichever method the micro LLP uses, it must be used consistently and must also result in a value which approximates cost.

Impairment

14.46 The fact that the micro LLP must measure stock at the lower of cost and estimated selling price less costs to complete and sell means that there is an implicit requirement for the micro LLP to assess whether inventories are impaired. Stock and work in progress is impaired when the carrying amount is not recoverable (in whole or in part); in other words, the carrying amount in the micro LLP's balance sheet is higher than recoverable amount. In such instances, the micro LLP must recognise an impairment loss in profit or loss.

It is possible to reverse a previously recognised impairment loss when the circumstances giving rise to the impairment loss no longer exist, or when there is clear evidence of an increase in selling price less costs to complete and sell. Care must be taken where the impairment reversal is concerned because it cannot exceed the value of the original impairment loss.

Recognition in profit or loss

14.47 Stock and work in progress is recognised as an expense in profit or loss in the period in which the related revenue is recognised.

Disclosures relating to stock and work in progress

14.48 A micro LLP must provide an indication of the nature and form of any items of stock given as security in respect of the micro LLP's commitments, guarantees and contingencies.

12 Joint ventures

14.49 There are three types of joint venture under the scope of FRS 105:

- jointly controlled operations;

- jointly controlled assets; and
- jointly controlled entities.

Jointly controlled entities are dealt with in Section 7 *Subsidiaries, Associates, Jointly Controlled Entities and Intermediate Payment Arrangements* in FRS 105 (see **14.20** which then directs preparers to Section 9 *Financial Instruments*, see **14.26**).

14.50 In a joint venture, there must be a **contractually agreed sharing of control** in existence. To meet the definition of a joint venture, the strategic financial and operating decisions which relate to the activity must require the unanimous consent of the parties sharing control (the venturers). No one party in a joint venture can have control because this would not constitute a joint venture.

Jointly controlled operations

14.51 A jointly controlled operation may involve the use of assets and/or other resources of the venturers rather than the creation of a separate vehicle (ie a company, partnership or other entity). In a jointly controlled operation, each venturer will use their own fixed assets and hold their own stock as well as incurring their own expenses and liabilities, including raising their own finance.

When a micro LLP enters into an arrangement which constitutes a jointly controlled operation, it recognises:

(a) the assets which it controls;

(b) the liabilities which it incurs; and

(c) the expenses that it incurs and its share of the income from the sale of goods or rendering of services.

Jointly controlled assets

14.52 A joint venture may involve a jointly controlled asset (such as an investment property). When a joint venture involves a jointly controlled asset, the venturer recognises in its financial statements:

(a) its share of the jointly controlled assets, which is classified in accordance with Section 4 *Statement of Financial Position* (see **14.16**);

(b) any liabilities which it has incurred (such as a loan);

(c) its share of any liabilities incurred jointly with other venturers in relation to the joint venture;

(d) any income from the sale or use of its share of the output of the joint venture, plus its share of any expenses incurred by the joint venture; and

(e) any expenses which it has incurred in respect of its interest in the joint venture.

Disclosures relating to joint ventures

14.53 The micro LLP must determine the amount of any financial commitments, guarantees and contingencies that are not on the balance sheet that arises from its jointly controlled operations and jointly controlled assets and disclose that amount within the total amount of financial commitments, guarantees and contingencies.

13 Property, plant and equipment

14.54 Property, plant and equipment is the terminology used in FRS 105 for tangible fixed assets and is dealt with in Section 12 *Property, Plant and Equipment* of the standard. Section 12 also relates to investment property held by a micro LLP. It does not, however, deal with biological assets which are related to agricultural activity as this is dealt with in Section 27 *Specialised Activities* (see **14.126** to **14.129**).

A micro LLP is only able to recognise an item of expense as property, plant and equipment (PPE) if, and only if:

(a) it is probable (ie more likely than not) that future economic benefits associated with the item will flow to the micro LLP; and

(b) the cost of the item can be reliably measured.

Some specific points to note in Section 12 are as follows.

Specific points

Major spare parts and standby equipment

14.55 A notable feature of FRS 105 is that it deals with the issue of major spare parts and standby equipment. FRS 105 says that when a micro LLP has major spare parts and standby equipment that it expects to use during more than one accounting period, it should classify them as PPE. In addition, where spare parts and servicing equipment can be used only in connection with an item of PPE, they, too, are considered to be PPE. This may result in more fixed assets being recognised on a micro LLP's balance sheet.

Replacement components

14.56 Some parts of an item of PPE or investment property might require replacement at regular intervals. Replacement components can be added to the cost of the asset if the replacement part is expected to provide incremental future benefits to the micro LLP. The carrying amount of the parts that are replaced are derecognised.

Major inspections

14.57 The operation of an item of PPE or investment property may be subject to it having regular major inspections for faults, regardless of whether parts of the item are replaced. As each major inspection is performed, the cost of the inspection is recognised in the carrying amount of PPE or investment property as a replacement if the recognition criteria are met. Any remaining carrying amount of the previous inspection is derecognised and is done regardless of whether the cost of the previous major inspection was identified in the transaction in which the item was acquired or constructed.

Land and buildings

14.58 Land and buildings are accounted for as separate assets, regardless of the fact that they may be acquired together. Land does not normally depreciate, but buildings do.

Measurement at initial recognition

14.59 All items of PPE or investment property are initially recognised at cost. The elements of 'cost' include:

- the purchase price, including legal and brokerage fees, import duties, non-refundable taxes (such as VAT if the micro LLP is not VAT-registered), and net of trade discounts and rebates;
- costs which are directly attributable to bringing the asset to the location and condition necessary for it to be capable in operating in the manner intended by the members (such as freight cost and testing of functionality); and
- an initial estimate of the costs of dismantling and removing the item and restoring the site on which it is located (this is recognised and measured in accordance with Section 16 *Provisions and Contingencies* – see **14.90** to **14.100**).

Costs which must not be capitalised, and hence recognised as an expense when they are incurred, include:

- the costs of opening a new facility;
- the costs of introducing a new product or service (including the cost of advertising and promotional activities);
- costs of conducting business in a new location or with a new class of customer, including staff training; and
- administration and other general overhead costs.

Focus

- The cost of an item of PPE is the cash price equivalent at the date of recognition. If payment is deferred beyond normal credit terms (hence a financing transaction), the cost is the cash price at the recognition date. The excess of the deferred payment amount over the cash price is recognised as interest over the deferred payment term.

Subsequent measurement

14.60 After initial recognition at cost, a micro LLP continues to measure items of PPE and investment property at cost less depreciation less any accumulated impairment losses. Day-to-day servicing and maintenance costs of items of PPE and investment property are recognised in profit or loss.

> **Focus**
>
> - There is no option available to carry items of PPE or investment property at fair value or at revaluation amounts under FRS 105.

Depreciation

14.61 FRS 105 places emphasis on component depreciation. Component depreciation is appropriate when the major components of an item of PPE or investment property have a significantly different pattern of consumption of economic benefit than the main asset itself. If this is the case, the micro LLP must depreciate each such component separately over its useful life. Other assets are depreciated as single assets over their useful economic lives.

> **Focus**
>
> - Land generally has an unlimited useful life and hence is not usually depreciated.

Depreciation charges in the accounting period are recognised in profit or loss. The exception may be where the micro LLP recognises depreciation of manufacturing PPE in the cost of inventories (although this is relatively uncommon in practice).

Depreciation of an item of PPE or investment property must begin when it is available for use. It ceases when the asset is derecognised but does not cease when the asset becomes idle or is retired from use, unless the asset is fully depreciated.

Depreciable amount

14.62 The depreciable amount of an asset is calculated as its cost price less residual value. The balance is then depreciated over the asset's useful economic life on a systematic basis.

> **Focus**
>
> - The residual value of an asset is based on its current price (not historic price as was the case under previous UK GAAP). Therefore, there is a likelihood that depreciation amounts may fluctuate from one accounting period to the next as the residual value increases or decreases.

Where there are indicators that the residual value of an asset has changed since the most recent reporting date, the micro LLP must review its previous estimates and, where current expectations differ, change the residual value, depreciation method or useful life. Such a change is a change in accounting estimate and will be applied prospectively.

Depreciation method

14.63 There is no 'one-size-fits-all' where depreciation methods are concerned. The two most commonly applied methods are the straight-line method and the reducing balance method (sometimes referred to as the 'diminishing balance method'). FRS 105 also recognises the 'usage method' of depreciation and under this particular method, the depreciation charge can be zero while there is no production.

Impairment

14.64 A micro LLP must review items of PPE and investment property at each balance sheet date for indicators of impairment. Section 22 *Impairment of Assets* deals with such issues (see **14.111** to **14.115**).

If the micro LLP is expecting to receive compensation from a third party due to the impairment of an asset (eg an insurance company for a car that has been written off in an accident), the micro LLP can only include the compensation as a receivable if the receipt is virtually certain.

Derecognising an item of PPE or investment property

14.65 A micro LLP derecognises an item of PPE or investment property when:

(a) the micro LLP disposes of the asset; or

(b) the micro LLP expects no future economic benefits from the asset's use or disposal.

The gain or loss on disposal is recognised in profit or loss (unless the arrangement constitutes a sale or leaseback (see **14.86** to **14.88**)).

Focus

- Gains on disposal of items of PPE or investment property must not be shown within the LLP's accounts as turnover.

Disclosures relating to items of property, plant and equipment and investment property

14.66 If the micro LLP has any financial commitments which have not been recognised in the balance sheet in respect of the acquisition of property, plant and equipment or investment property, that amount must be disclosed within the total amount of financial commitments, guarantees and contingencies.

In addition, the micro LLP must provide an indication of the nature and form of any items of property, plant and equipment or investment property which it has given as security for its commitments, guarantees and contingencies.

14 Intangible assets other than goodwill

14.67 The first point worthy of note in respect of intangible assets is that any internally-generated intangible assets are not to be recognised on the micro LLP's balance sheet. This includes development expenditure which must also be written off to profit or loss as the expense is incurred; there is no option available under FRS 105 to capitalise development costs.

In addition, FRS 105 prohibits the following types of expenditure from being capitalised as an intangible asset:

- research and development expenditure;
- internally generated brands, logos, publishing titles, customer lists and items which are similar in substance;
- start-up activities such as legal costs incurred in creating a new LLP, expenditure on opening a new facility and expenditure for starting new operations;
- training activities;
- advertising and promotional activities;
- relocating or reorganising part or all of a micro LLP; and
- internally-generated goodwill.

Initial measurement

14.68 When a micro LLP separately acquires an intangible asset, it is initially recognised at cost. Cost comprises:

(a) the purchase price, including import duties and non-refundable purchase taxes after the deduction of trade discounts and rebates; and

(b) any directly attributable cost of preparing the asset for its intended use.

Subsequent measurement

14.69 After initial recognition at cost, an intangible asset is recognised at cost less amortisation and less any accumulated impairment losses.

Amortisation

14.70 FRS 105 requires all intangible assets to be amortised over their useful economic life. An intangible asset cannot have an indefinite useful life.

When an intangible asset arises from contractual or other legal rights, the useful life must not exceed the period of the contractual or other legal rights. It may be shorter depending on the period over which the micro LLP expects to use the asset.

Example – limited term that can be renewed

A micro LLP acquires an intangible asset for a five-year period. After the five years has elapsed, the term can be renewed for a further three years. The financial controller is unsure as to what amortisation period to use for the acquired intangible asset.

In this scenario, the financial controller can only include the renewal period if there is evidence to support renewal by the micro LLP without significant cost. If this evidence is not available, the financial controller must amortise the intangible asset over a five-year period only.

Amortisation of an intangible asset must begin when the intangible asset is available for use. An intangible asset is available for use when it is usable in the manner intended by the members. Amortisation ceases when the asset is derecognised.

The amortisation method used by the micro LLP must reflect the pattern in which the micro LLP expects to consume the intangible asset's future economic benefits. If that pattern cannot be reliably determined, FRS 105 requires the straight-line method to be used.

Focus

- When the members of a micro LLP are unable to reliably measure the useful economic life of an intangible asset, the amortisation period must not exceed ten years. This ten-year cap is only expected to apply in exceptional circumstances and only applies when the members are unable to reliably estimate the intangible asset's useful economic life.

Residual values

14.71 Residual values for intangible assets are assumed to be zero. This assumption is not, however, absolute and a residual value may be assigned to an intangible asset if:

(a) there is a commitment by a third party to purchase the intangible asset at the end of its useful life; or

(b) there is an active market for the asset and:

   (i) a residual value can be determined by reference to that market; and

   (ii) it is probable that such a market will exist at the end of the intangible asset's useful life.

> **Focus**
>
> - An 'active market' is one in which all of the following conditions exist:
>   - — the items traded in the market are homogeneous;
>   - — willing buyers and sellers can normally be found at any time; and
>   - — prices are available to the public.

Review of amortisation periods and methods

14.72 There may be indicators that the useful life or residual value of an intangible asset has changed since the last reporting date. Where such indicators are present, the members must review previous estimates and where current expectations differ, the residual value, amortisation method or useful life must be changed accordingly. Such changes are changes in estimation technique and must be accounted for prospectively (ie there is no retrospective change applied).

Impairment

14.73 As with all other types of assets, the micro LLP must determine whether the intangible asset is impaired at the reporting date. Impairment reviews are done in accordance with Section 22 *Impairment of Assets* which are dealt with in **14.111** to **14.115**.

Derecognising an intangible asset

14.74 A micro LLP derecognises a separately acquired intangible asset and recognises a gain or loss in profit or loss when:

(a) the micro LLP disposes of the asset; or

(b) when there is no future economic benefit expected from its use or disposal.

Disclosures relating to intangible assets

14.75 The micro LLP must determine the amount of any financial commitments, guarantees and contingencies not recognised in the balance sheet in respect of its acquisition of separately acquired intangible assets and disclose that amount within the total amount of financial commitments, guarantees and contingencies.

The micro LLP must also provide an indication of the nature and form of any intangible assets given as security in respect of its commitments, guarantees and contingencies.

15 Business combinations and goodwill

14.76 Business combinations and goodwill are dealt with in Section 14 *Business Combinations and Goodwill*. Care must be taken because Section 14 says that if the micro

LLP acquires the trade and assets of another business, it must apply Section 19 *Business Combinations and Goodwill* in FRS 102, **except for the following:**

(a) a micro LLP must not separately identify and recognise intangible assets;

(b) a micro LLP must not recognise any amounts in respect of deferred tax;

(c) a micro LLP must apply paragraph 14.2 of FRS 105 (see **14.77** below) in respect of goodwill that arises in a trade and asset acquisition, not paragraph 19.23 of FRS 102; and

(d) a micro LLP is not required to provide any of the disclosures.

Goodwill in a trade and asset acquisition

14.77 When a micro LLP acquires goodwill in a trade and asset acquisition, it measures that goodwill at cost less accumulated amortisation and accumulated impairment losses.

In all cases, goodwill is considered to have a finite useful economic life and must be amortised over that useful life on a systematic basis. When the micro LLP is unable to make a reliable estimate of the useful life, the life must not exceed ten years (this is only expected to apply in exceptional circumstances).

Goodwill arising must also be tested for impairment at each reporting date following the principles in Section 22 *Impairment of Assets* in FRS 105 (see **14.111** to **14.115**).

Disclosures relating to trade and asset acquisitions

14.78 The micro LLP must determine the amount of any financial commitments, guarantees and contingencies which are not recognised in the balance sheet in respect of its trade and asset acquisitions and disclose that amount within the total of financial commitments, guarantees and contingencies.

16 Leases

14.79 Leasing transactions are dealt with in Section 15 *Leases* in FRS 105. Section 15 does not apply to licensing agreements for items such as motion picture films, video recordings, plays, manuscripts, patents and copyrights as these are dealt with in Section 13 *Intangible Assets other than Goodwill* (see **14.67** to **14.75**).

Classification of leases

14.80 The concept of 'finance' versus 'operating' lease features in FRS 105 and will apply to micro LLPs. A lease is classed as a finance lease if the lessor transfers substantially all the risks and rewards incidental to ownership to the lessee. This is because the lessee is required to apply substance over form to the transaction. In a finance lease, the lessee has acquired an asset for use in its business that has been financed through a leasing transaction, hence an asset is recorded on the balance sheet with a corresponding finance lease creditor.

FRS 105 outlines eight situations that would individually, or in combination, normally lead to a lease being classified as a finance lease as follows:

(a) the lease transfers ownership of the asset to the lessee by the end of the lease term;

(b) the lessee has the option to purchase the asset at a price which is expected to be sufficiently lower than the fair value at the date the option becomes exercisable and it is reasonably certain at the outset of the lease that this option will be exercised;

(c) the lease term is for the major part of the economic life of the asset even if title is not transferred;

(d) at the inception of the lease, the present value of the minimum lease payments equates to at least substantially all of the fair value of the leased asset;

(e) the leased assets are of such a specialised nature that only the micro LLP can use them;

(f) if the lessee can cancel the lease, the lessor's losses associated with the cancellation are borne by the lessee;

(g) gains or losses from the fluctuation in the residual value of the leased asset accrue to the lessee; and

(h) the lessee has the ability to continue the lease for a secondary period at a rent which is substantially lower than market rent.

Operating leases

14.81 Leases which are not finance leases are classed as operating leases. An operating lease arises when the risks and rewards incidental to ownership of the asset remain with the lessor.

Finance leases in the lessee's financial statements

14.82 In the financial statements of a micro LLP that is a lessee, an asset is recorded with a corresponding finance lease creditor. The asset's value will be the cash price of the asset on acquisition or, if lower, the present value of the minimum lease payments which are determined at the outset of the lease. Any initial costs directly attributable to arranging the lease are added to the amount recognised as an asset.

Therefore, the journal entries for a finance lease in the lessee's books are:

Dr Fixed assets	X
Cr Creditors	(X)

If incidental costs associated with the lease, such as legal fees are incurred, the entries in the book may be:

Dr Fixed assets	X
Cr Cash at bank/creditors	(X)

The asset is then depreciated over the asset's useful economic life or, if there is reasonable certainty that the lessee will obtain ownership at the end of the lease term, it is depreciated over the shorter of the lease term and its useful life.

The interest element of the finance lease is allocated to each period over the term of the lease so as to produce a constant periodic rate of interest on the remaining balance of the lease liability.

Operating leases in the lessee's financial statements

14.83 When a micro LLP enters into a lease that is an operating lease, the accounting treatment is inherently much easier than that of a finance lease. The payments to the lessor are recognised in profit or loss as they fall due as follows:

Dr Other charges	X
Cr Cash at bank/creditors	(X)

The lease payments under the operating lease are recognised as an expense over the term of the lease on a straight-line basis, unless another systematic basis is more representative of the time pattern of the user's benefit.

If the micro LLP has received a lease incentive, this is recognised as a reduction to the expense over the term of the lease on a straight-line basis. Another systematic basis can be used if the alternative basis is representative of the time pattern of the lessee's benefit from the use of the asset.

Finance leases in the lessor's financial statements

14.84 Micro LLPs which are lessors must recognise an asset held under a finance lease in the balance sheet as a debtor at an amount equivalent to the net investment in the lease.

Focus

- The net investment in the lease is the gross investment that is discounted at the interest rate implicit in the lease. The gross investment is the total of:
  - the minimum lease payments receivable by the lessor; and
  - any unguaranteed residual value accruing to the lessor.

After initial recognition, the lessor recognises finance income (interest) based on a pattern which reflects a constant periodic rate of return on the lessor's net investment in the finance lease. Lease payments which relate to the period (and exclude costs for services), are applied against this gross investment to reduce both the capital and unearned finance income. This is best illustrated using an example.

Example – Lessor accounting for a finance lease

Micro LLP (Micro) enters into a leasing transaction with its customer to lease a machine. The cash price of the machine is £10,000 and it has an expected useful life of five years and a residual value at the end of this five-year period of £1,000. Micro's customer will make five annual rental payments in advance of £2,100 per annum. No incremental costs have arisen in negotiating this lease.

Micro's gross investment in the lease is calculated as the total rents receivable of £10,500 (£2,100 × 5) plus the unguaranteed residual value at the end of the lease term of £1,000. Micro recognises a debtor at the outset of the lease of £10,000 which is the cash price of the machine and is also the present value of the gross investment in the lease discounted at the rate implicit in the lease of 6.62%. The finance income and debtor is shown below:

Year	Opening debtor	Rent received	Finance income at 6.62%	Gross investment at end of the year	Gross earnings to future years	Closing debtor
	£	£	£	£	£	£
1	10,000	2,100	523	9,400	977	8,423
2	8,423	2,100	419	7,300	558	6,742
3	6,742	2,100	307	5,200	251	4,949
4	4,949	2,100	189	3,100	62	3,038
5	3,038	2,100	62	1,000	–	1,000
		10,500	1,500			

Over the life of the lease, the gross investment comprises the total of the rents receivable in the future periods plus the unguaranteed residual of £1,000. For example, at the end of year 3, the gross investment is £5,200 which is two years' rentals at £2,100 plus the £1,000 unguaranteed residual. The closing debtor in Micro's books at the end of year 3 will be £4,949 which is the gross investment at the end of year 3 of £5,200 less the earnings allocated to years 4 and 5.

Operating leases in the lessor's financial statements

14.85 Lease income from operating leases is recognised in profit and loss on a straight-line basis over the lease term unless another systematic basis is representative of the time pattern of the lessee's benefit from using the asset. This can be the case even if the receipt of payments is not on that basis.

Lease incentives are recognised as reductions to income over the term of the lease on a straight-line basis (but another basis can be used if appropriate but alternative bases tend not to be used by micro LLPs).

The asset subject to the operating lease will be shown as a fixed asset in the lessor's balance sheet and all costs associated with the asset (including depreciation) are recognised as expenses. The depreciation policy for the asset must be consistent with the lessor's depreciation policy for similar assets.

Any incremental costs associated with negotiating the lease must be recognised as an expense over the term of the lease, which will be the same term as the income arising in the lease.

> **Focus**
>
> - As with all other types of assets, a micro LLP that is a lessor that has an asset in its balance sheet subject to an operating lease must apply the provisions in Section 22 *Impairment of Assets* at each reporting date. See **14.111** to **14.115**.

Sale and leaseback transactions

14.86 A sale and leaseback transaction can result in two outcomes:

- a sale and leaseback finance lease; or
- a sale and leaseback operating lease.

Sale and leaseback finance lease

14.87 The seller-lessee recognises any excess of sales proceeds over the carrying amount of the asset (ie the resulting gain) as income over the lease term. Any remaining balance is deferred.

Sale and leaseback operating lease

14.88 If the sale and leaseback operating lease has been carried out at fair value, the seller-lessee recognises any profit or loss immediately.

If the selling price is below fair value, any profit or loss is recognised immediately. However, if the seller-lessee is to be compensated for the loss by way of lease payments which are below market price, the seller-lessee must defer and amortise any loss in the transaction and recognise it in profit or loss in proportion to the lease payments over the period for which the asset is going to be used. When the selling price is higher than fair value of the asset, the seller-lessee defers the excess and amortises it to profit and loss over the period for which the asset is expected to be used.

Disclosures relating to leases

14.89 A micro LLP must determine the amount of any financial commitments, guarantees and contingencies not recognised in the balance sheet that have arisen from a sale and leaseback transaction and disclose that amount within the total of financial commitments, guarantees and contingencies.

17 Provisions and contingencies

14.90 A 'provision' is a liability of uncertain timing or amount. In order to recognise a provision, three criteria have to be met:

(a) the micro LLP must have an obligation at the reporting date as a result of a past event;

(b) it is probable (ie more likely than not) that the micro LLP will be required to transfer economic benefits in settlement; and

(c) the amount of the obligation can be reliably measured.

> **Focus**
>
> - The term 'provision' can be used interchangeably; for example, a 'provision' for bad debts or a 'provision' for depreciation. In this context, these are adjustments to carrying amounts in the micro LLP's accounts as opposed to the recognition of liabilities.

If the criteria for a provision cannot be met, the micro LLP does not recognise a provision but may have to disclose a contingent liability if the contingent liability is material.

An obligation

14.91 Part of the requirement to qualify for recognition of a provision is that the micro LLP must have an obligation at the reporting date. An 'obligation' can be of two guises:

(a) a 'legal' obligation; and

(b) a 'constructive' obligation.

A legal obligation is often clear-cut. Such obligations can arise due to court orders or the agreement to contract terms. A constructive obligation, on the other hand, can often be subjective and arises due to the micro LLP's published policies, past practices or specific statements that the micro LLP will accept its responsibilities and thus creates an expectation in the mind-sets of those affected that the micro LLP will discharge its obligations. A constructive obligation could arise if the micro LLP announces to its staff that it will pay them a bonus based on year-end profits prior to the year-end occurring. This announcement will create an expectation in the mind-sets of the employees that they will receive a bonus and hence it would be appropriate for the LLP to make provision in the year-end accounts for the costs of such a bonus.

Recognising a provision

14.92 A provision is recognised in the micro LLP's balance sheet as a liability and as an expense in the profit and loss account. The debit entry can be recognised as part of the cost of an asset (eg property, plant and equipment or inventories) if FRS 105 requires such accounting treatment. In the majority of cases, however, it is expected that the corresponding entry for a provision for liabilities will be recognised as an expense.

In situations where the effects of the time value of money are material, the amount of the provision is the present value expected to be required to settle the obligation. In practice, the need to discount provisions for a micro LLP is expected to be rare, but if it is needed, the discount rate to be applied will be the rate that reflects current market assessments of the time value of money and the risks which are liability-specific.

Focus

- The liability-specific risks must be reflected either in the discount rate OR in the estimation of the amounts expected to settle the liability but not both.

Reimbursement assets

14.93 There may be occasions when the amount required to settle a liability may be refunded (in whole, or in part) by a third party, such as an insurance company. In such cases, the reimbursement asset must only be recognised as an asset (ie not offset against the liability) when the receipt of the asset is **virtually certain**. This criteria is notably different than the criteria needed to recognise a liability (ie probable, which means more likely than not).

Focus

- While a reimbursement asset cannot be offset against a related liability in the balance sheet, FRS 105 does allow it to be offset in the profit and loss account and hence the expense will be shown net of the reimbursement asset.

Subsequent measurement

14.94 A micro LLP can only charge expenses against provisions for which the provision was originally recognised. In other words, amounts recognised as a provision cannot be used for other items of expenditure.

Provisions for liabilities must be reviewed at each reporting date by the members and adjusted accordingly to reflect the current best estimate of the amounts required to settle the obligation. Adjustments made to amounts previously recognised as a provision are recognised in profit or loss, unless the provision was originally recognised as part of the cost of an asset. Any unwinding of discounts used in measuring the cost of a provision are recognised in profit and loss in the period it arises.

Onerous contracts

14.95 A contract becomes onerous when the unavoidable payments exceed the value of the benefits to be received under the contract. When a micro LLP has an onerous contract, the unavoidable costs must reflect the least net cost of exiting the contract. This is the lower of the cost of fulfilling the contract and any compensation or penalties arising from failure to fulfil it.

Future operating losses

14.96 Provisions for future operating losses are not to be recognised in the micro LLPs accounts. This is because such future operating losses do not meet the definition of a liability, although the expectation of future operating losses might be an indicator that one, or more, assets are impaired.

Restructuring provisions

14.97 When a micro LLP is undergoing a restructuring, it can only recognise a restructuring provision when the following conditions are met:

(a) the micro LLP has a detailed formal plan for the restructuring, identifying at least:

   (i) the business or part of a business concerned;

   (ii) the principal locations affected;

   (iii) the location, function and approximate number of employees that will be compensated for terminating their services;

   (iv) the expenditures that will be undertaken;

   (v) when the plan will be implemented; and

(b) the micro LLP has raised a valid expectation in those affected (ie it has created a constructive obligation as per **14.91**) that it will carrying out the restructuring by starting to implement the plan or announce its main features to those affected by it.

Contingent liabilities

14.98 Contingent liabilities are not recognised in the financial statements because they do not meet the definition of a liability. The only exception to this rule is in respect of provisions for contingent liabilities of an acquiree in a trade and asset acquisition. The disclosure requirements in respect of contingent liabilities are outlined in **14.100**.

Focus

- When a micro LLP is jointly and severally liable for an obligation, the part of the obligation that is expected to be met by other parties is treated as a contingent liability.

Contingent assets

14.99 As with contingent liabilities, a contingent asset is also not recognised in the financial statements. When the receipt of a contingent asset becomes virtually certain, it is treated as a provision and hence is then recognised as a debtor in the micro LLP's balance sheet.

Disclosures in respect of contingencies

14.100 The micro LLP must determine the amount of any financial commitments, guarantees and contingencies that have not been recognised in the balance sheet and disclose this amount within the total amount of financial commitments, guarantees and contingencies. No disclosure is required as to the amount of a contingent liability where the possibility of an outflow of resources is remote.

18 Liabilities and equity

14.101 Section 17 *Liabilities and Equity* of FRS 105 outlines the principles involved in classifying financial instruments as either liabilities or equity.

Classification as liability or equity

14.102 For micro LLP's the issue of whether a financial instrument is debt or equity is often straightforward. If the micro LLP takes out a loan with its bank, then this creates a financial liability and it will be treated as such in the micro LLP's financial statements. A financial liability would also arise if the micro LLP entered into a hire purchase contract, or a fixed-rate interest loan with a member. In the broadest terms, Section 17 says that a financial liability arises when there is a contractual obligation on the part of the reporting entity to deliver cash or another asset; whilst an equity instrument arises where the issuer can be required to settle an obligation in cash or by way of another financial asset only in the event of the issuer's liquidation.

The issue for micro LLPs is usually when to treat members' capital as a liability or equity and the provisions in Section 17 will then apply. In such situations the importance of carefully scrutinising the members' agreement cannot be over-emphasised.

For micro LLP's this issue is likely to apply to members' capital and whether this is to be treated as a liability or equity. If there is an obligation for the micro LLP to repay members' capital, then it is treated as a liability and will be included within 'Loans and other debts due to members'. If there is no obligation to repay members' capital, it is treated as equity and is shown within 'Members' other interests'. This can be illustrated using illustrative micro LLP balance sheets as follows using a Format 1 balance sheet as follows (note the examples below assume the micro LLP has no prepayments or accrued income or accruals and deferred income during the year and hence are not shown):

Example – micro LLP balance sheet with no equity

	31 October 2017	
	£	£
Fixed assets		9,500
Current assets	37,000	

	31 October 2017	
	£	£
Creditors: amounts falling due within one year	(9,500)	
Net current assets		27,500
Total assets less current liabilities		37,000
Creditors: amounts falling due after more than one year		(4,000)
Provisions for liabilities		(6,500)
		26,500
Loans and other debts due to members		26,500

Example – micro LLP balance sheet with some equity

	31 October 2017	
	£	£
Fixed assets		9,500
Current assets	37,000	
Creditors: amounts falling due within one year	(9,500)	
Net current assets		27,500
Total assets less current liabilities		37,000
Creditors: amounts falling due after more than one year		(4,000)
Provisions for liabilities		(6,500)
		26,500
Loans and other debts due to members		14,000
Members' other interests		12,500
		26,500

Disclosures relating to equity and liabilities

14.103 There are no disclosure requirements under Section 17 of FRS 105.

19 Revenue

14.104 Revenue is dealt with in Section 18 *Revenue* in FRS 105. A micro LLP must measure revenue at the amount receivable but take into account any trade discounts, prompt settlement discounts and volume rebates which may be allowed to the micro LLP's customers.

> **Focus**
>
> - VAT is not accounted for in revenue if the micro LLP is VAT-registered as VAT is simply collected from the customer on behalf of HM Revenue and Customs. In addition, if there is an agency relationship (where the micro LLP (the agent) collects funds on behalf of the principal), such amounts collected are not recognised as revenue. Only the commission due to the agent is recognised as revenue.

Deferred revenue

14.105 If the micro LLP defers payment beyond normal credit terms, the amount of revenue that it recognises is equal to the cash price available on the date that the transaction occurs. Any excess of the deferred amount and the cash price available is treated as interest over the deferred payment term.

Sale of goods

14.106 If a micro LLP sells goods, it can only recognise revenue when **all** of the following conditions are satisfied:

(a) the micro LLP has transferred the significant risks and rewards of ownership of the goods to the buyer;

(b) the micro LLP retains neither continuing managerial involvement to the degree usually associated with ownership, nor effective control over the goods;

(c) the amount of revenue can be reliably measured;

(d) it is probable (ie more likely than not) that the micro LLP will receive economic benefit associated with the transaction; and

(e) the costs incurred (or to be incurred) in respect of the transaction can be reliably measured.

Paragraph 18.11 of FRS 105 outlines the situations in which a micro LLP might retain significant risks and rewards outlined in (a) as follows:

(a) when the micro LLP retains an obligation for unsatisfactory performance not covered by normal warranties;

(b) when the receipt of the revenue from a particular sale depends on the buyer selling the goods;

(c) when the goods are shipped but the micro LLP has to install them and installation is a significant part of the contract which has not yet been completed; and

(d) when the buyer has the right to rescind the purchase for a reason specified in the sales contract, or at the buyer's sole discretion without any reason, and the micro LLP is uncertain about the probability of return.

> **Focus**
>
> - A micro LLP can still retain an insignificant risk of ownership and recognise revenue. This might happen when the micro LLP retains legal title to goods to protect the collectability of the amount due to the micro LLP.

Rendering of services

14.107 The majority of LLPs usually operate in the service sector (ie professional firms). Revenue in respect of services fall under the scope of Section 18 of FRS 105 and paragraph 18.13 says that revenue should be recognised when the outcome of a transaction can be reliably estimated. Revenue is recognised by reference to the stage of completion (see **14.108**).

Paragraph 18.13 outlines four conditions which must be satisfied so as to conclude that the outcome of transaction can be reliably estimated:

(a) the amount of revenue can be measured reliably;

(b) it is probable (ie more likely than not) that the economic benefits associated with the transaction will flow to the micro LLP;

(c) the stage of completion of the transaction (see below at **14.108**) at the end of the reporting period can be measured reliably; and

(d) the costs incurred for the transaction and the costs to complete the transaction can be reliably measured.

Stage of completion

14.108 Micro LLPs are required to recognise revenue in a service contract according to the stage of completion having regard to a reliable estimate as to the outcome of the transaction. There are three possible outcomes where a service contract is concerned:

- the contract will make a profit;
- the contract will make a loss; or
- the outcome is uncertain.

Profit-making contracts

When the micro LLP is undertaking work which is expected to make a profit, revenue is recognised according to the stage of completion. The stage of completion can be estimated using various methods, including:

(a) the proportion that costs the micro LLP have incurred for the work performed to date bear to the estimated total costs. Costs incurred for such work performed today do not include costs which relate to future activity;

(b) surveys of work performed; and

(c) completion of a physical proportion of the contract work or the completion of a proportion of the service contract.

Example – profit-making contract

On 1 May 2017, a micro LLP begins work for a client at a fixed price of £5,000. Costs have been analysed at the start of the contract as follows:

	£
Materials to date plus additional costs	1,000
Labour and other overheads	1,200
Depreciation	900
	3,100

The estimated profit in the contract is expected to be £1,900 (£5,000 fixed price less £3,100 costs).

At the year-end 31 October 2017, the costs actually incurred were as follows:

	£
Purchase of materials	500
Labour and other overheads	600
Depreciation (£900 × 6/12)	450
Costs incurred at the year-end	1,550

On 31 October 2017, the contract was estimated as being 40% complete and a progress payment was made to the micro LLP amounting to £900 on that date.

As the contract is 40% complete and is profitable, 40% of the price can be recognised as revenue at the year-end together with 40% of the contract costs being recognised as follows:

	£
Revenue (40% × £5,000)	2,000
Cost of raw materials and consumables (40% x £3,100)	1,240
Gross profit (40% × £1,900)	760

In the micro LLP's balance sheet the amount recognised in current assets in respect of the gross amount due from the micro LLP's client is calculated as follows:

	£
Costs to date:	
Purchase of materials	500

	£
Labour and other overheads	600
Depreciation	450
Total costs to date	1,550
Contract profit recognised	760
	2,310
Less progress payment received	(900)
Gross amount due from client	1,410

Loss-making contract

When a contract is expected to make a loss, the micro LLP needs to exercise prudence and the expected loss must be recognised immediately when cost recovery is not probable.

Example – loss-making contract

A micro LLP has a fixed price contract of £5,000 and the members have assessed that it will make a loss of £900. At the year-end 31 October 2017, the project is 60% complete.

Revenue is recognised equivalent to 60% of the contract price (ie £3,000). The contract is expected to make a loss of £900 and hence cost of sales is a balancing figure to generate the required loss, hence:

	£
Revenue	3,000
Cost of raw materials and consumables	(3,900)
Gross loss	(900)

Uncertain outcome of a contract

When the outcome of a contract is uncertain, no profit is recognised. The stage of completion method is still used to identify the amount of revenue that can be recognised on the contract, but costs are again a balancing figure to generate a nil profit.

Example – uncertain contract

A micro LLP has a fixed price contract of £5,000 and the outcome is uncertain. At the year-end 31 October 2017, the contract is 60% complete.

Revenue is recognised as 60% of the contract price (ie £3,000). It is uncertain whether the contract will make a profit or a loss and therefore costs will also be £3,000 to generate a nil profit or loss.

Interest, royalties and dividends

14.109 A micro LLP may also receive revenue from asset-yielding interest, royalties and dividends. Revenue in respect of these items should only be recognised when:

(a) it is probable that economic benefits associated with the transaction will flow to the micro LLP; and

(b) the amount of the revenue can be measured reliably.

Revenue in respect of interest, royalties and dividends is recognised as follows:

Interest is recognised in accordance with Section 9 *Financial Instruments* (see **14.26**).

Royalties are recognised on an accrual basis in accordance with the substance of the relevant agreement.

Dividends are recognised when the micro LLP's right to receive payment is established.

20 Borrowing costs

14.110 Borrowing costs incurred by a micro LLP are recognised immediately in profit or loss in the period that they are incurred. There is no option in FRS 105 to capitalise such costs.

21 Impairment of assets

14.111 Micro LLPs must review assets in the balance sheet at each reporting date for indicators of impairment. Section 22 *Impairment of Assets* in FRS 105 outlines the guidance which should be followed by micro LLPs. There are, however, three types of assets which are not covered by Section 22:

- assets arising from construction contracts (Section 18 *Revenue* applies);
- financial assets under the scope of Section 9 *Financial Instruments*; and
- inventories (Section 10 *Inventories* applies).

Impairment

14.112 An asset is said to be impaired when its recoverable amount is higher than its carrying amount in the financial statements. If it is not possible to estimate the recoverable amount of an individual asset, the micro LLP should base recoverable amount on the cash-generating unit to which it belongs. This could, for example, be a group of machinery and an item in itself may not generate cash flows.

Impairment losses are recognised immediately in profit and loss and is calculated as the difference between recoverable amount and carrying amount.

Indicators that an asset is impaired

14.113 Indicators that an asset is impaired can come from two sources: external sources of information and internal sources of information:

External sources of information

- Market values of assets have declined significantly in excess of the amount which would be expected through normal passage of time or use.
- Adverse changes have taken place in the market to which the asset belongs.
- Market interest rates or returns on investments have increased during the period and these increases are likely to materially affect the discount rate the micro LLP has used to calculate the asset's value in use and hence decrease the asset's fair value less costs to sell.
- The carrying amount of the asset is more than the estimated fair value as a whole when, for example, valuing the LLP for potential sale.

Internal sources of information

- The asset is damaged or obsolete.
- The asset is likely to become idle due to adverse changes in the micro LLP which have taken, or are likely to take, place in the future.
- The micro LLP is planning to discontinue an operation of business.
- The micro LLP is planning to dispose of the asset before the previously anticipated disposal date.
- Evidence has become available suggesting the economic performance of the asset is worse than previously thought.

Focus

- Where indicators of impairment are present, the micro LLP should also review the remaining useful life, depreciation/amortisation method and residual value of the asset concerned and make appropriate adjustments even if no impairment loss is recognised.

Recoverable amount

14.114 An asset is impaired when its carrying amount in the micro LLP's financial statements is higher than its recoverable amount. Recoverable amount is the *higher* of an asset's fair value less costs to sell and its value in use.

Focus

- It is not always necessary to determine both fair value less costs to sell and value in use. This is because if *either* of these amounts are higher than the carrying amount, the asset in question is not impaired.

Fair value less costs to sell

This is likely to be the most common value used by micro LLPs. Fair value less costs to sell is the amount which an independent third party would be willing to pay for the asset in an arm's length transaction less directly attributable costs associated with the disposal. Fair value less costs to sell can usually be found in a binding sales agreement, or within an active market.

If there is no binding sales agreement or active market, fair value less costs to sell is based on the best information available to the micro LLP to reflect the amount which it could fetch in the open market.

Focus

- When considering fair value less costs to sell, the micro LLP must also take into consideration any restrictions imposed on that asset. Costs to sell would include the costs of relaxing the restriction so that the asset can be sold.

Value in use

Value in use calculations are generally quite complex for a micro LLP and in real-life are uncommon because fair value less costs to sell is easier to determine.

Value in use calculations involve discounting the present value of the future cash flows expected to be received from the asset. In practice, determining future cash flows for assets in a micro LLP will be difficult and hence where the micro LLP is undertaking a value in use calculation, it may want to use recent financial budgets or forecasts to estimate such cash flows (if these are available). Where they are available, the micro LLP could then extrapolate the projections using a steady or declining growth rate for subsequent years. A rising growth rate could be used, but only where this is justifiable.

Reversing impairment losses

14.115 When the reasons for the previously recognised impairment loss cease to apply, they can be reversed in subsequent accounting periods.

If the micro LLP has previously recognised an impairment loss which was based on the recoverable amount of an individually-impaired asset, the following must be applied:

(a) The micro LLP must estimate the recoverable amount of the asset as at the current balance sheet date.

(b) If the estimated recoverable amount of the asset exceeds its carrying amount, the micro LLP must increase the carrying amount to recoverable amount (subject to (c) below). This increase then represents the reversal of an impairment loss which is recognised immediately in profit and loss.

(c) An impairment loss cannot be reversed to the extent that it increases the asset above the carrying amount which would have been recognised (net of depreciation/amortisation) had no impairment been recognised previously.

(d) Once the impairment loss has been recognised, the micro LLP then adjusts the depreciation/amortisation charge for the asset in future periods so as to allocate the revised carrying amount, less residual value (if any) on a systematic basis over the remaining useful life.

22 Employee benefits

14.116 Employee benefits are dealt with in Section 23 *Employee Benefits* of FRS 105. Section 23 deals with four types of employee benefits:

- short-term employee benefits (other than termination benefits) which are expected to be settled within 12 months after the reporting date after the employee renders the service;
- post-employment benefits;
- long-term employment benefits; and
- termination benefits.

Short-term employee benefits include:

- wages and salaries;
- social security contributions;
- holiday pay;
- sick pay; and
- other non-monetary benefits, such as the provision of medical care, cars and housing.

When a micro LLP's employees have accrued employee benefits which have not been paid by the balance sheet date, the micro LLP recognises a liability together with a corresponding expense in profit and loss (unless FRS 105 requires the debit to be taken elsewhere, such as within property, plant and equipment).

Holiday pay

14.117 One of the most notable features of FRS 105 is that the standard specifically requires a micro LLP to make provisions for unpaid holiday pay accrued by its employees at the reporting date, but not paid until the subsequent accounting period. Whilst the term 'holiday pay accruals' seem to be the phrase that has been coined for such liabilities, they can also be prepayments.

Example – accrued holiday pay

Micro LLP has a year-end of 30 June 2017 and gives its employees 30 days' holiday entitlement per annum. Employees are also allowed to carry forward up to five days' holiday into the next holiday year. At the year-end an employee has taken 26 days' holiday.

An accrual should be made for four days' holiday entitlement which will be taken in the subsequent financial year.

Example – Holiday year not coterminous with the financial year

A micro LLP has a financial year which ends on 30 June 2017 and a holiday year which ends on 31 December 2016. An employee is given 30 days' holiday per annum and at the financial year-end had taken 20 days of her entitlement.

In this case, there will be a prepayment of five days' holiday ((30 days × 6/12) less 20 days).

Profit-sharing and bonus arrangements

14.118 A micro LLP can only recognise the cost of profit-sharing or bonus arrangements when two criteria have been met:

(a) the micro LLP has a present legal or constructive obligation to make such payments as a result of a past event; and

(b) a reliable estimate of the obligation can be made.

Post-employment benefits

14.119 The term 'post-employment benefits' refers to retirement benefits (pension plans) and other post-employment benefits such as post-employment life insurance and medical care.

There are two types of pension plan:

- defined contribution plans; and
- defined benefit plans.

Defined contribution plans

Contributions into a defined contribution pension plan or a defined benefit pension plan which are not expected to be settled within 12 months after the reporting date are discounted to present day values and it is this discounted amount which the micro LLP shall recognise in the financial statements. The difference between the settlement amount and the discounted amount is recognised as interest expense in profit and loss in the period which it arises. The discount rate used by the micro LLP must be arrived at by reference to market yields at the balance sheet date on high-quality corporate bonds.

Ordinarily, contributions into a defined contribution plan will be made on a regular basis (eg monthly) by the micro LLP. Contributions are then recognised in profit and loss as and when they arise and any contributions which are due but not paid are accrued in the financial statements. Usually such contributions will be payable within one year and classified as such in the micro LLP's accounts.

Defined benefit plans

Simplifications have been made to defined benefit pension plan accounting in FRS 105. The simplifications mean that a defined benefit pension plan (often referred to as a 'final salary plan') is accounted for in the same way as a defined contribution pension plan (ie the costs are recognised in profit and loss).

Focus

- While the accounting treatment for a defined benefit pension plan is consistent with the accounting treatment for a defined contribution pension plan in FRS 105, the standard requires that if the micro LLP has entered into an agreement with the plan which determines how the micro LLP will fund a deficit in the plan, it must recognise a liability in the balance sheet which reflects the contributions payable per the agreement to the extent that the contributions relate to the deficit. The corresponding expense is recognised in profit and loss.

Long-term employee benefits

14.120 There are five examples of long-term employee benefits under the scope of FRS 105:

- long-term absences such as long-service or sabbatical leave;
- other long-service benefits;
- long-term disability benefits;
- profit-sharing and bonuses; and
- deferred remuneration.

If a micro LLP enters into any of the above arrangements, it must recognise a liability which is measured at the present value of the obligation at the balance sheet date. The micro LLP must arrive at discount rate having regard to market yields on high-quality corporate bonds. The difference between the settlement amount and the discounted amount is recognised as interest expense in profit and loss in the period in which it arises.

Termination benefits

14.121 Termination benefits are always recognised in profit and loss. This is because such benefits will not provide the micro LLP with any future economic benefits.

In order to recognise a liability for the payment of termination benefits, the micro LLP must be demonstrably committed either:

- to terminate the employment of an employee (or a number of employees) before their normal retirement date; and
- be committed to providing termination benefits as a means of encouraging voluntary redundancy.

Focus

- The micro LLP will only be 'demonstrably committed' to a termination when the micro LLP has drawn up a detailed plan for the termination and is without realistic possibility of withdrawing from the plan.

Disclosure requirements for employee benefits

14.122 The micro LLP must disclose any commitment not recognised in the balance sheet concerning pensions separately from any other financial commitments, guarantees and contingencies.

23 Foreign currency translation

14.123 Section 25 *Foreign Currency Translation* deals with transactions a micro LLP may have which are denoted in a foreign currency. The micro LLP may enter into foreign currency transactions by:

- buying or selling goods or services in a foreign currency;
- borrowing or lending funds when the amounts payable or receivable are in a foreign currency; or
- acquiring or disposing of assets, or incurring and settling liabilities, which are in a foreign currency.

Example – purchase of goods

A micro LLP purchases some goods from a supplier based in Spain. The invoice received is denoted in Euros.

The micro LLP will translate the invoice into sterling using the exchange rate at the date of the transaction. It can also use the contracted rate where the transaction is to be settled using a contracted rate.

Translating amounts in foreign currency

14.124 Unless the micro LLP is using a contracted rate, at the balance sheet date the micro LLP must:

(a) translate foreign currency monetary items at the closing rate; and

(b) translate non-monetary items which are measured at historical cost and denoted in a foreign currency using the exchange rate at the date of the transaction.

Exchange differences are taken to profit and loss.

Example – translation of amounts in a foreign currency

A micro LLP purchases goods from a supplier located in an overseas country and the currency of the supplier is the Dinar (D). On 1 December 2017, the micro LLP purchases goods for D5,000. On this date the rate of exchange was £1:D1.20. Payment is due to the supplier on 31 January 2018 and on this date the rate of exchange was £1:D1.30 and there is no contracted rate. The transaction is recorded as follows:

<u>Record the purchase at the rate of exchange on the date of the transaction</u>

The purchase will be recorded in the purchase ledger at £4,167 (D5,000/1.20).

<u>Settlement of the invoice on 31 January 2018</u>

On settlement, the rate of exchange has moved from 1.20 to 1.30. The micro LLP will pay the supplier £3,846 (D5,000/1.30). This will result in an exchange gain of £321 (£4,167 less £3,846) because the rate of exchange has moved since the invoice was originally recognised. This gain is recognised in profit or loss on 31 January 2018.

If the year-end had been 31 December 2017, the creditor would be translated at the closing rate on 31 December 2017. Assuming this was £1:D1.25, the closing creditor would be £4,000 (D5,000/1.25) which would give rise to an exchange gain of £167 (£4,167 less £4,000). This exchange difference is recorded in profit and loss at the year-end.

---

24 Events after the end of the reporting period

14.125 The financial statements of a micro LLP should take into account all events between the balance sheet date and the date on which the financial statements are authorised for issue. This is because invariably the accounts will be prepared some time after the year-end and events can happen which might need to be reflected within the accounts. There are two types of events after the end of the reporting period (often referred to as 'post balance sheet events'):

- adjusting events; and
- non-adjusting events.

Adjusting events

Adjusting events are those events which provide evidence of conditions which existed at the balance sheet date and thus are reflected in the accounts even though they may have taken place after the balance sheet date. Examples of adjusting events are:

- the bankruptcy of a customer;
- sale of stock after the year-end which indicates that selling price is lower than cost;
- determination of amounts of profit-share and bonus arrangements paid after the balance sheet date where the micro LLP had a constructive obligation at the balance sheet date and hence made a provision; or
- discovery of fraud or error which show that the financial statements are incorrect.

Non-adjusting events

Non-adjusting events, by their definition, are not adjusted for in the financial statements. This is because their conditions did not exist at the balance sheet date. Examples of non-adjusting events include:

- the market value of some investments decline after the year-end; such a decline would reflect circumstances that have occurred subsequent to the year-end and hence are not adjusted; and
- a favourable judgement in respect of a court case occurs after the year-end but before the financial statements are authorised for issue. At the balance sheet date, the micro LLP would have a contingent asset; however, if the micro LLP and the third party agreed on an amount in settlement prior to the year-end which was not previously recognised because the amount of the settlement could not be reliably measured, this may indicate an adjusting event.

Going concern

14.126 The micro LLP should prepare its accounts on a going concern basis. However, if the members conclude after the balance sheet date that they intend to cease trading or liquidate the LLP (or they have no realistic alternative but to do so), the micro LLP must not use the going concern basis to prepare its financial statements. When the going concern basis is not appropriate to the micro LLP, the effect is usually so pervasive that it requires a fundamental change in the basis of accounting.

In such circumstances the financial statements are prepared on an alternative basis (usually the 'break-up' basis).

25 Specialised activities – agriculture

14.127 Agriculture is the only specialised activity within FRS 105 and hence if a micro LLP has a biological asset (a living animal or plant) or agricultural produce harvested from a biological asset, it accounts for such assets in accordance with Section 27 *Specialised Activities*.

Recognition of a biological asset or agricultural produce

14.128 There are three criteria which must be met before a micro LLP can recognise a biological asset or an item of agricultural produce:

(a) the micro LLP must control the asset as a result of past events;

(b) it is probable (ie more likely than not) that future economic benefits associated with the asset will flow to the micro LLP; and

(c) the cost of the asset can be reliably measured.

Subsequent measurement

14.129 After initial recognition at cost, the micro LLP can only measure biological assets at cost less accumulated depreciation and any impairment losses. Agricultural produce is measured at the point of harvest at the lower of cost and estimated selling price less costs to complete and sell. This will also be the cost price when applying Section 10 *Inventories* or another applicable section of FRS 105.

Disclosures relating to agriculture

14.130 The micro LLP must determine the cost of any financial commitments, guarantees and contingencies not recognised in the balance sheet for the acquisition of a biological asset and disclose that amount within the total of financial commitments, guarantees and contingencies.

The micro LLP must also provide an indication of the nature and form of any biological asset or item of agricultural produce given as security in respect of its commitments, guarantees and contingencies.

26 Transition to FRS 105

14.131 Section 28 *Transition to this FRS* requires the financial statements of a micro LLP to be restated to comply with the principles in FRS 105 retrospectively to the date of transition and in the comparative year. The 'date of transition' is the start date of the comparative period reported in the financial statements. Therefore, if a micro LLP has a year-end of 31 December 2016, the date of transition is 1 January 2015, being the start date of the comparative year reported in the micro LLP's accounts.

Process on transition

14.132 A micro LLP transitioning to FRS 105 for the first time is required to:

(a) recognise all assets and liabilities required by FRS 105 (eg holiday pay accruals);

(b) derecognise assets and liabilities not permitted by FRS 105;

(c) reclassify items which were recognised as one type of asset, liability or component of equity under the previous framework if they are a different type of asset, liability or component of equity under FRS 105; and

(d) apply FRS 105 going forward.

The LLP's accounting policies

14.133 The members of the micro LLP must consider the LLP's accounting policies and whether they are compliant with FRS 105 prior to transition. For example, if the micro LLP has an investment property carried at open market value, it must remove all previous revaluations and restate the investment property to the value it would have been carried at in the financial statements as at the date of transition and in the comparative year.

Any adjustments to the balance sheet at the date of transition should be reflected in loans and other debts due to members or members' other interests.

Mandatory exceptions from retrospective application

14.134 There are two mandatory exceptions from retrospective application which a micro LLP is required to apply on transition to FRS 105 in respect of:

- derecognition of financial assets and financial liabilities; and
- accounting estimates

Financial assets and financial liabilities which were derecognised under the previous financial reporting framework (eg the FRSSE (effective January 2015)) cannot be recognised upon transition to FRS 105.

For financial assets and financial liabilities which were recognised under previous UK GAAP, but which would have been derecognised under FRS 105, there are two choices available to a micro LLP:

- derecognise them on adoption of FRS 105; or
- continue recognising them until they are disposed of or settled.

Accounting estimates must not be changed on adoption of FRS 105 for the benefits of hindsight. Therefore, if a provision for a liability was included at the date of transition, the outcome of which is now known, the provision must not be changed to the actual amount paid in settlement.

Optional exemptions from retrospective application

14.135 There are seven optional exemptions from retrospective application which are applicable to micro LLPs and relate to

- business combinations and goodwill;

- investment properties;
- compound financial instruments;
- arrangements containing a lease;
- decommissioning liabilities included in the cost of property, plant and equipment or investment property;
- dormant companies; and
- lease incentives.

The optional exemption in FRS 105 relating to share-based payment transactions will not apply to micro LLPs.

Business combinations and goodwill

Where a business combination has taken place before the date of transition to FRS 105, a micro LLP is not required to apply Section 14 *Business Combinations and Goodwill*. However, if the micro LLP opts to apply Section 14 on first-time adoption of FRS 105, it must restate any later business combinations.

Where a first-time adopter does not apply Section 14 retrospectively, it must recognise and measure all the assets and liabilities acquired or assumed in a previous business combination at the date of transition in accordance with paragraph 28.7 to 28.9 or with the following paragraphs of this section, except that no adjustment must be made to the carrying amount of goodwill.

Investment properties

This is probably the area where some micro LLPs will be affected the most and care must be taken where a micro LLP has an investment property on its balance sheet because it might be that FRS 105 is not appropriate to use due to the impact it may have on the micro LLP's balance sheet. If FRS 105 is deemed inappropriate, the LLP must use FRS 102 as the next applicable financial reporting framework (and also comply with the provisions in the LLP SORP).

A first-time adopter does not have to apply paragraph 12.15 of FRS 105 to determine the depreciated cost of each of the major components of an investment property at the date of transition. Where advantage is taken of this exemption, a first-time adopter must:

1. Determine the total cost of the investment property (including all its components). Where the investment property was carried at open market value under the FRSSE (effective January 2015), this is arrived at by reversing any revaluation gains or losses previously recorded.
2. Separate the cost of the land from the buildings, where the land has a value. This is because land and buildings are accounted for separately under FRS 105.
3. Estimate the total depreciated cost of the investment property (excluding land) at the date of transition to FRS 105 by recognising accumulated depreciation since the date of initial acquisition. This is calculated on the basis of the useful life of the most

significant component of the item of investment property (eg the main structure of the investment property).

4. Some of the total depreciated cost calculated in 3 above is then allocated to each of the other major components of the investment property to determine their depreciated cost. This allocation is made on a basis which is reasonable and consistent.
5. Any amount of the total depreciated cost which is not allocated under 4 above is then allocated to the most significant component of the investment property (eg the main structure).

Compound financial instruments

A first-time adopter does not need to separate a compound financial instrument into its debt component and equity component if the liability component is not outstanding at the date of transition to FRS 105.

Arrangements containing a lease

A first-time adopter can assess whether an arrangement contains a lease, based on facts and circumstances which exist at the date of transition to FRS 105 rather than when the arrangement was entered into.

Decommissioning liabilities included in the cost of property, plant and equipment or investment property

Where the cost of an item of property, plant and equipment or investment property includes the initial estimate of costs of dismantling and removing the item and restoring the site on which the asset is located, a first-time adopter can measure this component of cost at the date of transition to FRS 105 as opposed to the date(s) when the obligation arose.

Dormant LLPs

A dormant LLP can elect to retain its accounting policies for reported assets, liabilities and equity at the date of transition to FRS 105 until there is a change to those balances, or the LLP undertakes new transactions.

Lease incentives

A first-time adopter continues the accounting treatment it previously used in respect of lease incentives for leases entered into before the date of transition to FRS 105.

Chapter summary

- LLPs are now able to use FRS 105, provided they meet the criteria and are not in a business which is precluded from using FRS 105.
- FRS 105 offers significantly reduced levels of disclosure. However, it is important that the appropriateness of FRS 105 is considered on a case-by-case basis.

- The accounting treatments are simplified in FRS 105 and there are no accounting policy options available to micro LLPs (other than some transitional options on first-time adoption of FRS 105).
- If FRS 105 is deemed inappropriate, a micro LLP can use FRS 102 and apply the presentation and disclosure requirements of Section 1A if it so wishes.

Appendix 1

LLP pro forma financial statements – group

XYZ LLP

Report and financial statements

For the year ended

31 March 201X

NOTE – in this example all profits require the approval of members before they are divided and division occurs after the year end. Capital is returned to members on their retirement.

The terminology used for the primary financial statements is that in FRS 102, although paragraph 3.22 to FRS 102 allows the use of alternative titles provided they are not misleading (hence the terms 'balance sheet' and 'profit and loss account' etc would still fall to be permissible).

Contents **Page**

Designated members and advisers

Designated members

A Designate
B Smith
C Jones

Registered office

1 The Long Street
Longtown
Longshire
LL1 1XY

Bankers

Big Bank plc
85 The Long Street
Longtown
Longshire
LL1 1YZ

Auditors

Stuart & Wilson LLP
5 The Short Street
Longtown
Longshire
LL2 1AB

Solicitors

Wright & Prentice LLP
25 The Short Street
Longtown
Longshire
LL2 1BC

Members' report

The members present their report and the financial statements for the year ended 31 March 201X.

Activities

The principal activity of the Group continues to be [ ].

Review of business

[The SORP requires disclosure of the principal activities of the LLP and its subsidiary undertakings, indicating any significant changes during the year. Whilst there are no statutory requirements with respect to additional information that might be included here, the members may wish to include further information about the performance of the LLP in support of the financial disclosures.]

Designated members

The following were designated members during the year:

A Designate
B Smith
C Jones

Members' drawings and the subscription and repayment of members' capital

During the year members receive monthly drawings representing payments on account of profits which may be allocated to them. The amount of such drawings is set at the beginning of each financial year, taking into account the anticipated cash needs of the LLP and may be reclaimed from members until such time as profits have been allocated to them.

Profits are determined, allocated and divided between members after the finalisation of the accounts. Prior to the allocation of profits and their division between members, drawings are included as 'amounts due from members' within debtors. Unallocated profits are included within equity as 'members' other interests'.

Capital requirements are determined by the designated members and are reviewed at least annually. All members are required to subscribe a proportion of that capital, with the amounts being determined by reference to experience.

On retirement, capital is repaid to members.

Auditors

[A resolution to reappoint Stuart & Wilson LLP as auditors will be proposed at the next members' meeting.] Or [Stuart & Wilson LLP have indicated their willingness to be reappointed and the members have made appropriate arrangements for them to be deemed reappointed as auditors].

Approved by the members

and signed on their behalf

A Designate

Designated member

Statement of members' responsibilities in respect of the financial statements[1]

The members are responsible for preparing the financial statements in accordance with applicable law and regulations.

The Limited Liability Partnerships (Accounts and Audit) (Application of Companies Act 2006) Regulations 2008 (the 2008 Regulations) requires the members to prepare financial statements for each financial year. Under the law the members have elected to prepare financial statements in accordance with United Kingdom Accounting Standards (United Kingdom Generally Accepted Accounting Practice). The financial statements are required by law to give a true and fair view of the state of affairs of the group and of the profit or loss of the group for that period. In preparing these financial statements, the members are required to:

- select suitable accounting policies and then apply them consistently;
- make judgements and accounting estimates that are reasonable and prudent;
- state whether applicable UK Accounting Standards have been followed, subject to any material departure disclosed and explained in the financial statements;
- prepare the financial statements on the going concern basis unless it is inappropriate to presume that the group will continue in business.

The members are responsible for keeping proper accounting records which disclose with reasonable accuracy at any time the financial position of the LLP and to enable them to ensure that the financial statements comply with the 2008 Regulations. They are also responsible for safeguarding the assets of the group and thence for taking reasonable steps for the prevention and detection of fraud and other irregularities.

These responsibilities are exercised by the designated members on behalf of the members.

Disclosure of information to the auditor

Each of the persons who is a member at the date of approval of this report confirms that:

- So far as the member is aware, there is no relevant audit information of which the group's auditor is unaware; and
- The member has taken all the steps that he/she ought to have taken as a member in order to make himself/herself aware of any relevant audit information and to establish that the group's auditor is aware of that information.

1 This statement can alternatively be included within the members' report and is only required where the LLP is subject to audit.

The following is an illustrative unqualified auditor's report

Independent auditor's report to the members of XYZ LLP

We have audited the financial statements of XYZ LLP for the year-ended 31 March 201X which comprise the principal accounting policies, the consolidated income statement, the consolidated statement of comprehensive income, the consolidated statement of financial position, the partnership statement of financial position, the consolidated statement of cash flows and related notes. The financial reporting framework that has been applied in their preparation is applicable law and United Kingdom Accounting Standards (United Kingdom Generally Accepted Accounting Practice).

Respective responsibilities of members and auditor

As explained more fully in the Members' Responsibilities Statement set out on page 305, the members are responsible for the preparation of the financial statements and for being satisfied that they give a true and fair view.

Our responsibility is to audit and express an opinion on the financial statements in accordance with applicable law and International Standards on Auditing (UK). Those standards require us to comply with the Financial Reporting Council's Ethical Standards for Auditors.[2] This report is made solely to the members of the partnership, as a body, in accordance with Chapter 3 of Part 16 of the Companies Act 2006, as applied by regulations 39 and 40 of the Limited Liability Partnerships (Accounts and Audit) (Application of Companies Act 2006) Regulations 2008. Our audit work has been undertaken so that we might state to the partnership's members those matters we are required to state to them in an auditor's report and for no other purpose. To the fullest extent permitted by law, we do not accept or assume responsibility to anyone other than the partnership and the partnership's members as a body for our audit work, for this report, or for the opinions we have formed.

Scope of the audit of the financial statements

A description of the scope of an audit of financial statements is provided on the Financial Reporting Council's website at www.frc.org.uk/auditscopeukprivate.

Opinion on the financial statements

In our opinion the financial statements:

- give a true and fair view of the state of the group's and the partnership's affairs as at 31 March 201X and of the group's profit for the year then ended;
- have been properly prepared in accordance with United Kingdom Generally Accepted Accounting Practice; and

2 This is still sometimes referred to as the 'Auditing Practices Board's Ethical Standards for Auditors' although the Auditing Practices Board now no longer exists.

- have been prepared in accordance with the requirements of the Companies Act 2006 as applied to limited liability partnerships by the Limited Liability Partnerships (Accounts and Audit) (Application of Companies Act 2006) Regulations 2008.

Matters on which we are required to report by exception

We have nothing to report in respect of the following maters where the Companies Act 2006 as applied to limited liability partnerships requires us to report to you if, in our opinion:

- adequate accounting records have not been kept by the partnership, or returns adequate for our audit have not been received from branches not visited by us; or
- the partnership financial statements are not in agreement with the accounting records and returns; or
- we have not received all the information and explanations we require for our audit.

A B Smith (Senior Statutory Auditor)

For and on behalf of Stuart & Wilson LLP

5 The Short Street

Longtown

Longshire

LL2 1AB

[insert date]

Consolidated income statement for the year ended 31 March 201X

	Notes	201X		201Y
		£'000	**£'000**	**£'000**
Turnover	3			
– Acquisitions				
Operating costs				
Staff costs	5			
Depreciation and other amounts written off tangible fixed assets				
Other operating charges				
Other operating income				
Operating profit				
– Acquisitions				
Share of operating profits of associated undertakings				
Profit/(loss) on sale of fixed asset investments				
Interest receivable and similar income				
Interest payable and similar expenses	6			
Profit on ordinary activities before taxation[3]	7			
Tax on profit on ordinary activities[3]	8			
Non-controlling interest				
Profit for the financial year before members' remuneration and profit shares				
Members' remuneration charged as an expense	4			
Retained profit for the financial year available for discretionary division among members[3]	4			

3 In circumstances where all profits are automatically divided before the year end this amount will be zero.

Consolidated statement of comprehensive income for the year ended 31 March 201X

	201X	**201Y**
	£'000	**£'000**
Retained profit for the financial year available for discretionary division among members		
Currency translation differences on net investment in group undertakings		
[Actuarial gain in respect of defined benefit pension schemes]		
Total comprehensive income for the year		

Registered number OC354321

Consolidated statement of financial position as at 31 March 201X

	Notes	201X £'000	201Y £'000
Fixed assets			
Intangible assets	10		
Tangible assets	11		
Investments	12		
Current assets			
Work in progress	13		
Debtors	14		
Cash at bank and in hand			
Creditors: amounts falling due within one year	15		
Net current assets/(liabilities)			
Total assets less current liabilities			
Creditors: amounts falling due after more than one year	16		
Provisions for liabilities	18		
Net assets attributable to members before pension fund surplus/(deficit)[4]			
[Pension fund surplus/(deficit)][4]	*20*		

4 Position of net pension fund surplus/(deficit) where the LLP has a defined benefit pension scheme. Although FRS 102 is not specific on where the pension asset or liability should be positioned.

	Notes	201X £'000	201Y £'000
Minority interest			
NET ASSETS ATTRIBUTABLE TO MEMBERS			
REPRESENTED BY			
Loans and other debts due to members within one year			
Members' capital classified as a liability[5]	19		
Other amounts	19		
Equity			
Members' other interests – other reserves classified as equity[6]	19		
Revaluation reserve	19		
Total members' interests			
Amounts due from members			
Loans and other debts due to members			
Members' other interests			

The financial statements were approved by the members on [ ] and were signed on its behalf by:

A Designate

Designated member

5 In this example members' capital is returned on retirement and is therefore a liability.
6 Profits which are only divided after the year end would be included within this balance.

Statement of financial position as at 31 March 201X

	Notes	201X £'000	201Y £'000
Fixed assets			
Intangible assets	10		
Tangible assets	11		
Investments	12		
Current assets			
Work in progress	13		
Debtors	14		
Cash at bank and in hand			
Creditors: amounts falling due within one year	15		
Net current assets/(liabilities)			
Total assets less current liabilities			
Creditors: amounts falling due after more than one year	16		
Provisions for liabilities	18		
Net assets attributable to members before pension fund surplus/(deficit)[4]			
Pension fund surplus/(deficit)[4]	20		

	Notes	201X	201Y
		£'000	**£'000**
NET ASSETS ATTRIBUTABLE TO MEMBERS			
REPRESENTED BY			
Loans and other debts due to members within one year			
Members' capital classified as a liability[5]	19		
Other amounts	19		
Equity			
Members' other interests – other reserves classified as equity[6]	19		
Revaluation reserve	19		
Total members' interests			
Amounts due from members			
Loans and other debts due to members			
Members' other interests			

The financial statements were approved by the members on [ ] and were signed on its behalf by:

A Designate

Designated member

Consolidated statement of cash flows for the year ended 31 March 201X

	Notes	201X £'000	201Y £'000
Net cash inflow/(outflow) from operating activities	a		
Cash flows from investing activities			
Interest received			
Purchase of intangible assets			
Purchase of property, plant and equipment			
Proceeds from sale of property, plant and equipment			
Purchase of subsidiary undertaking			
Net cash/(overdraft) acquired with subsidiary			
Purchase of interest in associate			
Net cash inflow/(outflow) from investing activities			
Transactions with members and former members			
Drawings and distributions to members			
Payments to former members			
Capital contributions by members			
Capital repayments to members			
Net cash inflow/(outflow) from transactions with members and former members			

	Notes	**201X**	**201Y**
		£'000	**£'000**
Cash flows from financing activities			
New long-term loans			
Repayment of long-term loans			
Repayment of capital element of finance lease rentals			
Net cash inflow/(outflow) from financing activities			
Increase/(decrease) in cash in the year	b		

Notes to the statement of cash flows

a	Reconciliation of operating profit/(loss) to net cash inflow/(outflow) from operating activities	201X £'000	201Y £'000
	Operating profit/(loss)		
	Depreciation		
	Amortisation of intangible assets		
	Loss/(profit) on sale of tangible fixed assets		
	Decrease/(increase) in work in progress		
	Decrease/(increase) in debtors		
	Increase/(decrease) in creditors		
	Increase/(decrease) in provisions		
	Interest paid		
	Net cash inflow/(outflow) from operating activities		

b	Cash and cash equivalents		
	Cash at bank and in hand		
	Less: bank overdraft		

Notes to the financial statements for the year ended 31 March 201X

1 Accounting policies[7]

The financial statements have been prepared in accordance with FRS 102 *The Financial Reporting Standard applicable in the UK and Republic of Ireland* and the requirements of the Statement of Recommended Practice 'Accounting by Limited Liability Partnerships'. A summary of the significant accounting policies adopted are described below.

Basis of accounting

The financial statements have been prepared under the historical cost convention.

[Where relevant the members should include appropriate disclosure about their reasons for adopting the going concern basis and any material uncertainties that cast significant doubt over the LLP's ability to continue as a going concern]

Basis of consolidation

The financial statements consolidate the results and the assets and liabilities of the LLP and its subsidiaries. The results of subsidiaries acquired or disposed of during the year are included in the consolidated income statement from the effective date of the business combination or up to the effective date of disposal, where appropriate.

Where necessary, adjustments are made to the financial statements of subsidiaries to bring the accounting policies used in line with those used by the Group.

All intra-group transactions, balances, income and expenses are eliminated on consolidation.

Business combinations

Business combinations during the year have been accounted for in accordance with Section 19 *Business Combinations and Goodwill* of FRS 102 and the LLP has applied the purchase method of accounting for the business combination.

On the acquisition of a business, fair values are attributed to the groups' share of net separable assets acquired. Where the cost of the business combination exceeds the fair values attributable to such net assets, the difference is treated as goodwill and capitalised in the consolidated statement of financial position in the year of the business combination. The results and cash flows relating to an acquired business are included in the consolidated income statement and statement of cash flows from the date of acquisition.

7 The accounting policies shown here are illustrative and the policies disclosed should be those that are specific to the LLP.

Goodwill and other intangible assets

Goodwill arising in a business combination is the difference between the fair value of the consideration given and the fair value of the net assets acquired. It is included on the consolidated statement of financial position and is being amortised over a period of ten years. The members have been able to reliably estimate the useful economic life of this goodwill by reference to the product lifecycles of the business and the stability of the acquired business.

Trademarks are included at cost of acquisition and are depreciated over their estimated useful life of three years.

Share of profits and losses of associated undertakings

Undertakings, other than subsidiary undertakings, over which the LLP exerts significant influence, are treated as associated undertakings and are accounted for under the equity method. Under the equity method of accounting, the consolidated income statement includes the LLP's share of the associate's results. For operating profit, this is disclosed separately. For items below operating profit, the LLP's share of the relevant amounts for associates is included within the amounts for the group. In the statement of financial position, the LLP's share of the net assets of the associate is included within investments.

Fixed assets

Depreciation is provided on cost or revalued amounts in equal annual instalments over the estimated useful lives of the assets concerned. The following annual rates are used.

Freehold land and buildings	-	in respect of buildings only, in equal instalments over 50 years
Short leasehold improvements	-	in equal instalments over the shorter of the term to lease expiry or to the date of the next break clause
Fixtures and fittings	-	15% reducing balance
Office equipment	-	20% reducing balance
Motor vehicles	-	25% reducing balance

Provisions for the estimated dilapidation costs at the end of a lease are built up over the final five years of a lease or to the date of the next break clause.

The LLP adopts the use of the cost model for its tangible fixed assets.

Investments

Investments are included at cost less any provision for impairment.

Professional indemnity insurance

Professional indemnity insurance premiums are charged as incurred and expensed to the income statement over the period of cover. Provision is made in respect of any uninsured excess that the group considers likely to be payable.

Taxation

The taxation payable on the profits of the limited liability partnership is the liability of the individual members. An amount is retained from each member to cover the members' estimated liability for income tax and social security contributions on their profit share. The amounts retained from allocated profits are included within 'loans and other debts due to members'.

Corporate subsidiaries of the LLP included within these consolidated financial statements are subject to UK corporation tax based on the profits of the accounting period which remains a liability of the company to which it relates (as opposed to the members). This tax charge is recorded in the profit and loss account under the heading 'tax on profit on ordinary activities' and any related liability is included as a creditor in the statement of financial position.

Deferred taxation

Deferred tax in respect of corporate subsidiaries of the LLP is provided for on a full provision basis on all timing differences which have arisen but not reversed at the reporting date. A deferred tax asset is not recognised to the extent that the transfer of economic benefit in the future is uncertain.

Members' remuneration[8]

Profits attributable to members are determined, allocated and divided between members after the year end and until that time are included as equity within members' other interests. Any drawings paid in respect of those profits are included as 'amounts due from members' within debtors.

The terms of the members' agreement require that capital be returned to a member on his or her retirement. Capital is accordingly accounted for as a liability of the LLP.

Pensions and other post-retirement benefits

The defined benefit pension scheme is accounted for in accordance with Section 28 *Employee Benefits*. The scheme is funded with the assets of the scheme held separately from those of the group in separate trustee administered funds. The scheme is closed to new members.

8 The accounting policy reflects the particular profit sharing and capital arrangements of the LLP in this example.

Current service costs and curtailment gains are recognised in arriving at operating profit. The interest cost in respect of scheme liabilities, net of the expected return on scheme assets, is included in either 'interest receivable' or 'interest payable and similar expenses'. Differences between amounts charged to the income statement and amounts funded are shown in either provisions or prepayments in the statement of financial position.

Scheme assets are measured at fair value and scheme liabilities are measured on an actuarial basis and discounted at a rate equivalent to a high quality Sterling bond with a term equivalent to the scheme liabilities. Changes in the scheme deficit arising from actuarial gains and losses are recognised immediately in other comprehensive income.

Contributions to defined contribution schemes are charged to the income statement as they become payable in accordance with the rules of the scheme.

Under the terms of the members' agreement, former members are entitled to an annuity payment based on a formula directly linked to the profits of the LLP. Provision is made in the accounts for the estimated present value of the expected future payments to that member. Amounts in respect of current members are included within 'members' remuneration charged as an expense', and amounts with respect to former members are included within 'staff costs'. The liability with respect to current members is included within 'loans and other amounts due to members' and the liability to former members is included within 'provisions for liabilities'.

Leases

Assets held under finance leases are included in fixed assets and the capital element of the related lease commitment is shown within creditors as 'obligations under finance leases'. The lease rentals are treated as consisting of capital and interest elements. The capital element is applied to reduce the outstanding obligations and the interest element is charged against profit using the effective interest method. The finance charge is allocated to each period during the term of the lease so as to produce a constant periodic rate of interest on the remaining balance of the liability.

Rental costs under operating leases are charged to the income settlement on a straight-line basis over the lease term.

Foreign currencies

Transactions denominated in a foreign currency are translated into Sterling at the rate of exchange ruling at the date of the transaction. At the reporting date, monetary assets and liabilities denominated in foreign currency are translated at the rate ruling at that date. Resulting exchange differences are dealt with in the income statement.

The income statements of overseas subsidiaries are translated at average rates of exchange for the financial year.

Exchange differences arising from the retranslation at the closing rate of the opening net investment in overseas subsidiaries and of their results for the year are taken to other comprehensive income and accumulated in equity.

Work in progress

Where work has been performed in relation to which revenue will be recognised in a later period, work in progress is recognised at the lower of cost and estimated selling price less costs to complete.

Cost comprises direct staff costs and a share of overhead appropriate to the relevant state of completion of the related project. The relevant proportion of the salaried remuneration of members is included within cost. Members' profit allocations are excluded.

Revenue recognition

Turnover represents the value of fees and commissions earned in the period, net of VAT.

Where fees for professional work have been unconditionally earned but not invoiced at the period end, these amounts are included within accrued income.

Revenue in respect of professional services is recognised by reference to the fair value of the services provided at the reporting date as a proportion of the total value of the engagement. Unbilled revenue is included within debtors as accrued income.

Critical accounting judgements and key sources of estimation uncertainty

In the application of the group's accounting policies, which are described above, the members are required to make judgements, estimates and assumptions about the carrying values of assets and liabilities which are not readily apparent from other sources. The members base such estimates on historical experience and other factors that are considered to be relevant. Actual results may differ from these estimates.

The estimates and underlying assumptions are reviewed on an ongoing basis. Revisions to accounting estimates are recognised in the period in which the estimate is revised if the revisions only affect that period. If the revisions affect both the current and future periods, it is recognised in the current and subsequent periods.

The key sources of estimation uncertainty which have a significant effect on the amounts recognised in the financial statements are described below:

[Describe the relevant sources of estimation uncertainty which have had a significant effect on the amounts recognised in the financial statements (eg valuation of land and buildings, estimates of work in progress etc)].

2 Business combination

On [ ], the LLP acquired the entire share capital of ABC Limited for cash consideration of £[ ]. In addition, the former shareholders of ABC Limited have been offered an enhanced allocation of profits in addition to that available to all members, which is calculated by reference to a formula linked to the financial performance of ABC Limited. An amount of £[ ], being the current best estimate of the amounts payable, is included in 'members' other interests' within loans and other debts due to members. The business combination has been accounted for using the purchase method of accounting. The amount of goodwill arising as a result of the acquisition is £[ ].

The income statement of ABC Limited for the period from 1 April 201Y to the date of acquisition and for the previous financial year were as follows[9]

	1 April 201Y to date of acquisition	**Preceding financial year ended 31 March 201Y**
	£'000	**£'000**
Turnover		
Operating profit		
Profit before tax		
Taxation		
Profit after tax		

9 This example assumes that the acquisition is significant to the group.

2 **Business combination** ***(continued)***

The following table summarises the adjustments made to the book value of the major categories of assets and liabilities acquired to arrive at the fair values included in the consolidated financial statements at the date of acquisition.

	Book value £'000	**Fair value adjustments £'000**	**Fair value £'000**
Tangible fixed assets			
Current assets			
Creditors			
Consideration			
Cash (including acquisition costs of £[ ])			
Contingent consideration			
Goodwill			

The fair value adjustments comprise [ ]

3 **Turnover**[10]

	201X £'000	**201Y £'000**
United Kingdom		
Rest of the World		

10 This segment analysis is not required by FRS 102 although some LLPs do choose to include a segment analysis hence is shown here for completeness.

4 Information in relation to members

	201X Number	201Y Number
The average number of members during the year was		
	£'000	*£'000*
[*The average members' remuneration during the year was*][11]		
	£'000	£'000
Salaried remuneration of members		
Paid under employment contract		
Paid under the terms of the LLP agreement		
The amount of profit attributable to the member with the largest entitlement was		

Profit attributable to the member with the largest entitlement is determined by reference to [ ]

11 This disclosure is optional.

5 Employee information and staff costs

The average number of persons (including members with contracts of employment) employed by the LLP during the year was:

	201X Number	201Y Number
Selling and distribution		
Administration		

	201X £'000	201Y £'000
Staff costs for the above persons were:		
Wages and salaries		
Social security costs		
Pension costs		

6 Interest payable and similar expenses

	201X £'000	201Y £'000
Bank loans and overdrafts		
Finance leases		
Net return on pension and other retirement schemes		

7 **Profit on ordinary activities before taxation**

Profit on ordinary activities before taxation is stated after charging/(crediting):	**£'000**	**£'000**
Depreciation		
– owned assets		
– assets held under finance leases		
Goodwill amortisation		
Amortisation of intangible assets		
Operating leases – property		
– other		

The analysis of auditors' remuneration is as follows:	**201X** **£'000**	**201Y** **£'000**
Fees payable to the LLP's auditors for the audit of the LLP's annual accounts		
Fees payable to the LLP's auditors and their associates for other services to the group		
Fees payable in respect of the audit of the LLP's subsidiaries pursuant to legislation		
Total audit fees		
Tax services		
Corporate finance services		
Other services		
Total non-audit fees		
Fess payable to the LLP's auditors in respect of associated pension schemes		
Audit		

8[3] Tax on profit on ordinary activities

	£	£
UK corporation tax at [ ]%		
Under/(over) provision in respect of prior years		
Deferred tax		
Share of associated undertakings tax charge		
Tax charge for the year		

The standard rate of tax for the year, based on the UK standard rate of corporation tax is [ ]%. The actual tax charge for the current and previous year is less than the standard rate for the reasons set out in the following reconciliation:

	201X	201Y
	£	£
Profit on ordinary activities before tax		
Tax on profit on ordinary activities at the standard rate		
Factors affecting charge for the period:		
Profits of LLP not chargeable to corporation tax		
Capital allowances for period in excess of depreciation		
Expenses not allowable for tax purposes		
Other timing differences		
Adjustments to tax charge in respect of prior periods		

9 Profit of the LLP

As permitted by section 408 of the Companies Act 2006 as applied to LLPs, the LLP is exempt from presenting its own profit and loss account. The profit of the LLP for the financial year amounted to £[ ] (201Y: £[ ]).

10 **Intangible fixed assets**

Group

	Goodwill £'000	Trademarks £'000	Total £'000
Cost			
At 1 April 201Y			
Additions			
At 31 March 201X			
Amortisation			
At 1 April 201Y			
Charge for year			
At 31 March 201X			
Net book value			
At 31 March 201X			
At 31 March 201Y			

10 **Intangible fixed assets *(continued)***

LLP

	Trademarks £'000
Cost	
At 1 April 201Y	
Additions	
At 31 March 201X	
Amortisation	
At 1 April 201Y	
Charge for the year	
At 31 March 201X	
Net book value	
At 31 March 201X	
At 31 March 201Y	

11 Tangible fixed assets

Group	Freehold land and buildings	Short leasehold improve-ments	Office fixtures and fittings	Motor vehicles	Total
	£'000	£'000	£'000	£'000	£'000
Cost or valuation					
At 1 April 201Y					
Additions					
Acquired with subsidiary					
Disposals					
At 31 March 201X					
Depreciation					
At 1 April 201Y					
Charge for the year					
Disposals					
At 31 March 201X					
Net book value					
At 31 March 201X					
At 31 March 201Y					

The net book value of the group's office fixtures and fittings includes £[ ] (201Y: £[ ]) in respect of assets held under finance leases.

11 **Tangible fixed assets *(continued)***

LLP	**Freehold land and buildings**	**Short leasehold improve-ments**	**Office fixtures and fittings**	**Motor vehicles**	**Total**
	£'000	**£'000**	**£'000**	**£'000**	**£'000**
Cost or valuation					
At 1 April 201Y					
Additions					
Disposals					
At 31 March 201Y					
Depreciation					
At 1 April 201Y					
Charge for the year					
Disposals					
At 31 March 201Y					
Net book value					
At 31 March 201Y					
At 31 March 201Y					

The net book value of the LLP's office fixtures and fittings includes £[ ] (201Y: £[ ]) in respect of assets held under finance leases.

12 **Investments**

Group

	Interest in associated undertakings £'000
At 1 April 201Y	
Group share of result for the period	
At 31 March 201X	

LLP

	Investment in associated undertakings £'000	Investment in subsidiary undertakings £'000	Total £'000
At 1 April 201Y			
Additions			
Disposals			
At 31 March 201X			

12 **Investments *(continued)***

The principal undertakings in which the group's interest in the ordinary share capital at the year end is more than 20% are as follows:

Subsidiary undertakings	**Country of registration**	**Activity**	**Portion of ordinary shares held**
ABC Limited	[ ]	[ ]	[ ]
XYZ Limited	[ ]	[ ]	[ ]
Associated undertakings			
123 Limited	[ ]	[ ]	[ ]

13 **Work in progress**

	Group		LLP	
	201X	**201Y**	**201X**	**201Y**
	£'000	**£'000**	**£'000**	**£'000**
Work in progress				

14 **Debtors**

	Group		LLP	
	201X	**201Y**	**201X**	**201Y**
	£'000	**£'000**	**£'000**	**£'000**
Trade debtors				
Amounts owed by subsidiary undertakings				
Amounts owed by associates				
Amounts due from members				
Other debtors				
Prepayments and accrued income				

15 **Creditors:** amounts falling due within one year

	Group		LLP	
	201X	**201Y**	**201X**	**201Y**
	£'000	**£'000**	**£'000**	**£'000**
Bank loans and overdrafts				
Obligations under finance leases				
Trade creditors				
Amounts owed to subsidiary undertakings				
Corporation tax				
Other taxation and social security				
[Retirement benefits due to former members][12]				
Other creditors				
Accruals and deferred income				

16 **Creditors:** amounts falling due after more than one year

	Group		LLP	
	201X	**201Y**	**201X**	**201Y**
	£	**£**	**£**	**£**
Bank loans and overdrafts				
Obligations under finance leases				
Retirement benefits due to former members				

12 Where the amount of retirement benefits to former members is fixed it should be included within creditors (split between due within and due after one year) rather than be included within provisions

17 **Borrowings**

	Group		**LLP**	
	201X	**201Y**	**201X**	**201Y**
	£	**£**	**£**	**£**
Bank overdraft				
Bank loan				
(secured [ ]% above LIBOR)				
Obligations under finance leases				
Due within one year				
Due after one year				
Maturity analysis				
Within one year or on demand				
More than one year but less than two years				
More than two years but not less than five years				
More than five years				

[Bank loans and overdrafts are secured by fixed and floating charges over the assets of the LLP and its subsidiary undertakings].

18 **Provisions for liabilities**

Group and LLP

	Post-retirement payments to former members £'000	Provisions for dilapidations £'000	Total £'000
At 1 April 201Y			
Subsidiary acquired			
Income statement charge			
Amounts utilised			
At 31 March 201X			

19 Reconciliation of members' interests – Group

	EQUITY				DEBT			
	Members' Other interests				Loans and other debts due to members less any amounts due from members in debtors			TOTAL MEMBERS' INTERESTS
	Members' capital (classified as equity)	Revaluation reserve	Other reserves	Total	Members' capital (classified as debt)	Other amounts	Total	Total
	£'000	£'000	£'000	£'000	£'000	£'000	£'000	£'000
Amounts due to members								
Amounts due from members								
Members' interests at 1 April 201Y								
Members' remuneration charged as an expense								
Profit for the financial year available for discretionary division among members								
Members' interests after profit for the year								
Other divisions of profits/losses								
Exchange movements								
Surplus arising on revaluation of fixed assets								
Introduced by members								
Repayments of capital								
Repayment of debt								
Drawings								
Other movements								
Amounts due to members								
Amounts due from members								
Members' interests at 31 March 201X								

Amounts due to members will rank pari pasu with other unsecured creditors in the event of a winding up. In such a circumstance, the members have subordinated their rights to payments of amounts owed to them in preference to external creditors.

19 Reconciliation of members' interests – LLP

	EQUITY				DEBT			
	Members' other interests				Loans and other debts due to members less any amounts due from members in debtors			TOTAL MEMBERS' INTERESTS
	Members' capital (classified as equity)	Revaluation reserve	Other reserves	Total	Members' capital (classified as debt)	Other amounts	Total	Total
	£'000	£'000	£'000	£'000	£'000	£'000	£'000	£'000
Amounts due to members								
Amounts due from members								
Members' interests at 1 April 201Y								
Members' remuneration charged as an expense								
Profit for the financial year available for discretionary division among members								
Members' interests after profit for the year								
Other divisions of profits/losses								
Surplus arising on revaluation of fixed assets								
Introduced by members								
Repayments of capital								
Repayment of debt								
Drawings								
Other movements								
Amounts due to members								
Amounts due from members								
Members' interests at 31 March 201X								

20 **Pension costs**

Section 28 requires considerable disclosures with respect to pension costs relating to defined benefit schemes. Where relevant, reference should be had to the standard.

21 **Operating lease commitments**

At 31 March 201X the LLP had annual commitments under non-cancellable operating leases as follows:

	201X Property £'000	201Y Property £'000	201X Other £'000	201Y Other £'000
For leases expiring:				
Within one year				
Between two and five years				
In excess of five years				

22 **Capital commitments**

	201X £	201Y £
Contracted but not provided for		

23 **Contingent liabilities**

The LLP has guaranteed the borrowings of individual members taken out in order to fund their capital interests in the LLP. At 31 March 201X the total amount guaranteed was £[ ]. 201Y £[ ].

24 **Related party transactions**

The LLP has taken advantage of the exemption in Section 33 *Related Party Disclosures* from reporting related party transactions with its wholly-owned subsidiaries.

[Related party transactions of the group and the parent (except for those with its wholly-owned subsidiary) should be disclosed here]

25 **Controlling party**

In the opinion of the members there is no controlling party.

26 **Events after the reporting date**

[Material non-adjusting events after the reporting date should be disclosed in accordance with Section 32 *Events after the End of the Reporting Period*.]

Appendix 2

LLP pro forma financial statements – single LLP

XYZ LLP

Report and financial statements

For the year ended

31 March 201X

NOTE – in this example all profits require the approval of members before they are divided and division occurs after the year end. Capital is returned to members on their retirement.

These illustrative financial statements use the terminology found in FRS 102 (eg 'statement of financial position' instead of 'balance sheet'). Alternative titles can be used for the financial statements according to paragraph 3.22 of FRS 102 provided they are not misleading, hence the term 'balance sheet' and 'profit and loss account' may still be used.

Contents **Page**

Designated members and advisers

Designated members

A Designate
B Smith
C Jones

Registered office

1 The Long Street
Longtown
Longshire
LL1 1XY

Bankers

Big Bank plc
85 The Long Street
Longtown
Longshire
LL1 1YZ

Auditors

Stuart & Wilson LLP
5 The Short Street
Longtown
Longshire
LL2 1AB

Solicitors

Wright & Prentice LLP
25 The Short Street
Longtown
Longshire
LL2 1BC

Members' report

The members present their report and the financial statements for the year ended 31 March 201X.

Activities

The principal activity of the LLP continues to be [ ].

Review of business

[The SORP requires disclosure of the principal activities of the LLP and its subsidiary undertakings, indicating any significant changes during the year. Whilst there are no statutory requirements with respect to additional information that might be included here, the members may wish to include further information about the performance of the LLP in support of the financial disclosures.]

Designated members

The following were designated members during the year:

A Designate
B Smith
C Jones

Members' drawings and the subscription and repayment of members' capital

During the year members receive monthly drawings representing payments on account of profits which may be allocated to them. The amount of such drawings is set at the beginning of each financial year, taking into account the anticipated cash needs of the LLP and may be reclaimed from members until such time as profits have been allocated to them.

Profits are determined, allocated and divided between members after the finalisation of the accounts. Prior to the allocation of profits and their division between members, drawings are included as 'amounts due from members' within debtors. Unallocated profits are included within equity as 'members' other interests'.

Capital requirements are determined by the designated members and are reviewed at least annually. All members are required to subscribe a proportion of that capital, with the amounts being determined by reference to experience.

On retirement, capital is repaid to members.

Auditors

[A resolution to reappoint Stuart & Wilson LLP as auditors will be proposed at the next members' meeting.] Or [Stuart & Wilson LLP have indicated their willingness to be reappointed and the members have made appropriate arrangements for them to be deemed reappointed as auditors].

Approved by the members

and signed on their behalf

A Designate

Designated member

Statement of members' responsibilities in respect of the financial statements[1]

The members are responsible for preparing the Annual Report and the financial statements in accordance with applicable law and regulations.

The Limited Liability Partnerships Regulations 2008 requires the members to prepare financial statements for each financial year which give a true and fair view of the state of affairs of the LLP and of the profit or loss of the LLP for that period in accordance with United Kingdom Generally Accepted Accounting Practice. In preparing these financial statements, the members are required to:

- select suitable accounting policies and then apply them consistently;
- make judgements and estimates that are reasonable and prudent;
- state whether applicable UK Accounting Standards have been followed, subject to any material departure disclosed and explained in the financial statements;
- prepare the accounts on the going concern basis unless it is inappropriate to presume that the LLP will continue in business.

The members are responsible for keeping adequate accounting records which disclose with reasonable accuracy at any time the financial position of the LLP and to enable them to ensure that the accounts comply with the Limited Liability Partnerships Regulations. They are also responsible for safeguarding the assets of the LLP and thence for taking reasonable steps for the prevention and detection of fraud and other irregularities.

These responsibilities are exercised by the designated members on behalf of the members.

Disclosure of information to the auditor

Each of the persons who is a member at the date of approval of this report confirms that:

- so far as the member is aware, there is no relevant audit information of which the auditor is unaware; and
- the member has taken all the steps that he/she ought to have taken as a member in order to make himself/herself aware of any relevant audit information and to establish that the auditor is aware of that information.

1 This statement can alternatively be included within the members' report and is only required where the LLP is subject to audit.

The following is an illustrative unqualified audit report

Independent auditor's report to the members of XYZ LLP

We have audited the financial statements of XYZ LLP (the 'LLP') for the year-ended 31 March 201X which comprise the income statement, statement of financial position, statement of cash flows and related notes. The financial reporting framework that has been applied in their preparation is applicable law and United Kingdom Accounting Standards (United Kingdom Generally Accepted Accounting Practice).

This report is made solely to the LLP's members, as a body, in accordance with Chapter 3 of Part 16 of the Companies Act 2006, as applied to limited liability partnerships by the Limited Liability Partnerships (Accounts and Audit) (Application of Companies Act 2006) Regulations 2008. Our audit work has been undertaken so that we might state to the LLP's members those matters we are required to state to them in an auditor's report and for no other purpose. To the fullest extent permitted by law, we do not accept or assume responsibility to anyone other than the LLP and the LLP's members as a body, for our audit work, for this report, or for the opinions we have formed.

Respective responsibilities of members and auditor

As explained more fully in the Members' Responsibilities Statement, the members are responsible for the preparation of the financial statements and for being satisfied that they give a true and fair view. Our responsibility is to audit and express an opinion on the financial statements in accordance with applicable law and International Standards on Auditing (UK). Those standards require us to comply with the Financial Reporting Council's Ethical Standard for Auditors.[2]

Scope of the audit of the financial statements

An audit involves obtaining evidence about the amounts and disclosures in the financial statements sufficient to give reasonable assurance that the financial statements are free from material misstatement, whether caused by fraud or error. This includes an assessment of: whether the accounting policies are appropriate to the LLP and have been consistently applied and adequately disclosed; the reasonableness of significant accounting estimates made by the members; and the overall presentation of the financial statements. In addition, we read all the financial and non-financial information in the annual report to identify material inconsistencies with the audited financial statements. If we become aware of any apparent material misstatements or inconsistencies we consider the implications for our report.

2 The Auditing Practices Board is no longer in existence and some firms refer to the Auditing Practices Board. It is preferable to follow the guidance in the relevant guidance issued by the FRC on the wording in the audit report.

Opinion on financial statements

In our opinion the financial statements:

- give a true and fair view of the state of the LLP's affairs as at 31 March 201X and of its profit for the year then ended;
- have been properly prepared in accordance with United Kingdom Generally Accepted Accounting Practice; and
- have been prepared in accordance with the requirements of the Companies Act 2006 as applied to limited liability partnerships.

Matters on which we are required to report by exception

We have nothing to report in respect of the following matters where the Companies Act 2006 as applied to limited liability partnerships requires us to report to you if, in our opinion:

- adequate accounting records have not been kept by the LLP, or returns adequate for our audit have not been received from branches not visited by us; or
- the LLPs financial statements are not in agreement with the accounting records and returns; or
- we have not received all the information and explanations we require for our audit.

J J Smith (Senior Statutory Auditor)

For and on behalf of Stuart & Wilson LLP

5 The Short Street

Longtown

Longshire

LL2 1AB

[Insert date of report]

Income statement for the year ended 31 March 201X

	Notes	201X		201Y
		£'000	**£'000**	**£'000**
Turnover	2			
Operating costs				
Staff costs	4			
Depreciation and other amounts written off tangible fixed assets				
Other operating charges				
Other operating income				
Operating profit				
Interest receivable and similar income				
Interest payable and similar expenses	5			
Profit for the financial year before members' remuneration and profit shares	6			
Members' remuneration charged as an expense	3			
Retained profit for the financial year available for discretionary division among members[3]	3			

3 In circumstances where all profits are automatically divided before the year end this amount will be zero.

Registered number OC354321

Statement of financial position as at 31 March 201X

	Notes	201X £'000	201Y £'000
Fixed assets			
Intangible assets	7		
Tangible assets	8		
Current assets			
Work in progress	9		
Debtors	10		
Cash at bank and in hand			
Creditors: amounts falling due within one year	11		
Net current assets/(liabilities)			
Total assets less current liabilities			
Creditors: amounts falling due after more than one year	12		
Provisions for liabilities	14		
NET ASSETS ATTRIBUTABLE TO MEMBERS			
REPRESENTED BY			
Loans and other debts due to members within one year			
Members' capital classified as a liability			
Other amounts			
Equity			
Members' other interests – other reserves classified as equity			
Total members' interests			
Amounts due from members			
Loans and other debts due to members			
Members' other interests			

The financial statements were approved by the members on [ ] and were signed on its behalf by:

A Designate

Designated member

Statement of cash flows for the year ended 31 March 201X

	Notes	201X £'000	201Y £'000
Net cash inflow/(outflow) from operating activities	a		
Cash flows from investing activities			
Interest received			
Purchase of intangible assets			
Purchase of property, plant and equipment			
Proceeds from sale of property, plant and equipment			
Net cash inflow/(outflow) from investing activities			
Transactions with members and former members			
Drawings and distributions to members			
Payments to former members			
Capital contributions by members			
Capital repayments to members			
Net cash inflow/(outflow) from transactions with members and former members			
Cash flows from financing activities			
New long-term loans			
Repayment of long-term loans			
Repayment of capital element of finance lease rentals			
Net cash inflow/(outflow) from financing activities			
Increase/(decrease) in cash in the year	b		

Notes to the statement of cash flows

a	**Reconciliation of operating profit/(loss) to net cash inflow/(outflow) from operating activities**	**201X £'000**	**201Y £'000**
	Operating profit/(loss)		
	Depreciation		
	Amortisation of intangible assets		
	Loss/(profit) on sale of tangible fixed assets		
	Decrease/(increase) in work in progress		
	Decrease/(increase) in debtors		
	Increase/(decrease) in creditors		
	Increase/(decrease) in provisions		
	Interest paid		
	Net cash inflow/(outflow) from operating activities		

b	**Cash and cash equivalents**		
	Cash at bank and in hand		
	Less bank overdraft		

Notes to the financial statements for the year ended 31 March 201X

1 Accounting policies[4]

The accounts have been prepared in accordance with FRS 102 *The Financial Reporting Standard applicable in the UK and Republic of Ireland* and the requirements of the Statement of Recommended Practice 'Accounting by Limited Liability Partnerships'. A summary of the significant accounting policies adopted are described below.

Basis of accounting

The accounts have been prepared under the historical cost convention [Where relevant the members should include appropriate disclosure about their reasons for adopting the going concern basis and any material uncertainties that cast significant doubt over the LLP's ability to continue as a going concern]

Intangible assets

Trademarks are included at cost of acquisition and are depreciated over their estimated useful life of three years.

Fixed assets

Depreciation is provided on cost in equal annual instalments over the estimated useful lives of the assets concerned. The following annual rates are used.

Freehold land and buildings	-	in respect of buildings only, in equal instalments over 50 years
Short leasehold improvements	-	in equal instalments over the shorter of the term to lease expiry or to the date of the next break clause
Fixtures and fittings	-	15% reducing balance
Office equipment	-	20% reducing balance
Motor vehicles	-	25% reducing balance

Provisions for the estimated dilapidation costs at the end of a lease are built up over the final five years of a lease or to the date of the next break clause.

The LLP adopts the use of the cost model for all its tangible fixed assets.

Investments

Investments are included at cost less any provision for impairment

4 The accounting policies shown here are illustrative and the policies disclosed should be those that are specific to the LLP.

Professional indemnity insurance

Professional indemnity insurance premiums are charged as incurred and expensed to the income statement over the period of cover. Provision is made in respect of any uninsured excess that the LLP considers likely to be payable.

Taxation

The taxation payable on the profits of the limited liability partnership is the liability of the individual members. An amount is retained from each member to cover the members' estimated liability for income tax and social security contributions on their profit share. The amounts retained from allocated profits are included within 'loans and other debts due to members'.

Members' remuneration[5]

Profits attributable to members are determined, allocated and divided between members after the year end and until that time are included as equity within members' other interests. Any drawings paid in respect of those profits are included as 'amounts due from members' within debtors.

The terms of the members' agreement require that capital be returned to a member on his or her retirement. Capital is accordingly accounted for as a liability of the LLP.

Pensions and other post-retirement benefits

Contributions to defined contribution schemes are charged to the income statement as they become payable in accordance with the rules of the scheme.

Under the terms of the members' agreement, former members are entitled to an annuity payment based on a formula directly linked to the profits of the LLP. Provision is made in the financial statements for the estimated present value of the expected future payments to that member. Amounts in respect of current members are included within 'members' remuneration charged as an expense', and amounts with respect to former members are included within 'staff costs'. The liability with respect to current members is included within 'loans and other amounts due to members' and the liability to former members is included within 'provisions for liabilities'.

Leases

Assets held under finance leases are included in fixed assets and the capital element of the related lease commitment is shown within creditors as 'obligations under finance leases'. The lease rentals are treated as consisting of capital and interest elements. The capital element is applied to reduce the outstanding obligations and the interest element is charged against profit using the effective interest method. The finance charge is allocated to each period during the term of the lease so as to produce a constant periodic rate of interest on the remaining balance of the liability.

Rental costs under operating leases are charged to the income statement on a straight-line basis over the lease term.

Foreign currencies

Transactions denominated in a foreign currency are translated into Sterling at the rate of exchange ruling at the date of the transaction. At the reporting date, monetary assets and liabilities denominated in foreign currency are translated at the rate ruling at that date. Resulting exchange differences are dealt with in the income statement.

Work in progress

Where work has been performed in relation to which revenue will be recognised in a later period, work in progress is recognised at the lower of cost and estimated selling price less costs to complete.

5 The accounting policy reflects the particular profit sharing and capital arrangements of the LLP in this example.

Cost comprises direct staff costs and a share of overhead appropriate to the relevant state of completion of the related project. The relevant proportion of the salaried remuneration of members is included within cost. Members' profit allocations are excluded.

Revenue recognition

Turnover represents the value of fees and commissions earned in the period, net of VAT.

Where fees for professional work have been unconditionally earned but not invoiced at the reporting date, these amounts are included within accrued income.

Revenue in respect of professional services is recognised by reference to the fair value of the services provided at the reporting date as a proportion of the total value of the engagement. Unbilled revenue is included within debtors as accrued income.

Critical accounting estimates and key sources of estimation uncertainty

In the application of the LLP's accounting policies, which are described above, the members are required to make judgements, estimates and assumptions about the carrying values of assets and liabilities which are not readily apparent from other sources. The members base such estimates on historical experience and other factors that are considered to be relevant. Actual results may differ from these estimates.

The estimates and underlying assumptions are reviewed on an ongoing basis. Revisions to accounting estimates are recognised in the period in which the estimate is revised if the revisions only affect that period. If the revisions affect both the current and future periods, it is recognised in the current and subsequent periods.

The key sources of estimation uncertainty which have a significant effect on the amounts recognised in the financial statements are described below:

[Describe the relevant sources of estimation uncertainty which have had a significant effect on the amounts recognised in the financial statements (eg valuation of land and buildings, estimates of work in progress etc)].

2 **Turnover**[6]

	201X	201Y
	£'000	£'000
United Kingdom		
Rest of the World		

6 This segment analysis is not required under FRS 102 but is included for completeness as some LLPs choose to make this disclosure.

3 Information in relation to members

	201X Number	**201Y Number**
The average number of members during the year was		
	£'000	*£'000*
[*The average members' remuneration during the year was*[7]]		]
	£'000	£'000
Salaried remuneration of members		
Paid under employment contract		
Paid under the terms of the LLP agreement		
The amount of profit attributable to the member with the largest entitlement was		

Profit attributable to the member with the largest entitlement is determined by reference to [ ]

7 This disclosure is optional.

4 Employee information and staff costs

The average number of persons (including members with contracts of employment) employed by the LLP during the year was:

	201X Number	201Y Number
Selling and distribution		
Administration		

	£'000	£'000
Staff costs for the above persons were:		
Wages and salaries		
Social security costs		
Pension costs		

5 Interest payable and similar expenses

	201X £'000	201Y £'000
Bank loans and overdrafts		
Finance leases		

6 Profit for the financial year before members' remuneration and profit shares

	£'000	£'000
Profit for the financial year before members' remuneration and profit shares is stated after charging/(crediting):		
Depreciation		
– owned assets		
– assets held under finance leases		
Amortisation of intangible assets		
Operating leases – property		
– other		

6 **Profit for the financial year before members' remuneration and profit shares *(continued)***

The analysis of auditors' remuneration is as follows:	**201X**	**201Y**
	£'000	**£'000**
Fees payable to the LLP's auditors for the audit of the LLP's annual accounts		
Fees payable to the LLP's auditors and their associates for other services to the LLP		
Total audit fees		
Tax services		
Corporate finance services		
Other services		
Total non-audit fees		

7 Intangible fixed assets

	Trademarks £'000
Cost	
At 1 April 201Y	
Additions	
At 31 March 201X	
Amortisation	
At 1 April 201Y	
Charge for the year	
At 31 March 201X	
Net book value	
At 31 March 201X	
At 31 March 201Y	

8 Tangible fixed assets

	Freehold land and buildings	Short leasehold improvements	Office fixtures and fittings	Motor vehicles	Total
	£'000	£'000	£'000	£'000	£'000
Cost or valuation					
At 1 April 201Y					
Additions					
Disposals					
At 31 March 201X					
Depreciation					
At 1 April 200Y					
Charge for the year					
Disposals					
At 31 March 201X					
Net book value					
At 31 March 201X					
At 31 March 201Y					

The net book value of the LLP's office fixtures and fittings includes £[ ] (201Y: £[ ]) in respect of assets held under finance leases.

9 Work in progress

	201X £'000	201Y £'000
Work in progress		

10 Debtors

	201X £'000	201Y £'000
Trade debtors		
Amounts due from members		
Other debtors		
Prepayments and accrued income		

11 **Creditors:** amounts falling due within one year

	201X £'000	201Y £'000
Bank loans and overdrafts		
Obligations under finance leases		
Trade creditors		
Other taxation and social security		
[Retirement benefits due to former members][8]		
Other creditors		
Accruals and deferred income		

8 Where the amount of retirement benefits to former members is fixed it should be included within creditors (split between due within and due after one year) rather than provisions.

12 **Creditors:** amounts falling due after more than one year

	LLP	
	201X	**201Y**
	£	**£**
Bank loans and overdrafts		
Obligations under finance leases		
[Retirement benefits due to former members][8]		

13 **Borrowings**

	201X	**201Y**
	£	**£**
Bank overdraft		
Bank loan		
(secured [ ]% above LIBOR)		
Obligations under finance leases		
Due within one year		
Due after one year		
Maturity analysis		
Within one year or on demand		
More than one year but less than two years		
More than two years but not less than five years		
More than five years		

[Bank loans and overdrafts are secured by fixed and floating charges over the assets of the LLP].

14 **Provisions for liabilities**

	Post-retirement payments to former members	Provisions for dilapidations	Total
	£'000	£'000	£'000
At 1 April 201Y			
Profit and loss account charge			
Amounts utilised			
At 31 March 201X			

15 **Reconciliation of members' interests**

	EQUITY Members' other interests			**DEBT Loans and other debts due to members less any amounts due from members in debtors**			**TOTAL MEMBERS' INTERESTS**
	Members' capital (classified as equity)	**Other reserves**	**Total**	**Members' capital (classified as debt)**	**Other amounts**	**Total**	**Total**
	£'000	**£'000**	**£'000**	**£'000**	**£'000**	**£'000**	**£'000**
Amounts due to members							
Amounts due from members							
Members' interests at 1 April 201Y							
Members' remuneration charged as an expense							
Profit for the financial year available for discretionary division among members							
Members' interests after profit for the year							

	EQUITY Members' other interests			DEBT Loans and other debts due to members less any amounts due from members in debtors			TOTAL MEMBERS' INTERESTS
	Members' capital (classified as equity) £'000	Other reserves £'000	Total £'000	Members' capital (classified as debt) £'000	Other amounts £'000	Total £'000	Total £'000
Other divisions of profits/losses							
Introduced by members							
Repayments of capital							
Repayment of debt							
Drawings							
Other movements							
Amounts due to members							
Amounts due from members							
Members' interests at 31 March 201X							

Amounts due to members will rank pari pasu with other unsecured creditors in the event of a winding up. In such a circumstance, the members have subordinated their rights to payments of amounts owed to them in preference to external creditors.

16 **Operating lease commitments**

At 31 March 201X the LLP had annual commitments under non-cancellable operating leases as follows:

	201X Property £'000	201Y Property £'000	201X Other £'000	201Y Other £'000
For leases expiring:				
Within one year				
Between two and five years				
In excess of five years				

17 **Capital commitments**

	201X £	201Y £
Contracted but not provided for		

18 **Contingent liabilities**

The LLP has guaranteed the borrowings of individual members taken out in order to fund their capital interests in the LLP. At 31 March 201X the total amount guaranteed was £[ ]. 201Y £[ ].

19 **Related party transactions**

There were no related party transactions as defined by Section 33 *Related Party Disclosures* during the year.

20 **Controlling party**

In the opinion of the members there is no controlling party.

21 **Events after the reporting date**

[Material non-adjusting events after the reporting date should be disclosed in accordance with Section 32 *Events after the Reporting Period*].

Index

[*All references are to paragraph number and appendices*]